# PRAISE FOR *BOX OF BONES*

"As a lifelong horror lover who savo ⎯⎯⎯⎯⎯⎯⎯⎯⎯⎯ cts
with Black history and family lore, ⎯⎯⎯⎯⎯⎯ ᴮᴼˣ ᴼꜰ ᴮᴼᴺᴱˢ and
marveled at every page. Ayize Jama-Everett and John Jennings have
created a revolutionary, unforgettable journey I was happy to risk
the nightmares for."

### TANANARIVE DUE
American Book Award winner, author of
*Ghost Summer: Stories,*
*The Good House,* and *The Between*

"Centuries of oppression, of violence, of torture, but
still we don't let it loose. What might happen if we did?
The price for revenge is too high, this is
the thing we guard. The real helter skelter.
This is the *Box of Bones.*"

### NALO HOPKINSON
World Fantasy Award winner, author of *Skin Folk,*
*Brown Girl in the Ring,* and
DC Comics' *House of Whispers*

" *Box of Bones* is a brilliantly disturbing nightmare. It manages to
be both beautiful and disgusting with every turn of the page as it
explores a gruesome horror that I've never seen in comics before."

### DAVID WALKER
Eisner and Ringo Award winner, author of *Bitter Root,*
*The Life of Frederick Douglas,* and
*The Black Panther Party: A Graphic Novel History*

*Published by*
*Rosarium Publishing*
*P.O. Box 544*
*Greenbelt, MD 20768-0544*
*www.rosariumpublishing.com*

# BOX OF BONES

## BOOK ONE

### CHAPTER ONE - *"THE TROUBLES I'VE SEEN"*
STORY- JOHN JENNINGS AND AYIZE JAMA EVERETT
WRITER- AYIZE JAMA EVERETT
ART- JOHN JENNINGS
LETTERING- DAMIAN DUFFY
COLOR PRODUCTION - ANTHONY MONCADA

### CHAPTER TWO - *"WRETCHED BLOOD"*
STORY- JOHN JENNINGS AND AYIZE JAMA EVERETT
WRITER- AYIZE JAMA EVERETT
ART- SOLE REBEL / JOHN JENNINGS /
DAMIAN DUFFY / TOMMY NGUYEN
LETTERING- JEREMY MARSHALL
COLOR PRODUCTION - ANTHONY MONCADA

### CHAPTER THREE - *"CITY OF DARKNESS"*
STORY- JOHN JENNINGS AND AYIZE JAMA EVERETT
WRITER- AYIZE JAMA EVERETT
ART- BRYAN CHRISTOPHER MOSS
LETTERING- JEREMY MARSHALL
COLOR PRODUCTION - ANTHONY MONCADA

### CHAPTER FOUR - *"PLANTATION"*
STORY- JOHN JENNINGS AND AYIZE JAMA EVERETT
WRITER- AYIZE JAMA EVERETT
ART- FRANCES OLIVIA LIDDELL-RODRIGUEZ
COLORS- ANTHONY MONCADA
LETTERING- JEREMY MARSHALL
COLOR PRODUCTION -STANFORD CARPENTER

### CHAPTER FIVE - *"SUFFERING ON THE HILL"*
STORY- JOHN JENNINGS AND AYIZE JAMA EVERETT
WRITER- AYIZE JAMA EVERETT
ART- JAMAL AND JARMEL WILLIAMS
LETTERING- JEREMY MARSHALL
COLOR PRODUCTION AND FINAL COLORS - ALEX BATCHELOR
SERIES EDITOR AND PUBLISHER- BILL CAMPBELL

# OPENING THE BOX

The enduring potential of an artifact is that once it is created it takes on an existence all its own, moving through space and time, all the while rendering its creators less and less visible.

*Box of Bones* is an artifact of our imagination.

You don't see us. Writers, pencillers, inkers, colorists, and letterers slogging away – channeling our experiences and skills – in an elaborate game of exquisite corpse in which we receive pages in various stages of production that we add on to, alter, erase, enhance, and otherwise edit. Giving a little bit here. Taking a little bit from there. Taking things, in whole or in part, and reconfiguring them to make something …. else. In anthropology it's called this bricolage, in music it's called remixing, and in other parts it's called it racecraft. Regardless, the task of channeling and harnessing experiences, histories, memories in the service of making things … the process of transforming ideas about the world into things in the world … is all the more difficult when the ideas are tied to trauma.

Imagine waking up in the morning and receiving pages that force you to reconcile the trauma of the person who sent them even as the process demands that you pour a little bit of your own trauma onto the page before you send it to the next person.

*Box of Bones* is a recitation on racial trauma told from the perspective of a woman in search of an artifact. It is the story of Black experiences embodied in some … not quite living things … that remind us. Even as they hurtle though space and ever-transforming time, their identities in constant flux, their world bounded by six walls … the inside of an artifact in the shape of a box. They are trauma given form, crafted from the echoes of moments long gone and pain everlasting, named and identified:

**The Dark.** Fashioned from the dark essence of a servant from a slave ship and creator of the Box of Bones, he is the essence of every indignity, every injury, every slight, and all of the pain of black servitude past, present, and future.

**The Nobody.** A living wound created from the hollowing out of Black culture perpetually existing in a state of knowing of but not actually remembering what was lost.

**The Wretched.** A sentient lynching tree nurtured in the most wretched of earth infused with the blood, sweat, tears, torn flesh, burnt bones, and last cries of every violent act committed on a Black body.

**The Suffering.** The embodiment of Black masculinity in its most demonized iteration, the ultimate Black buck contorted, twisted, wracked with anger and rage with no other outlet than the sheer violence its strength enables.

The Dark, The Nobody, The Wretched, and The Suffering call the Box of Bones home. Inside the Box of Bones, the moaning, crying, and screaming are so constant, so ever present, so much a part of the background that they pass for this world's notion of silence … only to be disrupted by the call. Chants, conjuring, a cacophony of voices from outside that cause the walls to shake, tremble, and peel away at the edges letting in shafts of otherworldly light followed by a rush of air. Suction. Pulling the denizens of the Box of Bones from there dark cramped space of yearning into a different world, the world where the traumas that made what passes for their flesh were originally conceived.

The Box of Bones is a driving force in a quintessentially EthnoGothic landscape that serves as a warning to us all about just how dangerous our traumas can be. We bear witness to the transformation of experiences into things. Things forged from emotional turmoil and physical pain rooted in Black experiences. Things that take on a life of their own that serves to project some of the most horrific aspects of the Black experience into the future. And in so doing rendering these experiences as things that follow, haunt, and stalk the Blackest, the Whitest, all of us.

*Box of Bones* forces us to look at trauma differently. Too often we speak of trauma in terms of cycles, this idea that history is an ever-repeating set of stories. But the making of things, the giving of life to trauma is most horrific in its evolutionary implications. These things go on to live in ways we don't want to acknowledge. They seek their own comfort, they eat, they rest, they experience joy, they feel pain, they love, and they give birth … to new things, things that are not responsible for their existence, their nature. Things that that could be nurtured but rarely ever are. New life that carries with it the existential horror of at once embodying our trauma and being without any sin of their own making.

What do we make of our traumas given form moving and multiplying through space and time?

What do we make of these vehicles, these artifacts of our imagination that speed them along?

How do we live with this?

*-Stanford Carpenter, PhD*
*Chicago, IL, October, 2020*

---

**STANFORD CARPENTER, PhD** is a Cultural Anthropologist, Comic Scholar, Comic Creator, and former Archaeologist. Dr. Carpenter is co-creator of the forthcoming NPR Affiliate podcast *Brother-Story and the Correspondent*, an ethnographic and journalistic take on comics, culture, and the lives of the people who create and consume them. He is on the advisory boards of Abrams ComicArts' Megascope imprint advisory board, the Black & Brown Comix Arts Festival, and Pocket Con Team.

# CHAPTER ONE

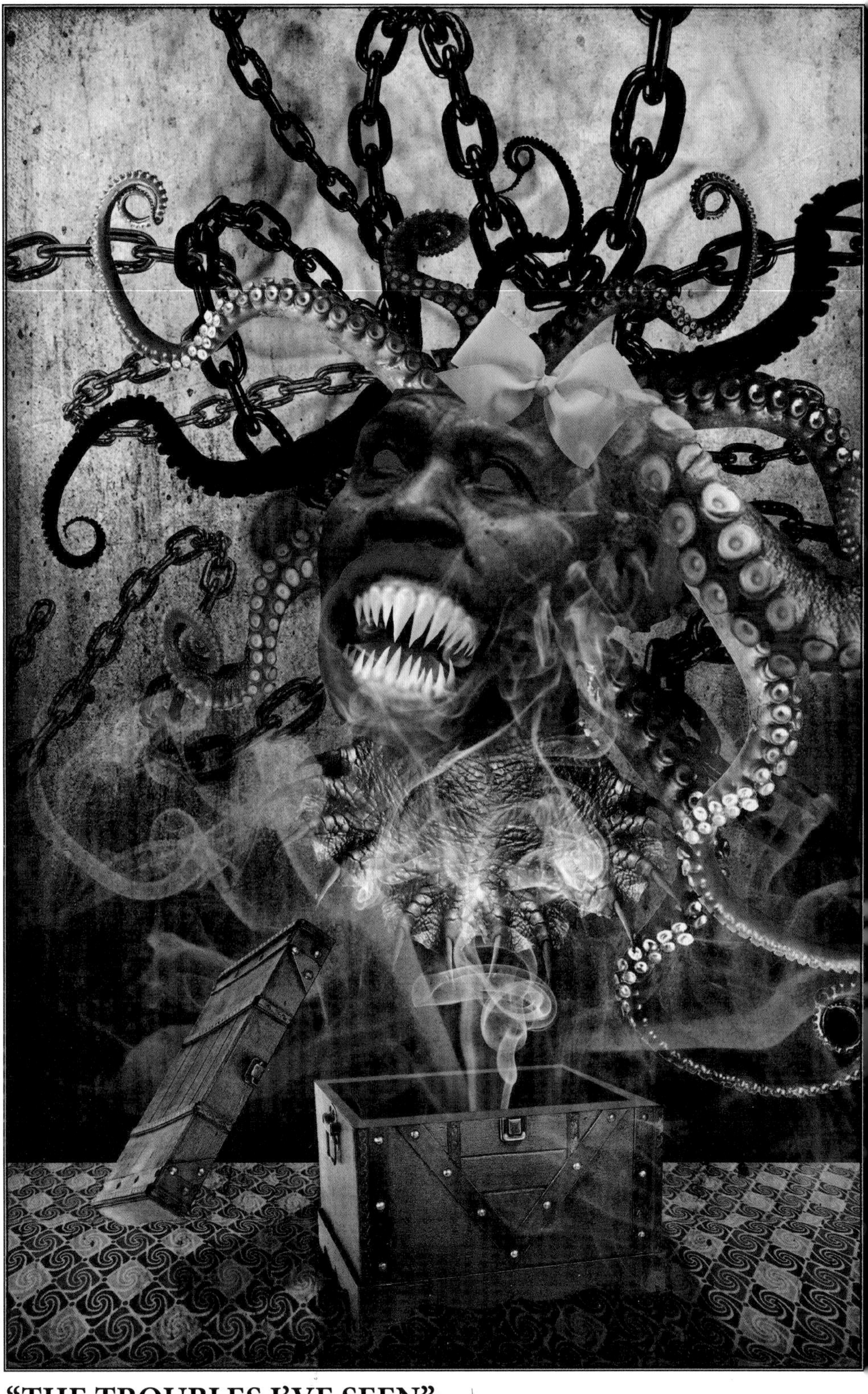

"THE TROUBLES I'VE SEEN"

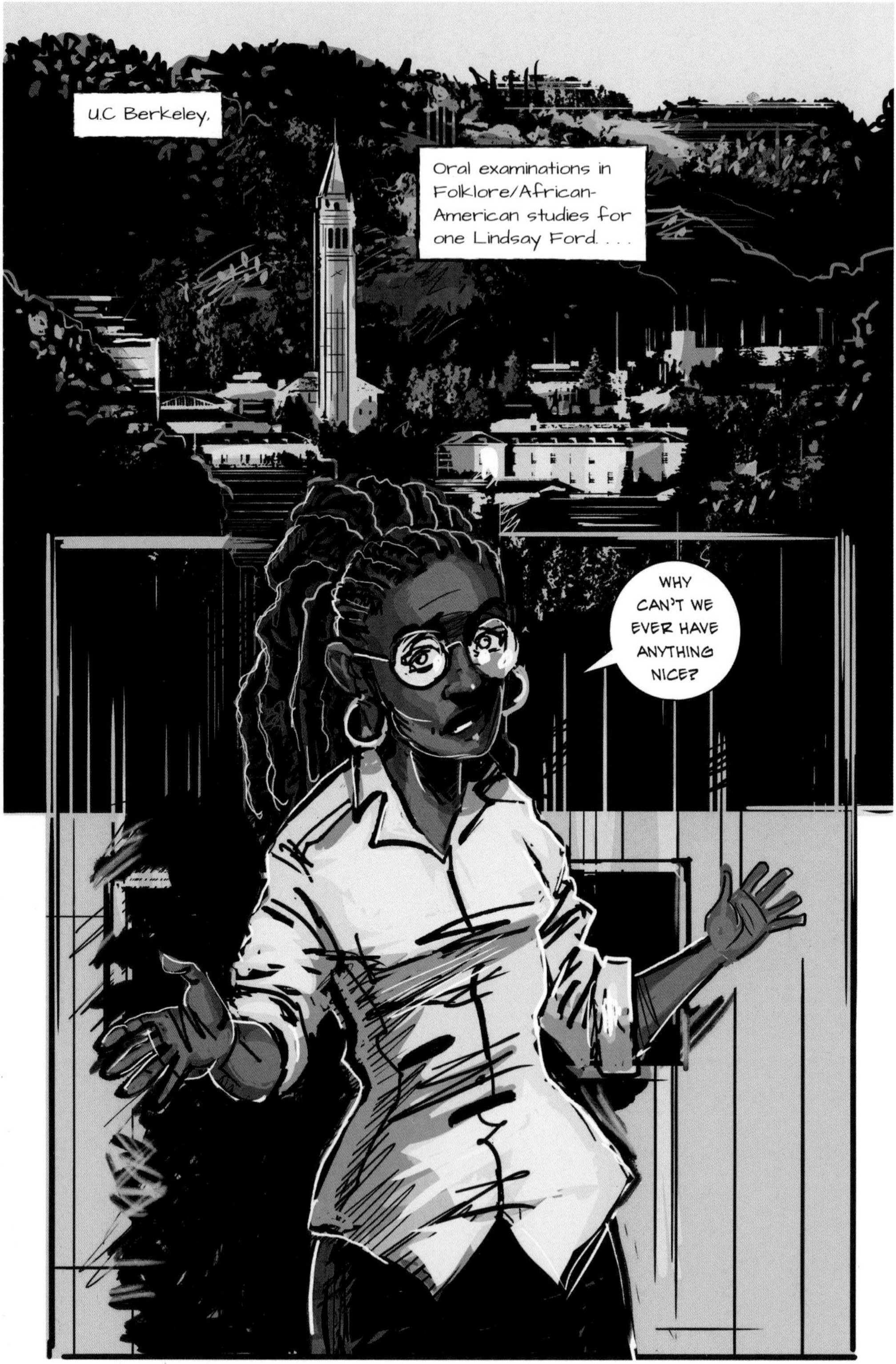
U.C Berkeley,
Oral examinations in Folklore/African-American studies for one Lindsay Ford. . .
WHY CAN'T WE EVER HAVE ANYTHING NICE?

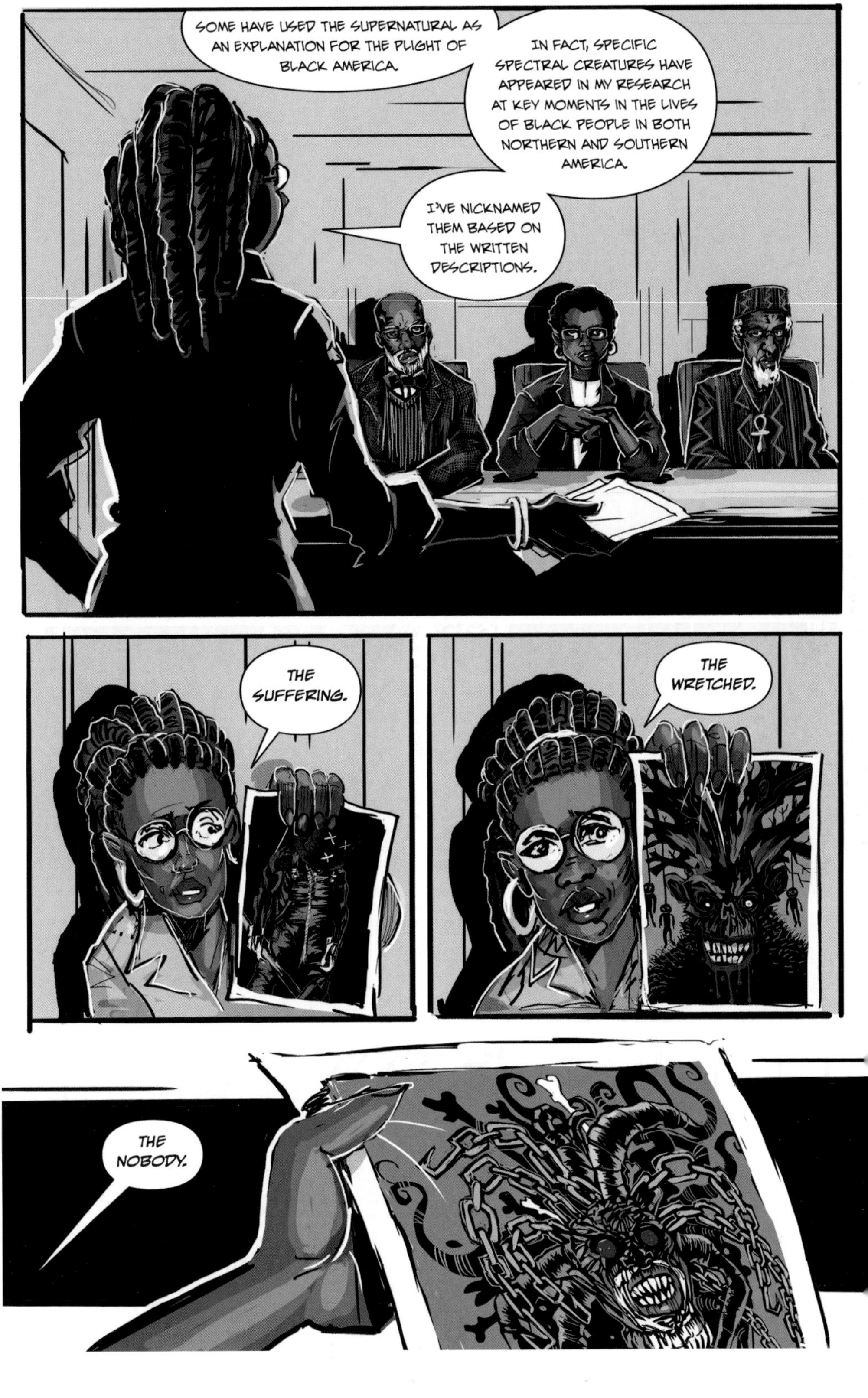
SOME HAVE USED THE SUPERNATURAL AS AN EXPLANATION FOR THE PLIGHT OF BLACK AMERICA.
IN FACT, SPECIFIC SPECTRAL CREATURES HAVE APPEARED IN MY RESEARCH AT KEY MOMENTS IN THE LIVES OF BLACK PEOPLE IN BOTH NORTHERN AND SOUTHERN AMERICA.
I'VE NICKNAMED THEM BASED ON THE WRITTEN DESCRIPTIONS.
THE SUFFERING.
THE WRETCHED.
THE NOBODY.

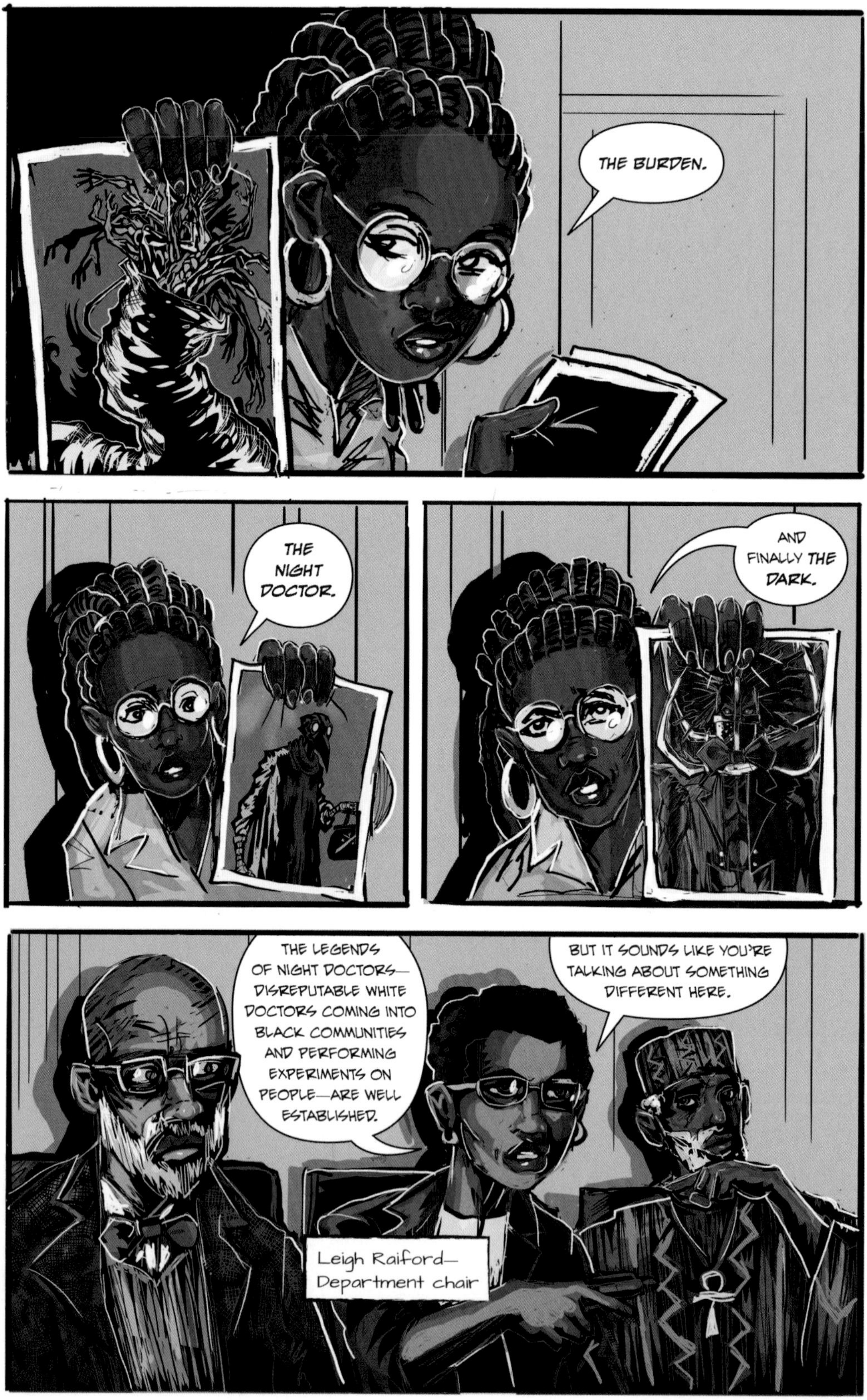
THE BURDEN.
THE NIGHT DOCTOR.
AND FINALLY THE DARK.
THE LEGENDS OF NIGHT DOCTORS—DISREPUTABLE WHITE DOCTORS COMING INTO BLACK COMMUNITIES AND PERFORMING EXPERIMENTS ON PEOPLE—ARE WELL ESTABLISHED.
BUT IT SOUNDS LIKE YOU'RE TALKING ABOUT SOMETHING DIFFERENT HERE.
Leigh Raiford—
Department chair

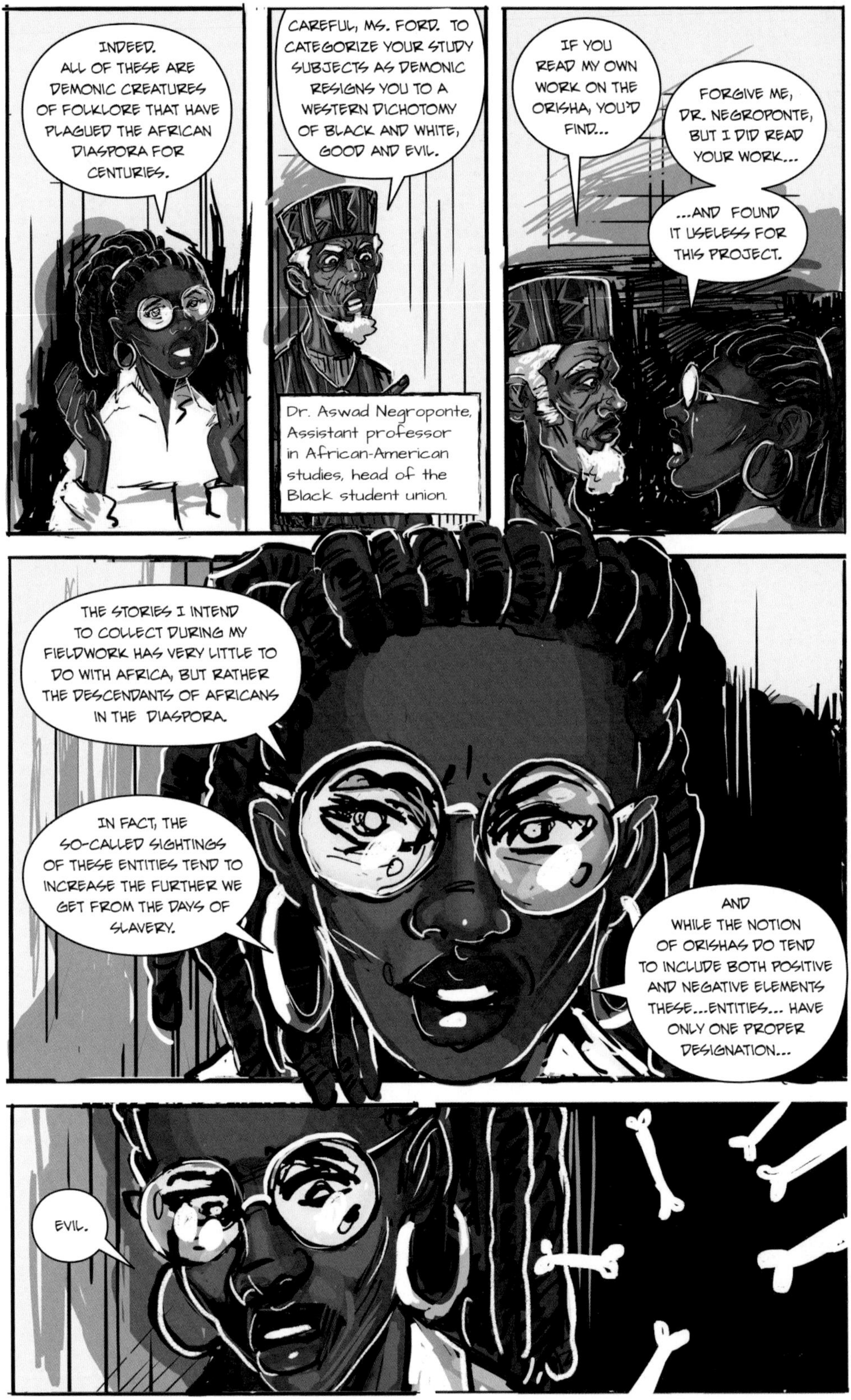
INDEED. ALL OF THESE ARE DEMONIC CREATURES OF FOLKLORE THAT HAVE PLAGUED THE AFRICAN DIASPORA FOR CENTURIES.
CAREFUL, MS. FORD. TO CATEGORIZE YOUR STUDY SUBJECTS AS DEMONIC RESIGNS YOU TO A WESTERN DICHOTOMY OF BLACK AND WHITE, GOOD AND EVIL.
Dr. Aswad Negroponte, Assistant professor in African-American studies, head of the Black student union.
IF YOU READ MY OWN WORK ON THE ORISHA, YOU'D FIND...
FORGIVE ME, DR. NEGROPONTE, BUT I DID READ YOUR WORK...
...AND FOUND IT USELESS FOR THIS PROJECT.
THE STORIES I INTEND TO COLLECT DURING MY FIELDWORK HAS VERY LITTLE TO DO WITH AFRICA, BUT RATHER THE DESCENDANTS OF AFRICANS IN THE DIASPORA.
IN FACT, THE SO-CALLED SIGHTINGS OF THESE ENTITIES TEND TO INCREASE THE FURTHER WE GET FROM THE DAYS OF SLAVERY.
AND WHILE THE NOTION OF ORISHAS DO TEND TO INCLUDE BOTH POSITIVE AND NEGATIVE ELEMENTS THESE...ENTITIES... HAVE ONLY ONE PROPER DESIGNATION...
EVIL.

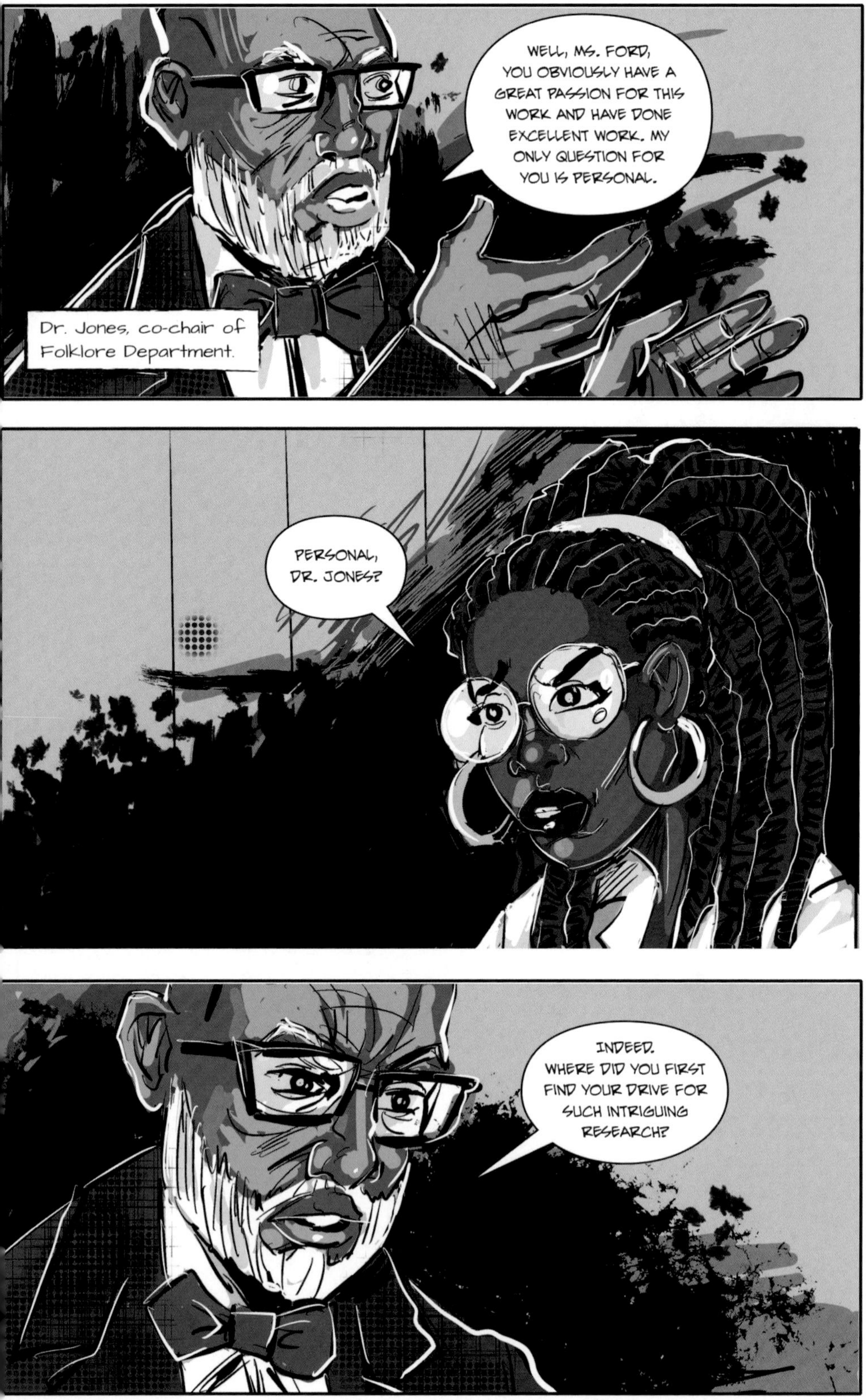
WELL, MS. FORD, YOU OBVIOUSLY HAVE A GREAT PASSION FOR THIS WORK AND HAVE DONE EXCELLENT WORK. MY ONLY QUESTION FOR YOU IS PERSONAL.
Dr. Jones, co-chair of Folklore Department.
PERSONAL, DR. JONES?
INDEED. WHERE DID YOU FIRST FIND YOUR DRIVE FOR SUCH INTRIGUING RESEARCH?

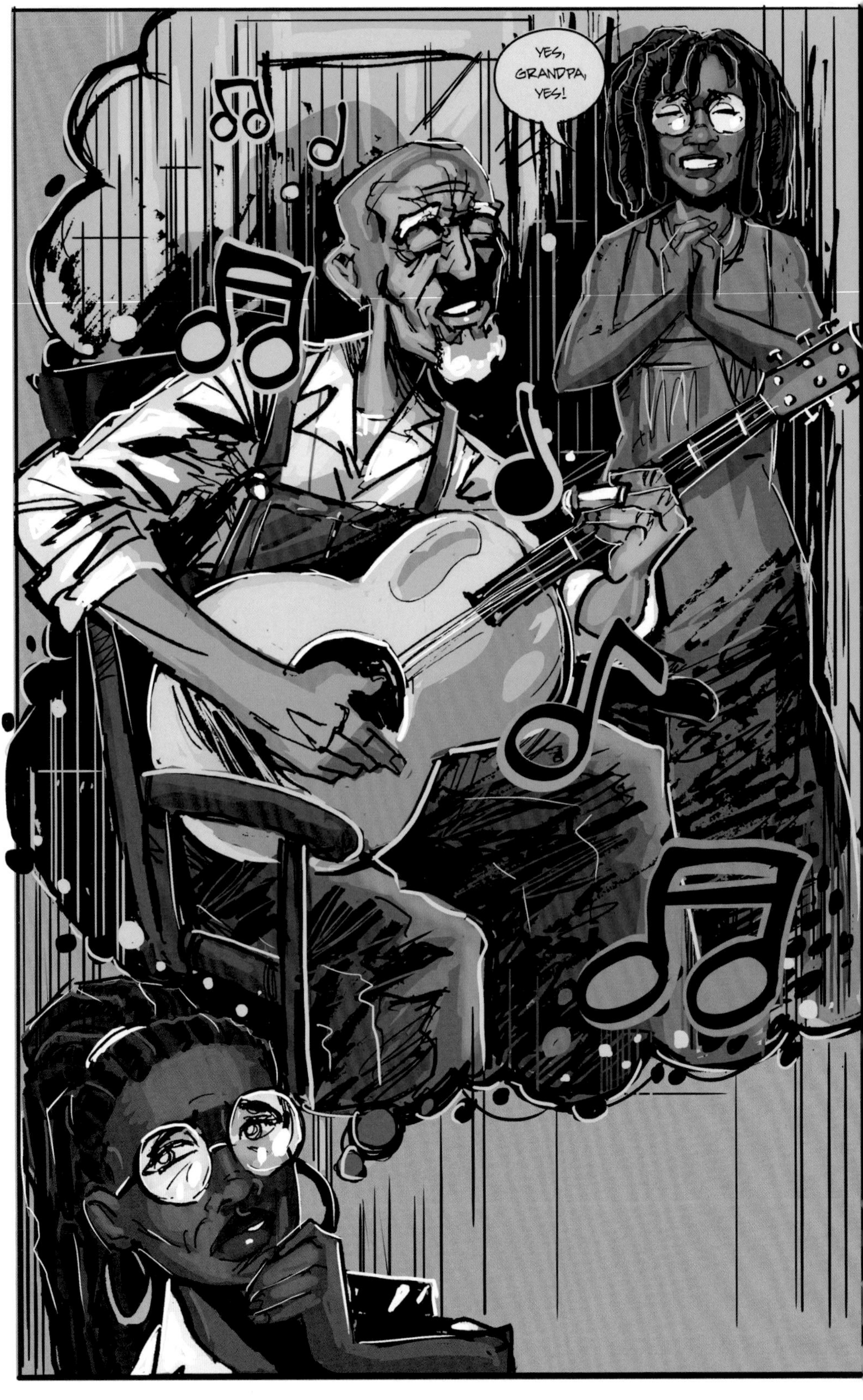
YES, GRANDPA, YES!

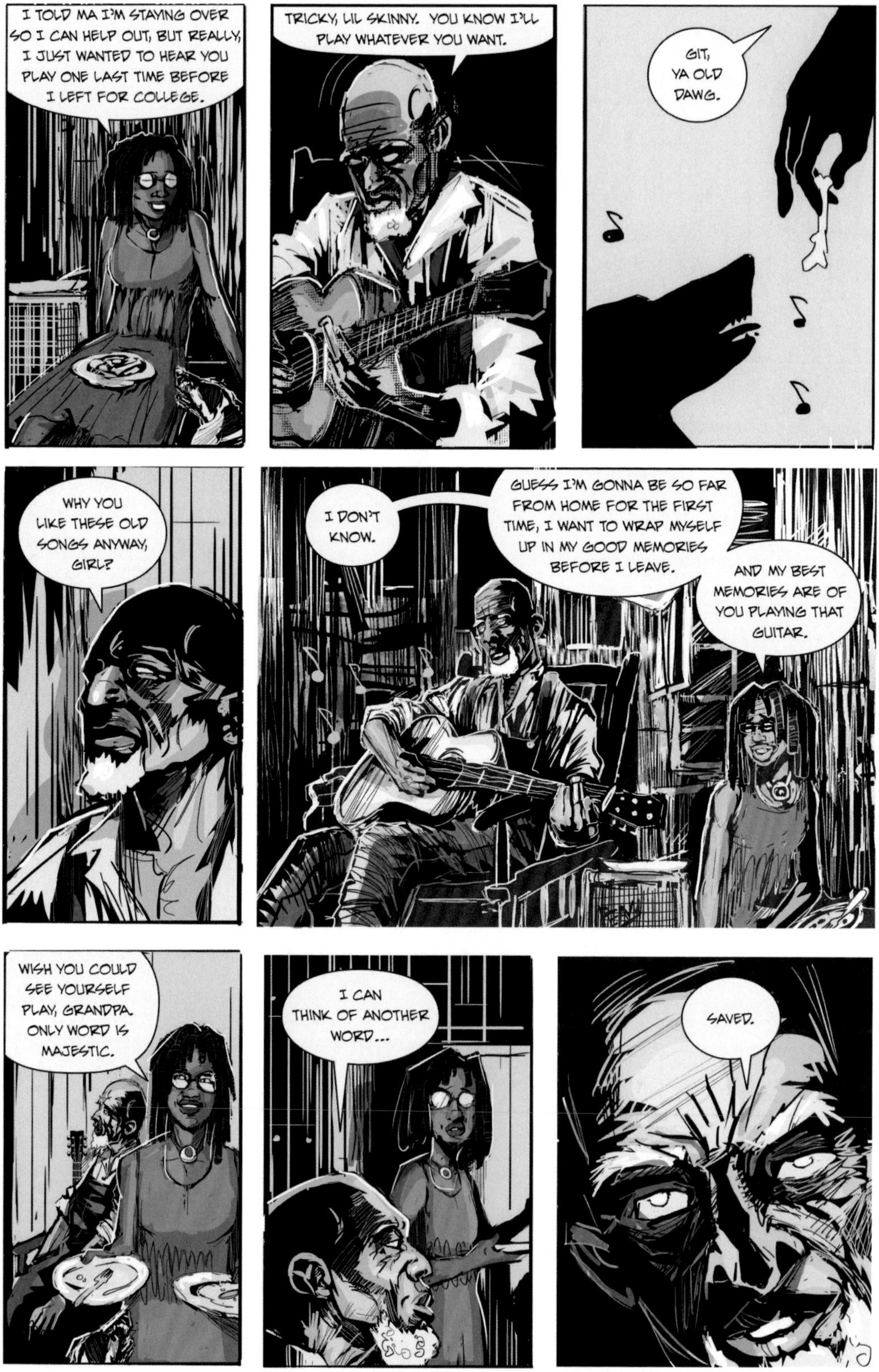
I TOLD MA I'M STAYING OVER SO I CAN HELP OUT, BUT REALLY, I JUST WANTED TO HEAR YOU PLAY ONE LAST TIME BEFORE I LEFT FOR COLLEGE.
TRICKY, LIL SKINNY. YOU KNOW I'LL PLAY WHATEVER YOU WANT.
GIT, YA OLD DAWG.
WHY YOU LIKE THESE OLD SONGS ANYWAY, GIRL?
I DON'T KNOW.
GUESS I'M GONNA BE SO FAR FROM HOME FOR THE FIRST TIME, I WANT TO WRAP MYSELF UP IN MY GOOD MEMORIES BEFORE I LEAVE.
AND MY BEST MEMORIES ARE OF YOU PLAYING THAT GUITAR.
WISH YOU COULD SEE YOURSELF PLAY, GRANDPA. ONLY WORD IS MAJESTIC.
I CAN THINK OF ANOTHER WORD...
SAVED.

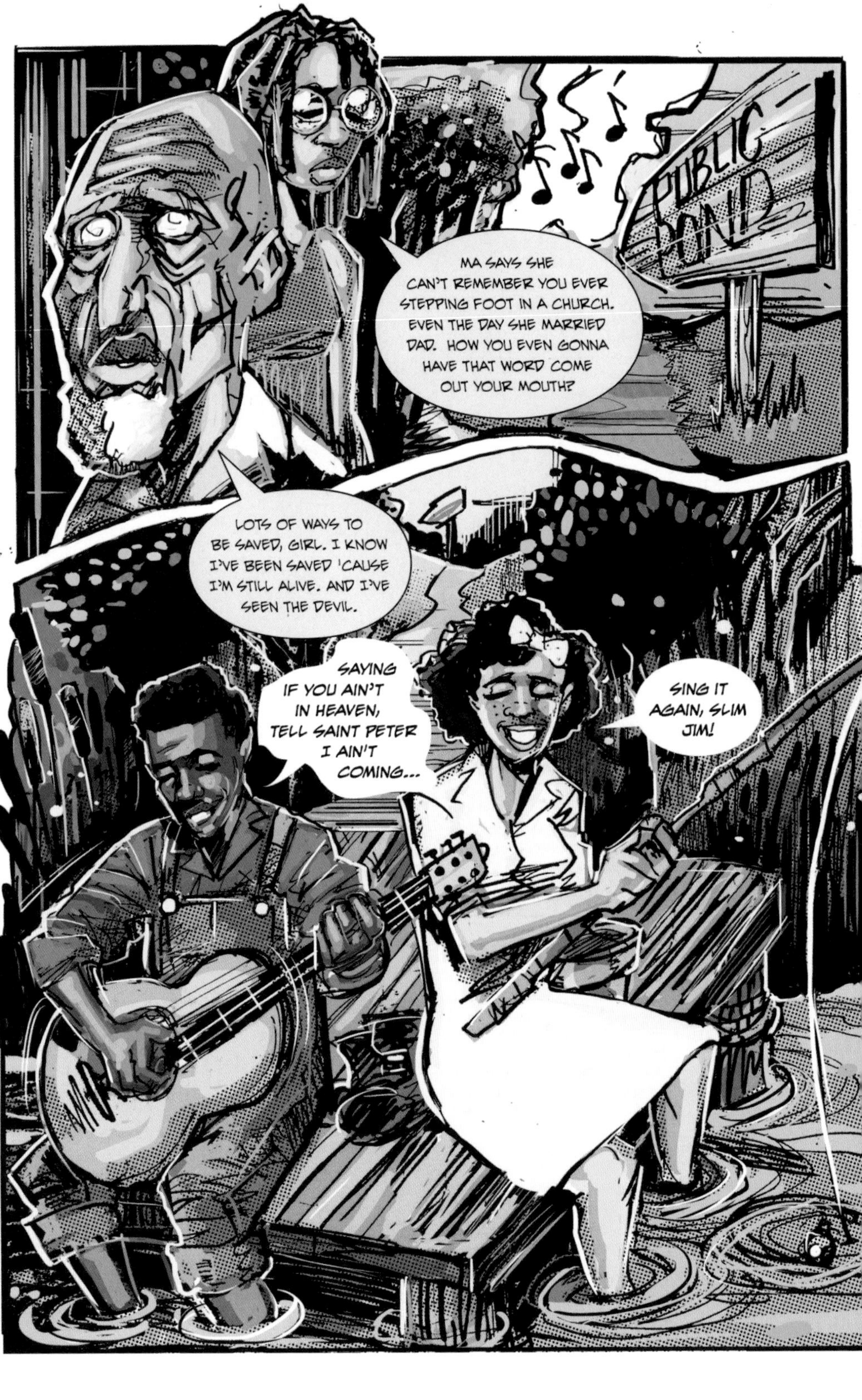
PUBLIC POND
MA SAYS SHE CAN'T REMEMBER YOU EVER STEPPING FOOT IN A CHURCH. EVEN THE DAY SHE MARRIED DAD. HOW YOU EVEN GONNA HAVE THAT WORD COME OUT YOUR MOUTH?
LOTS OF WAYS TO BE SAVED, GIRL. I KNOW I'VE BEEN SAVED 'CAUSE I'M STILL ALIVE. AND I'VE SEEN THE DEVIL.
SAYING IF YOU AIN'T IN HEAVEN, TELL SAINT PETER I AIN'T COMING...
SING IT AGAIN, SLIM JIM!

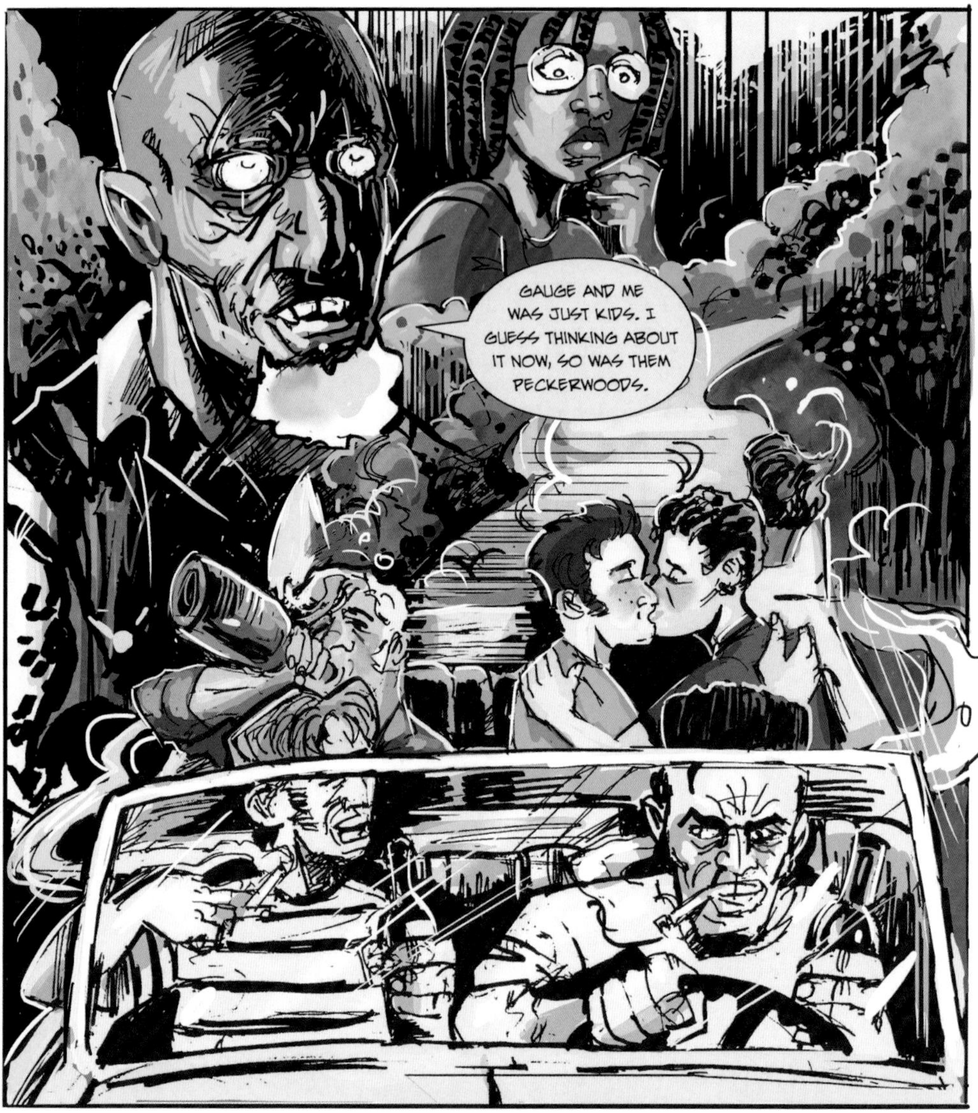
GAUGE AND ME WAS JUST KIDS. I GUESS THINKING ABOUT IT NOW, SO WAS THEM PECKERWOODS.

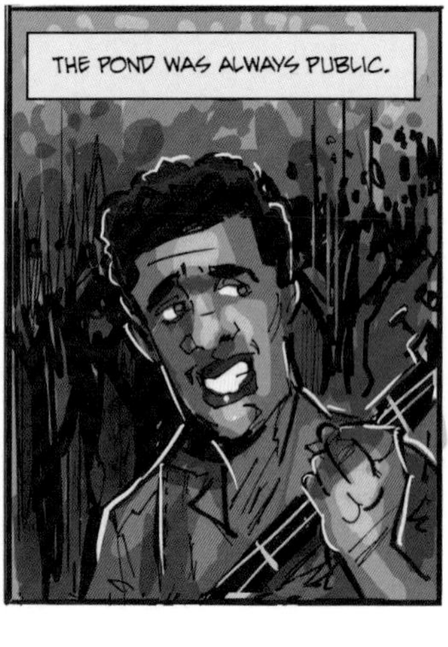
THE POND WAS ALWAYS PUBLIC.

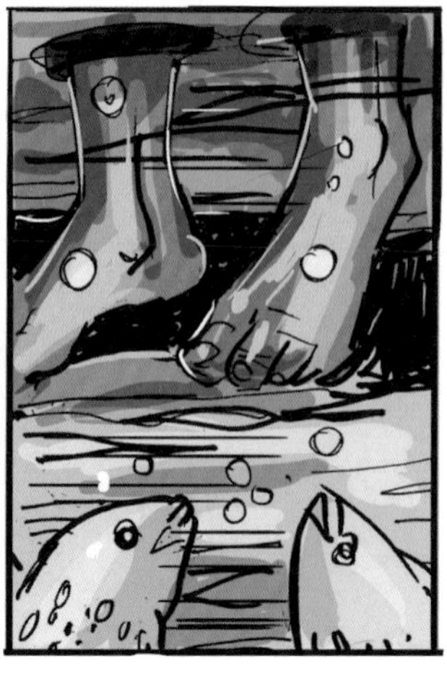

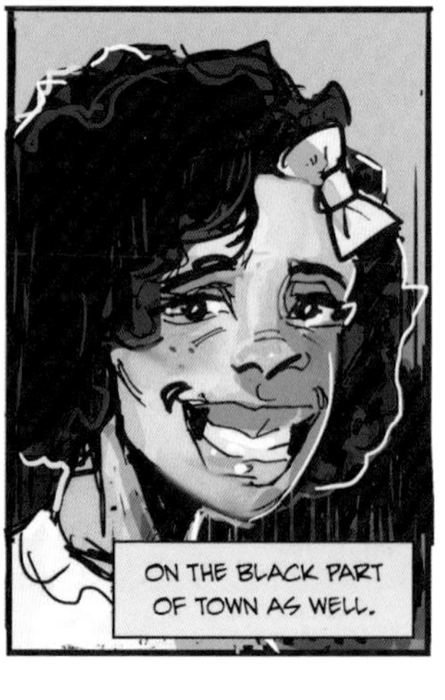
ON THE BLACK PART OF TOWN AS WELL.

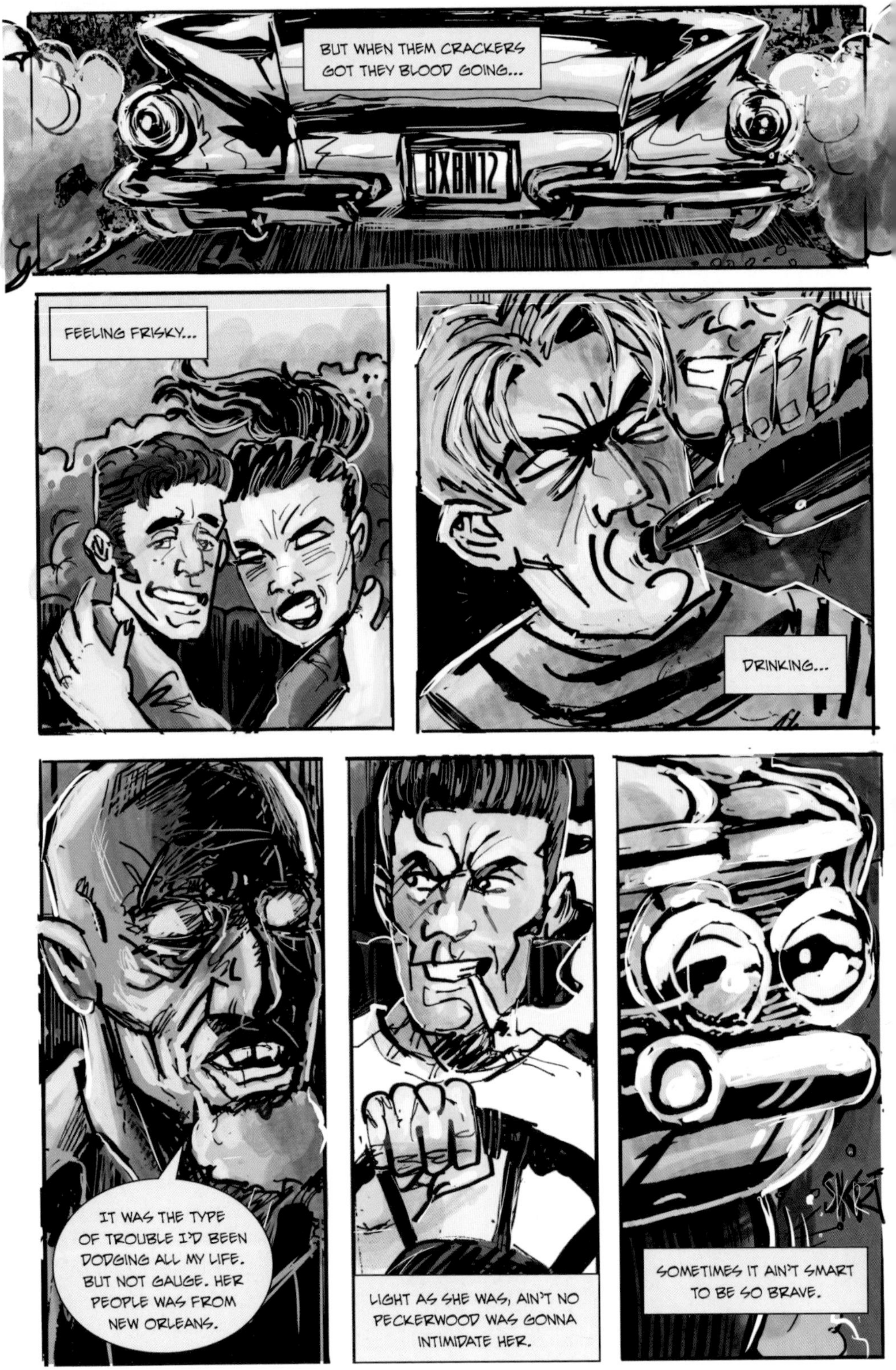
BUT WHEN THEM CRACKERS GOT THEY BLOOD GOING...
BXBN12
FEELING FRISKY...
DRINKING...
IT WAS THE TYPE OF TROUBLE I'D BEEN DODGING ALL MY LIFE. BUT NOT GAUGE. HER PEOPLE WAS FROM NEW ORLEANS.
LIGHT AS SHE WAS, AIN'T NO PECKERWOOD WAS GONNA INTIMIDATE HER.
SKRT
SOMETIMES IT AIN'T SMART TO BE SO BRAVE.

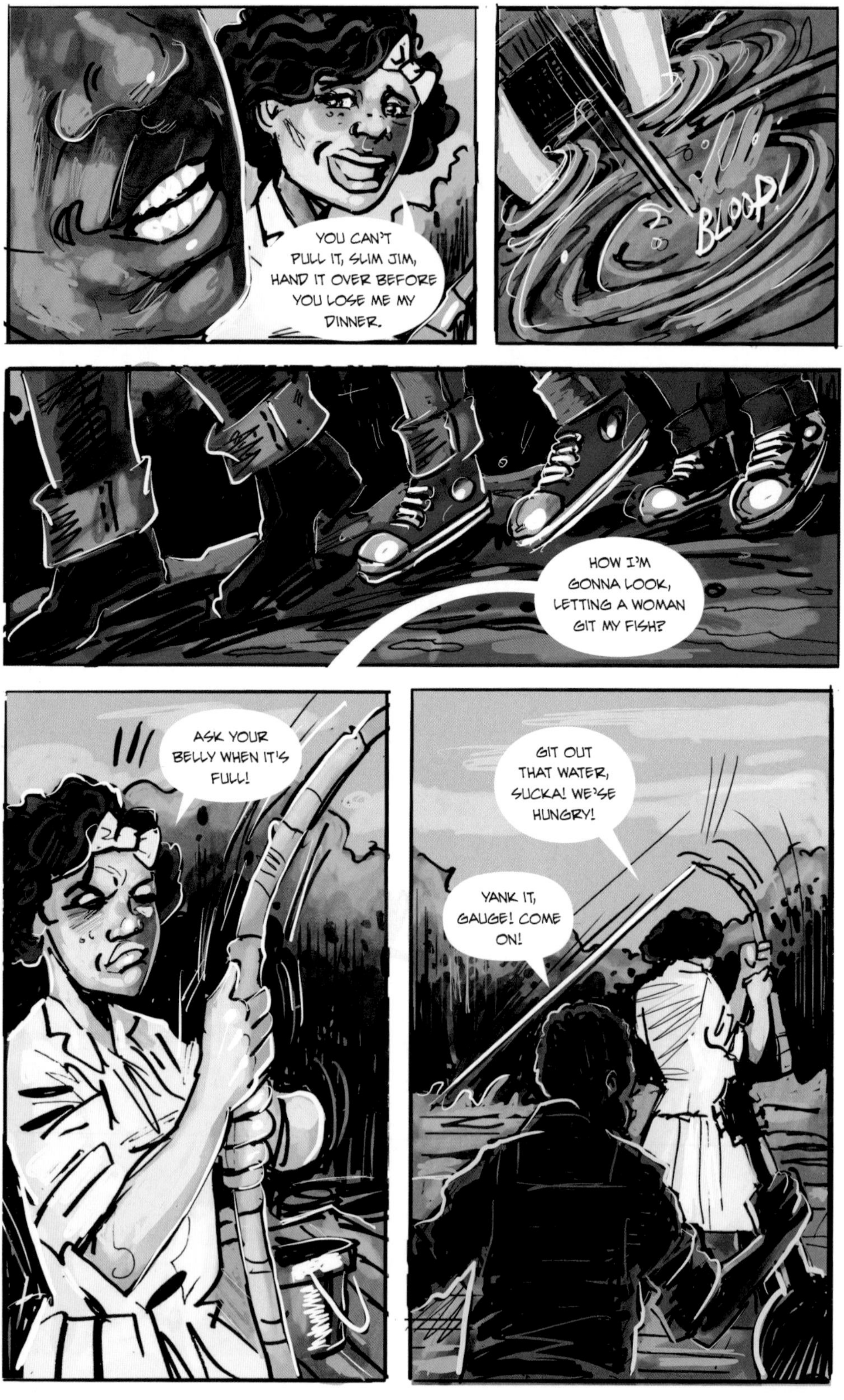
YOU CAN'T PULL IT, SLIM JIM, HAND IT OVER BEFORE YOU LOSE ME MY DINNER.
BLOOP!
HOW I'M GONNA LOOK, LETTING A WOMAN GIT MY FISH?
ASK YOUR BELLY WHEN IT'S FULL!
GIT OUT THAT WATER, SUCKA! WE'SE HUNGRY!
YANK IT, GAUGE! COME ON!

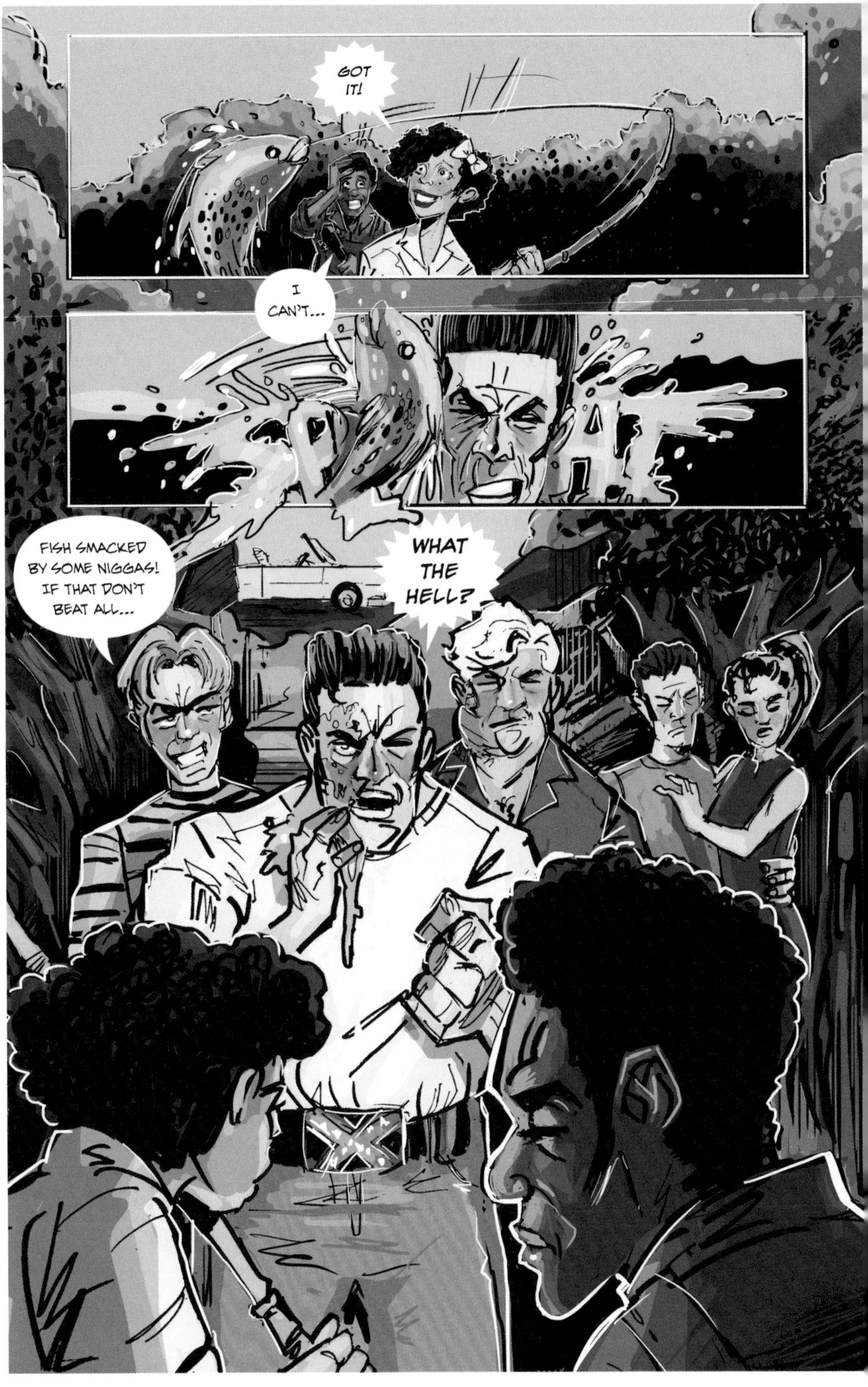
GOT IT!
I CAN'T...
WHAT THE HELL?
FISH SMACKED BY SOME NIGGAS! IF THAT DON'T BEAT ALL...

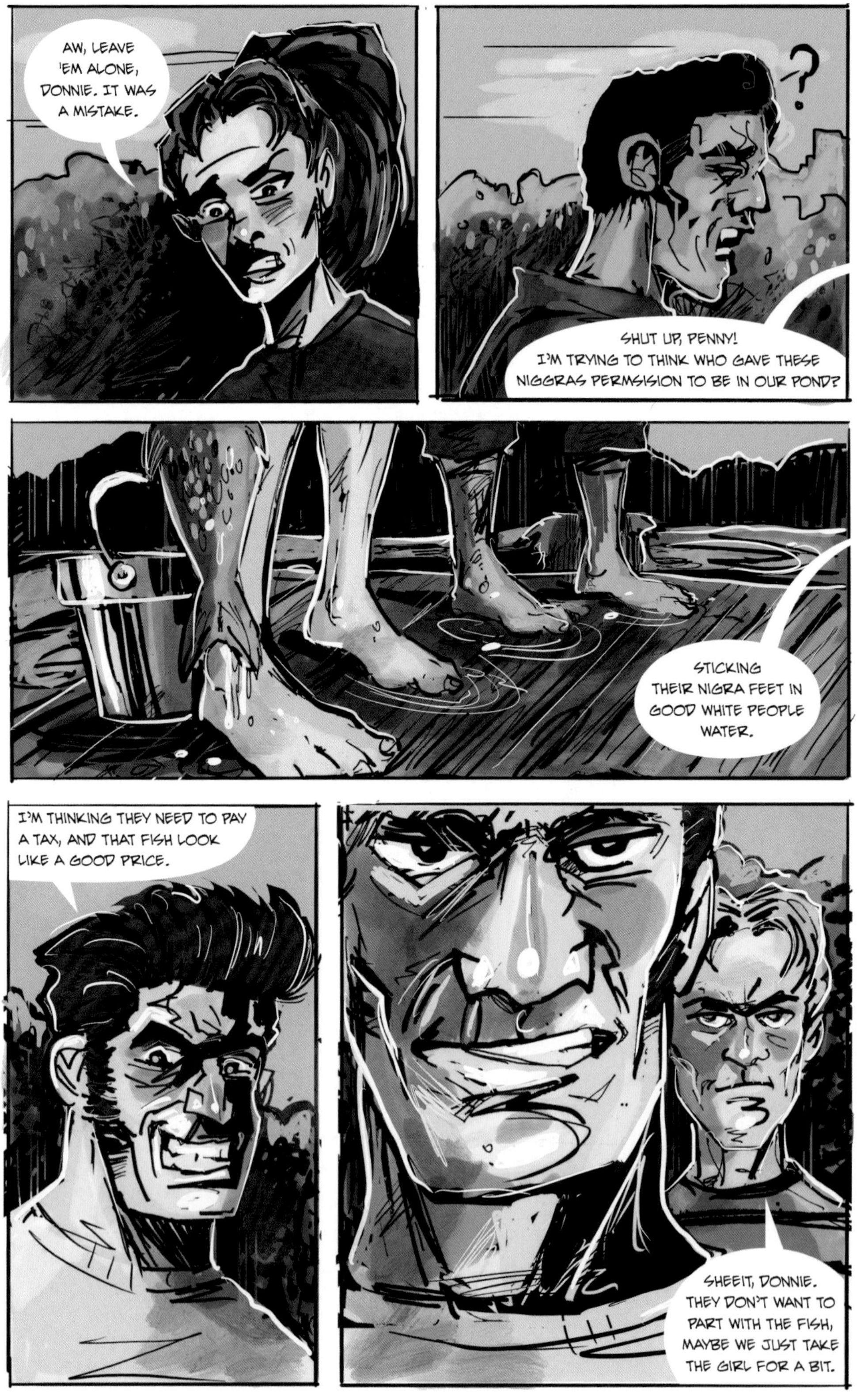
AW, LEAVE 'EM ALONE, DONNIE. IT WAS A MISTAKE.
?
SHUT UP, PENNY! I'M TRYING TO THINK WHO GAVE THESE NIGGRAS PERMSISION TO BE IN OUR POND?
STICKING THEIR NIGRA FEET IN GOOD WHITE PEOPLE WATER.
I'M THINKING THEY NEED TO PAY A TAX, AND THAT FISH LOOK LIKE A GOOD PRICE.
SHEEIT, DONNIE. THEY DON'T WANT TO PART WITH THE FISH, MAYBE WE JUST TAKE THE GIRL FOR A BIT.

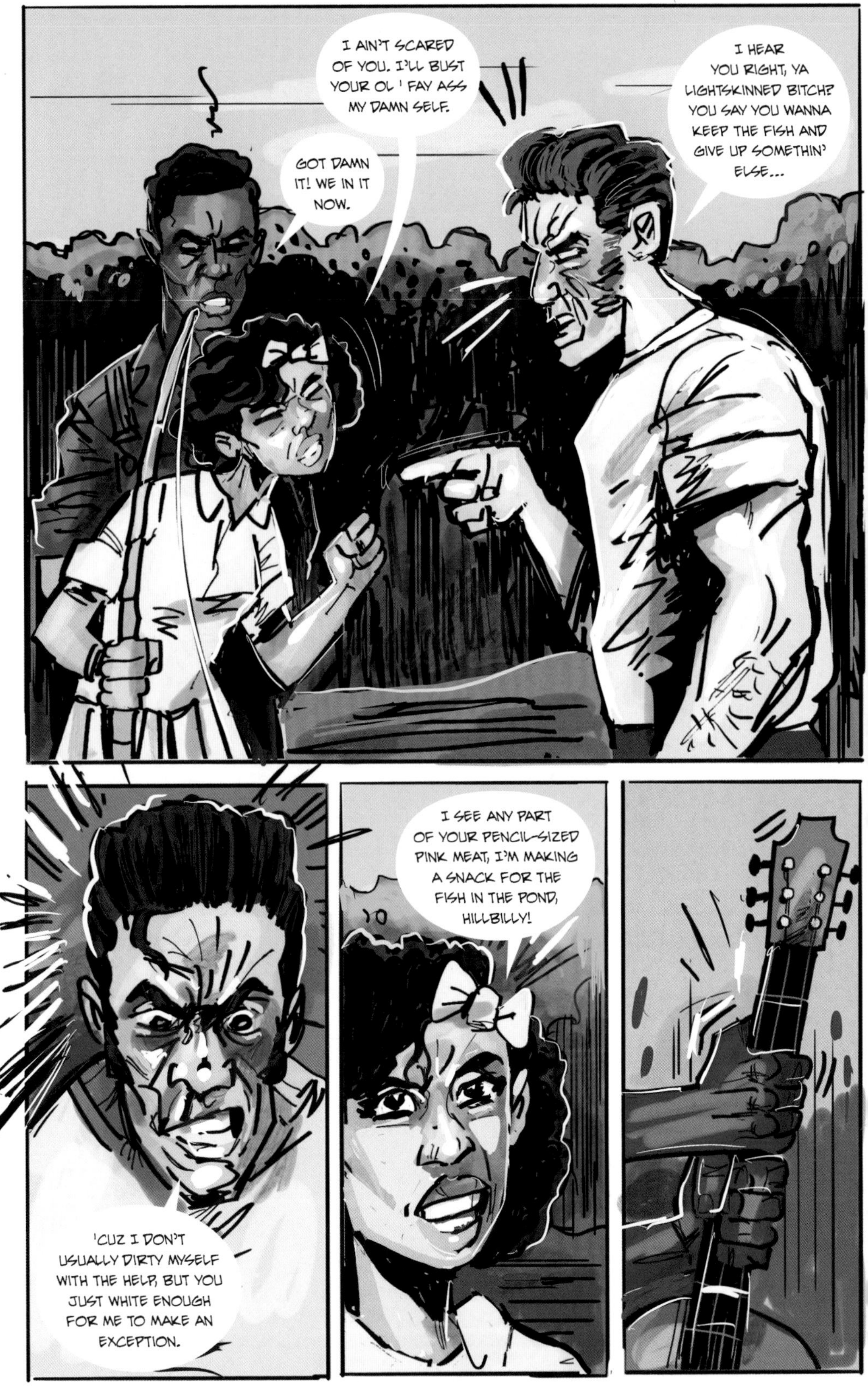
GOT DAMN IT! WE IN IT NOW.
I AIN'T SCARED OF YOU. I'LL BUST YOUR OL' FAY ASS MY DAMN SELF.
I HEAR YOU RIGHT, YA LIGHTSKINNED BITCH? YOU SAY YOU WANNA KEEP THE FISH AND GIVE UP SOMETHIN' ELSE...
'CUZ I DON'T USUALLY DIRTY MYSELF WITH THE HELP, BUT YOU JUST WHITE ENOUGH FOR ME TO MAKE AN EXCEPTION.
I SEE ANY PART OF YOUR PENCIL-SIZED PINK MEAT, I'M MAKING A SNACK FOR THE FISH IN THE POND, HILLBILLY!

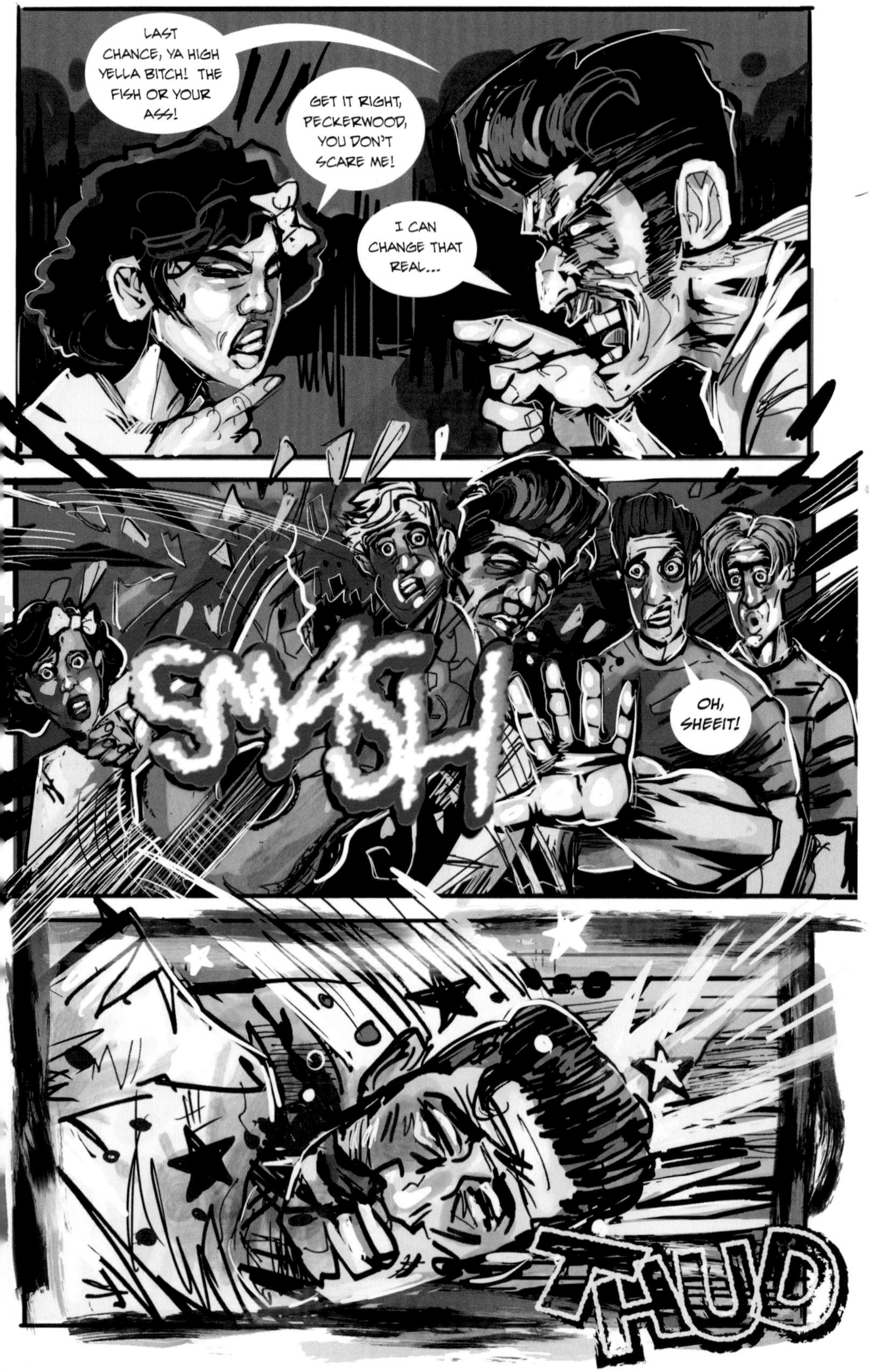
LAST CHANCE, YA HIGH YELLA BITCH! THE FISH OR YOUR ASS!
GET IT RIGHT, PECKERWOOD, YOU DON'T SCARE ME!
I CAN CHANGE THAT REAL...
SMASH
OH, SHEEIT!
THUD

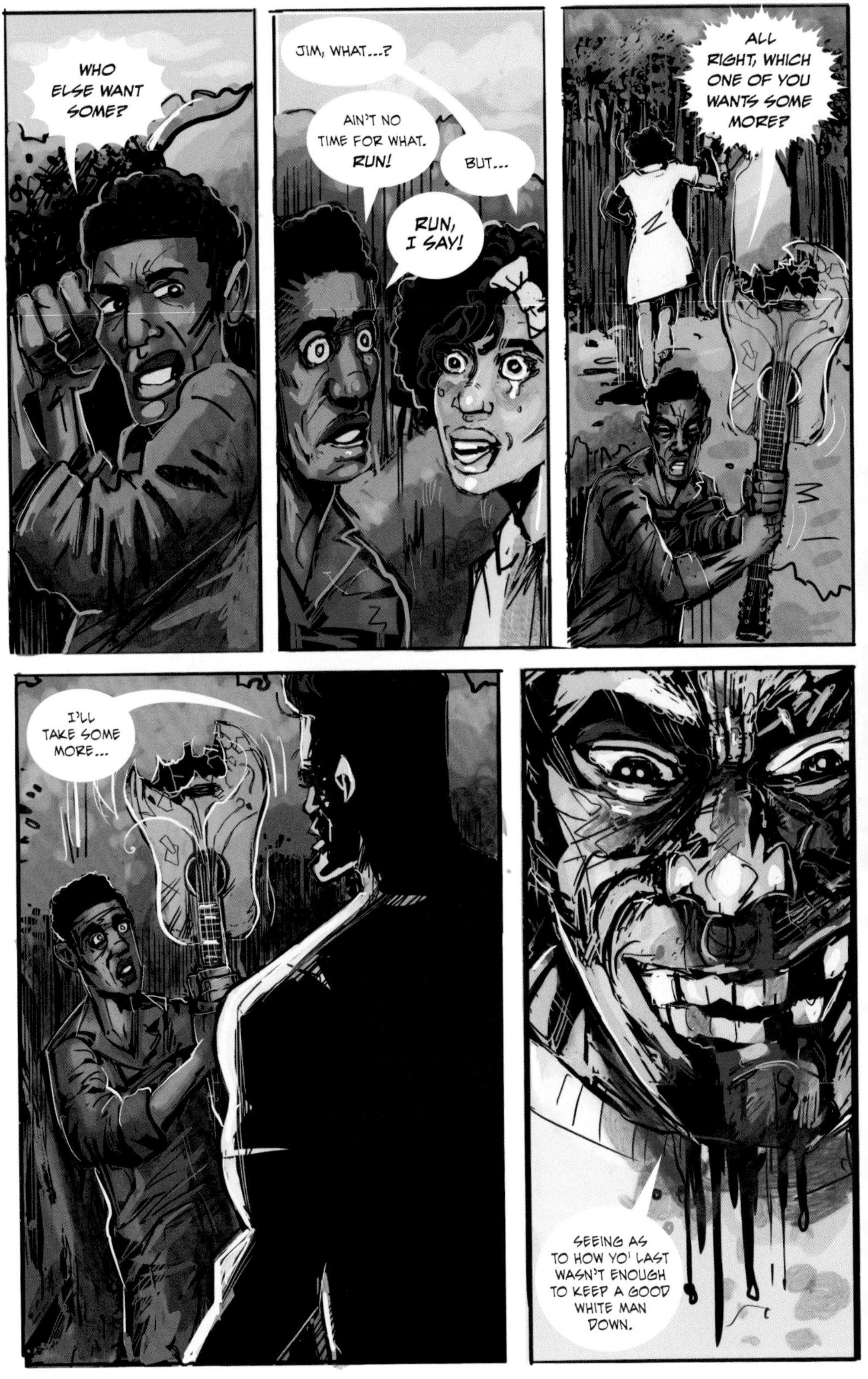
WHO ELSE WANT SOME?
JIM, WHAT...?
AIN'T NO TIME FOR WHAT. RUN!
BUT...
RUN, I SAY!
ALL RIGHT, WHICH ONE OF YOU WANTS SOME MORE?
I'LL TAKE SOME MORE...
SEEING AS TO HOW YO' LAST WASN'T ENOUGH TO KEEP A GOOD WHITE MAN DOWN.

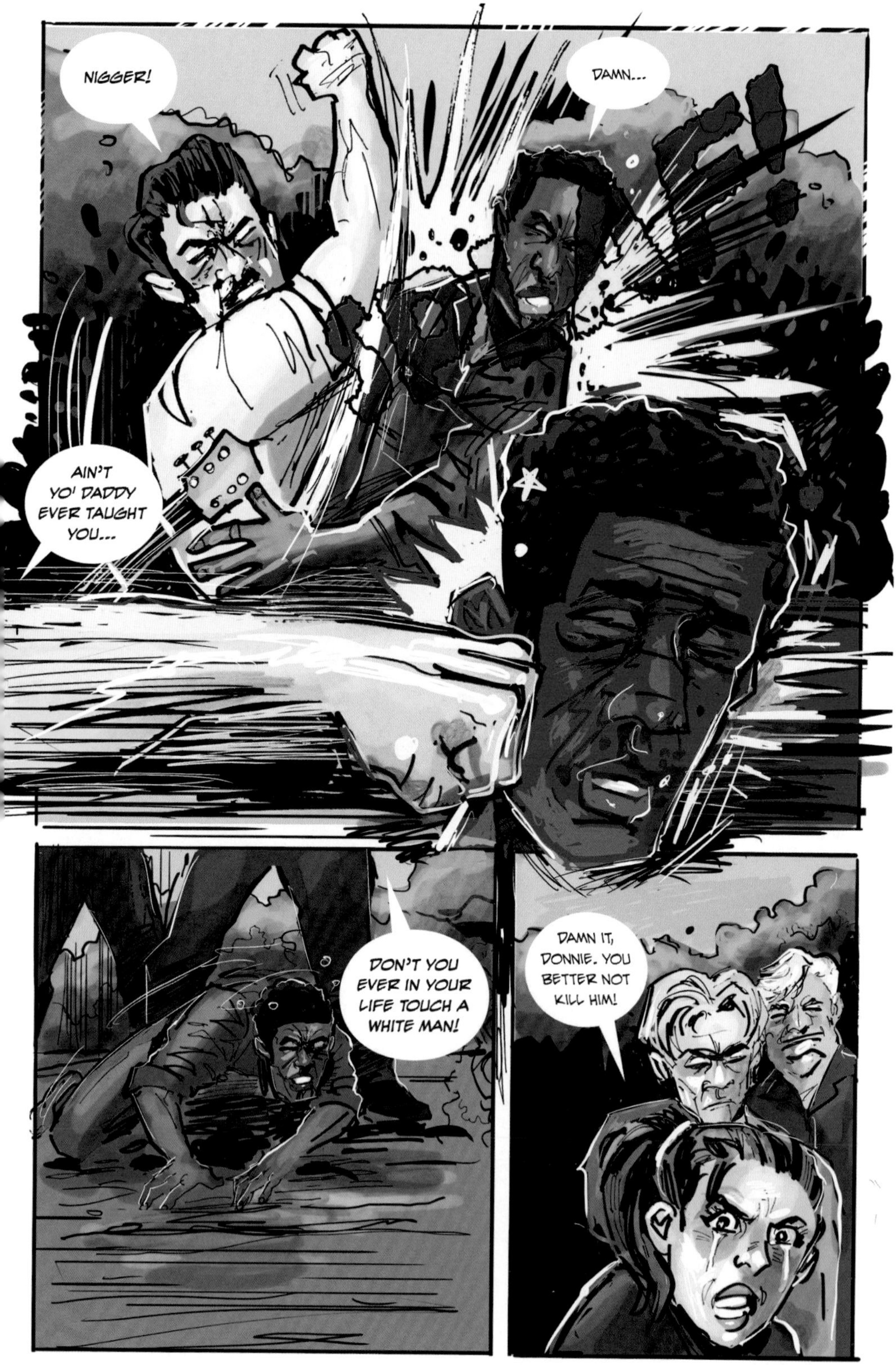
NIGGER!
DAMN...
AIN'T YO' DADDY EVER TAUGHT YOU...
DON'T YOU EVER IN YOUR LIFE TOUCH A WHITE MAN!
DAMN IT, DONNIE. YOU BETTER NOT KILL HIM!

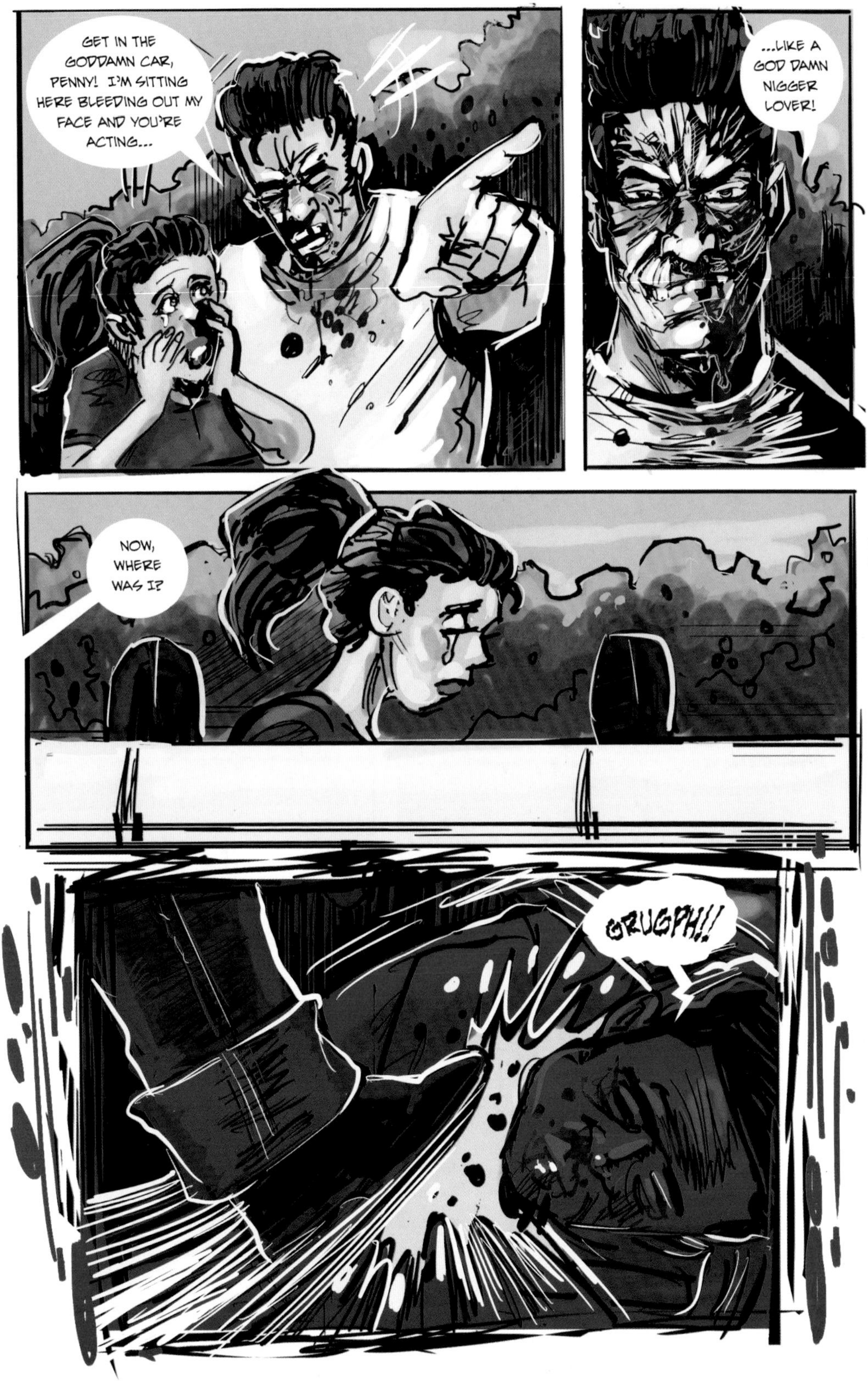
GET IN THE GODDAMN CAR, PENNY! I'M SITTING HERE BLEEDING OUT MY FACE AND YOU'RE ACTING...
...LIKE A GOD DAMN NIGGER LOVER!
NOW, WHERE WAS I?
GRUGPH!!

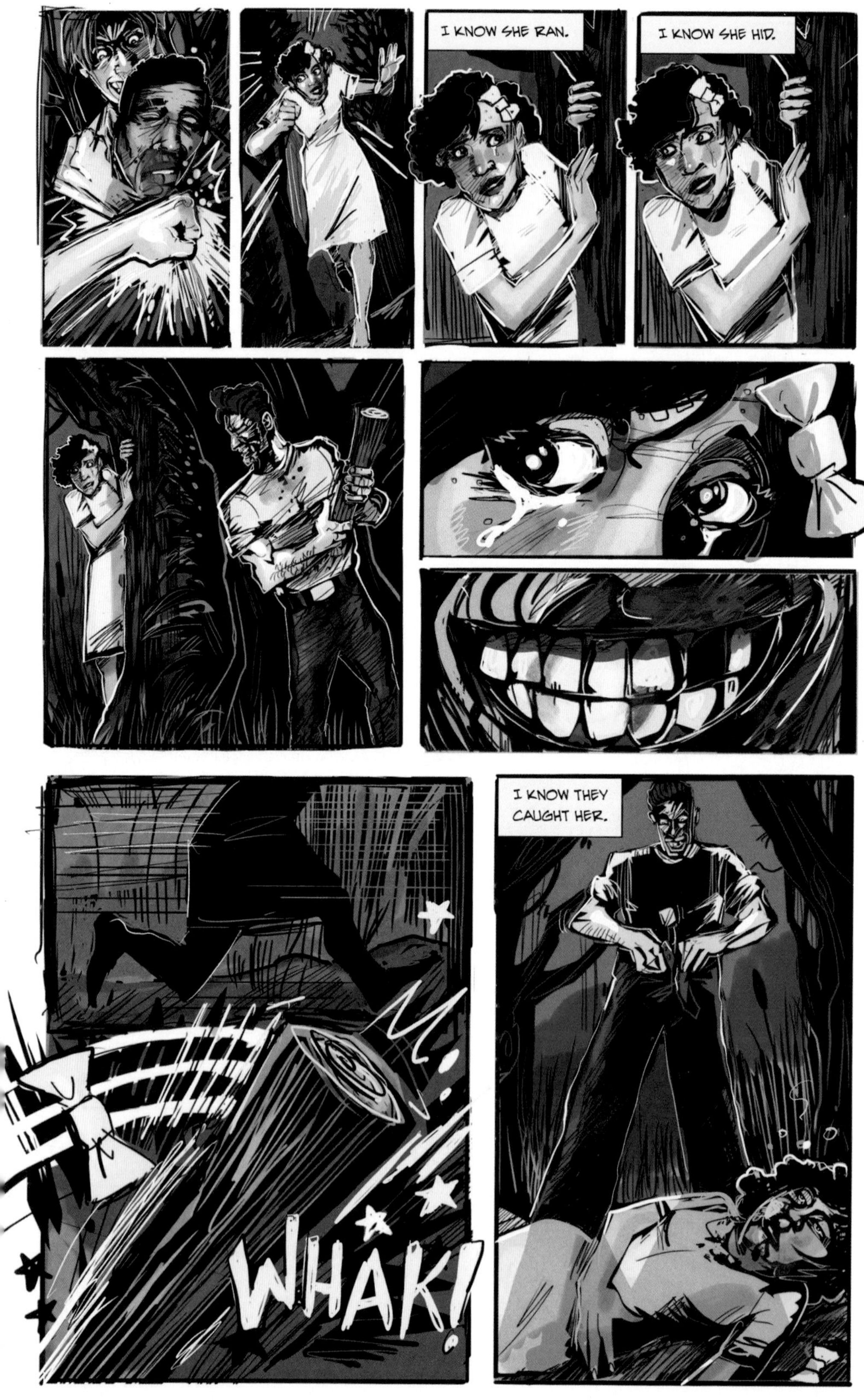
I KNOW SHE RAN.
I KNOW SHE HID.
WHAK!
I KNOW THEY CAUGHT HER.

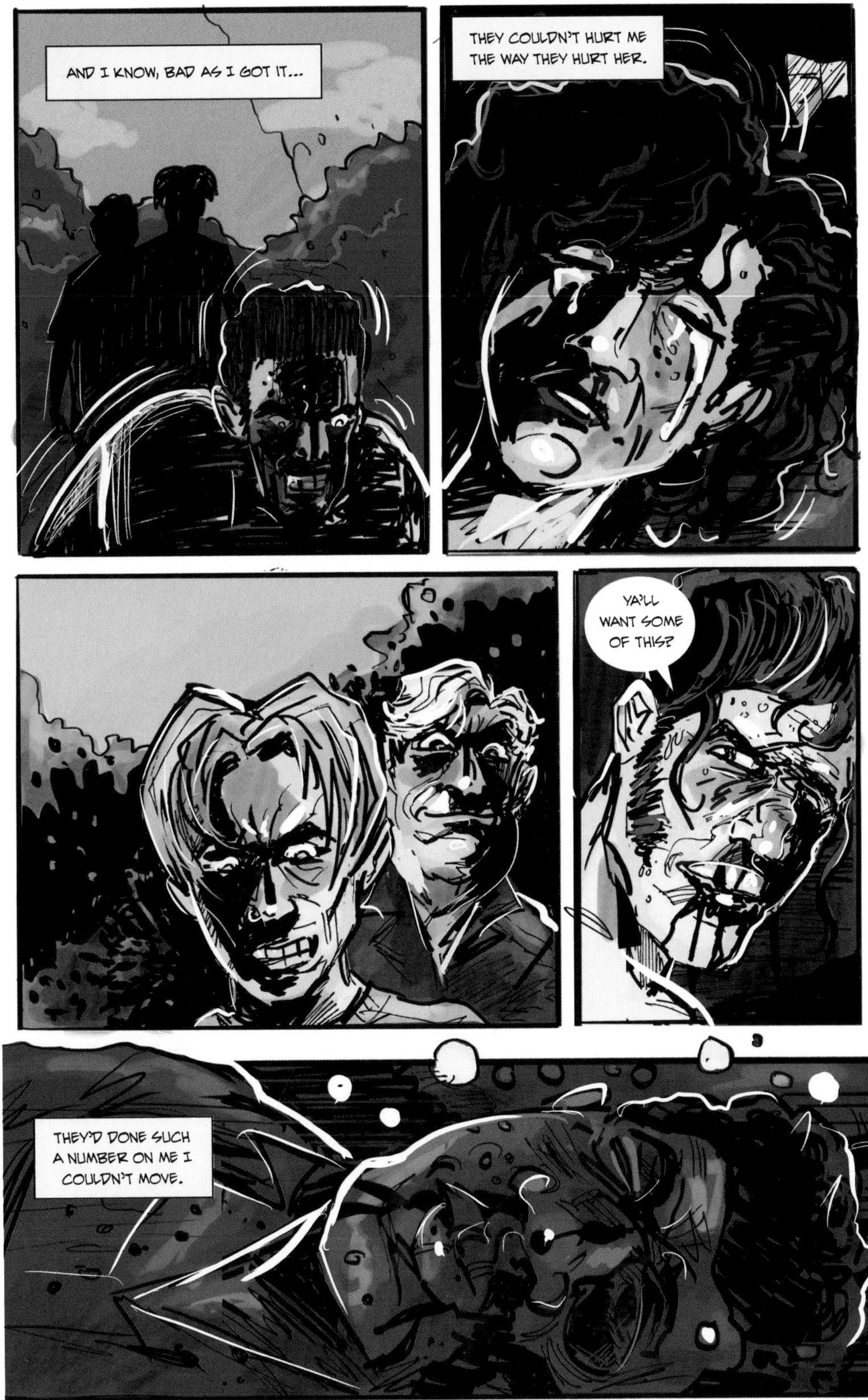
AND I KNOW, BAD AS I GOT IT...
THEY COULDN'T HURT ME THE WAY THEY HURT HER.
YA'LL WANT SOME OF THIS?
THEY'D DONE SUCH A NUMBER ON ME I COULDN'T MOVE.

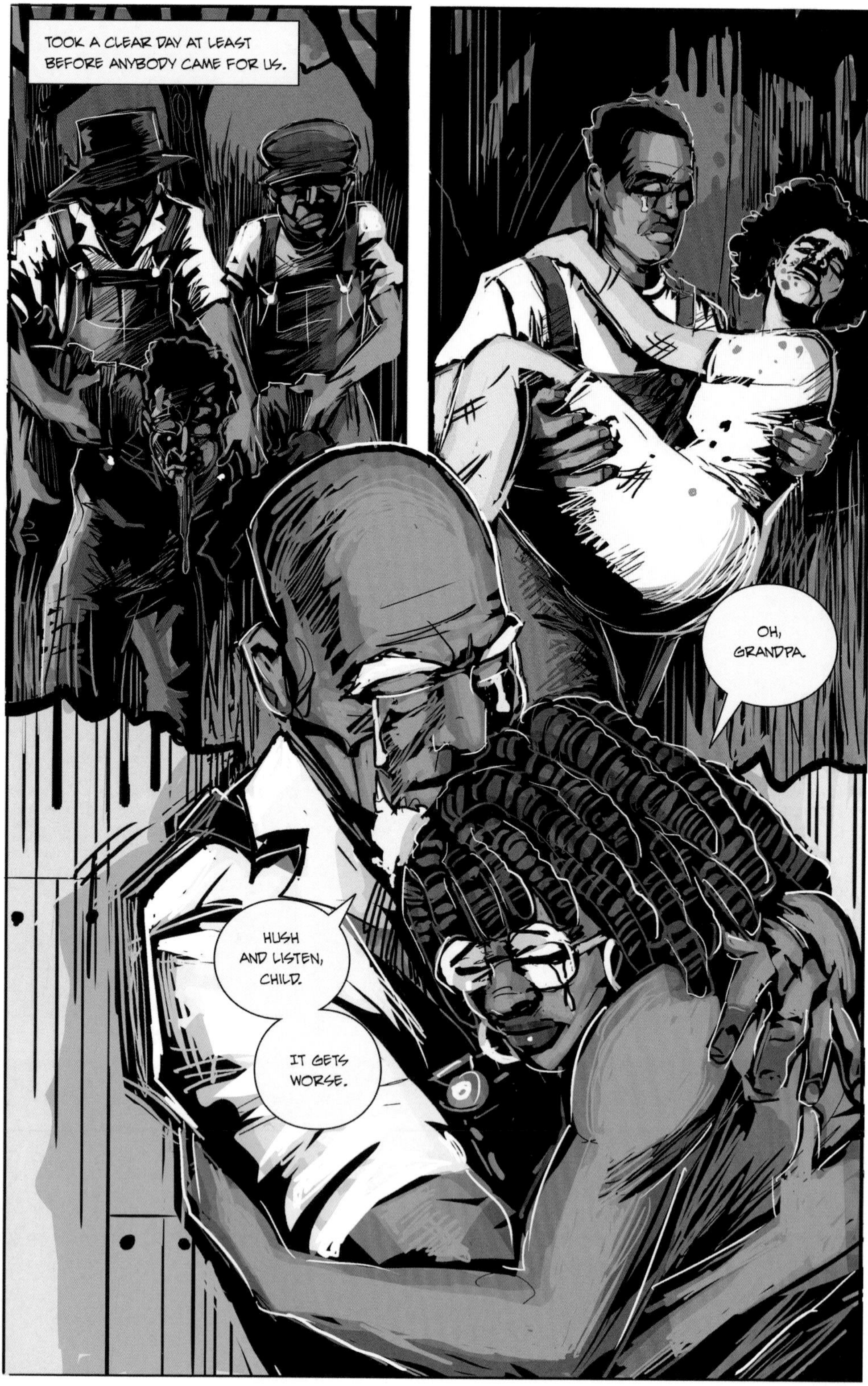
TOOK A CLEAR DAY AT LEAST BEFORE ANYBODY CAME FOR US.
OH, GRANDPA.
HUSH AND LISTEN, CHILD.
IT GETS WORSE.

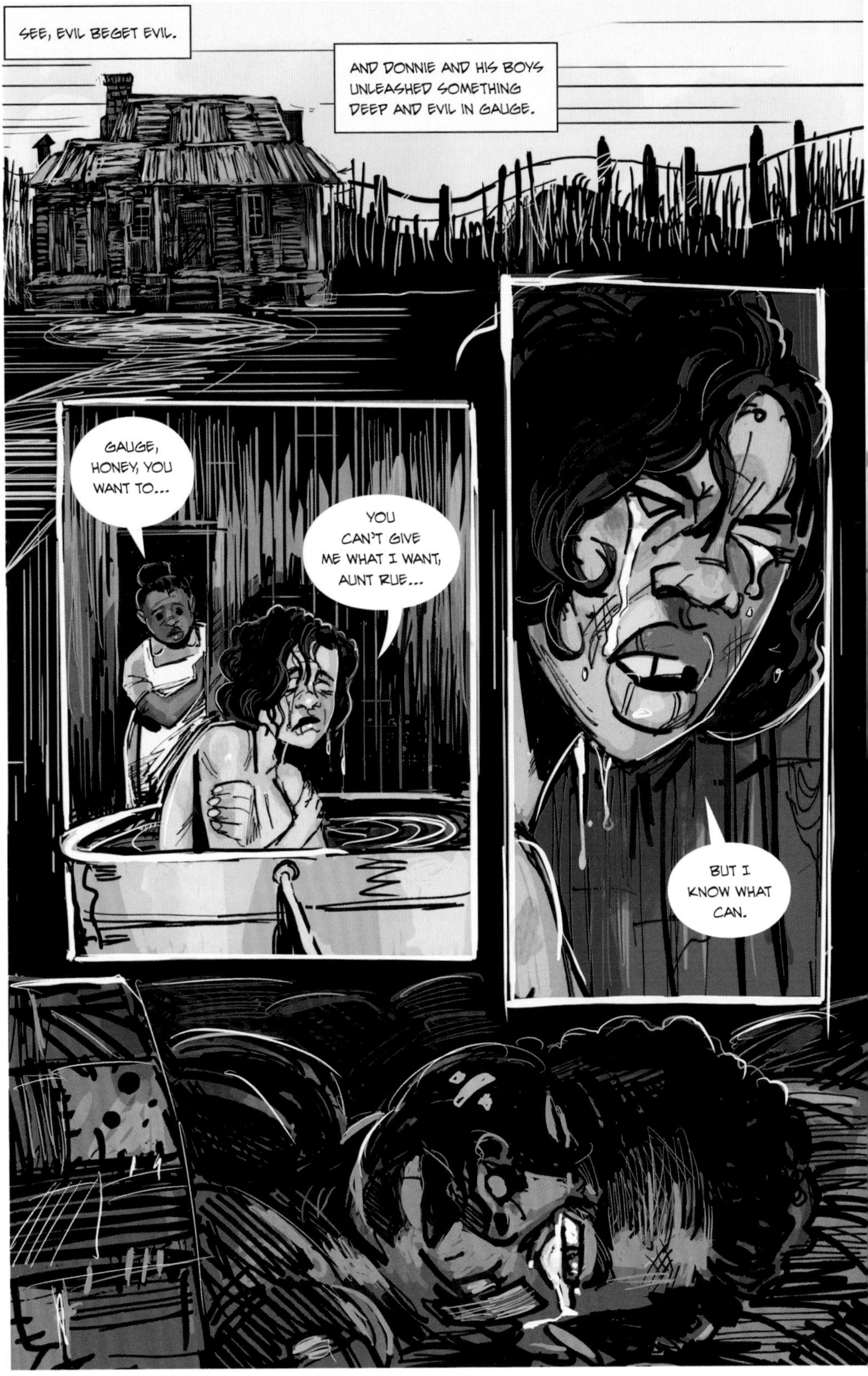
SEE, EVIL BEGET EVIL.
AND DONNIE AND HIS BOYS UNLEASHED SOMETHING DEEP AND EVIL IN GAUGE.
GAUGE, HONEY, YOU WANT TO...
YOU CAN'T GIVE ME WHAT I WANT, AUNT RUE...
BUT I KNOW WHAT CAN.

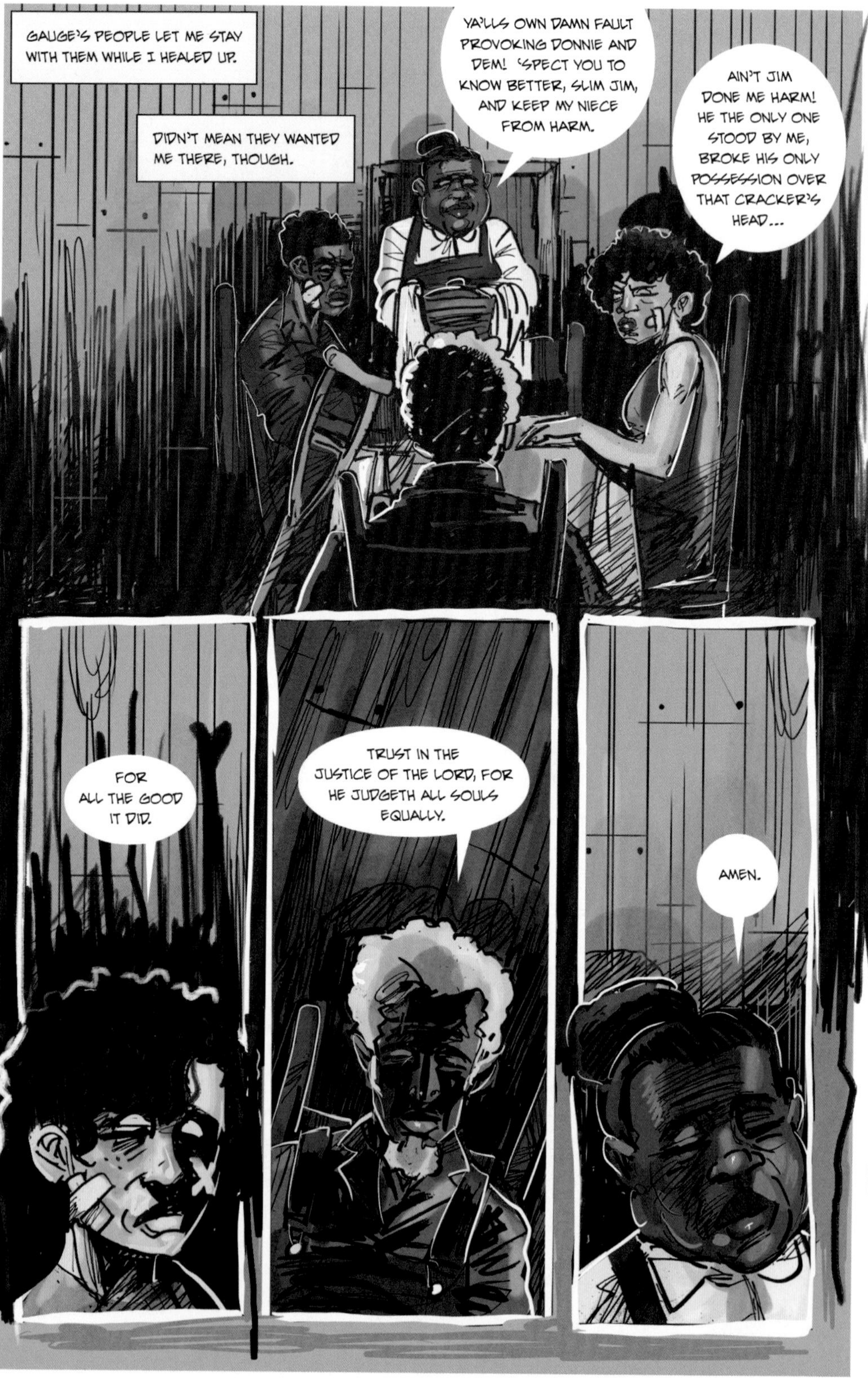
GAUGE'S PEOPLE LET ME STAY WITH THEM WHILE I HEALED UP.
DIDN'T MEAN THEY WANTED ME THERE, THOUGH.
YA'LLS OWN DAMN FAULT PROVOKING DONNIE AND DEM! 'SPECT YOU TO KNOW BETTER, SLIM JIM, AND KEEP MY NIECE FROM HARM.
AIN'T JIM DONE ME HARM! HE THE ONLY ONE STOOD BY ME, BROKE HIS ONLY POSSESSION OVER THAT CRACKER'S HEAD...
FOR ALL THE GOOD IT DID.
TRUST IN THE JUSTICE OF THE LORD, FOR HE JUDGETH ALL SOULS EQUALLY.
AMEN.

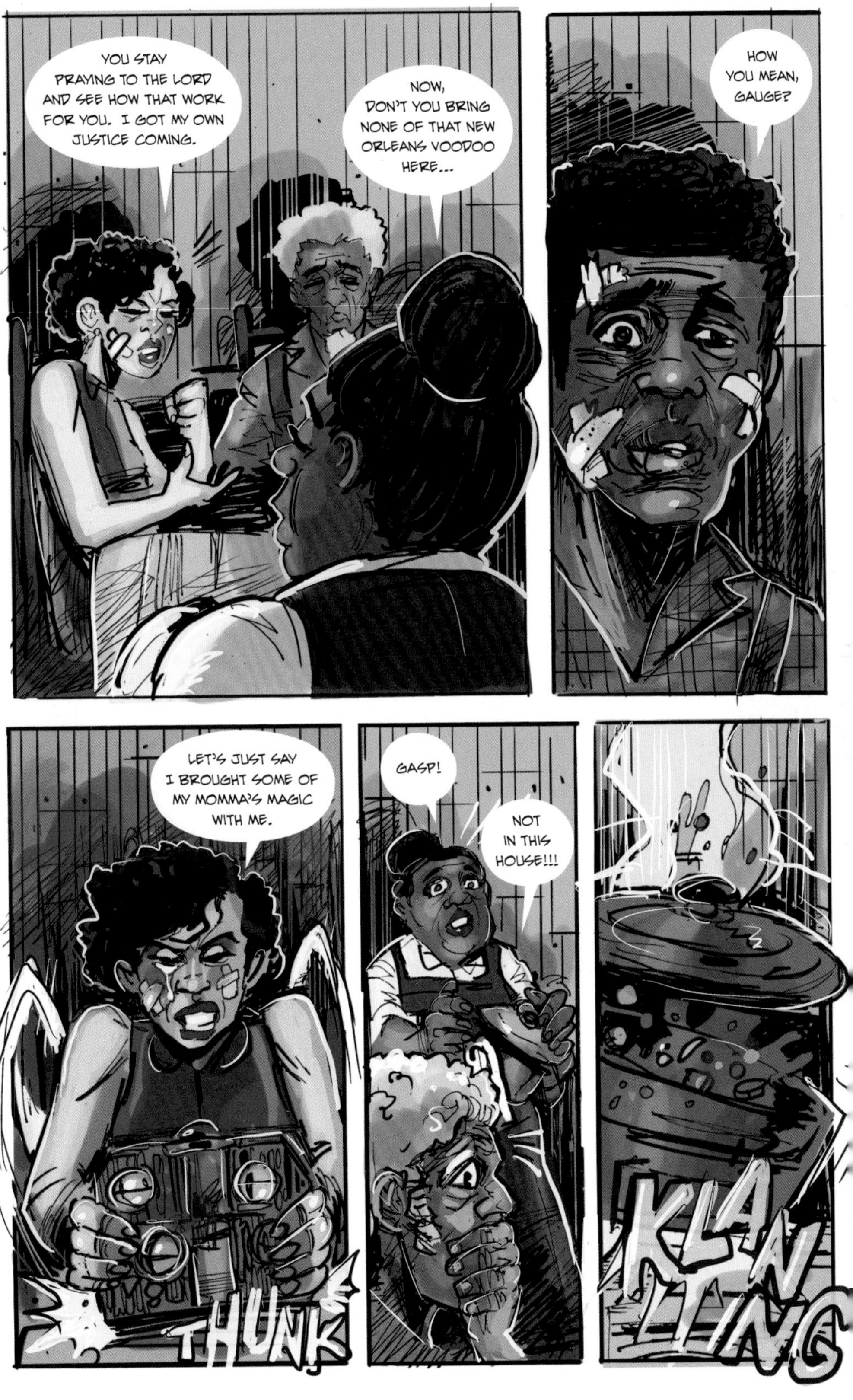
YOU STAY PRAYING TO THE LORD AND SEE HOW THAT WORK FOR YOU. I GOT MY OWN JUSTICE COMING.
NOW, DON'T YOU BRING NONE OF THAT NEW ORLEANS VOODOO HERE...
HOW YOU MEAN, GAUGE?
LET'S JUST SAY I BROUGHT SOME OF MY MOMMA'S MAGIC WITH ME.
THUNK
GASP!
NOT IN THIS HOUSE!!!
KLAN LING

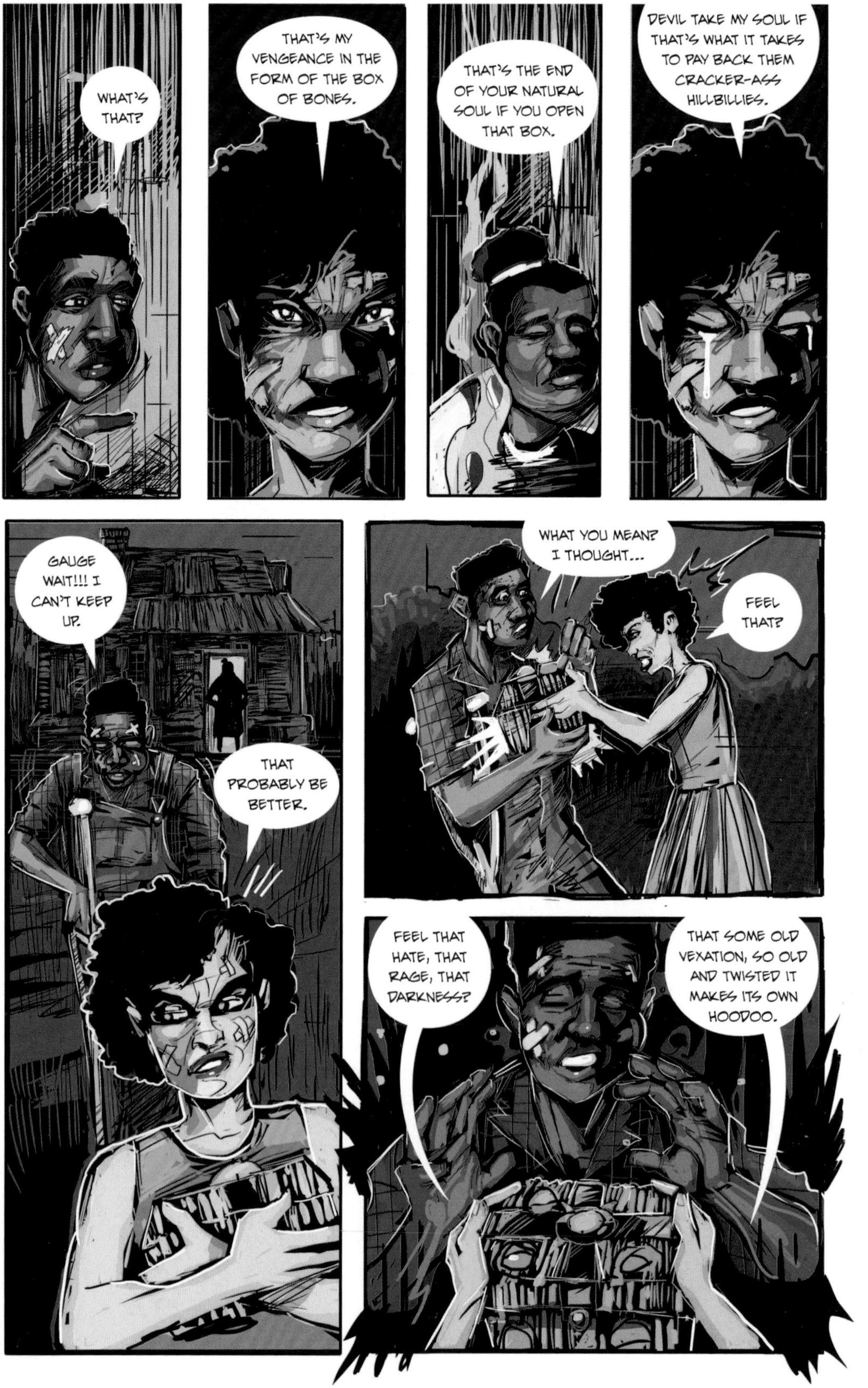
WHAT'S THAT?
THAT'S MY VENGEANCE IN THE FORM OF THE BOX OF BONES.
THAT'S THE END OF YOUR NATURAL SOUL IF YOU OPEN THAT BOX.
DEVIL TAKE MY SOUL IF THAT'S WHAT IT TAKES TO PAY BACK THEM CRACKER-ASS HILLBILLIES.
GAUGE WAIT!!! I CAN'T KEEP UP.
THAT PROBABLY BE BETTER.
WHAT YOU MEAN? I THOUGHT...
FEEL THAT?
FEEL THAT HATE, THAT RAGE, THAT DARKNESS?
THAT SOME OLD VEXATION, SO OLD AND TWISTED IT MAKES ITS OWN HOODOO.

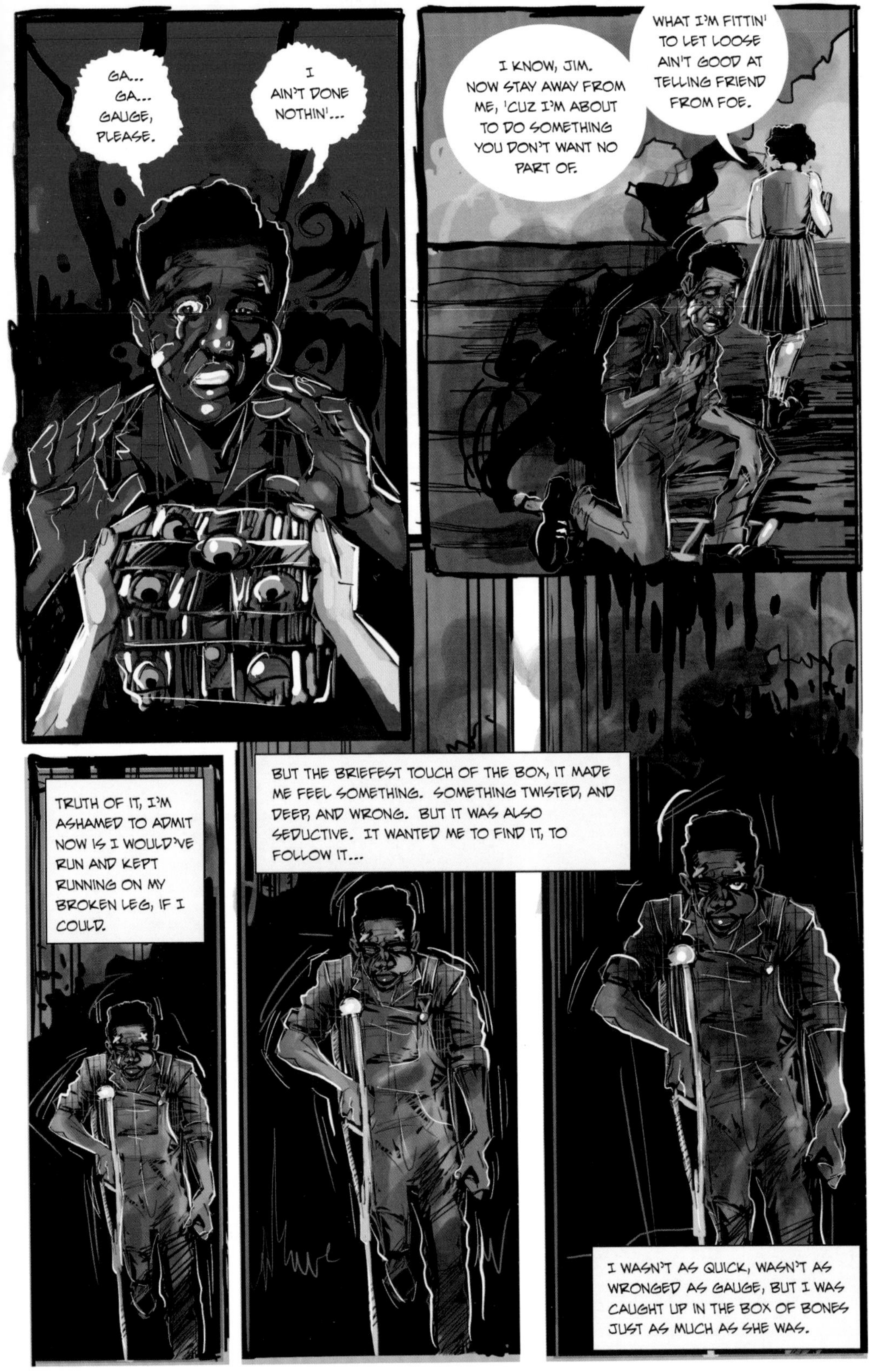
GA... GA... GAUGE, PLEASE.
I AIN'T DONE NOTHIN'...
I KNOW, JIM. NOW STAY AWAY FROM ME, 'CUZ I'M ABOUT TO DO SOMETHING YOU DON'T WANT NO PART OF.
WHAT I'M FITTIN' TO LET LOOSE AIN'T GOOD AT TELLING FRIEND FROM FOE.
TRUTH OF IT, I'M ASHAMED TO ADMIT NOW IS I WOULD'VE RUN AND KEPT RUNNING ON MY BROKEN LEG, IF I COULD.
BUT THE BRIEFEST TOUCH OF THE BOX, IT MADE ME FEEL SOMETHING. SOMETHING TWISTED, AND DEEP, AND WRONG. BUT IT WAS ALSO SEDUCTIVE. IT WANTED ME TO FIND IT, TO FOLLOW IT...
I WASN'T AS QUICK, WASN'T AS WRONGED AS GAUGE, BUT I WAS CAUGHT UP IN THE BOX OF BONES JUST AS MUCH AS SHE WAS.

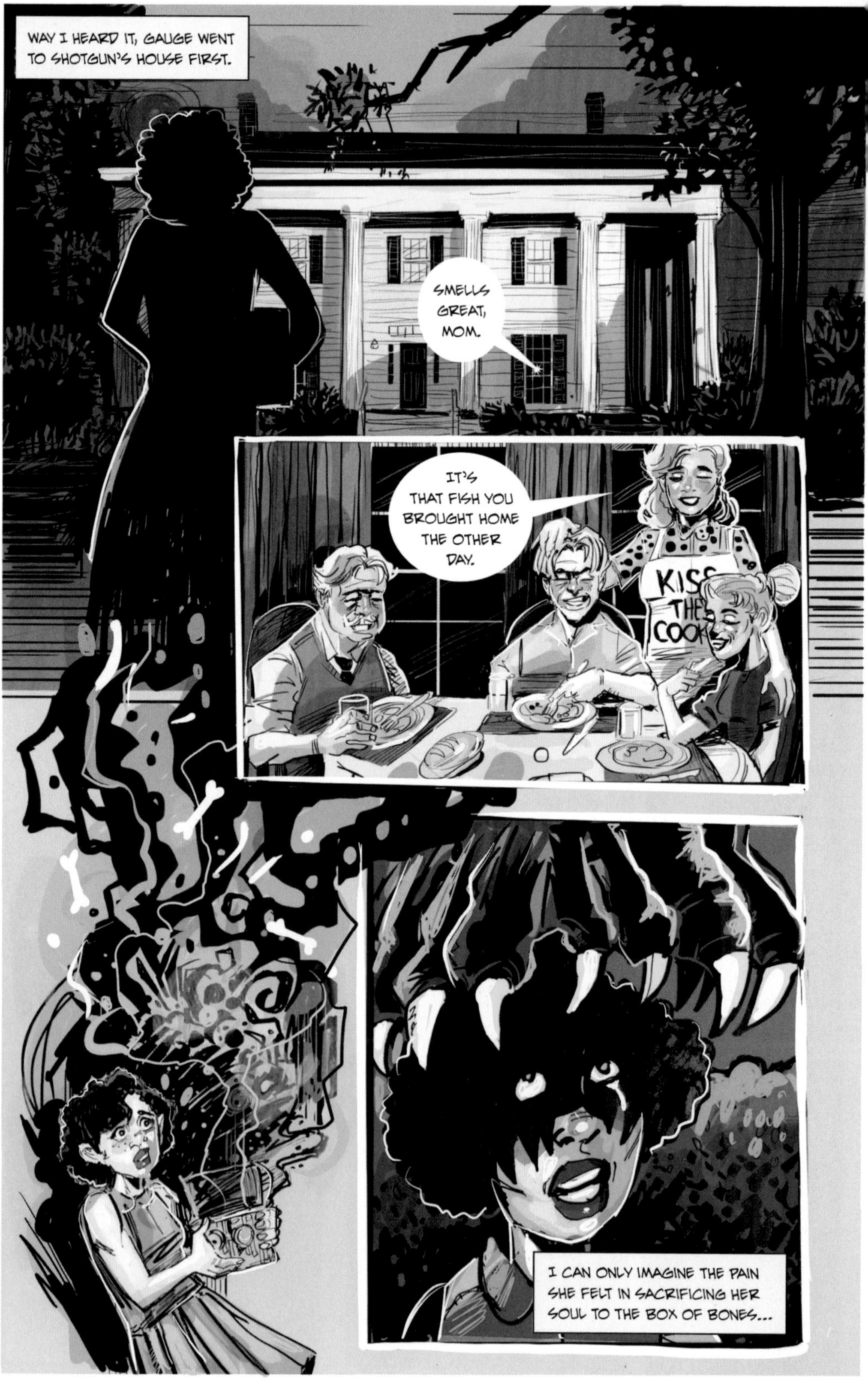
WAY I HEARD IT, GAUGE WENT TO SHOTGUN'S HOUSE FIRST.
SMELLS GREAT, MOM.
IT'S THAT FISH YOU BROUGHT HOME THE OTHER DAY.
KISS THE COOK
I CAN ONLY IMAGINE THE PAIN SHE FELT IN SACRIFICING HER SOUL TO THE BOX OF BONES...

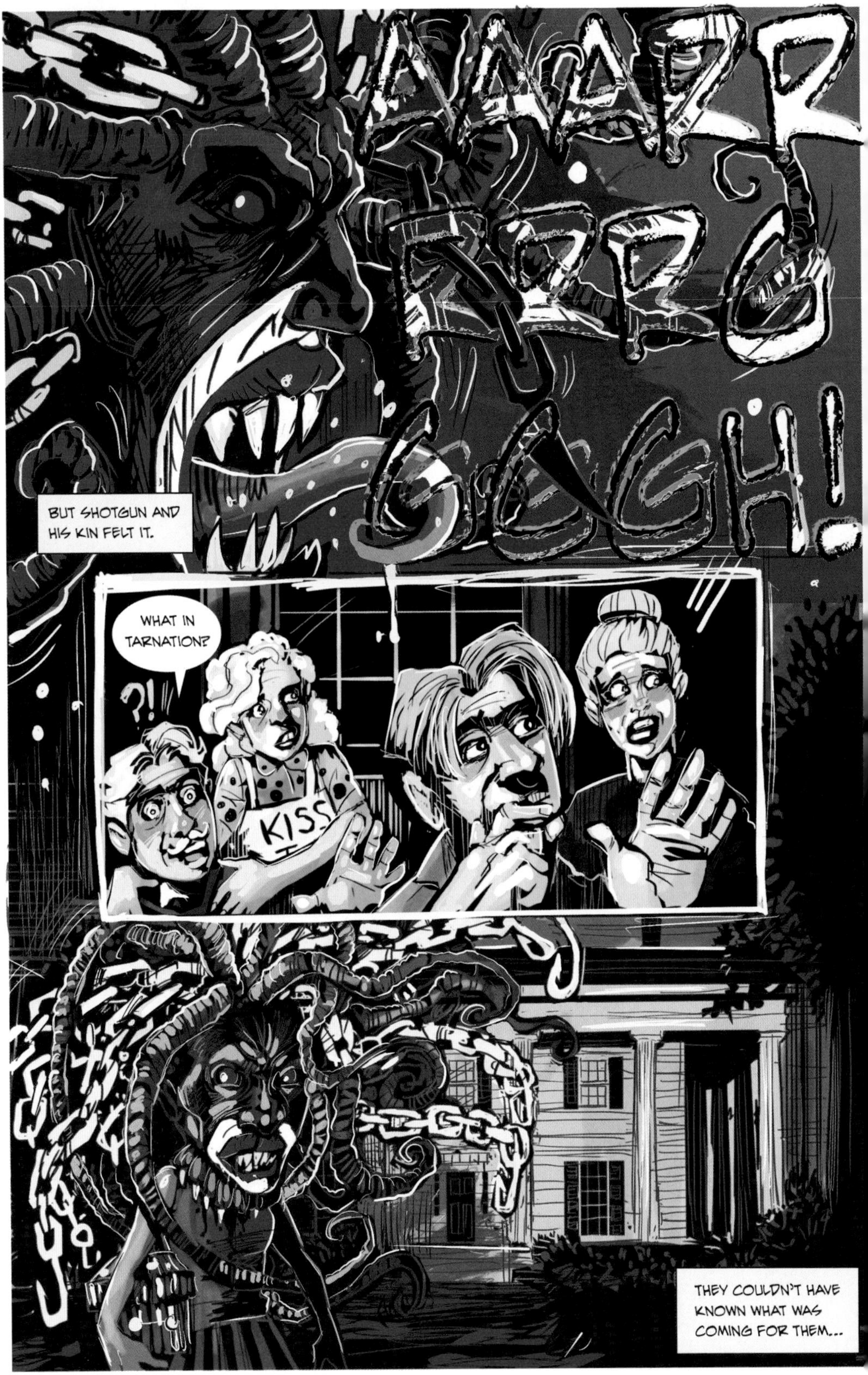
BUT SHOTGUN AND HIS KIN FELT IT.
WHAT IN TARNATION?
?!
KISS
THEY COULDN'T HAVE KNOWN WHAT WAS COMING FOR THEM...

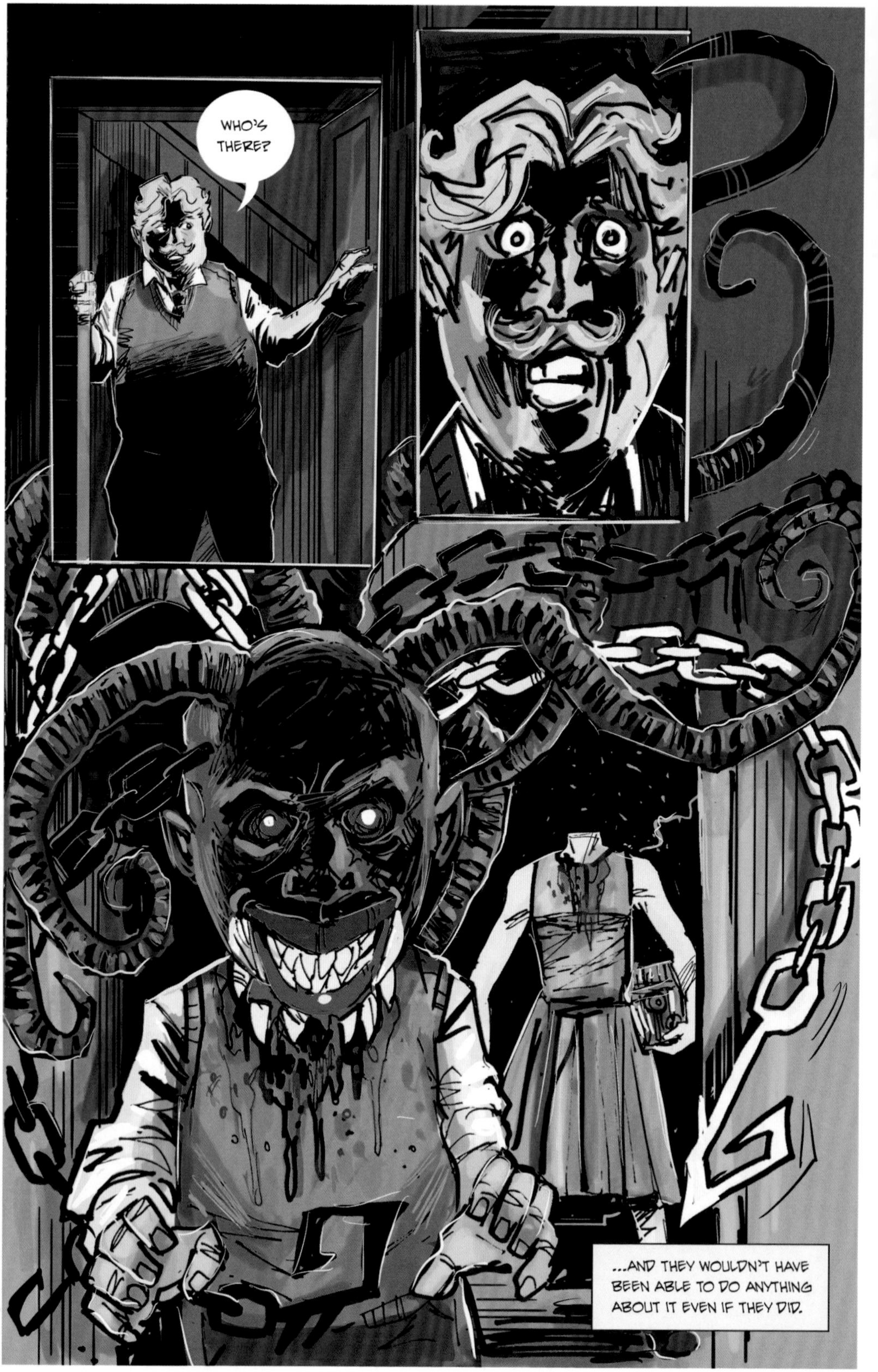
WHO'S THERE?
...AND THEY WOULDN'T HAVE BEEN ABLE TO DO ANYTHING ABOUT IT EVEN IF THEY DID.

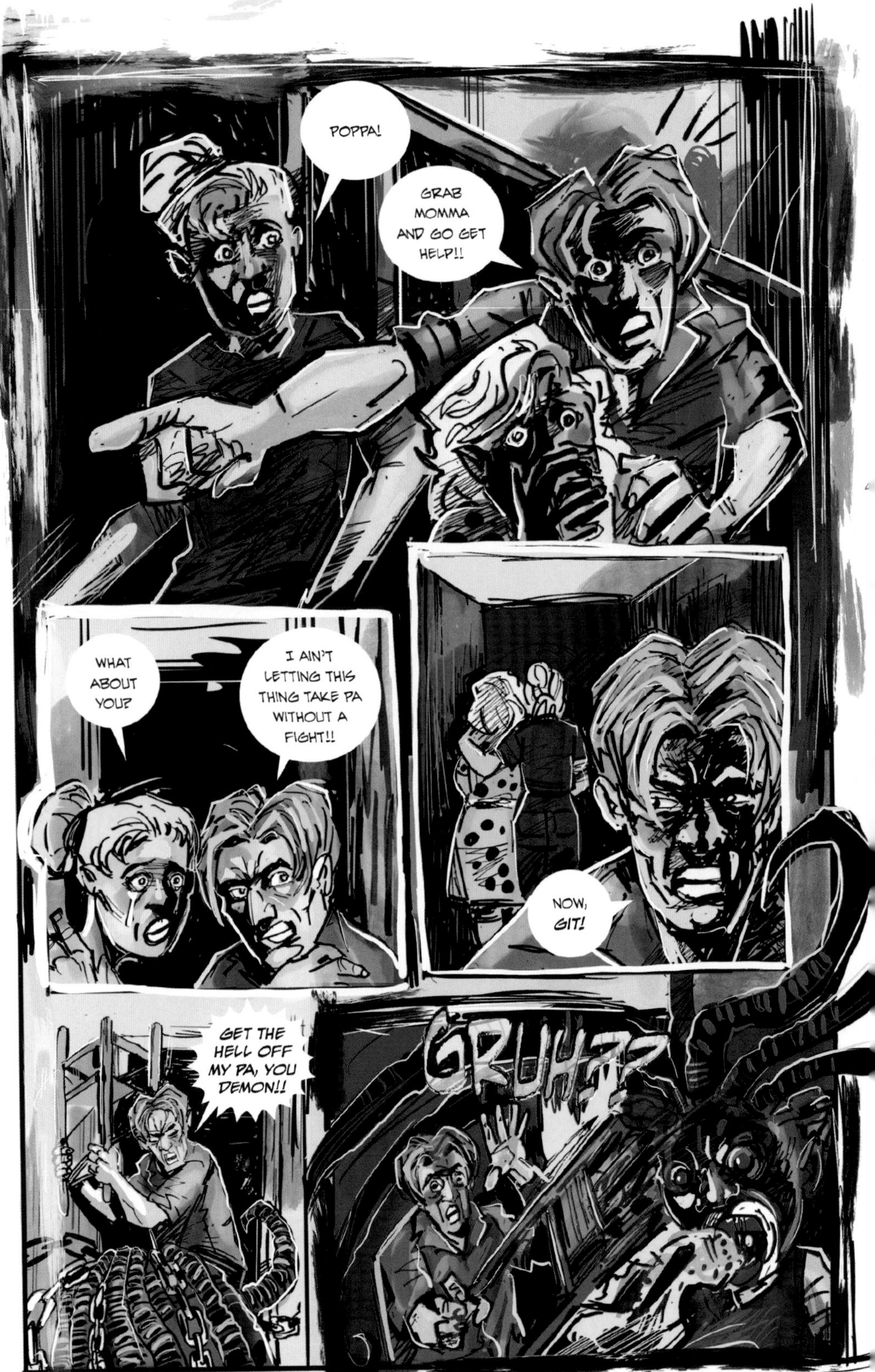
POPPA!
GRAB MOMMA AND GO GET HELP!!
WHAT ABOUT YOU?
I AIN'T LETTING THIS THING TAKE PA WITHOUT A FIGHT!!
NOW, GIT!
GET THE HELL OFF MY PA, YOU DEMON!!
GRUH?!?

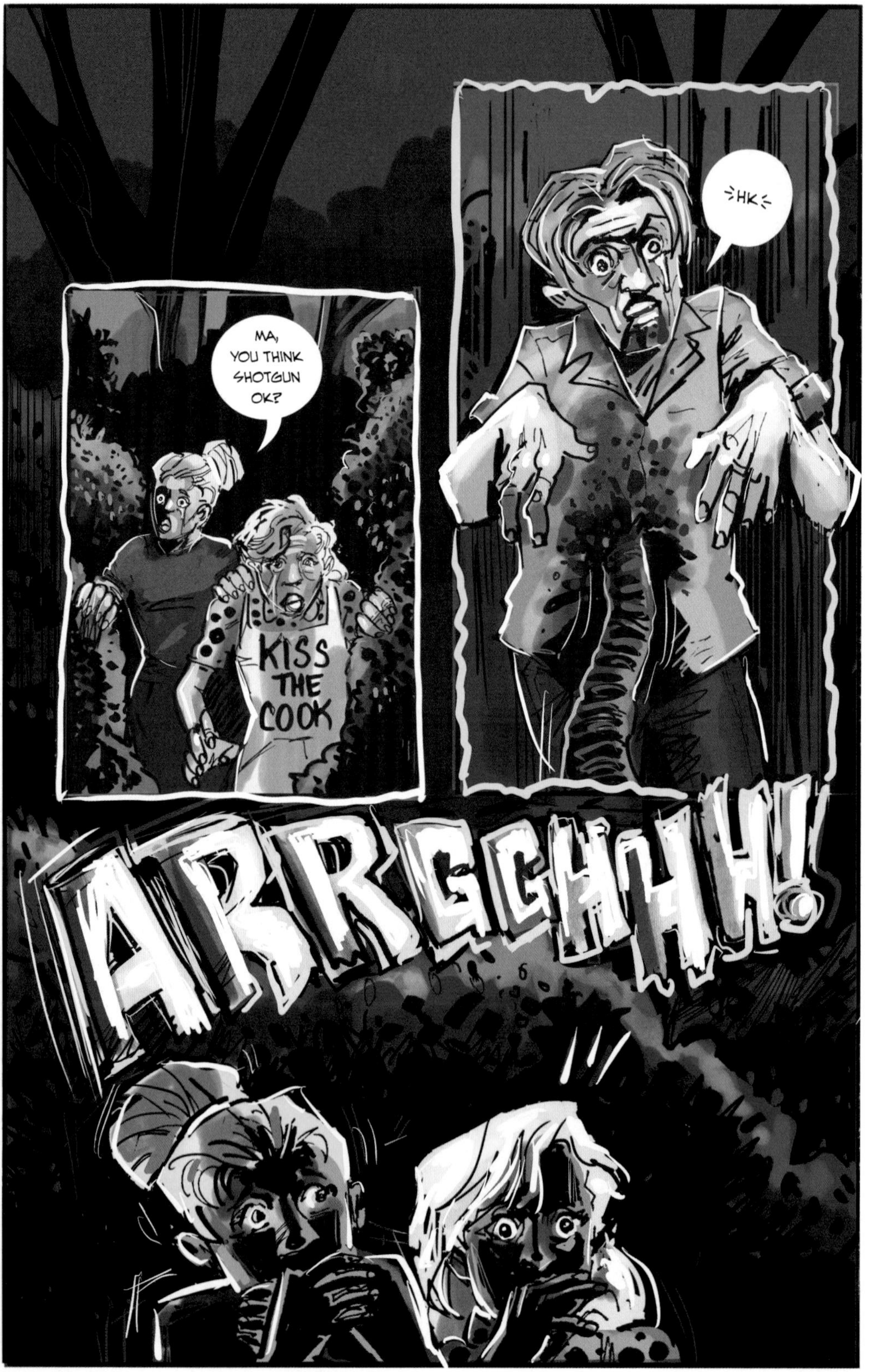
MA, YOU THINK SHOTGUN OK?
KISS THE COOK
HK
ARRGGHHH!

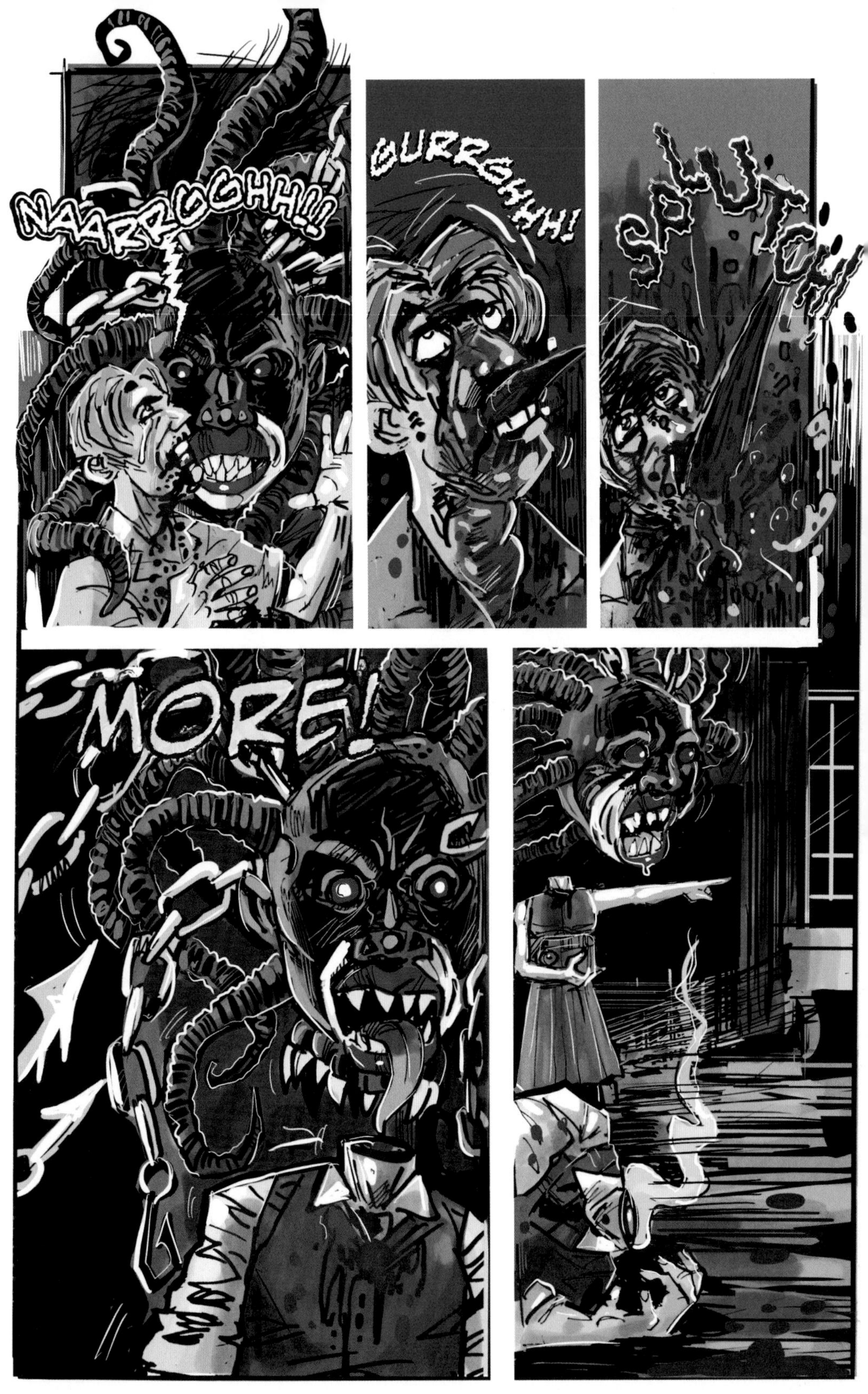
NAARRGGHH!!!
GURRGHHH!
SPLUTCH!!
MORE!

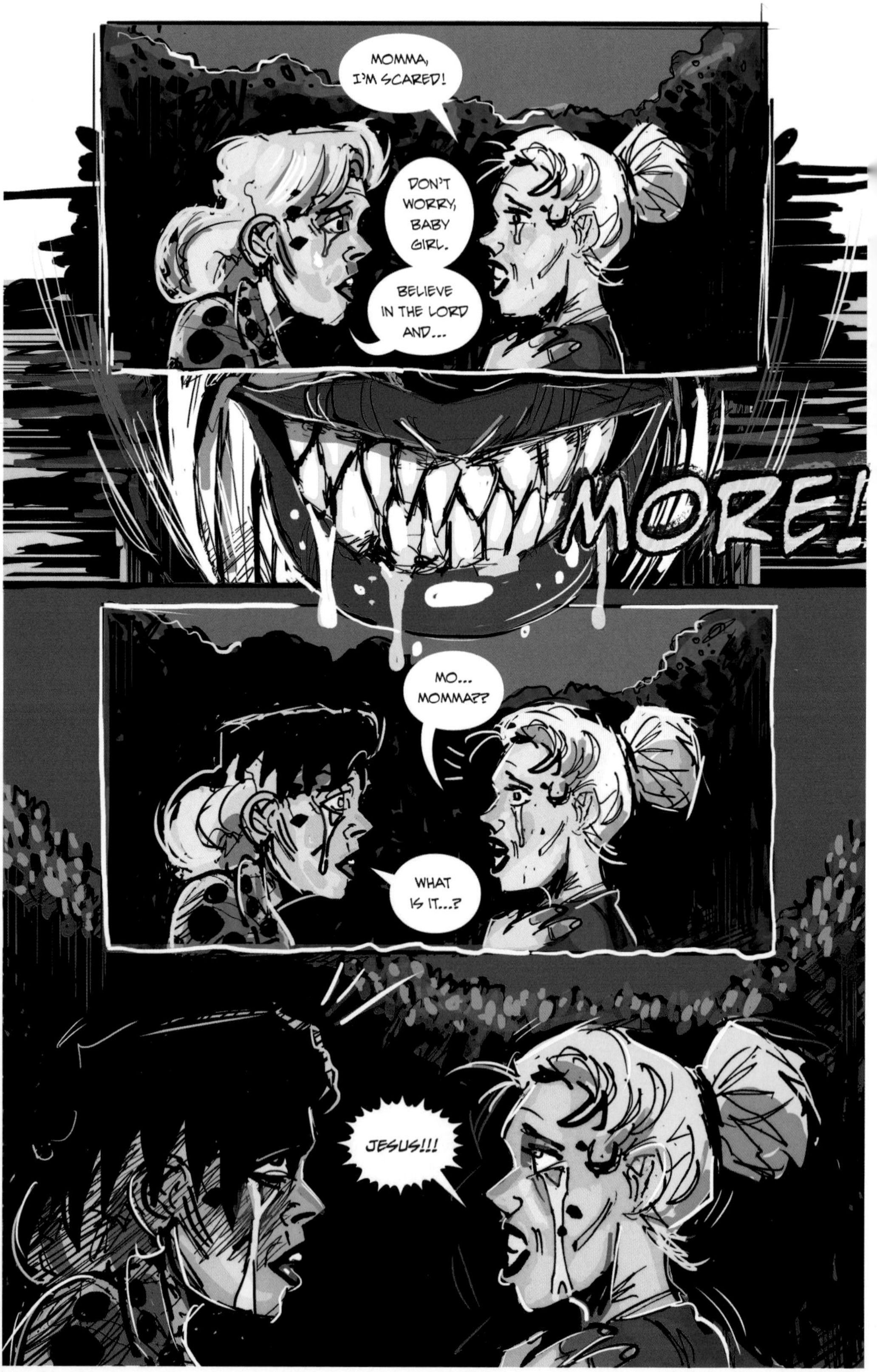
MOMMA, I'M SCARED!
DON'T WORRY, BABY GIRL.
BELIEVE IN THE LORD AND...
MORE!
MO... MOMMA??
WHAT IS IT...?
JESUS!!!

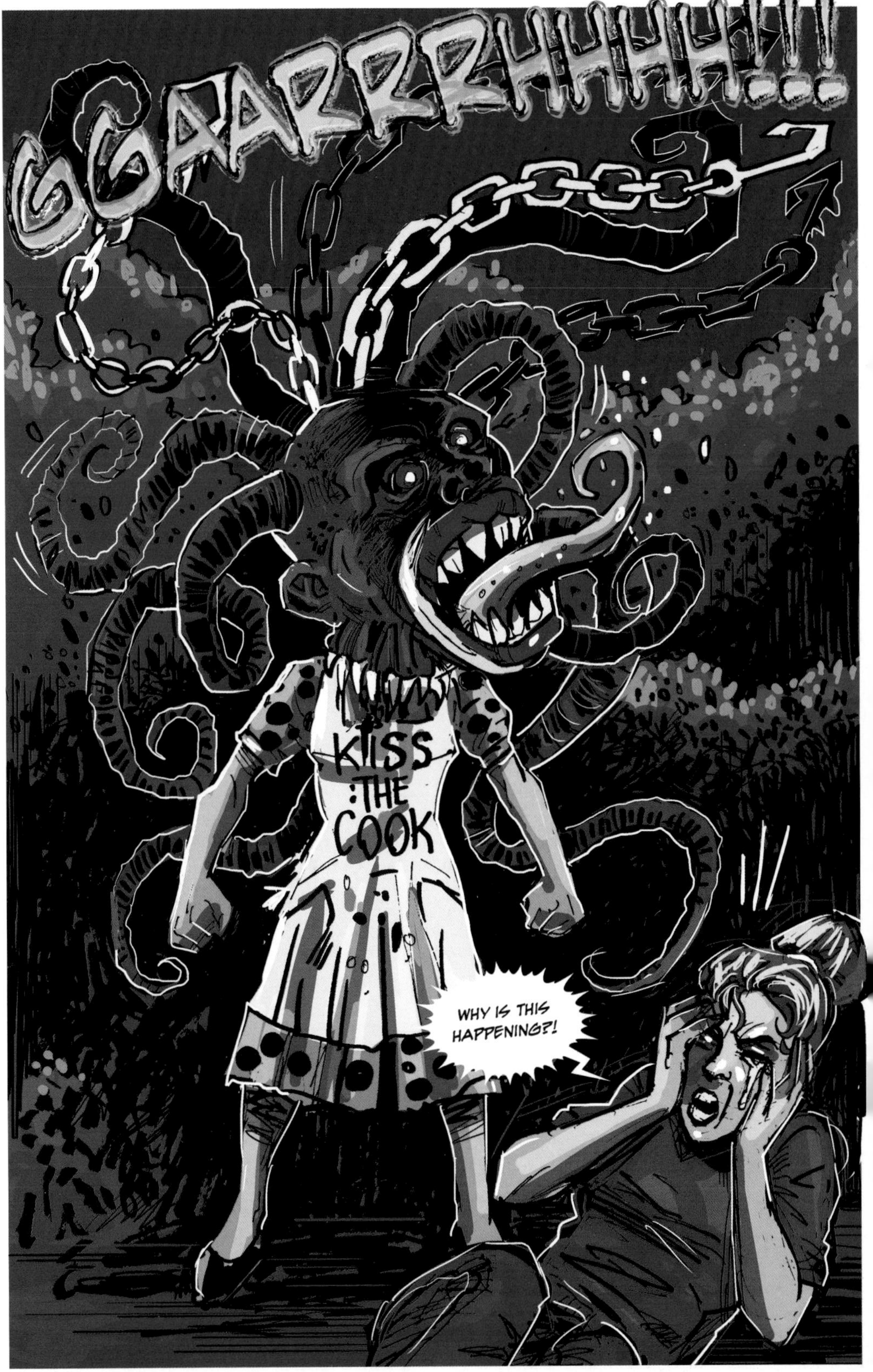
GGAARRRHHHH!!!
KISS THE COOK
WHY IS THIS HAPPENING?!

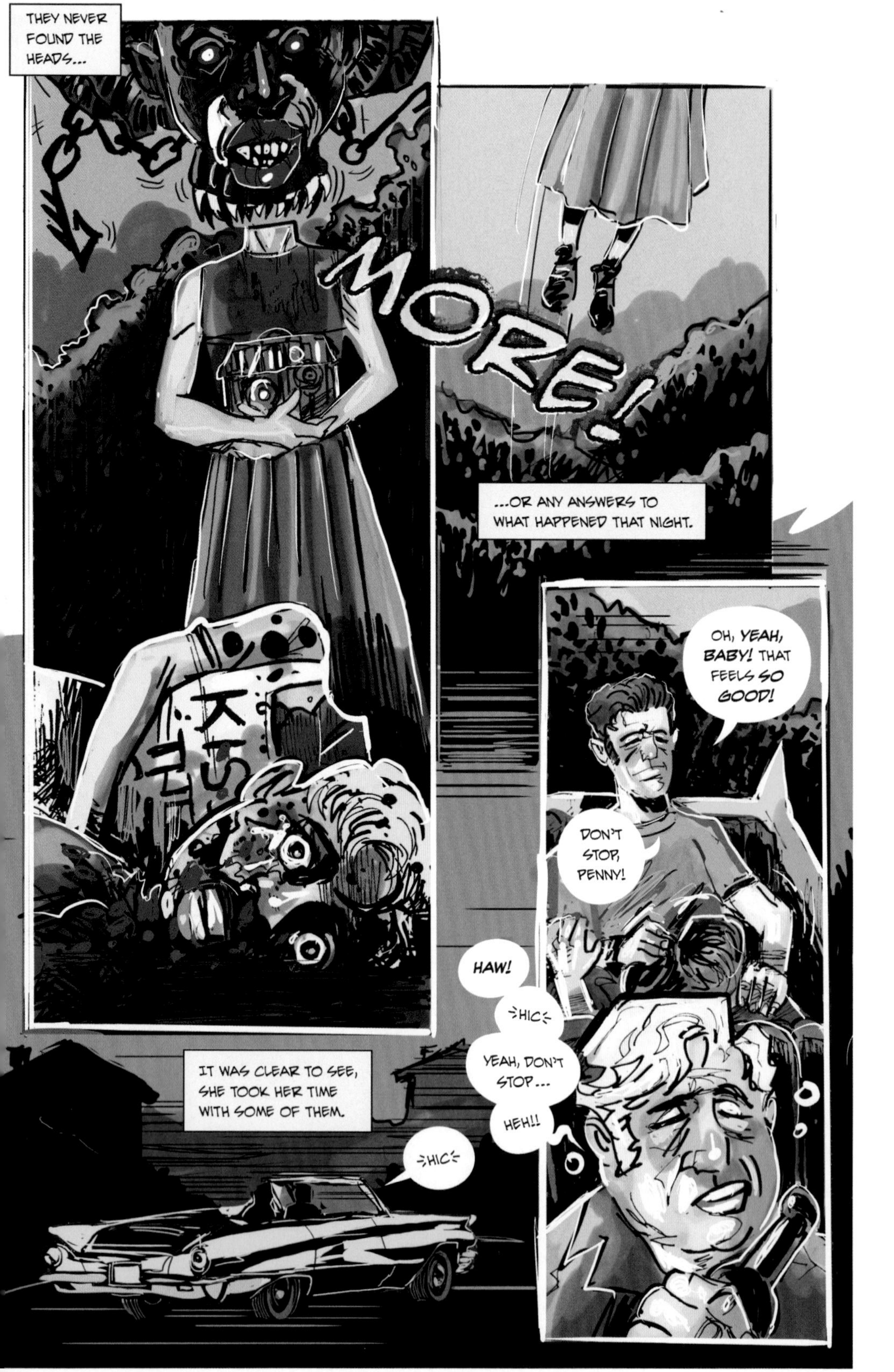
THEY NEVER FOUND THE HEADS...
MORE!
...OR ANY ANSWERS TO WHAT HAPPENED THAT NIGHT.
OH, YEAH, BABY! THAT FEELS SO GOOD!
DON'T STOP, PENNY!
IT WAS CLEAR TO SEE, SHE TOOK HER TIME WITH SOME OF THEM.
HIC
HAW!
HIC
YEAH, DON'T STOP...
HEH!!

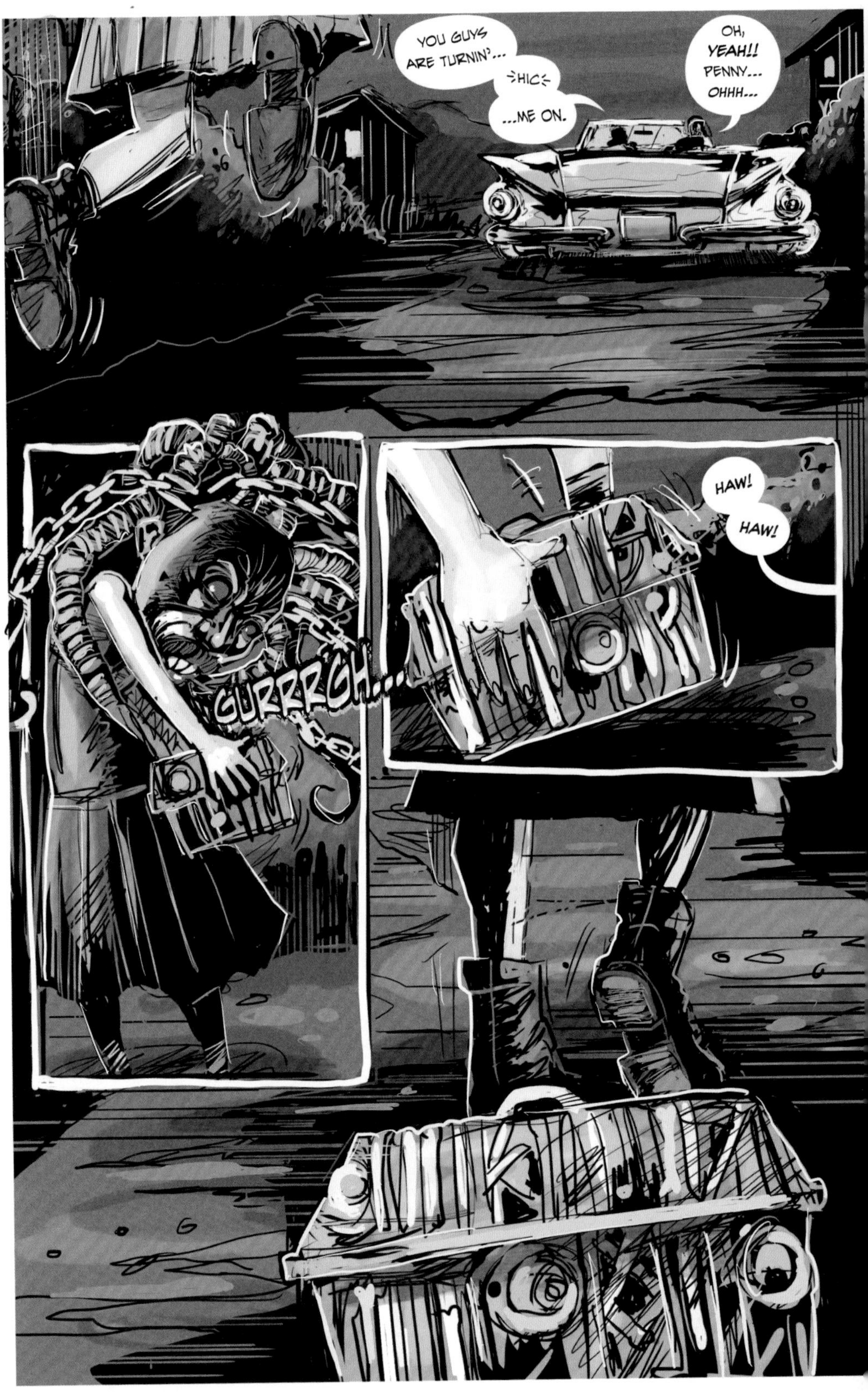
YOU GUYS ARE TURNIN'...
HIC
...ME ON.
OH, YEAH!! PENNY... OHHH...
GURRRGH...
HAW!
HAW!

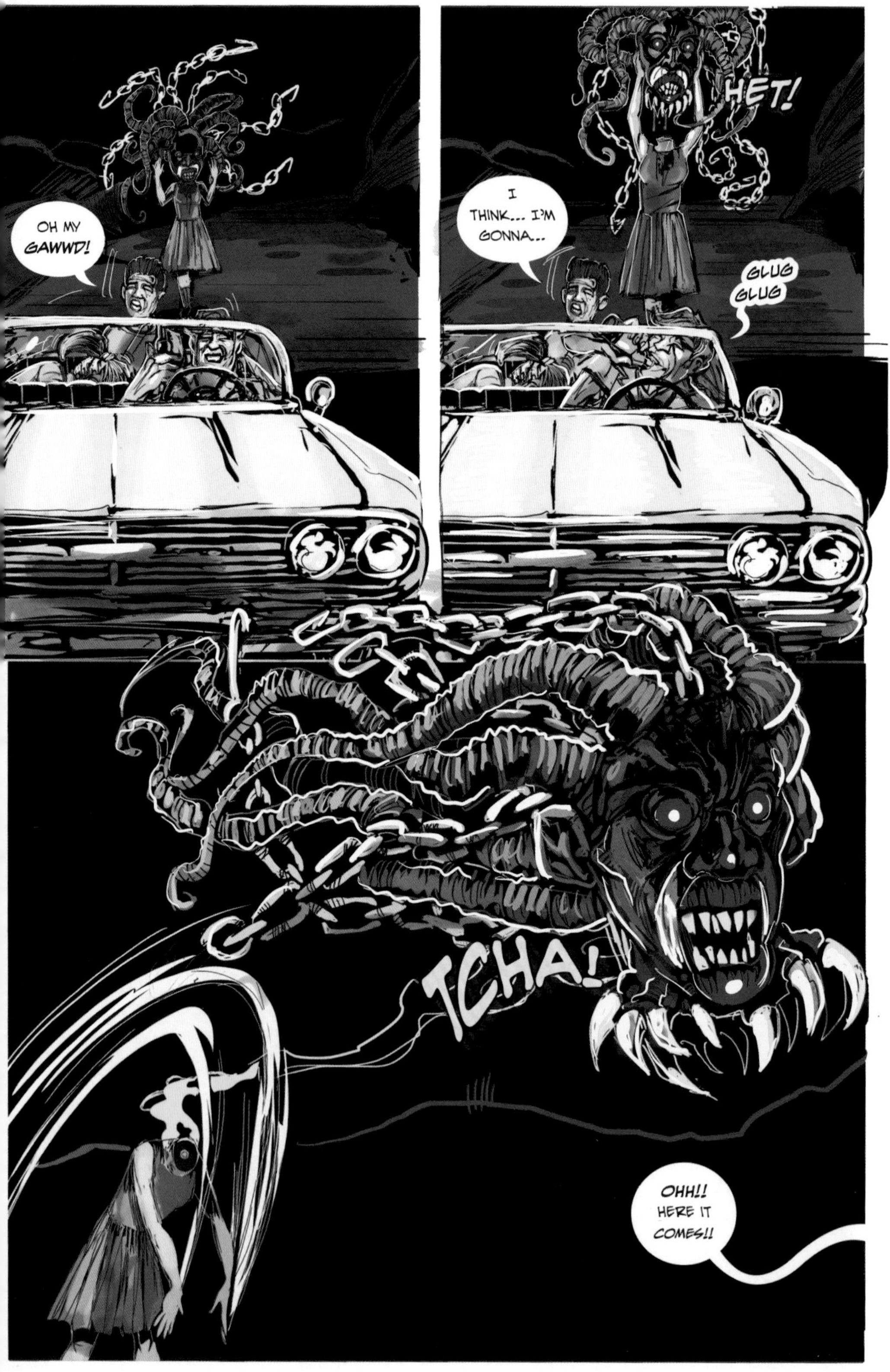
OH MY GAWWD!
I THINK... I'M GONNA...
HET!
GLUG GLUG
TCHA!
OHH!! HERE IT COMES!!

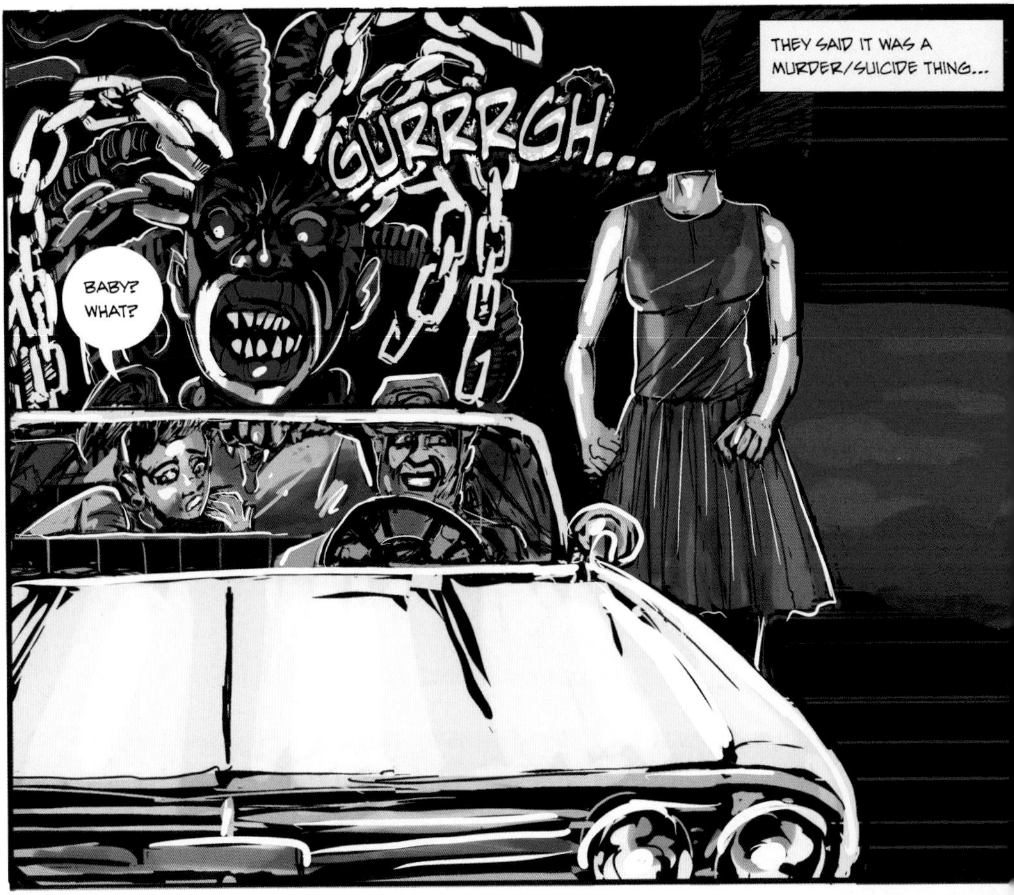
THEY SAID IT WAS A MURDER/SUICIDE THING...
GURRRGH...
BABY? WHAT?
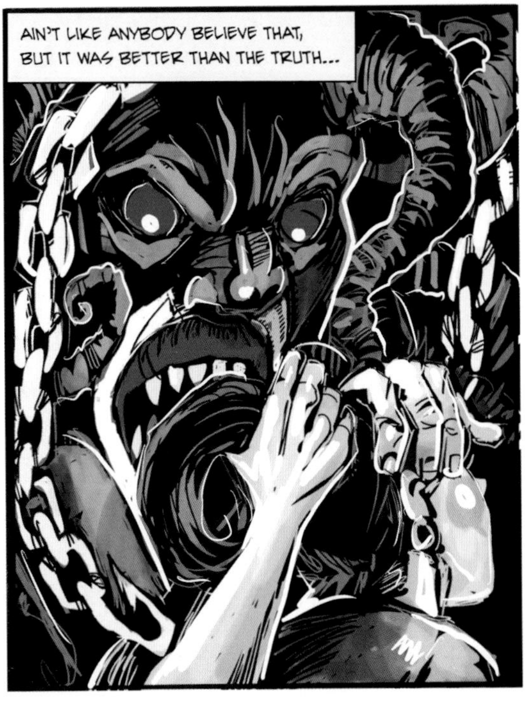
AIN'T LIKE ANYBODY BELIEVE THAT, BUT IT WAS BETTER THAN THE TRUTH...
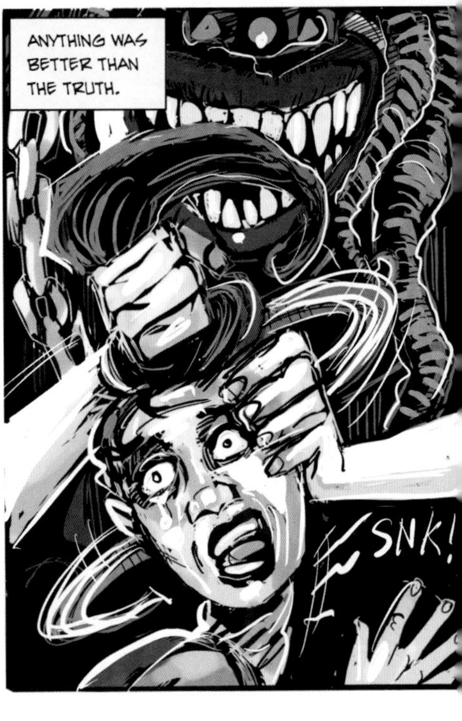
ANYTHING WAS BETTER THAN THE TRUTH.
SNK!

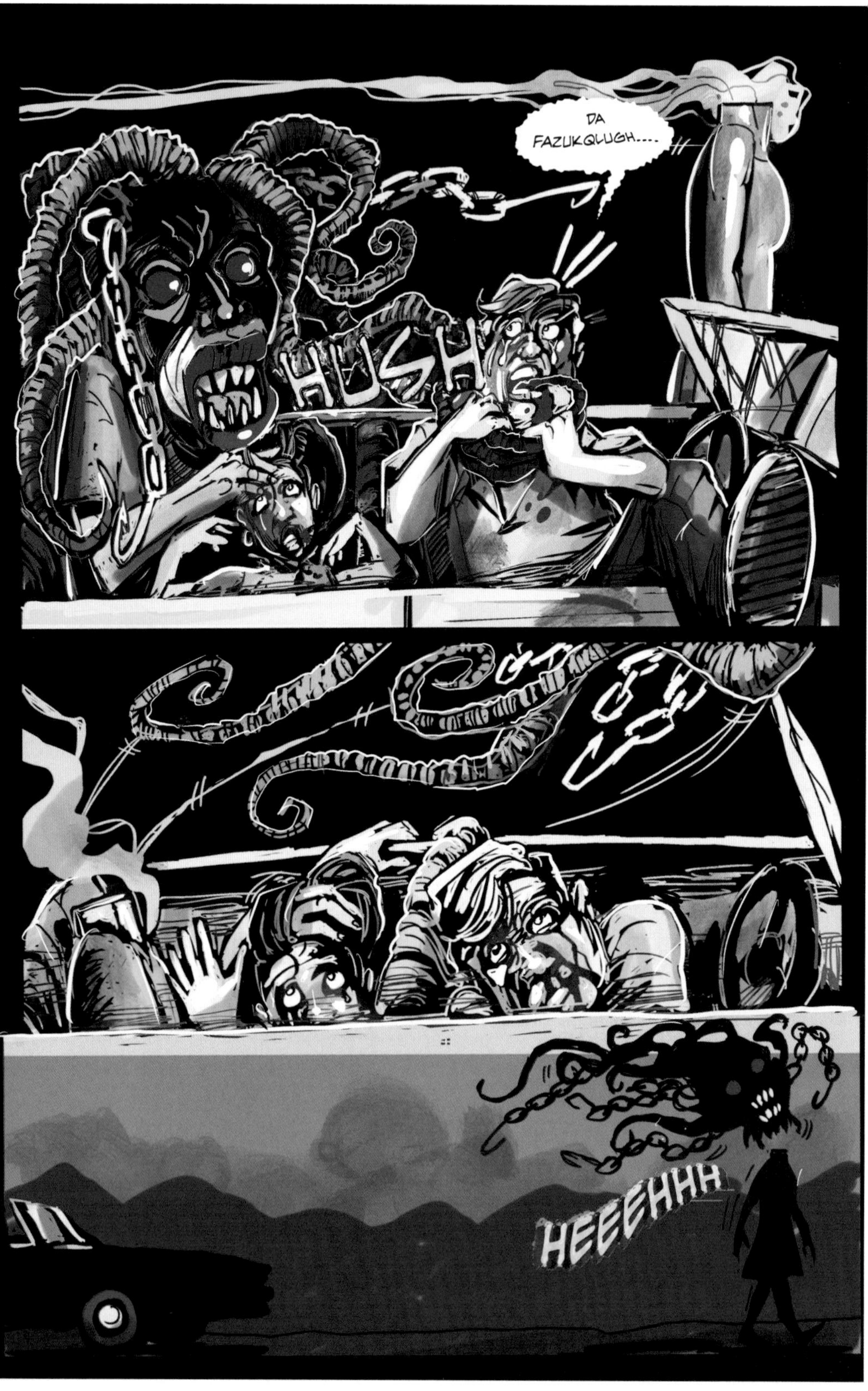
DA FAZUKQLUGH....
HUSH
HEEEHHH

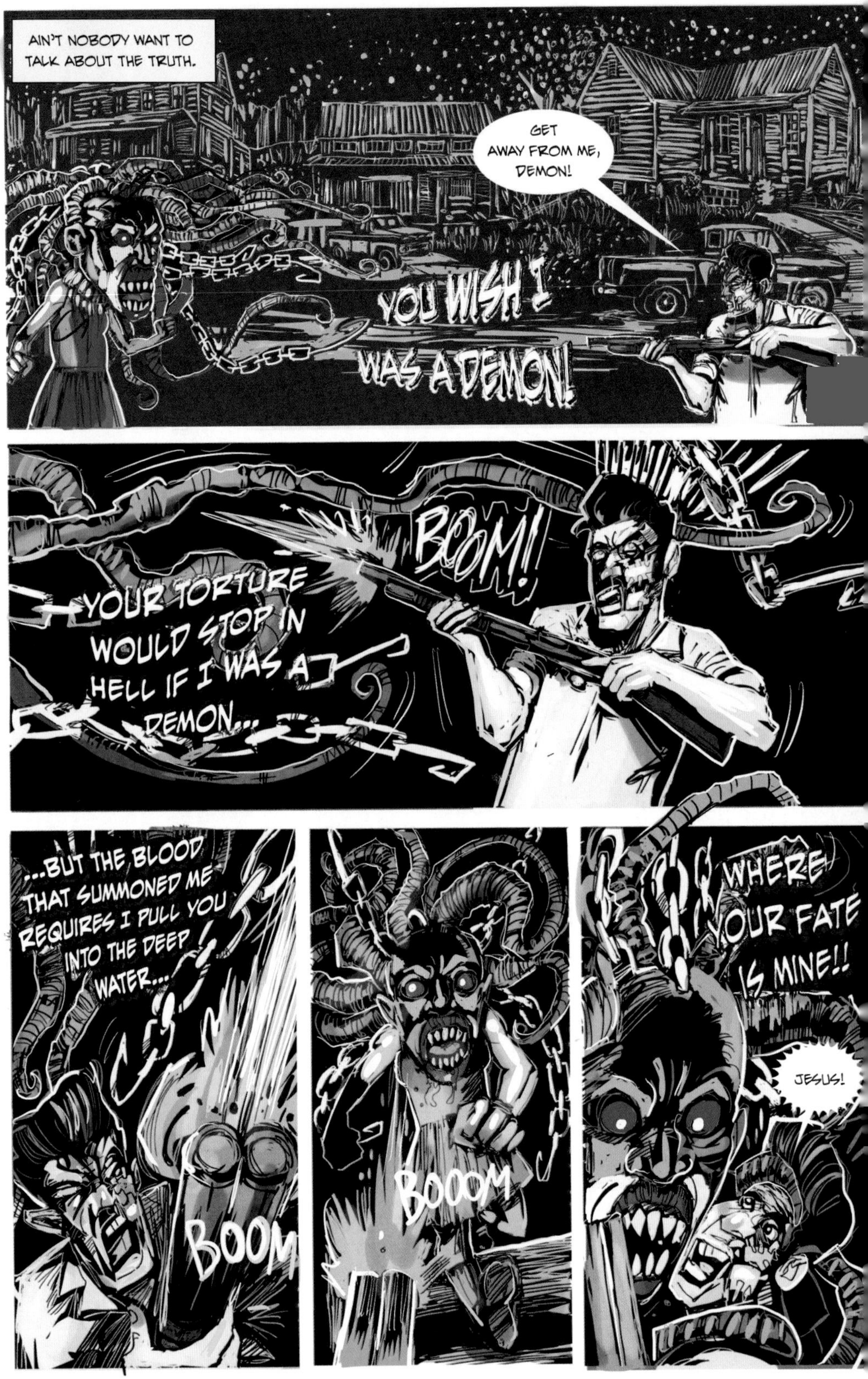
AIN'T NOBODY WANT TO TALK ABOUT THE TRUTH.
GET AWAY FROM ME, DEMON!
YOU WISH I WAS A DEMON!
BOOM!
YOUR TORTURE WOULD STOP IN HELL IF I WAS A DEMON...
...BUT THE BLOOD THAT SUMMONED ME REQUIRES I PULL YOU INTO THE DEEP WATER...
BOOM
BOOOM
WHERE YOUR FATE IS MINE!!
JESUS!

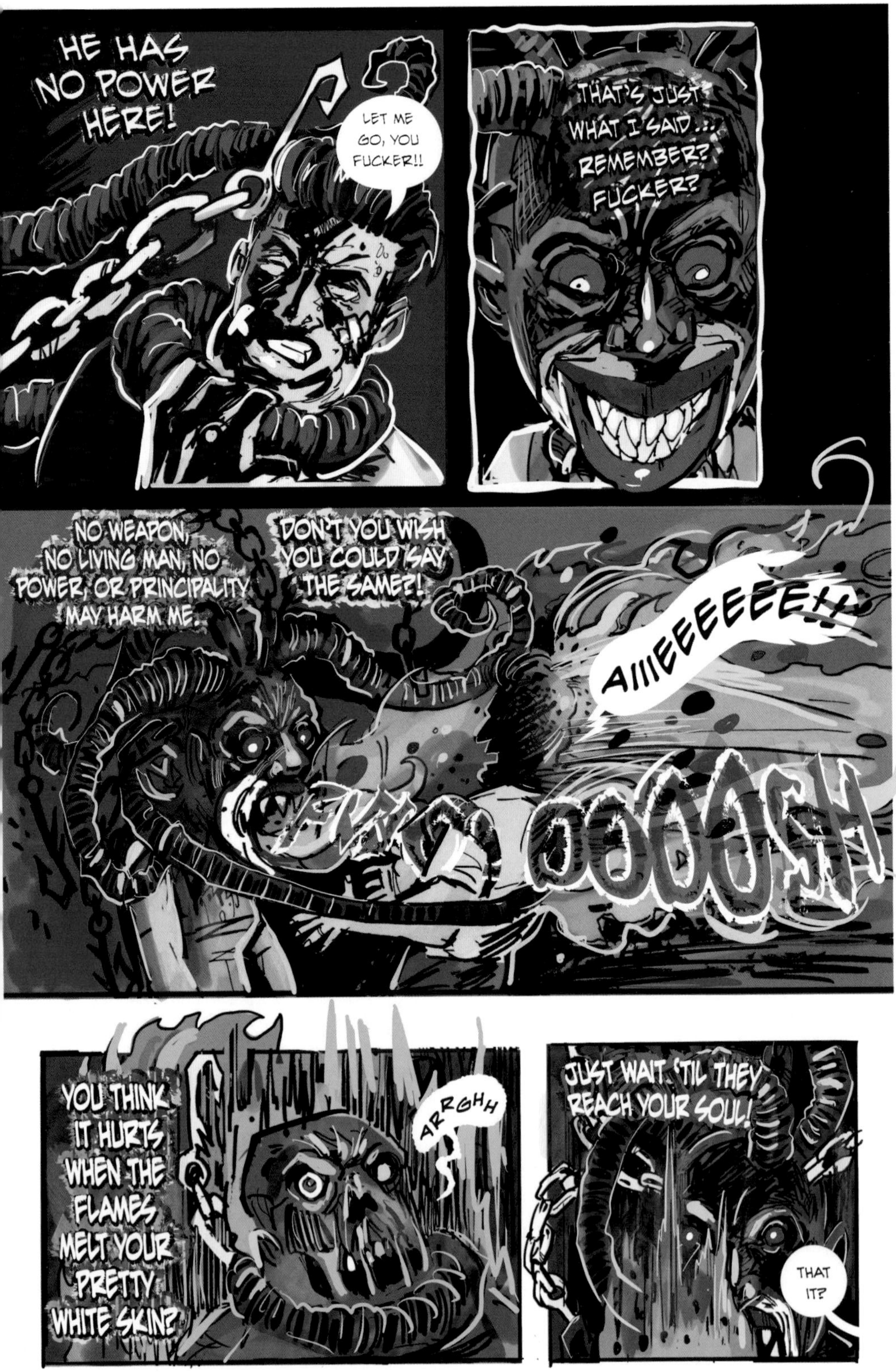
HE HAS NO POWER HERE!
LET ME GO, YOU FUCKER!!
THAT'S JUST WHAT I SAID... REMEMBER? FUCKER?
NO WEAPON, NO LIVING MAN, NO POWER, OR PRINCIPALITY MAY HARM ME.
DON'T YOU WISH YOU COULD SAY THE SAME?!
AIIIEEEEEEE!!
FWOOOOOSH
YOU THINK IT HURTS WHEN THE FLAMES MELT YOUR PRETTY WHITE SKIN?
ARRGHH
JUST WAIT 'TIL THEY REACH YOUR SOUL!
THAT IT?

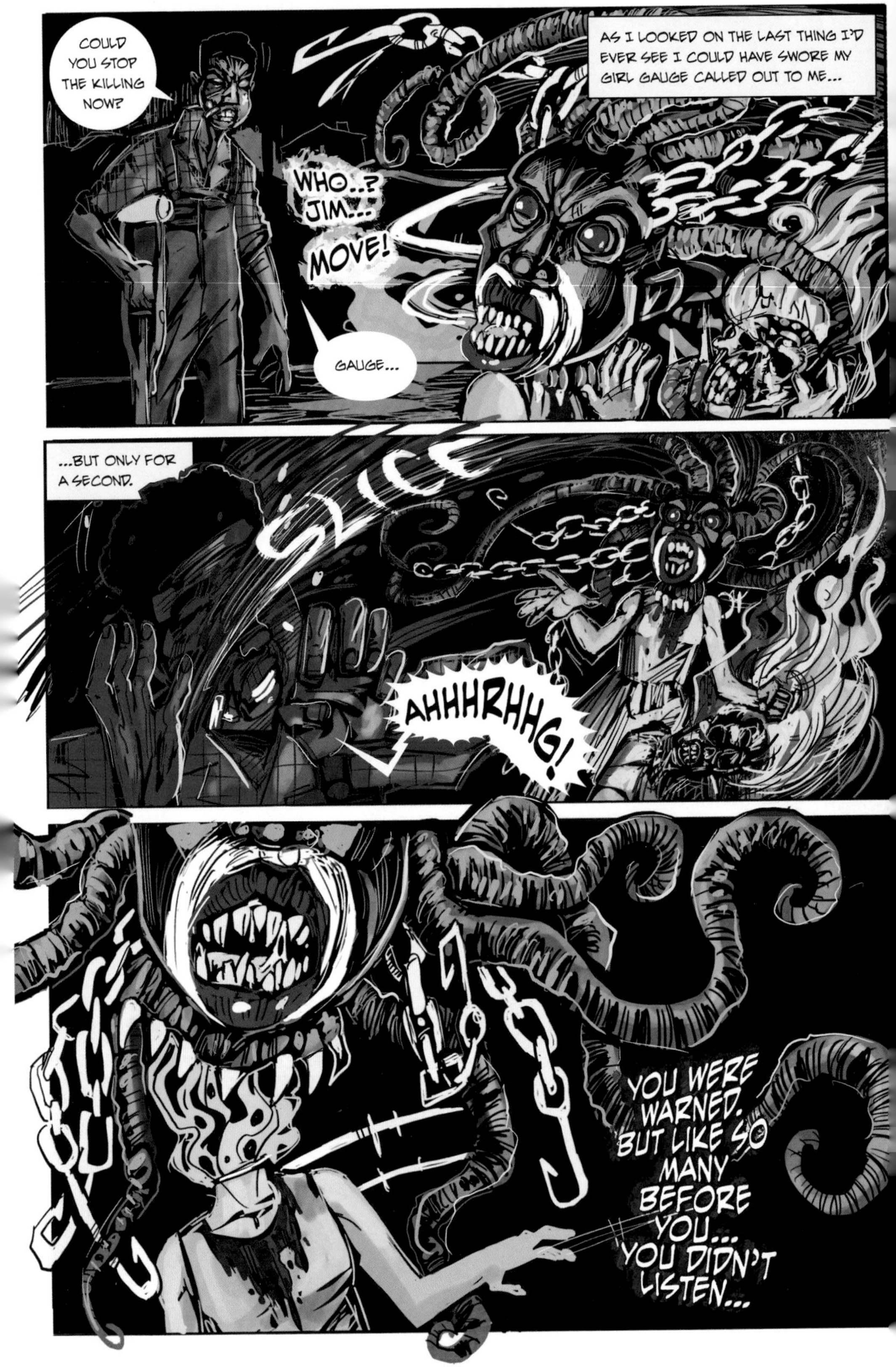
COULD YOU STOP THE KILLING NOW?
AS I LOOKED ON THE LAST THING I'D EVER SEE I COULD HAVE SWORE MY GIRL GAUGE CALLED OUT TO ME...
WHO..? JIM...
MOVE!
GAUGE...
...BUT ONLY FOR A SECOND.
SLICE
AHHHRHHG!
YOU WERE WARNED. BUT LIKE SO MANY BEFORE YOU... YOU DIDN'T LISTEN...

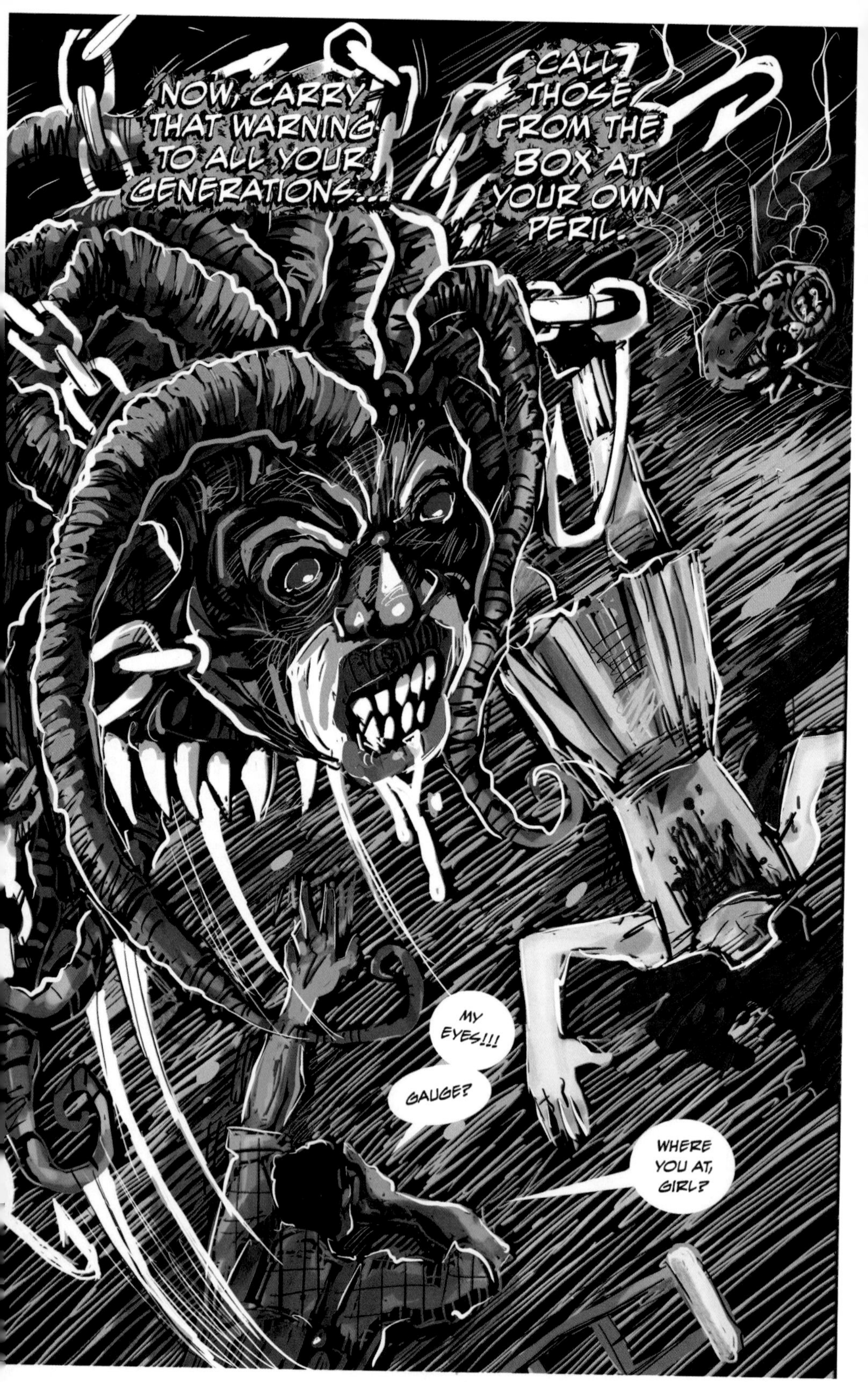
NOW, CARRY THAT WARNING TO ALL YOUR GENERATIONS...
CALL THOSE FROM THE BOX AT YOUR OWN PERIL.
MY EYES!!!
GAUGE?
WHERE YOU AT, GIRL?

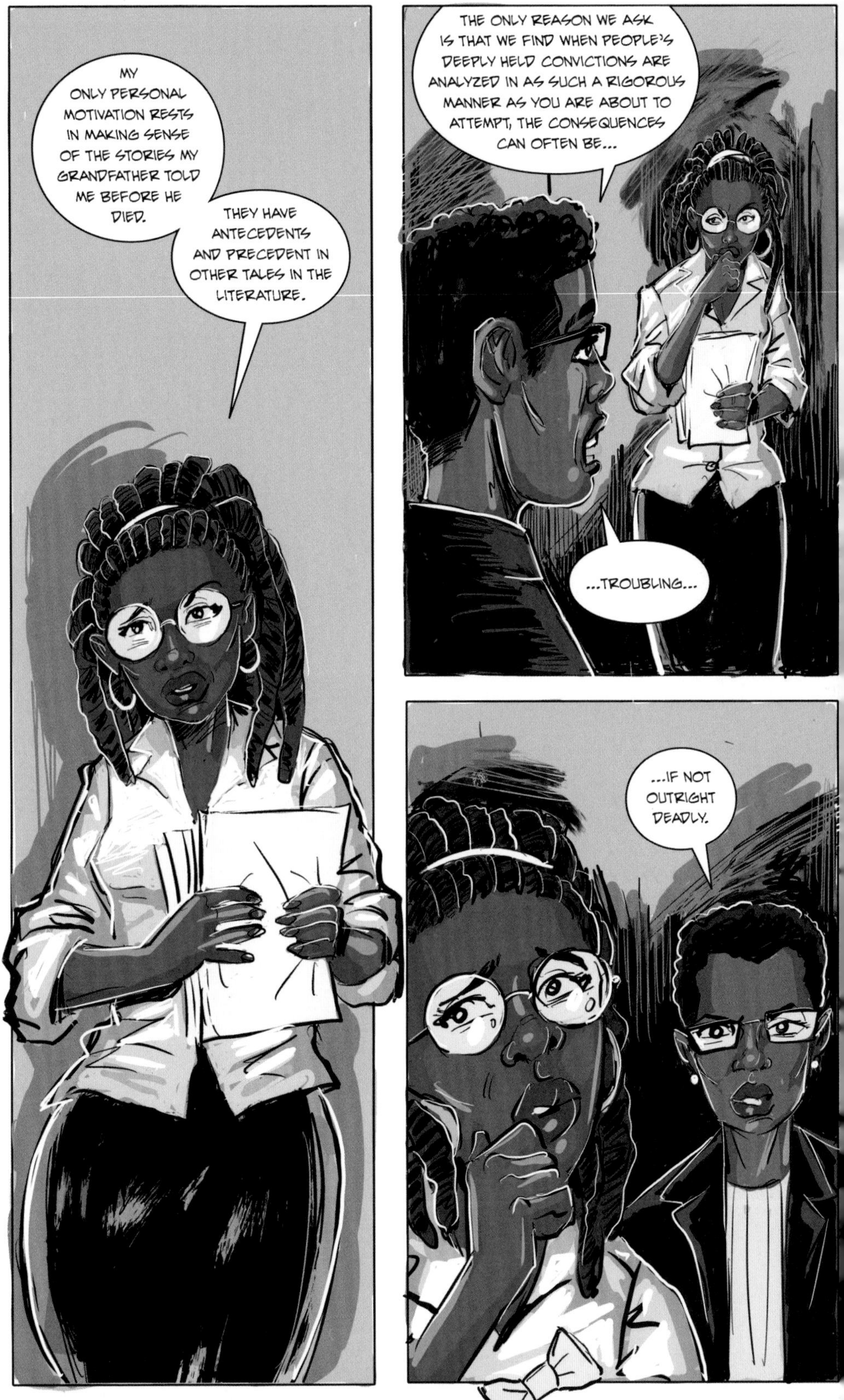
MY ONLY PERSONAL MOTIVATION RESTS IN MAKING SENSE OF THE STORIES MY GRANDFATHER TOLD ME BEFORE HE DIED.
THEY HAVE ANTECEDENTS AND PRECEDENT IN OTHER TALES IN THE LITERATURE.
THE ONLY REASON WE ASK IS THAT WE FIND WHEN PEOPLE'S DEEPLY HELD CONVICTIONS ARE ANALYZED IN AS SUCH A RIGOROUS MANNER AS YOU ARE ABOUT TO ATTEMPT, THE CONSEQUENCES CAN OFTEN BE...
...TROUBLING...
...IF NOT OUTRIGHT DEADLY.

# CHAPTER TWO

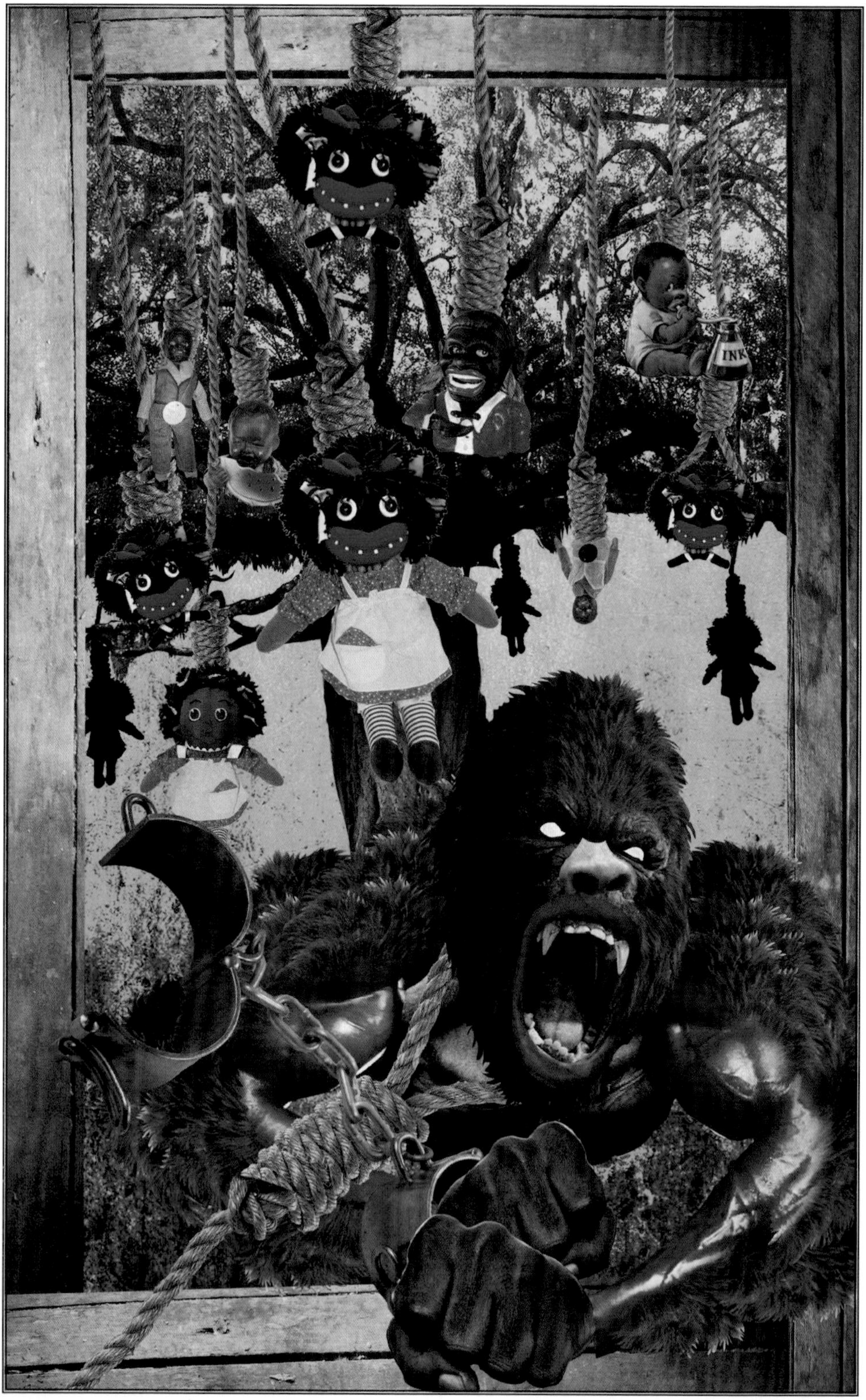
INK

# “WRETCHED BLOOD”

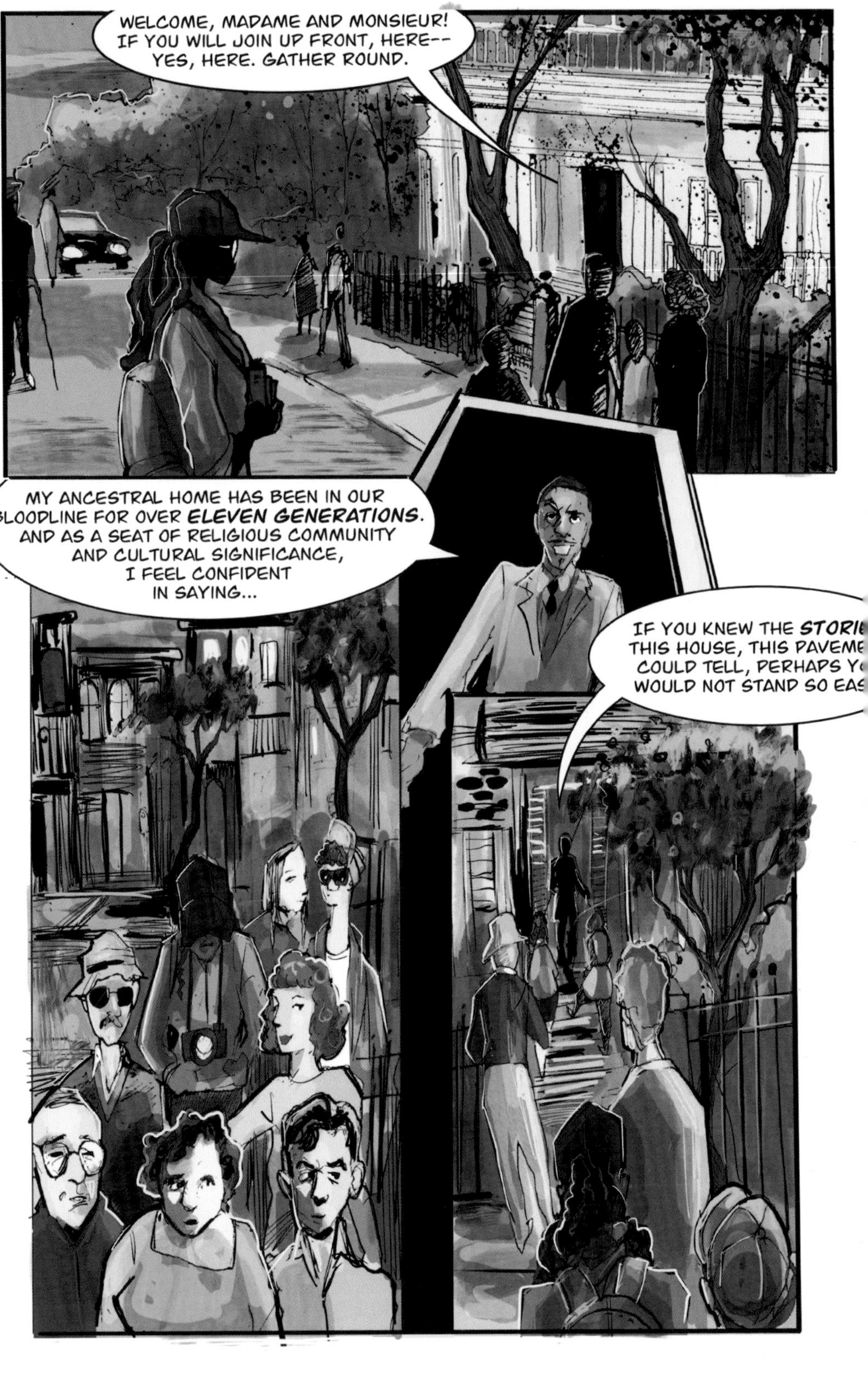
WELCOME, MADAME AND MONSIEUR! IF YOU WILL JOIN UP FRONT, HERE-- YES, HERE. GATHER ROUND.
MY ANCESTRAL HOME HAS BEEN IN OUR BLOODLINE FOR OVER ELEVEN GENERATIONS. AND AS A SEAT OF RELIGIOUS COMMUNITY AND CULTURAL SIGNIFICANCE, I FEEL CONFIDENT IN SAYING...
IF YOU KNEW THE STORI THIS HOUSE, THIS PAVEME COULD TELL, PERHAPS Y WOULD NOT STAND SO EAS

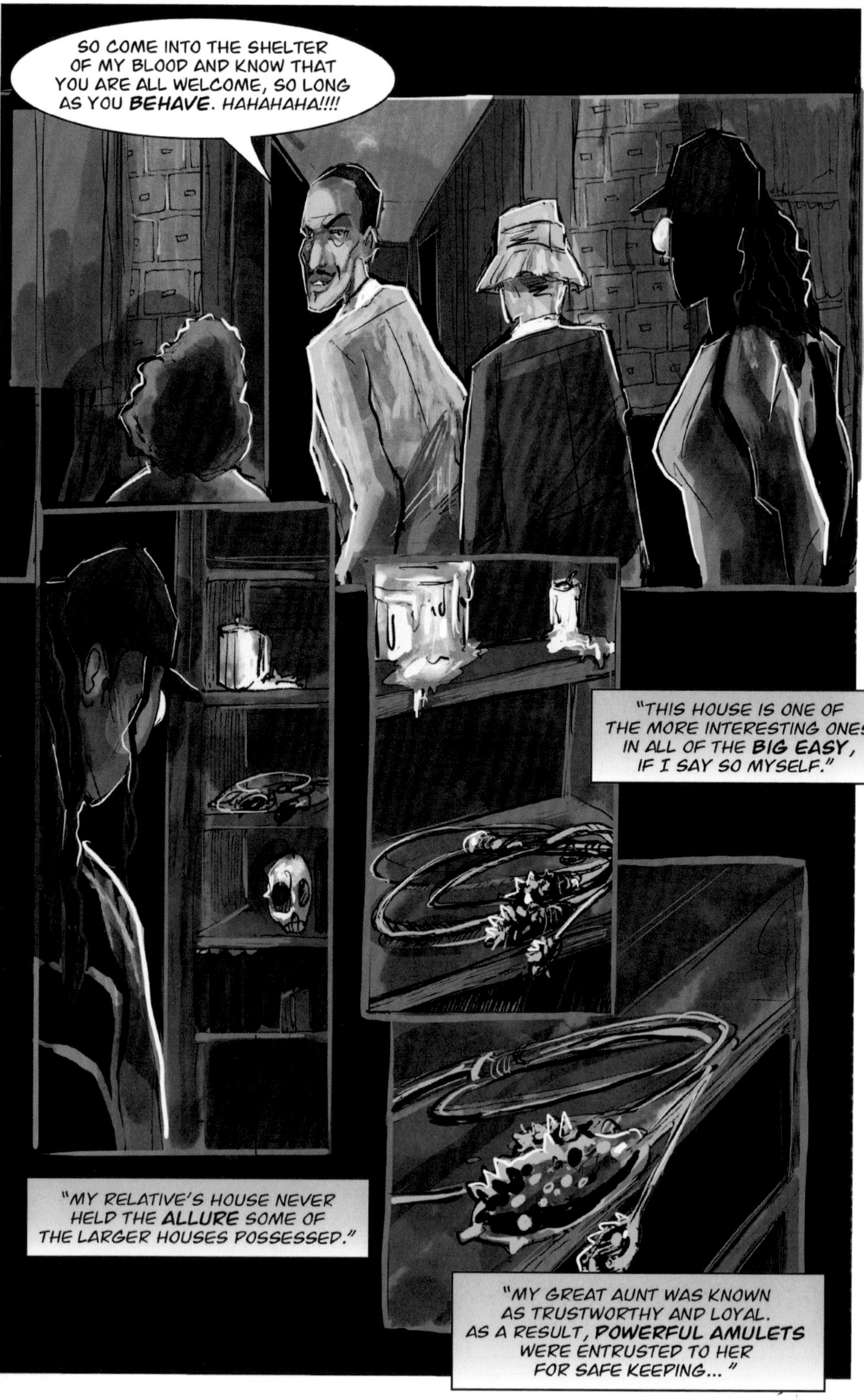
SO COME INTO THE SHELTER OF MY BLOOD AND KNOW THAT YOU ARE ALL WELCOME, SO LONG AS YOU BEHAVE. HAHAHAHA!!!!
"THIS HOUSE IS ONE OF THE MORE INTERESTING ONES IN ALL OF THE BIG EASY, IF I SAY SO MYSELF."
"MY RELATIVE'S HOUSE NEVER HELD THE ALLURE SOME OF THE LARGER HOUSES POSSESSED."
"MY GREAT AUNT WAS KNOWN AS TRUSTWORTHY AND LOYAL. AS A RESULT, POWERFUL AMULETS WERE ENTRUSTED TO HER FOR SAFE KEEPING..."

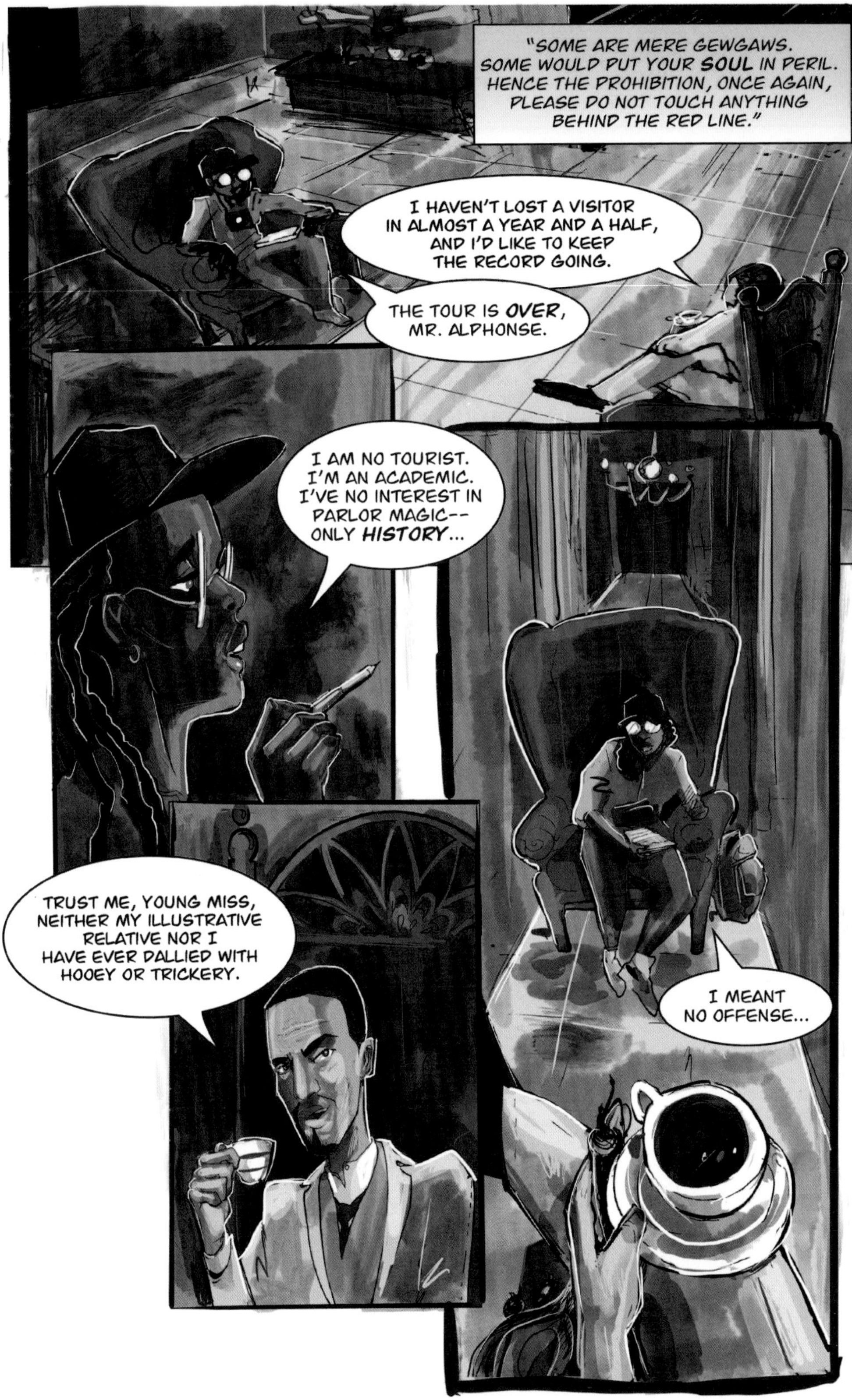
"SOME ARE MERE GEWGAWS. SOME WOULD PUT YOUR **SOUL** IN PERIL. HENCE THE PROHIBITION, ONCE AGAIN, PLEASE DO NOT TOUCH ANYTHING BEHIND THE RED LINE."
I HAVEN'T LOST A VISITOR IN ALMOST A YEAR AND A HALF, AND I'D LIKE TO KEEP THE RECORD GOING.
THE TOUR IS ***OVER***, MR. ALPHONSE.
I AM NO TOURIST. I'M AN ACADEMIC. I'VE NO INTEREST IN PARLOR MAGIC-- ONLY ***HISTORY***...
TRUST ME, YOUNG MISS, NEITHER MY ILLUSTRATIVE RELATIVE NOR I HAVE EVER DALLIED WITH HOOEY OR TRICKERY.
I MEANT NO OFFENSE...

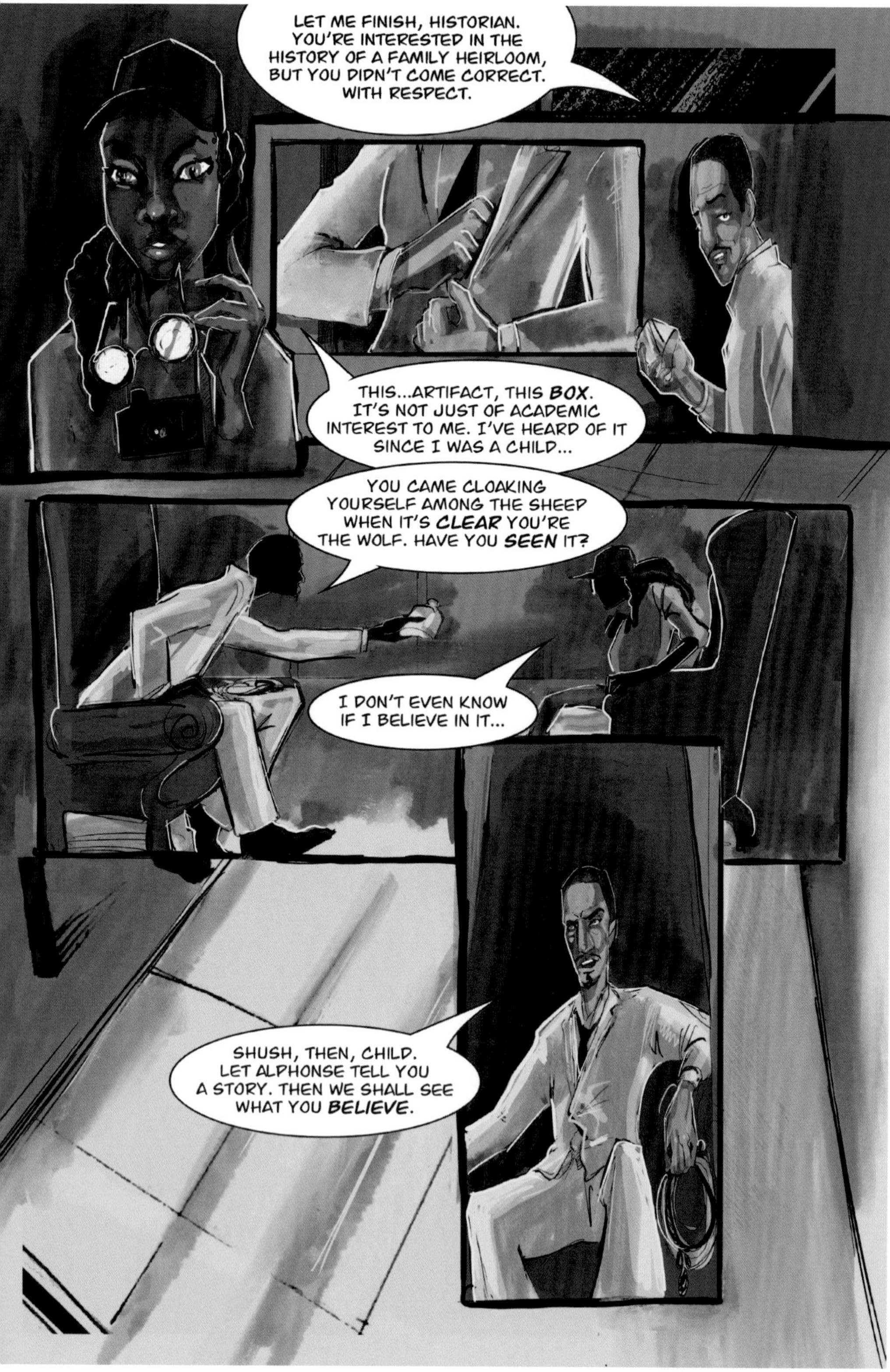
LET ME FINISH, HISTORIAN. YOU'RE INTERESTED IN THE HISTORY OF A FAMILY HEIRLOOM, BUT YOU DIDN'T COME CORRECT. WITH RESPECT.
THIS...ARTIFACT, THIS BOX. IT'S NOT JUST OF ACADEMIC INTEREST TO ME. I'VE HEARD OF IT SINCE I WAS A CHILD...
YOU CAME CLOAKING YOURSELF AMONG THE SHEEP WHEN IT'S CLEAR YOU'RE THE WOLF. HAVE YOU SEEN IT?
I DON'T EVEN KNOW IF I BELIEVE IN IT...
SHUSH, THEN, CHILD. LET ALPHONSE TELL YOU A STORY. THEN WE SHALL SEE WHAT YOU BELIEVE.

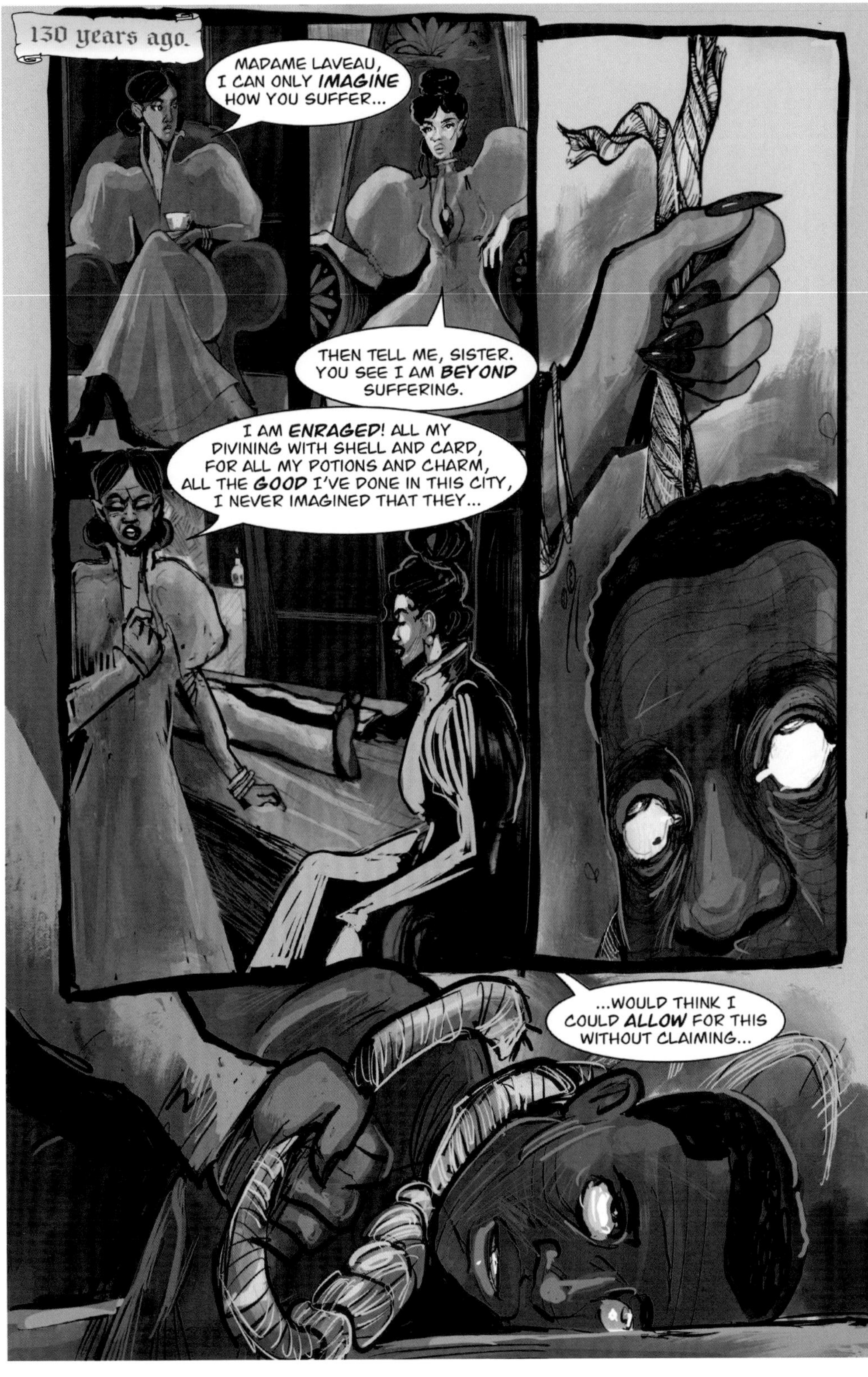
130 years ago.
MADAME LAVEAU, I CAN ONLY IMAGINE HOW YOU SUFFER...
THEN TELL ME, SISTER. YOU SEE I AM BEYOND SUFFERING.
I AM ENRAGED! ALL MY DIVINING WITH SHELL AND CARD, FOR ALL MY POTIONS AND CHARM, ALL THE GOOD I'VE DONE IN THIS CITY, I NEVER IMAGINED THAT THEY...
...WOULD THINK I COULD ALLOW FOR THIS WITHOUT CLAIMING...

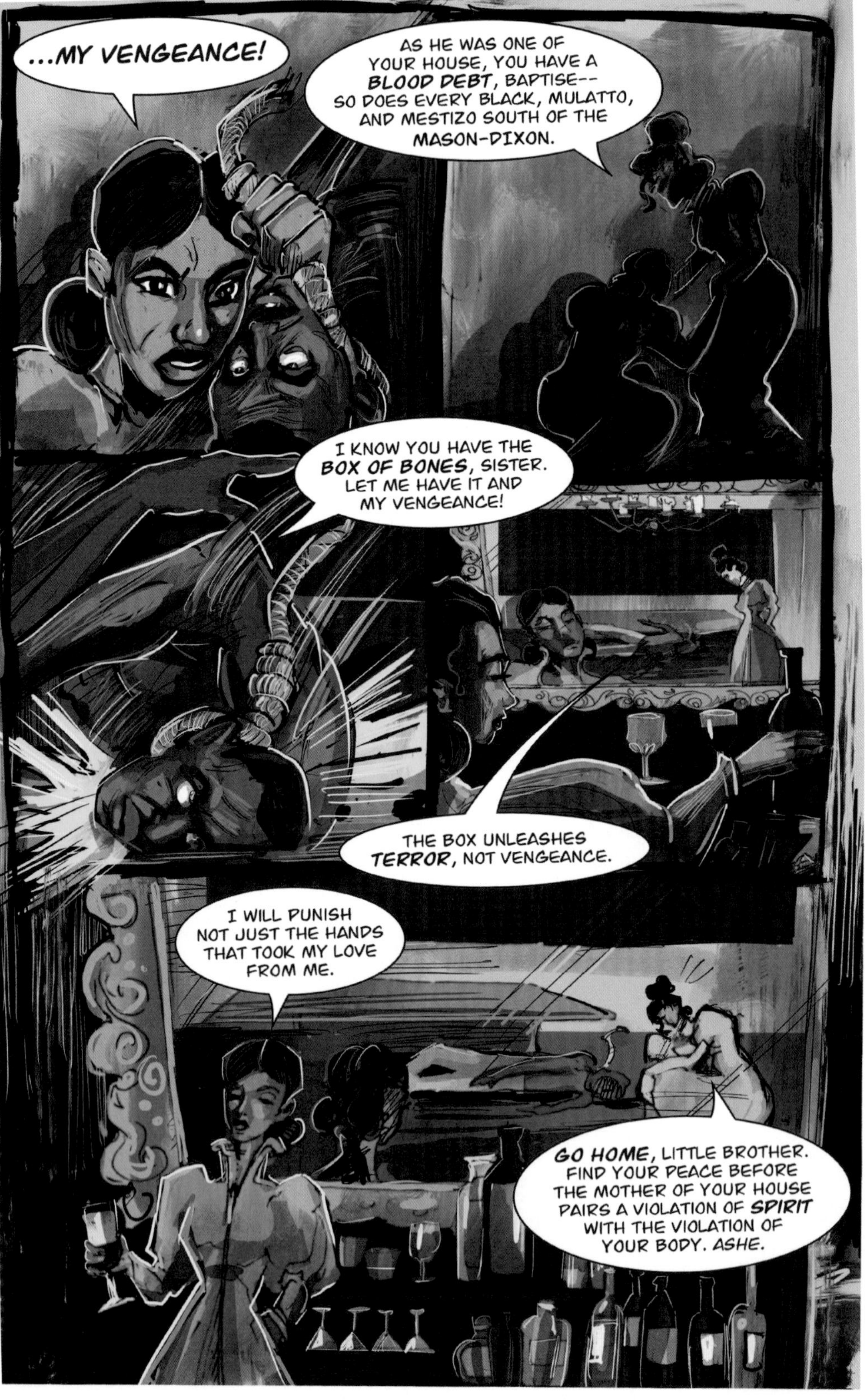
...MY VENGEANCE!
AS HE WAS ONE OF YOUR HOUSE, YOU HAVE A BLOOD DEBT, BAPTISE-- SO DOES EVERY BLACK, MULATTO, AND MESTIZO SOUTH OF THE MASON-DIXON.
I KNOW YOU HAVE THE BOX OF BONES, SISTER. LET ME HAVE IT AND MY VENGEANCE!
THE BOX UNLEASHES TERROR, NOT VENGEANCE.
I WILL PUNISH NOT JUST THE HANDS THAT TOOK MY LOVE FROM ME.
GO HOME, LITTLE BROTHER. FIND YOUR PEACE BEFORE THE MOTHER OF YOUR HOUSE PAIRS A VIOLATION OF SPIRIT WITH THE VIOLATION OF YOUR BODY. ASHE.

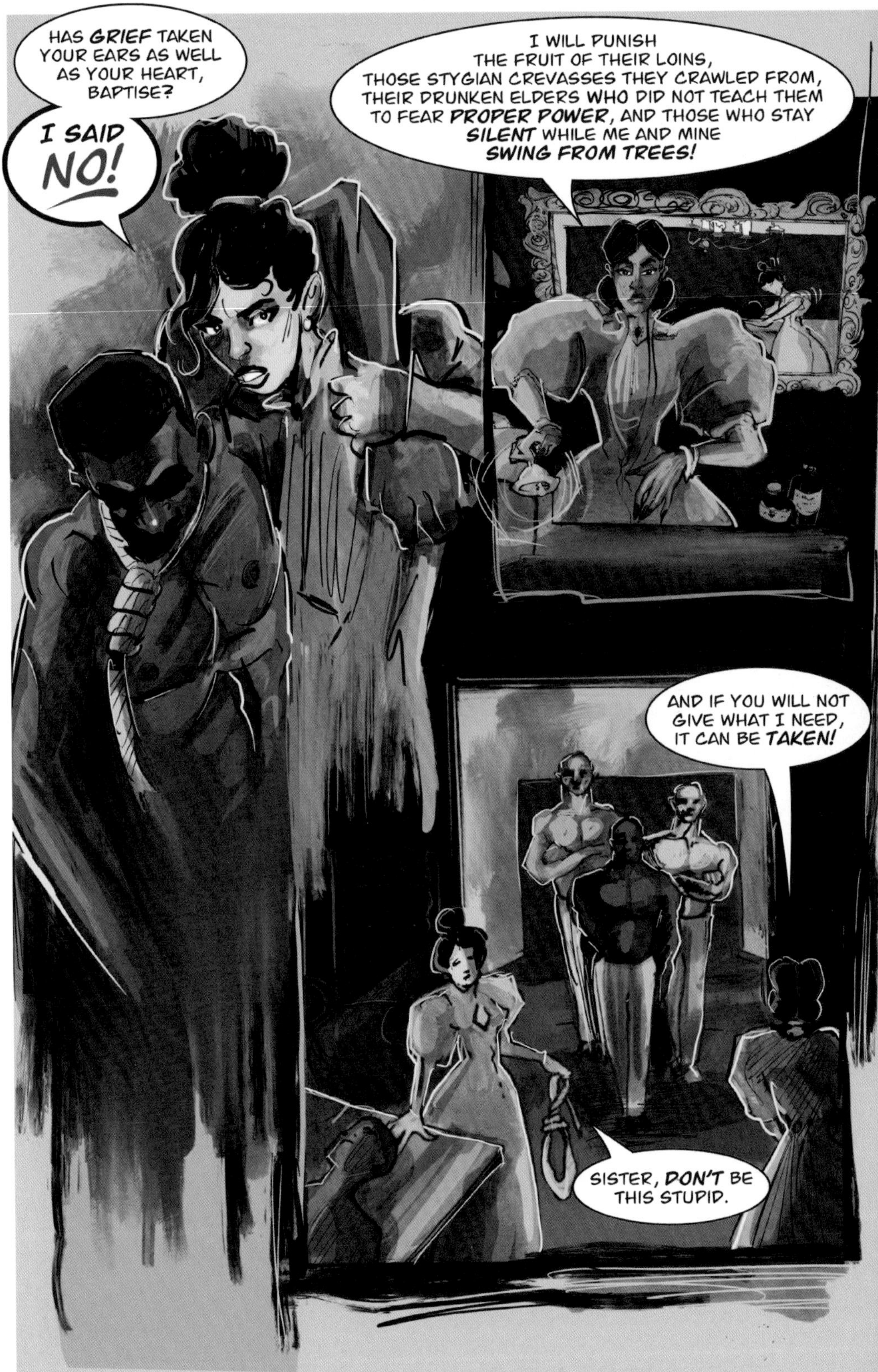
HAS GRIEF TAKEN YOUR EARS AS WELL AS YOUR HEART, BAPTISE?
I SAID NO!
I WILL PUNISH THE FRUIT OF THEIR LOINS, THOSE STYGIAN CREVASSES THEY CRAWLED FROM, THEIR DRUNKEN ELDERS WHO DID NOT TEACH THEM TO FEAR PROPER POWER, AND THOSE WHO STAY SILENT WHILE ME AND MINE SWING FROM TREES!
AND IF YOU WILL NOT GIVE WHAT I NEED, IT CAN BE TAKEN!
SISTER, DON'T BE THIS STUPID.

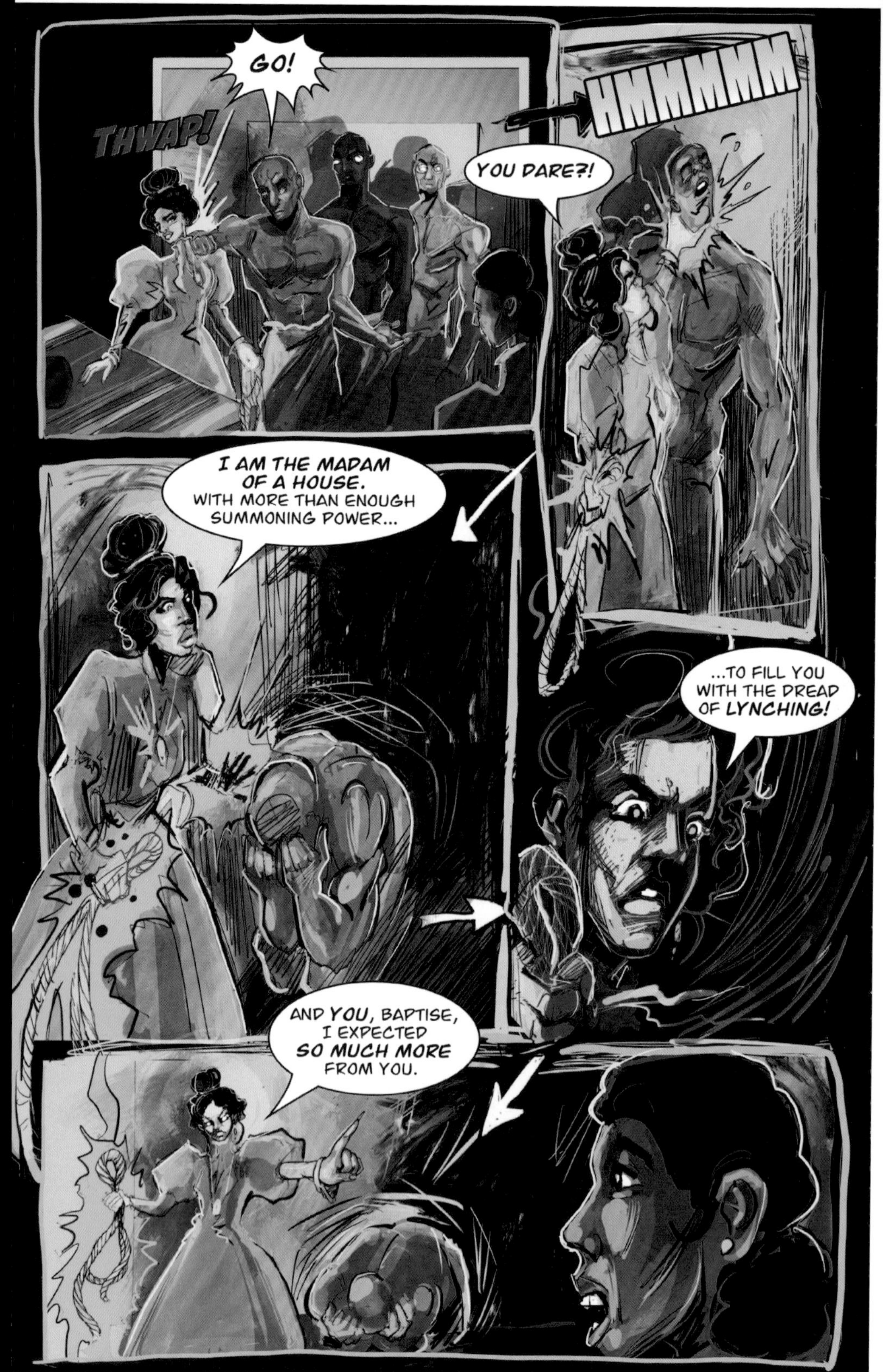
GO!
THWAP!
HMMMMM
YOU DARE?!
I AM THE MADAM OF A HOUSE. WITH MORE THAN ENOUGH SUMMONING POWER...
...TO FILL YOU WITH THE DREAD OF LYNCHING!
AND YOU, BAPTISE, I EXPECTED SO MUCH MORE FROM YOU.

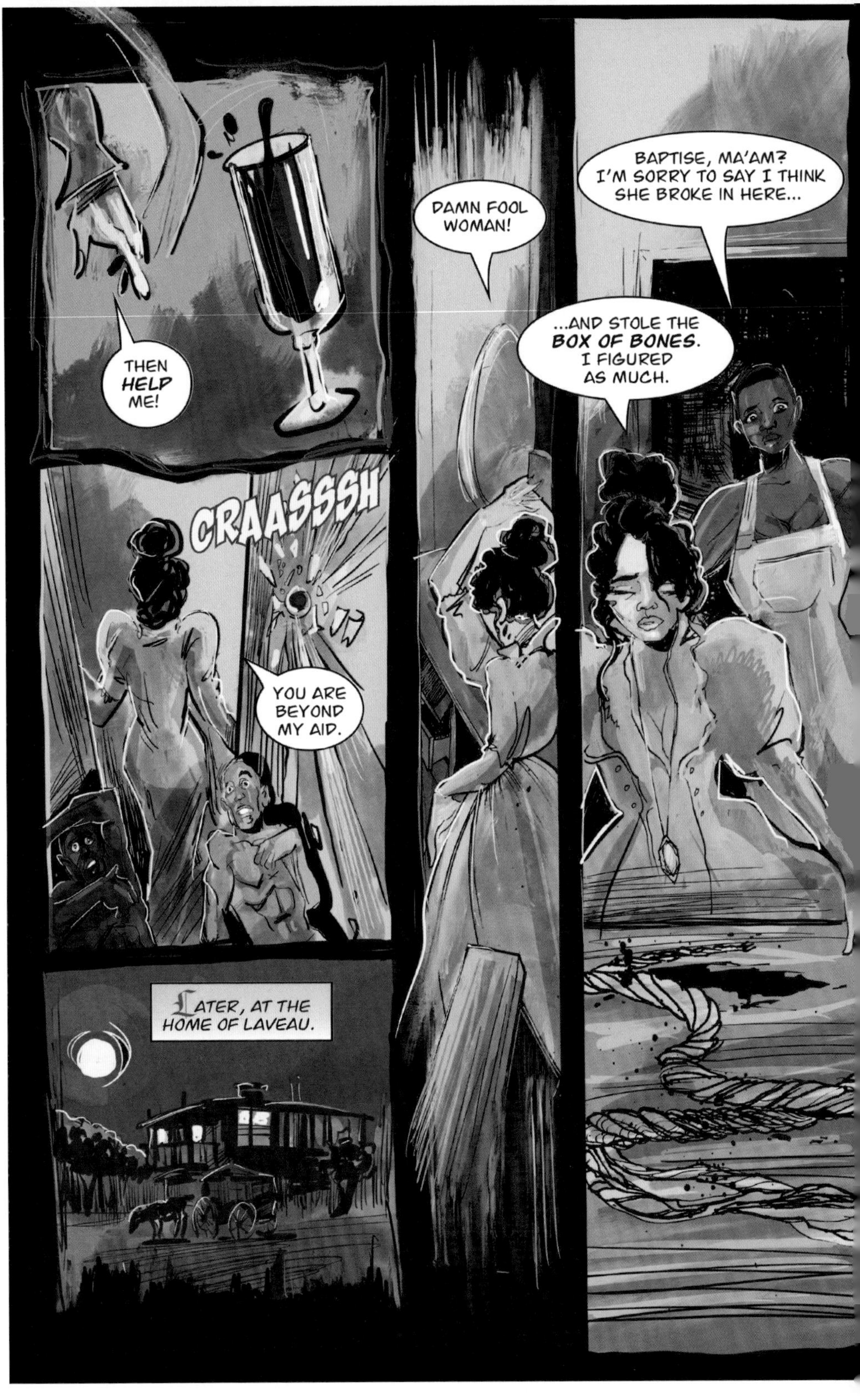
THEN HELP ME!
CRAASSSH
YOU ARE BEYOND MY AID.
LATER, AT THE HOME OF LAVEAU.
DAMN FOOL WOMAN!
BAPTISE, MA'AM? I'M SORRY TO SAY I THINK SHE BROKE IN HERE...
...AND STOLE THE BOX OF BONES. I FIGURED AS MUCH.

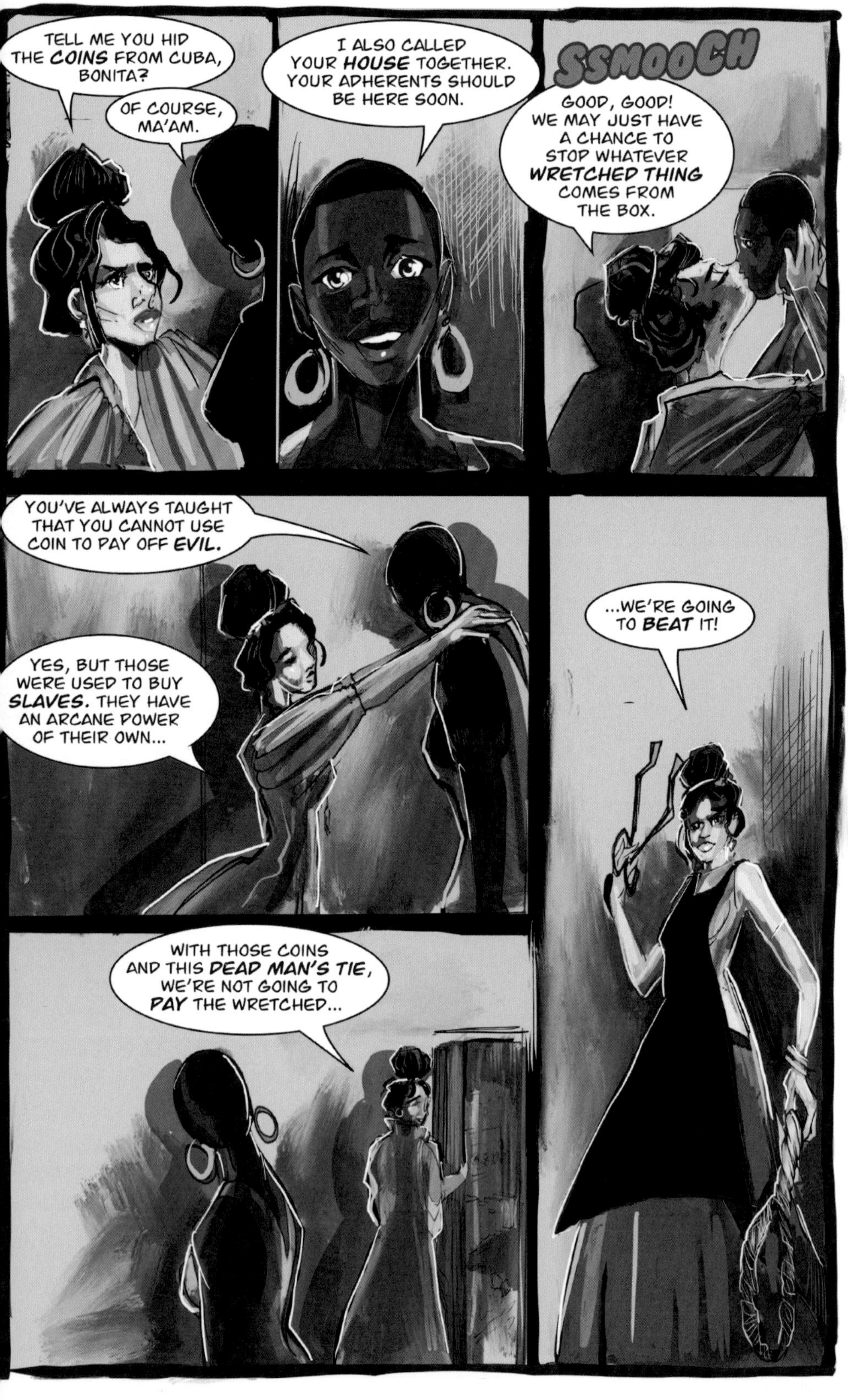
TELL ME YOU HID THE COINS FROM CUBA, BONITA?
OF COURSE, MA'AM.
I ALSO CALLED YOUR HOUSE TOGETHER. YOUR ADHERENTS SHOULD BE HERE SOON.
SSMOOCH
GOOD, GOOD! WE MAY JUST HAVE A CHANCE TO STOP WHATEVER WRETCHED THING COMES FROM THE BOX.
YOU'VE ALWAYS TAUGHT THAT YOU CANNOT USE COIN TO PAY OFF EVIL.
YES, BUT THOSE WERE USED TO BUY SLAVES. THEY HAVE AN ARCANE POWER OF THEIR OWN...
WITH THOSE COINS AND THIS DEAD MAN'S TIE, WE'RE NOT GOING TO PAY THE WRETCHED...
...WE'RE GOING TO BEAT IT!

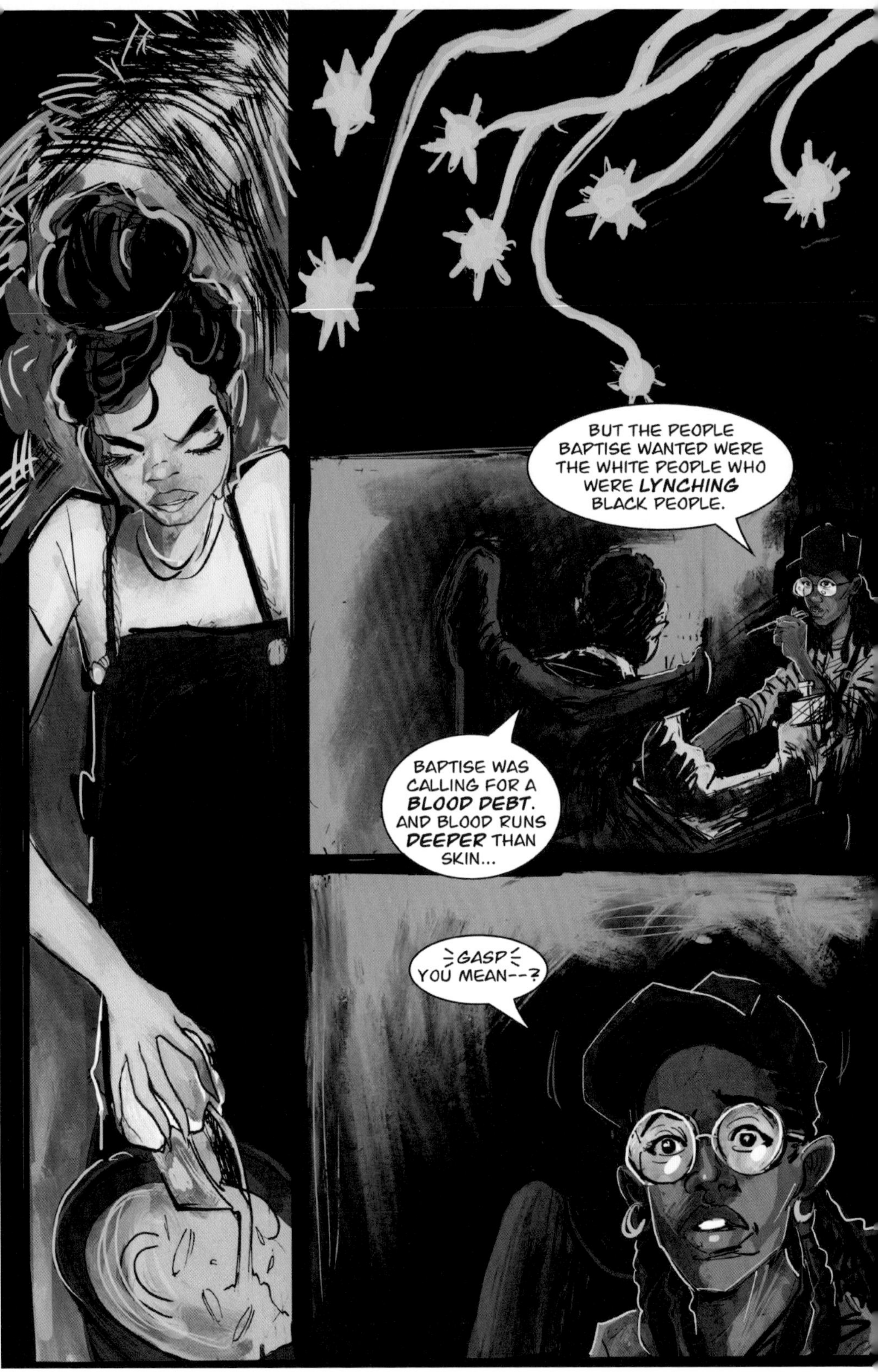
BUT THE PEOPLE BAPTISE WANTED WERE THE WHITE PEOPLE WHO WERE **LYNCHING** BLACK PEOPLE.
BAPTISE WAS CALLING FOR A **BLOOD DEBT**. AND BLOOD RUNS **DEEPER** THAN SKIN...
GASP
YOU MEAN--?

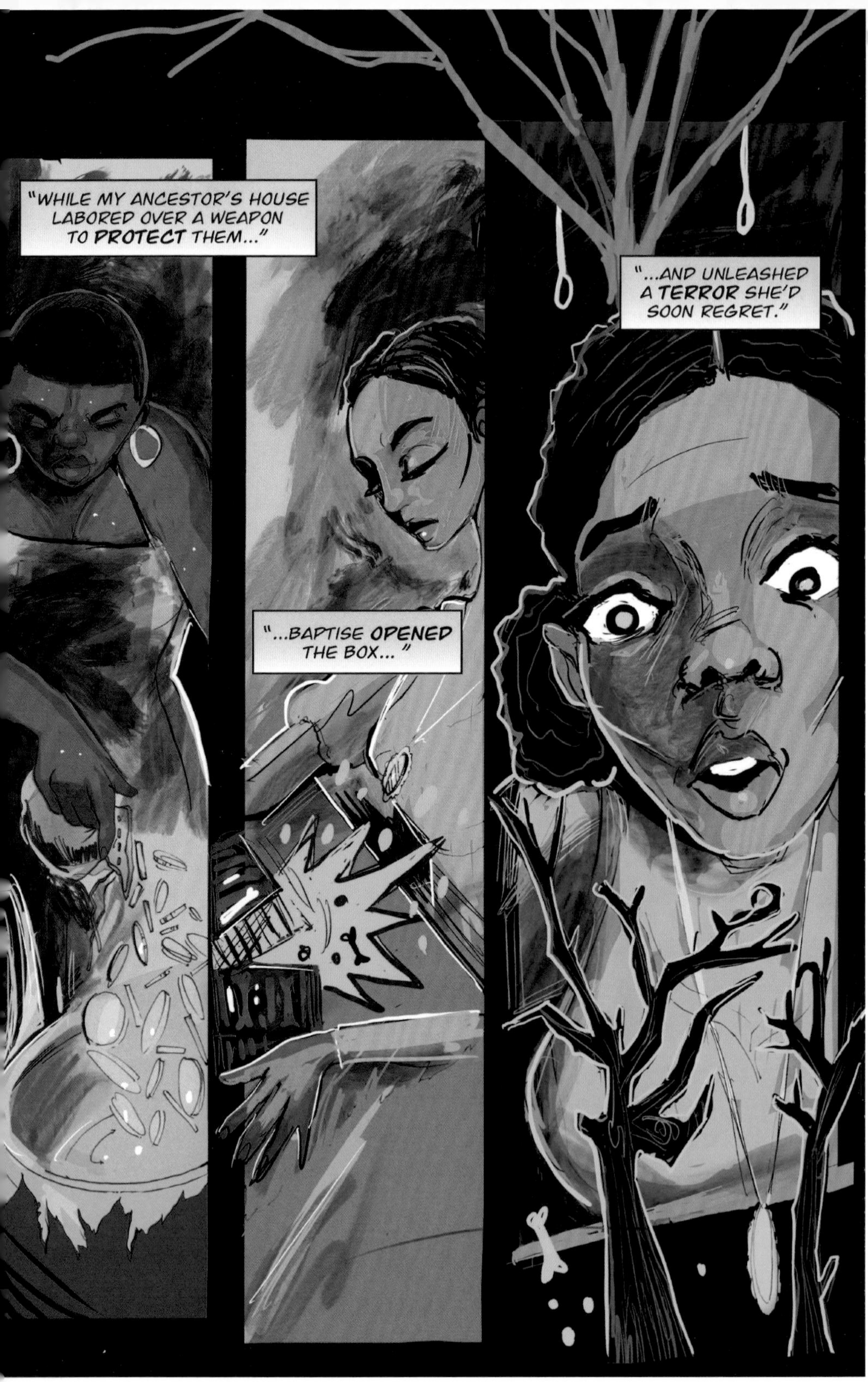
"WHILE MY ANCESTOR'S HOUSE LABORED OVER A WEAPON TO PROTECT THEM..."
"...BAPTISE OPENED THE BOX..."
"...AND UNLEASHED A TERROR SHE'D SOON REGRET."

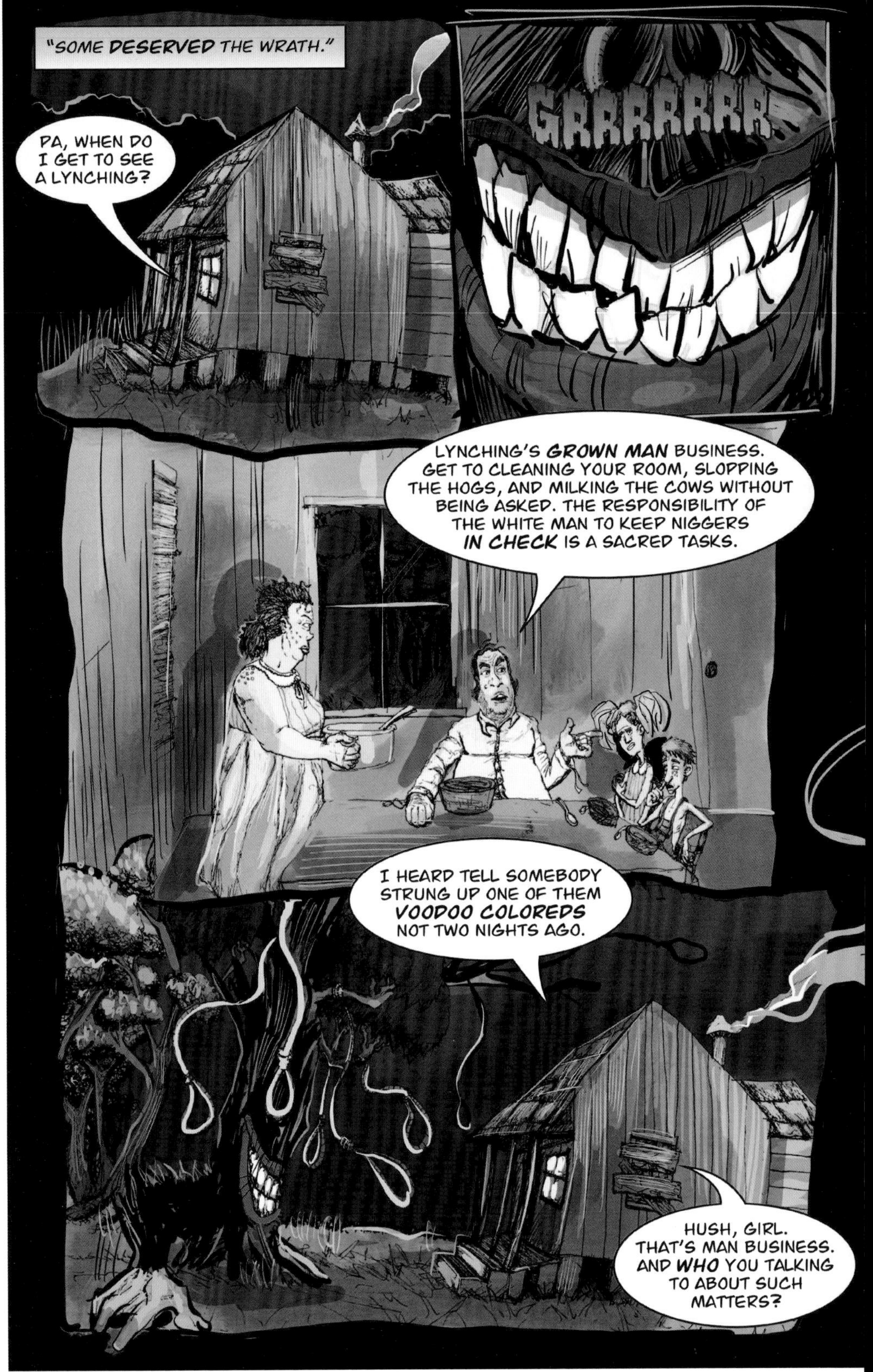
"SOME DESERVED THE WRATH."
PA, WHEN DO I GET TO SEE A LYNCHING?
GRRRRRRR
LYNCHING'S GROWN MAN BUSINESS. GET TO CLEANING YOUR ROOM, SLOPPING THE HOGS, AND MILKING THE COWS WITHOUT BEING ASKED. THE RESPONSIBILITY OF THE WHITE MAN TO KEEP NIGGERS IN CHECK IS A SACRED TASKS.
I HEARD TELL SOMEBODY STRUNG UP ONE OF THEM VOODOO COLOREDS NOT TWO NIGHTS AGO.
HUSH, GIRL. THAT'S MAN BUSINESS. AND WHO YOU TALKING TO ABOUT SUCH MATTERS?

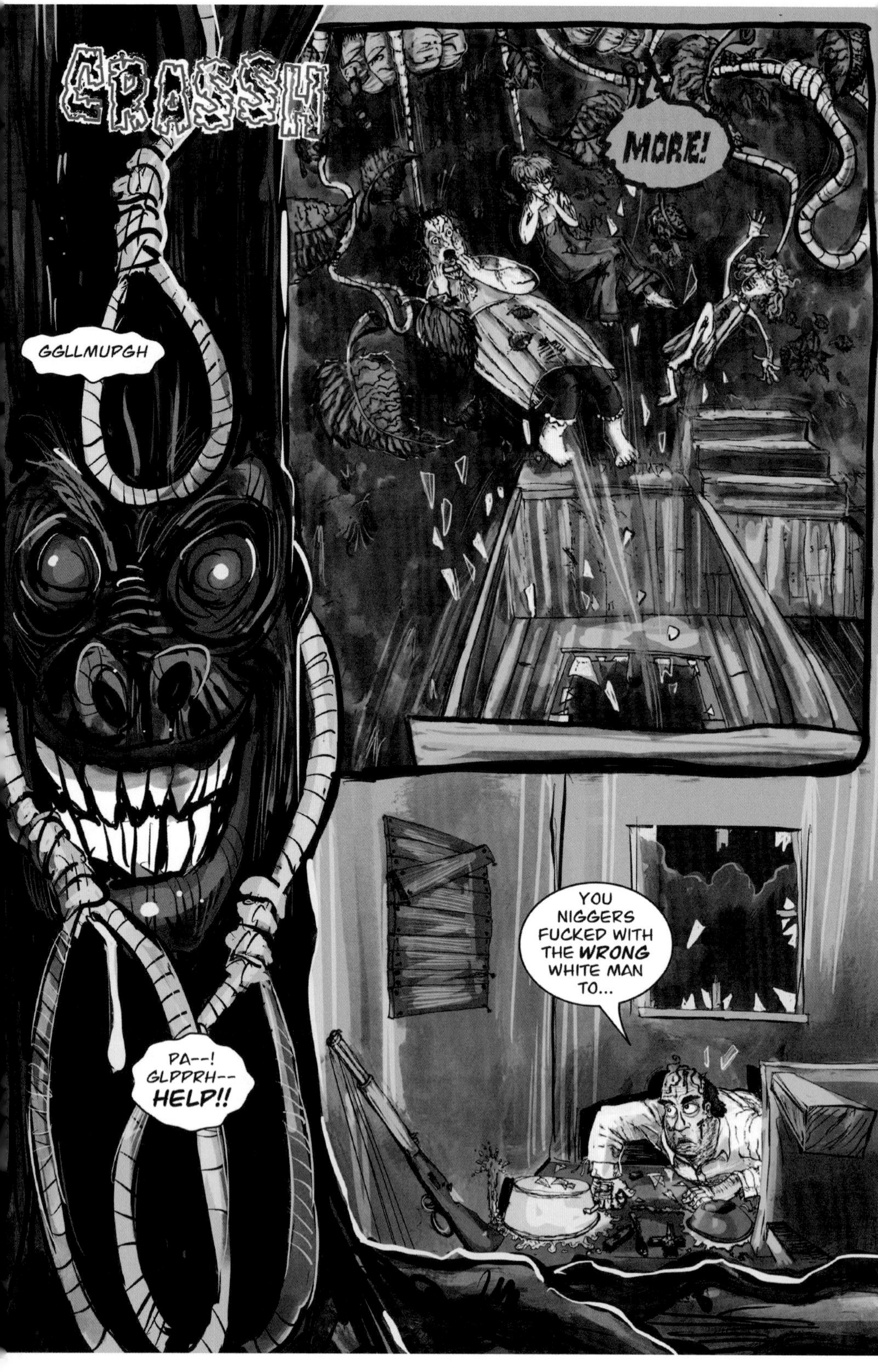
CRASSH
MORE!
GGLLMUPGH
PA--! GLPPRH-- HELP!!
YOU NIGGERS FUCKED WITH THE WRONG WHITE MAN TO...

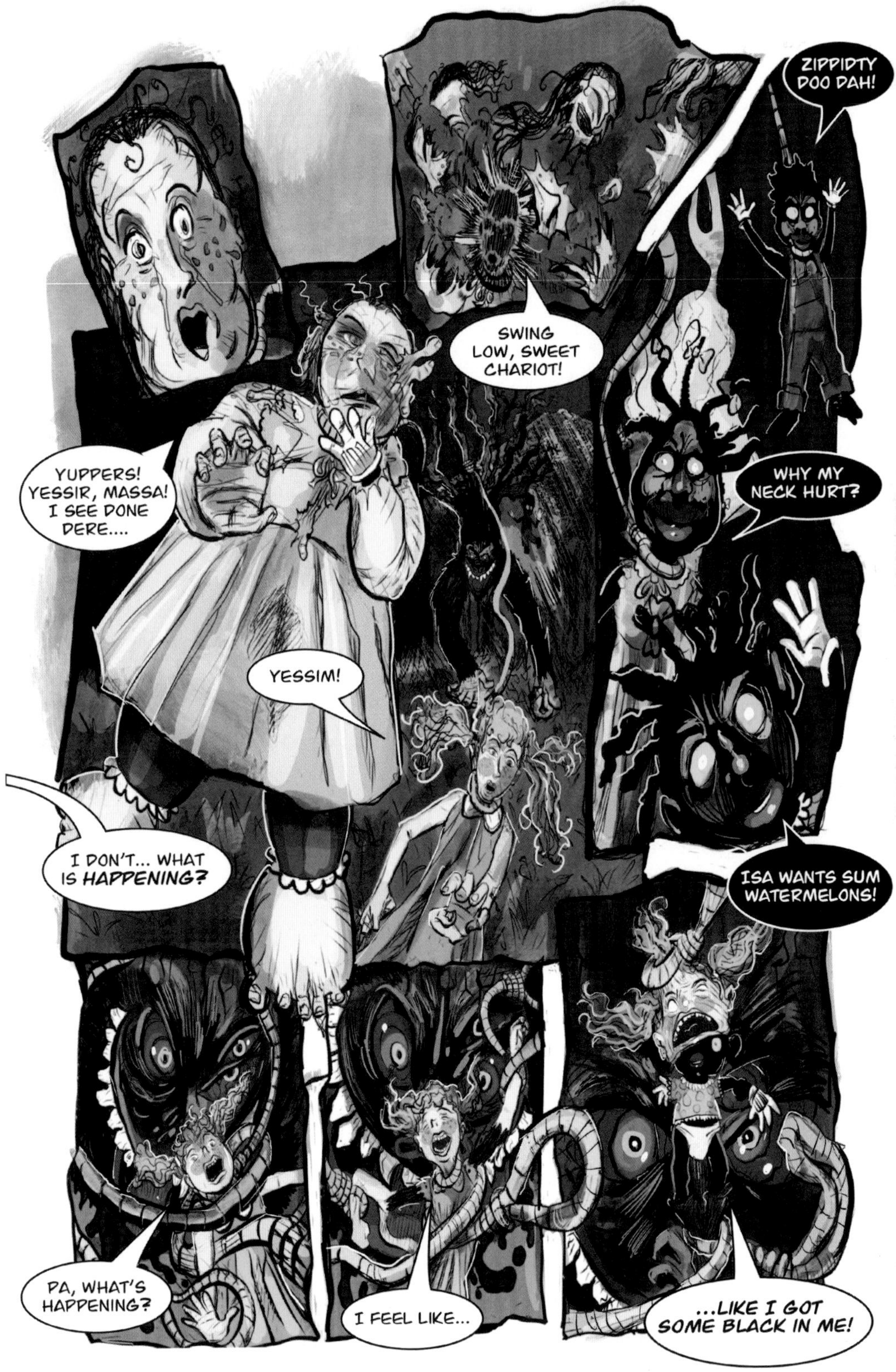

ZIPPIDTY DOO DAH!
SWING LOW, SWEET CHARIOT!
YUPPERS! YESSIR, MASSA! I SEE DONE DERE....
WHY MY NECK HURT?
YESSIM!
I DON'T... WHAT IS HAPPENING?
ISA WANTS SUM WATERMELONS!
PA, WHAT'S HAPPENING?
I FEEL LIKE...
...LIKE I GOT SOME BLACK IN ME!

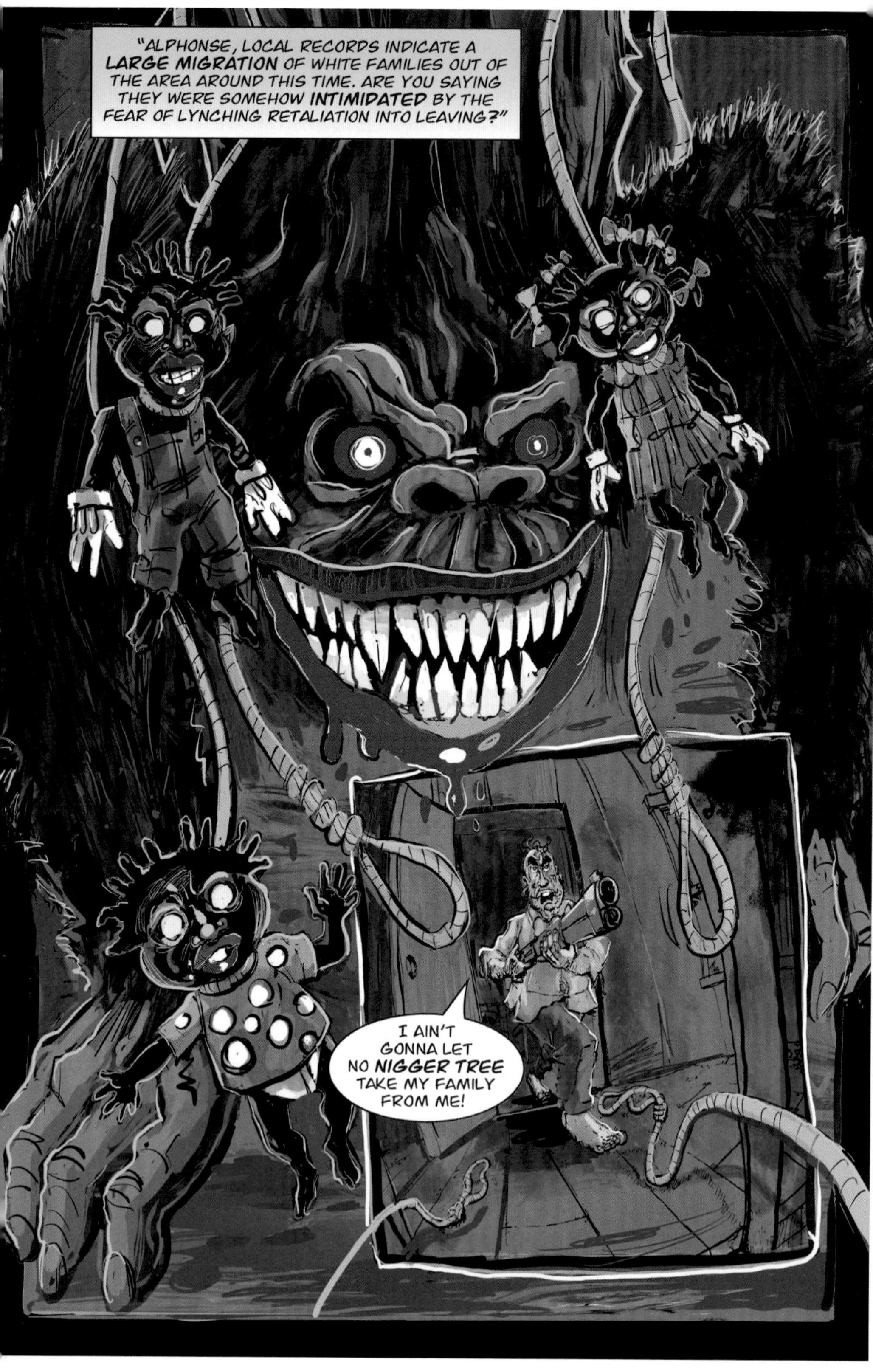
"ALPHONSE, LOCAL RECORDS INDICATE A **LARGE MIGRATION** OF WHITE FAMILIES OUT OF THE AREA AROUND THIS TIME. ARE YOU SAYING THEY WERE SOMEHOW **INTIMIDATED** BY THE FEAR OF LYNCHING RETALIATION INTO LEAVING?"
I AIN'T GONNA LET NO ***NIGGER TREE*** TAKE MY FAMILY FROM ME!

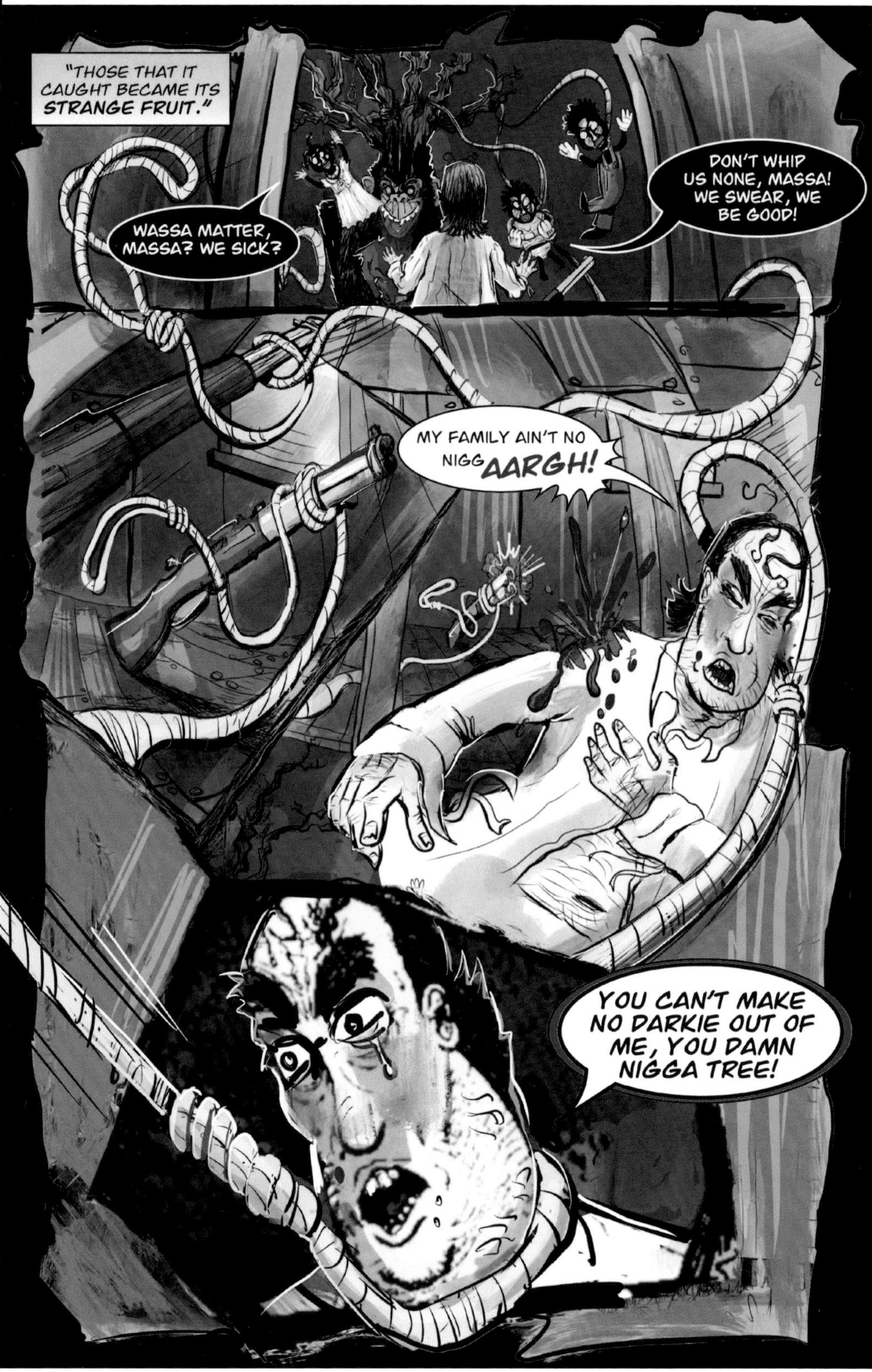
"THOSE THAT IT CAUGHT BECAME ITS STRANGE FRUIT."
WASSA MATTER, MASSA? WE SICK?
DON'T WHIP US NONE, MASSA! WE SWEAR, WE BE GOOD!
MY FAMILY AIN'T NO NIGG AARGH!
YOU CAN'T MAKE NO DARKIE OUT OF ME, YOU DAMN NIGGA TREE!

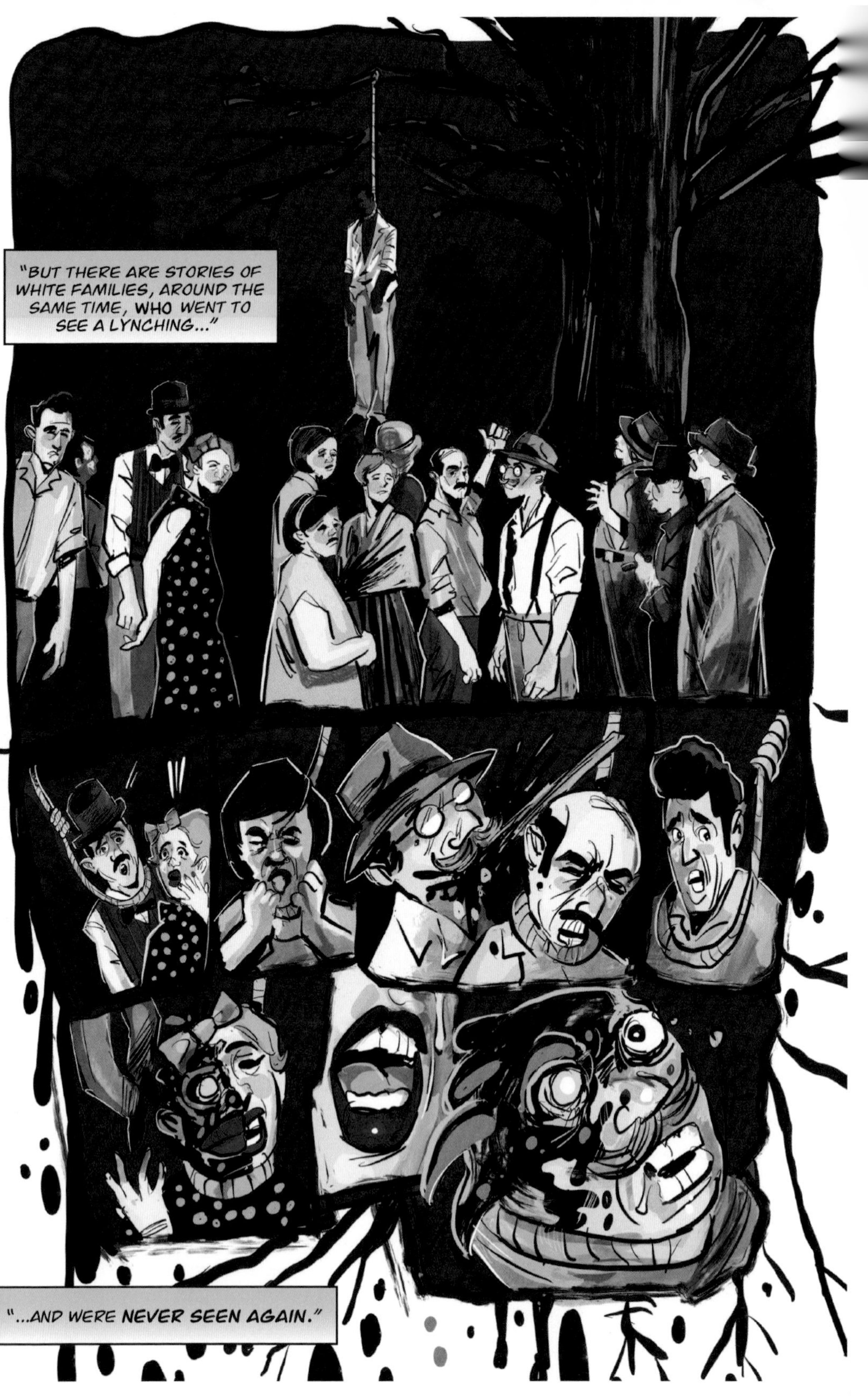
"BUT THERE ARE STORIES OF WHITE FAMILIES, AROUND THE SAME TIME, WHO WENT TO SEE A LYNCHING..."
"...AND WERE NEVER SEEN AGAIN."

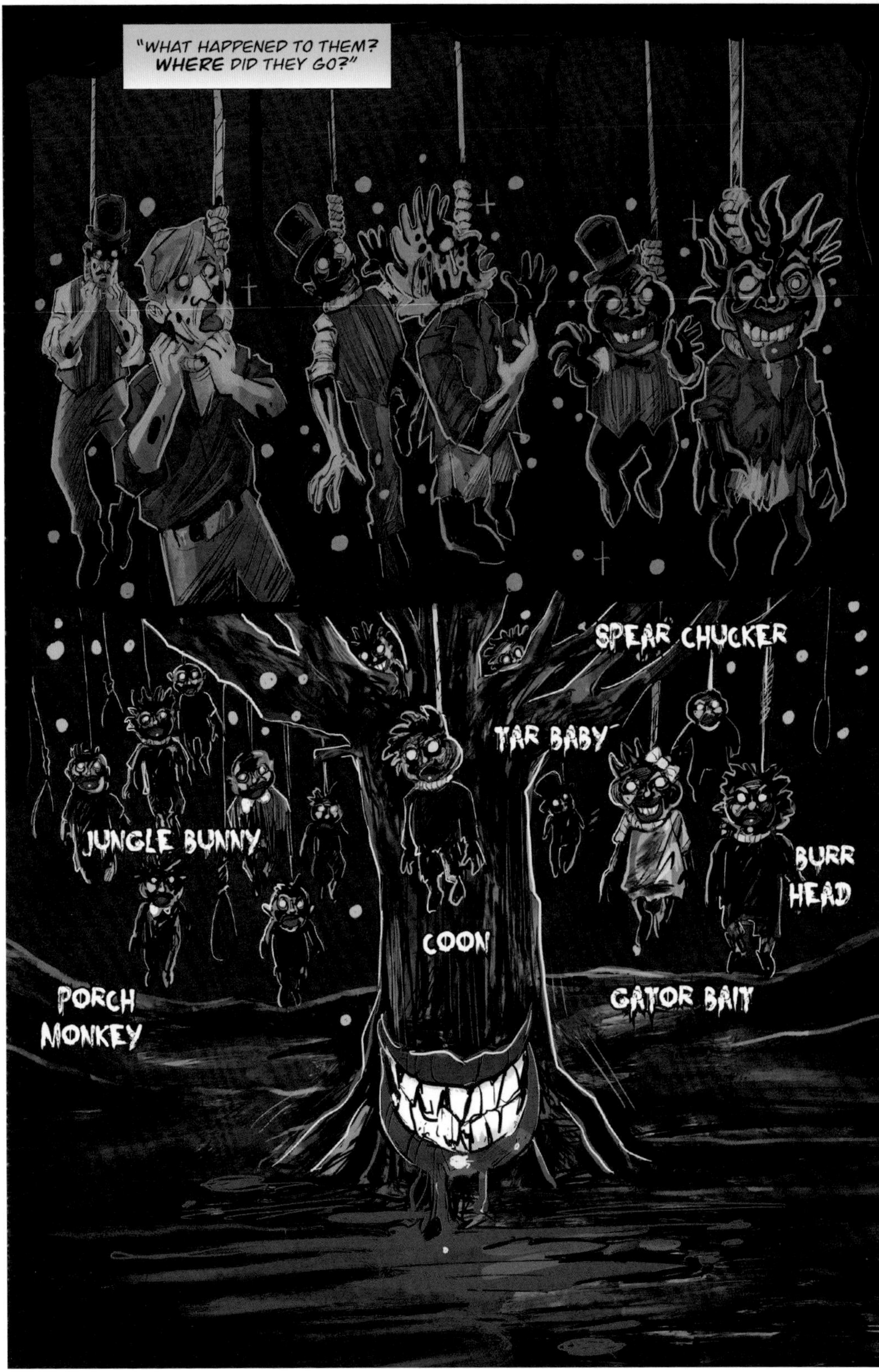
"WHAT HAPPENED TO THEM? WHERE DID THEY GO?"
SPEAR CHUCKER
TAR BABY
JUNGLE BUNNY
BURR HEAD
COON
PORCH MONKEY
GATOR BAIT

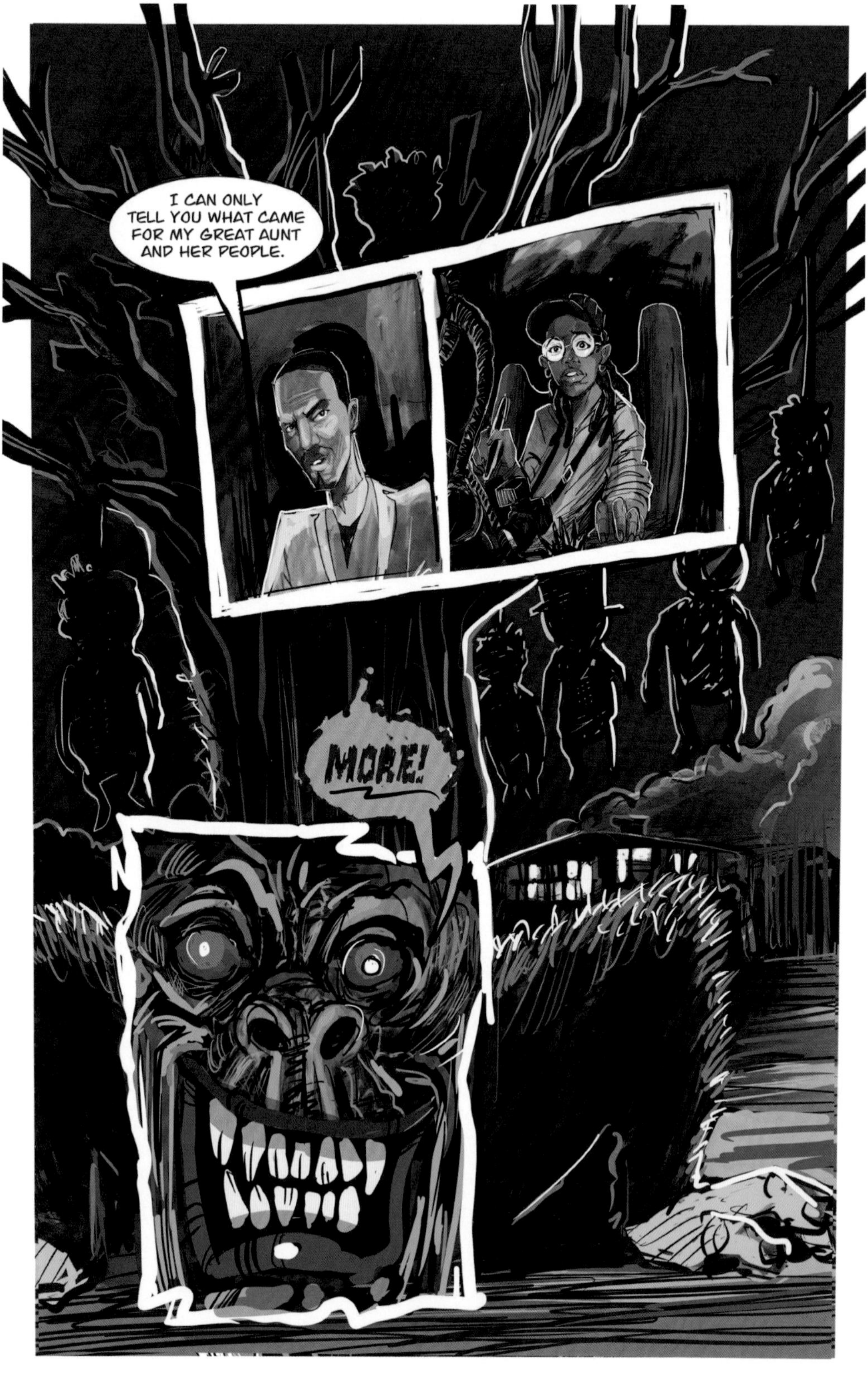
I CAN ONLY TELL YOU WHAT CAME FOR MY GREAT AUNT AND HER PEOPLE.
MORE!

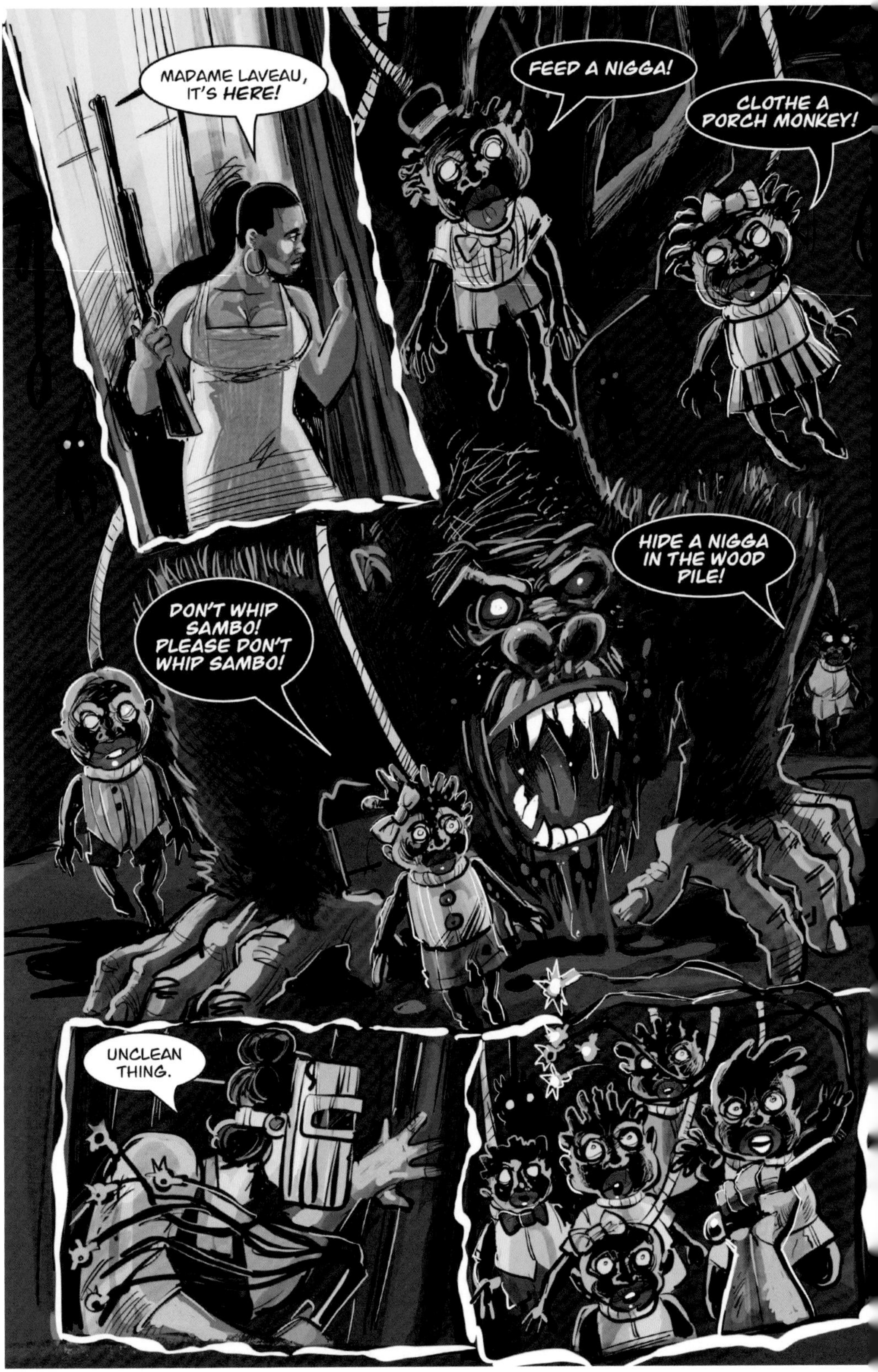
MADAME LAVEAU, IT'S HERE!
FEED A NIGGA!
CLOTHE A PORCH MONKEY!
HIDE A NIGGA IN THE WOOD PILE!
DON'T WHIP SAMBO! PLEASE DON'T WHIP SAMBO!
UNCLEAN THING.

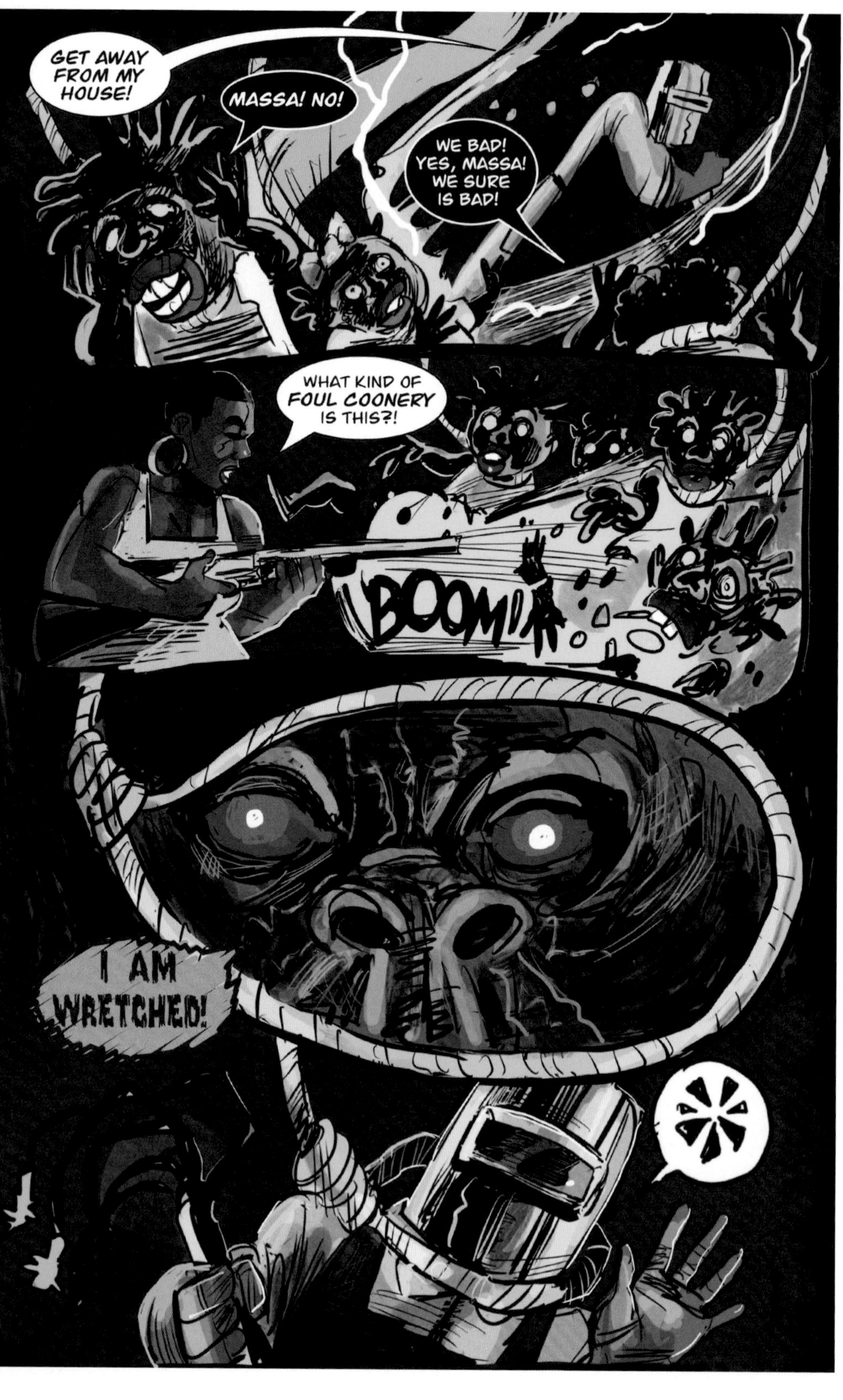
GET AWAY FROM MY HOUSE!
MASSA! NO!
WE BAD! YES, MASSA! WE SURE IS BAD!
WHAT KIND OF FOUL COONERY IS THIS?!
BOOM!
I AM WRETCHED!

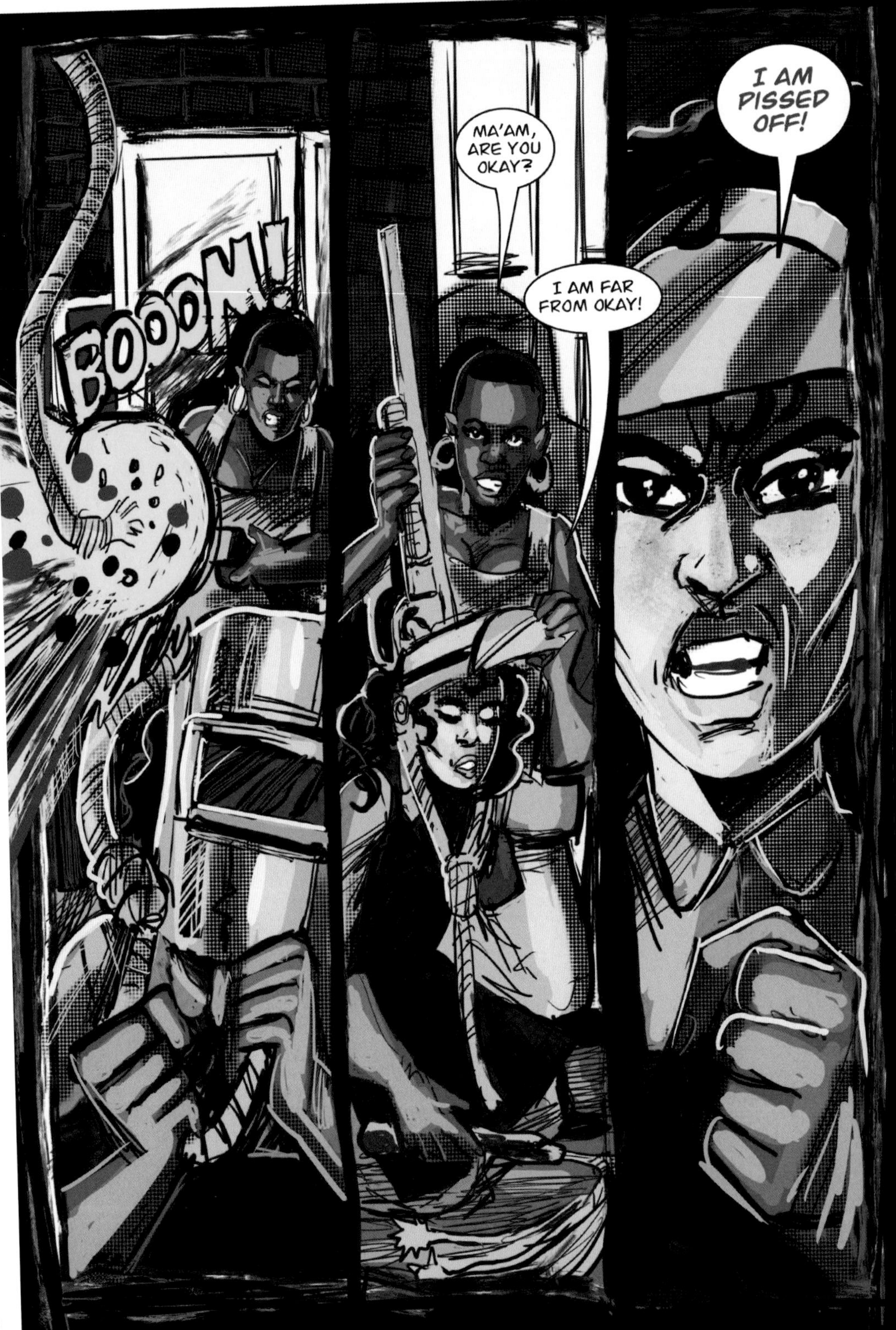
BOOOM!
MA'AM, ARE YOU OKAY?
I AM FAR FROM OKAY!
I AM PISSED OFF!

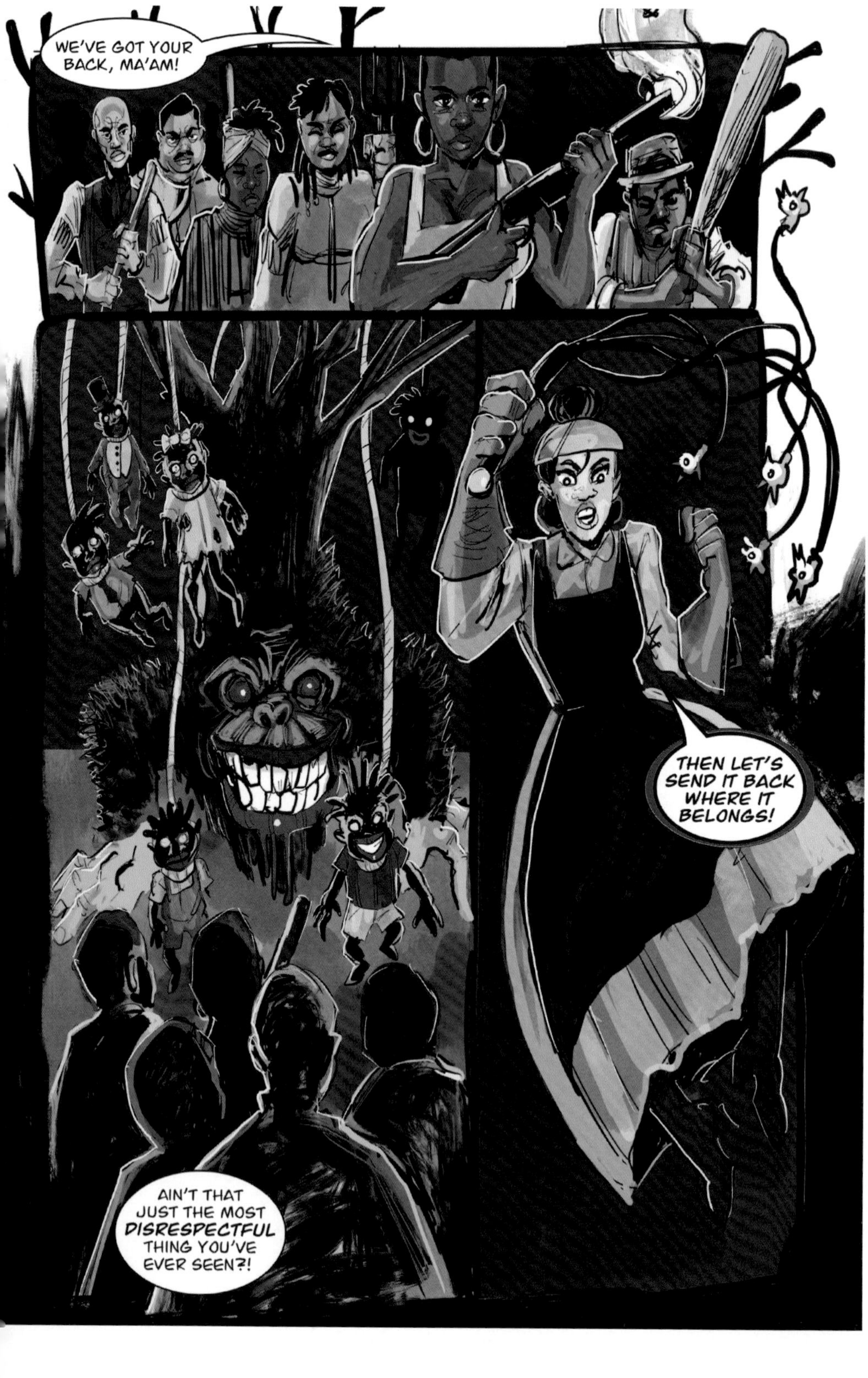
WE'VE GOT YOUR BACK, MA'AM!
THEN LET'S SEND IT BACK WHERE IT BELONGS!
AIN'T THAT JUST THE MOST DISRESPECTFUL THING YOU'VE EVER SEEN?!

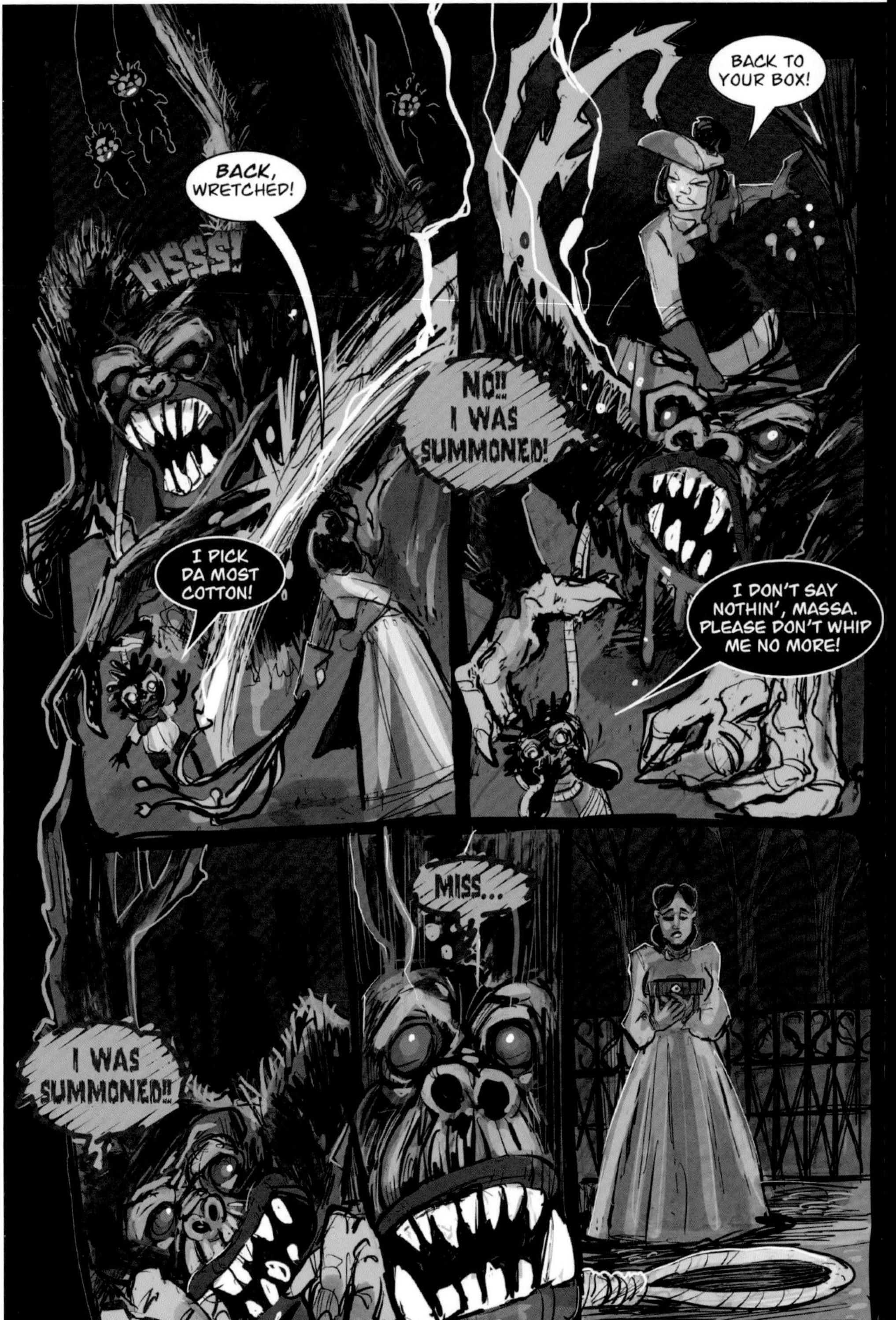
BACK, WRETCHED!
HSSS!
I PICK DA MOST COTTON!
BACK TO YOUR BOX!
NO!! I WAS SUMMONED!
I DON'T SAY NOTHIN', MASSA. PLEASE DON'T WHIP ME NO MORE!
MISS...
I WAS SUMMONED!!

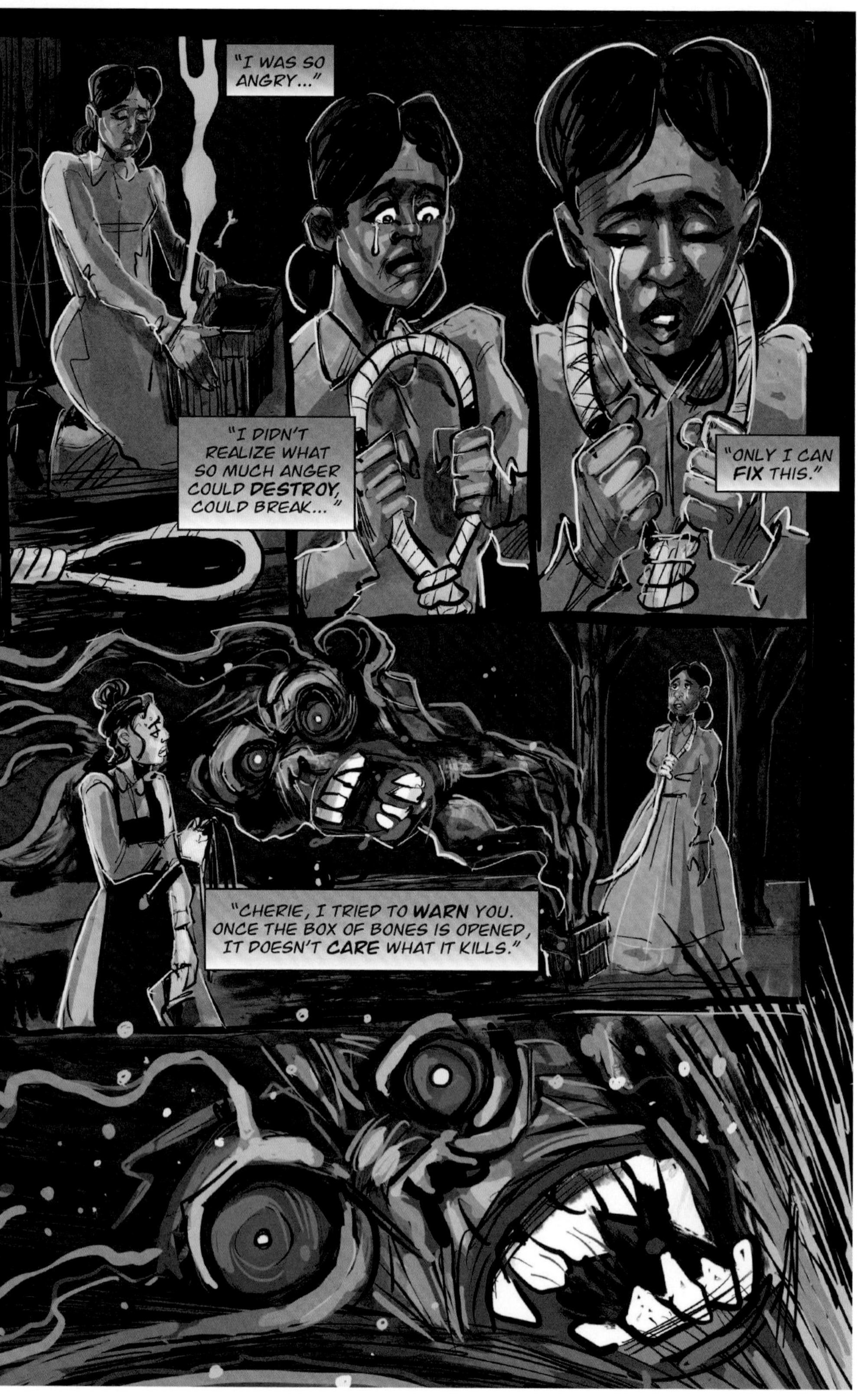
"I WAS SO ANGRY..."
"I DIDN'T REALIZE WHAT SO MUCH ANGER COULD **DESTROY**, COULD BREAK..."
"ONLY I CAN **FIX** THIS."
"CHERIE, I TRIED TO **WARN** YOU. ONCE THE BOX OF BONES IS OPENED, IT DOESN'T **CARE** WHAT IT KILLS."

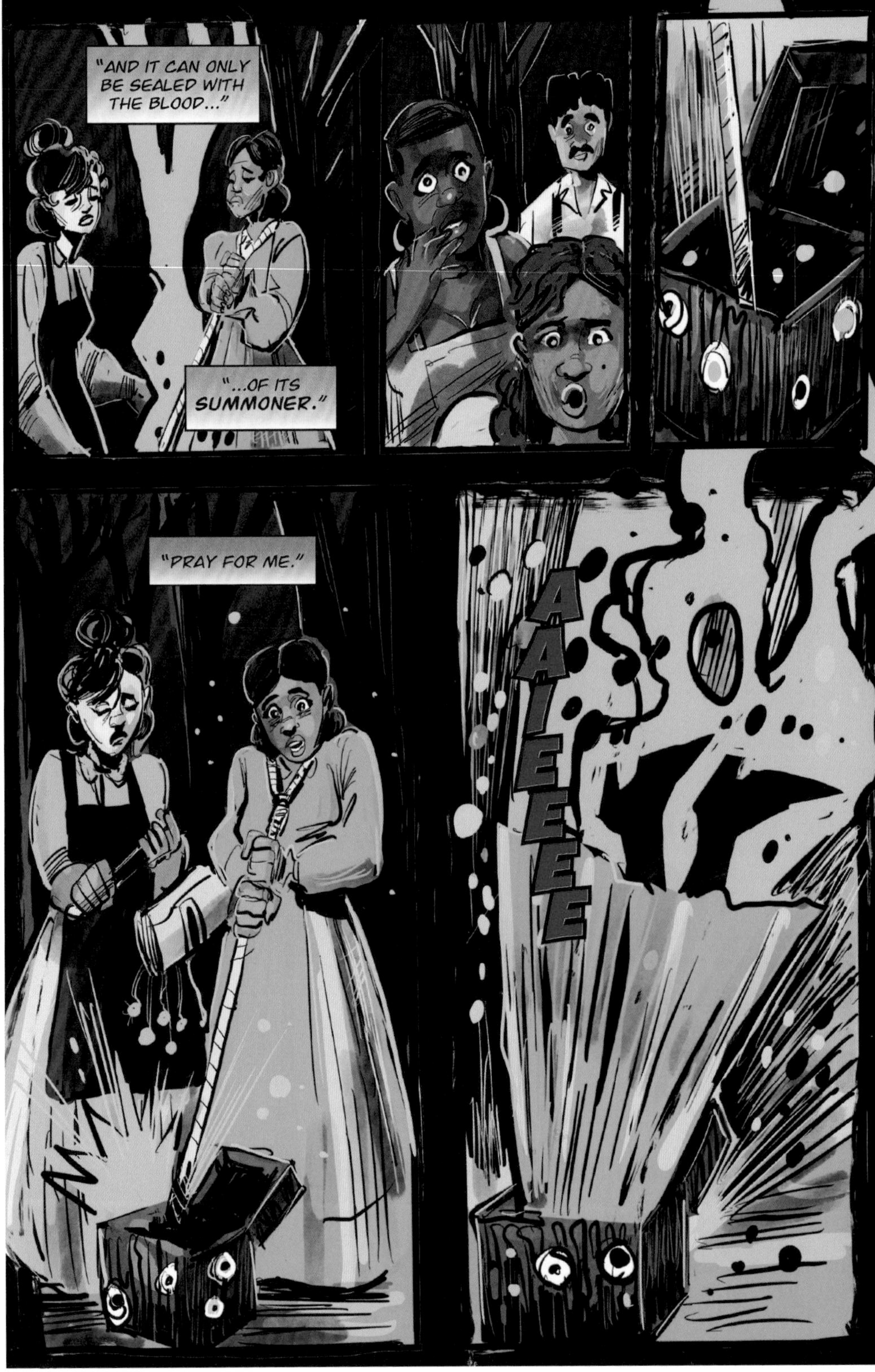
"AND IT CAN ONLY BE SEALED WITH THE BLOOD..."
"...OF ITS SUMMONER."
"PRAY FOR ME."
AAIEEEE

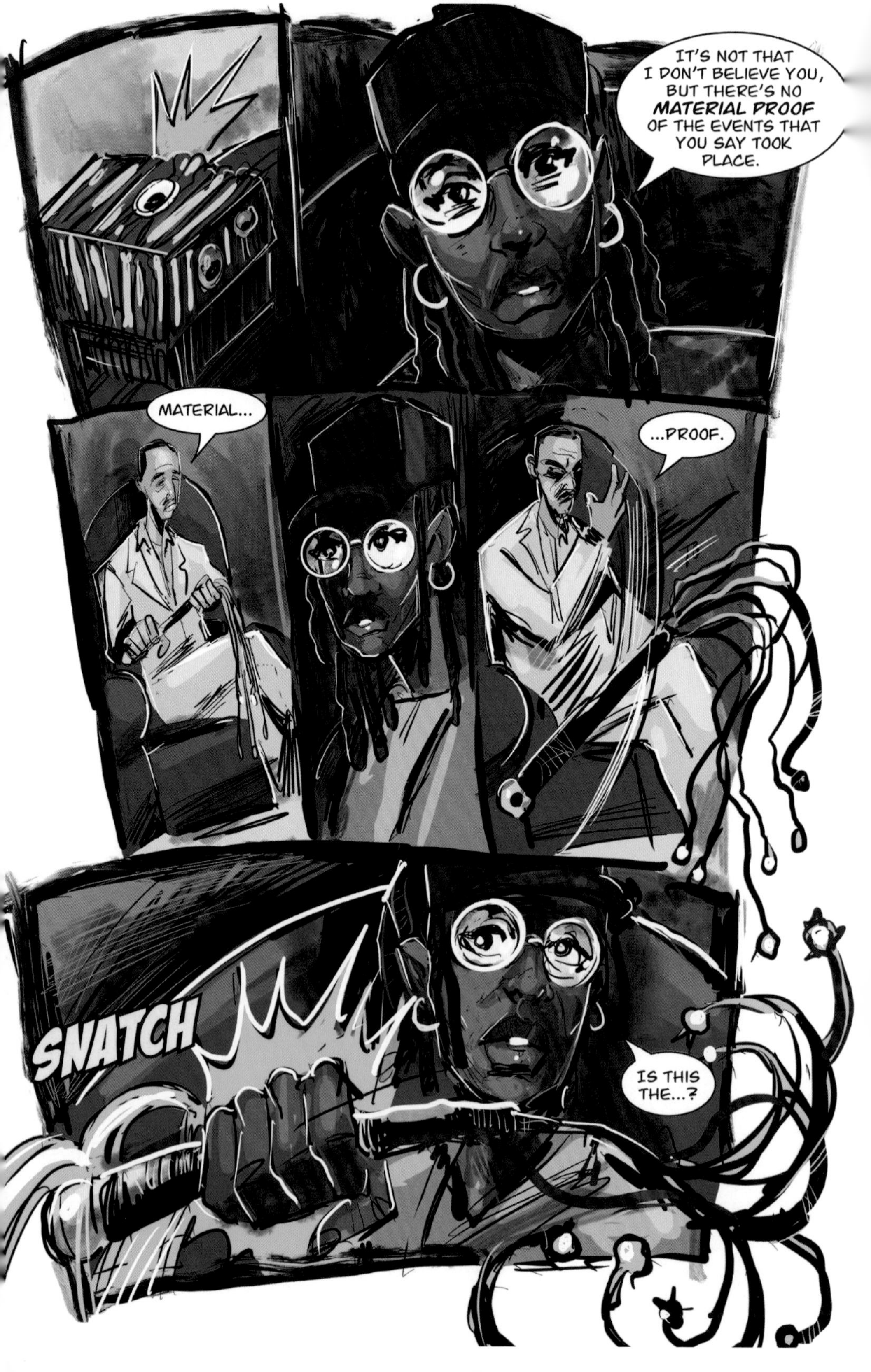
IT'S NOT THAT I DON'T BELIEVE YOU, BUT THERE'S NO **MATERIAL PROOF** OF THE EVENTS THAT YOU SAY TOOK PLACE.
MATERIAL...
...PROOF.
SNATCH
IS THIS THE...?

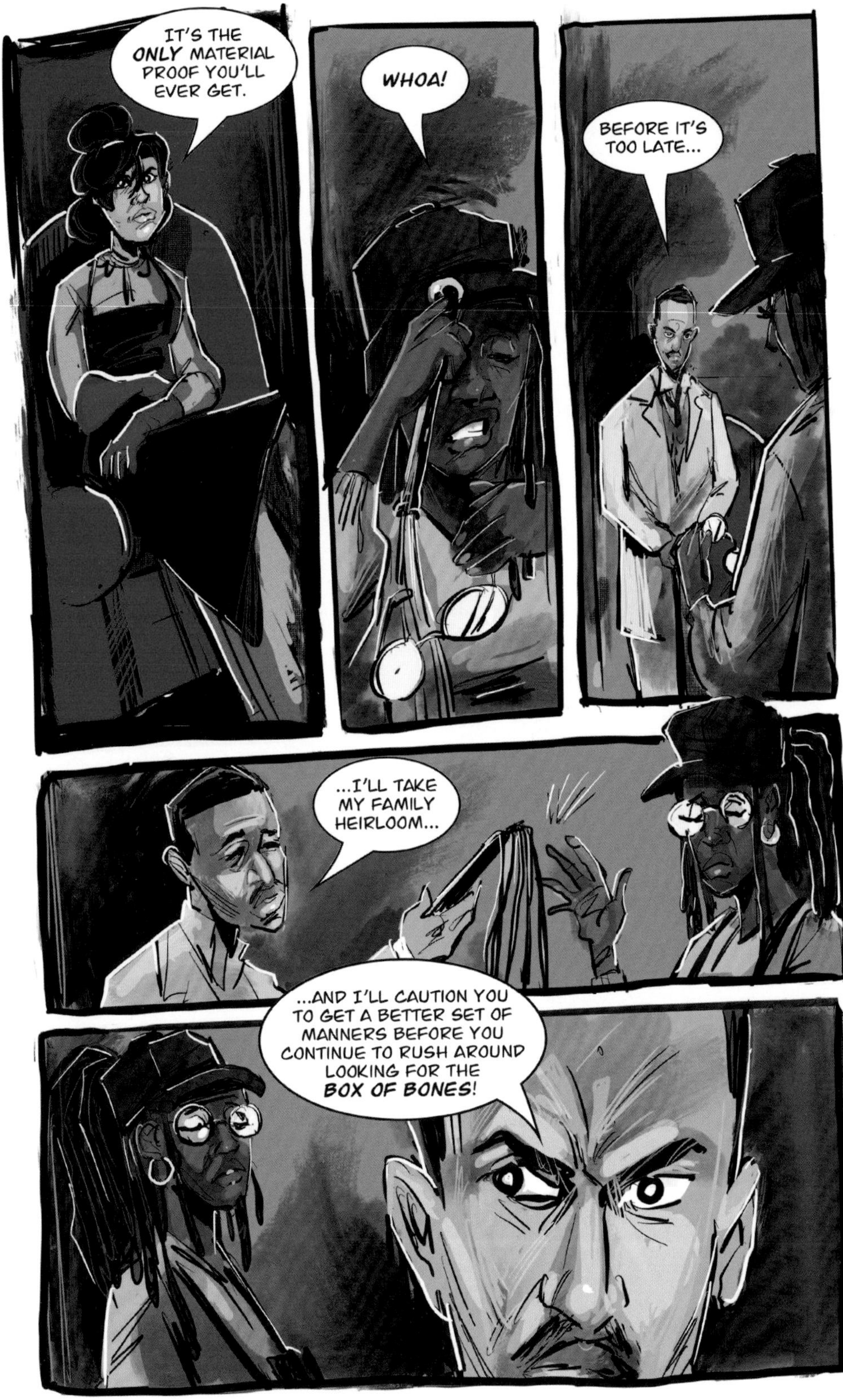
IT'S THE ONLY MATERIAL PROOF YOU'LL EVER GET.
WHOA!
BEFORE IT'S TOO LATE...
...I'LL TAKE MY FAMILY HEIRLOOM...
...AND I'LL CAUTION YOU TO GET A BETTER SET OF MANNERS BEFORE YOU CONTINUE TO RUSH AROUND LOOKING FOR THE BOX OF BONES!

# CHAPTER THREE

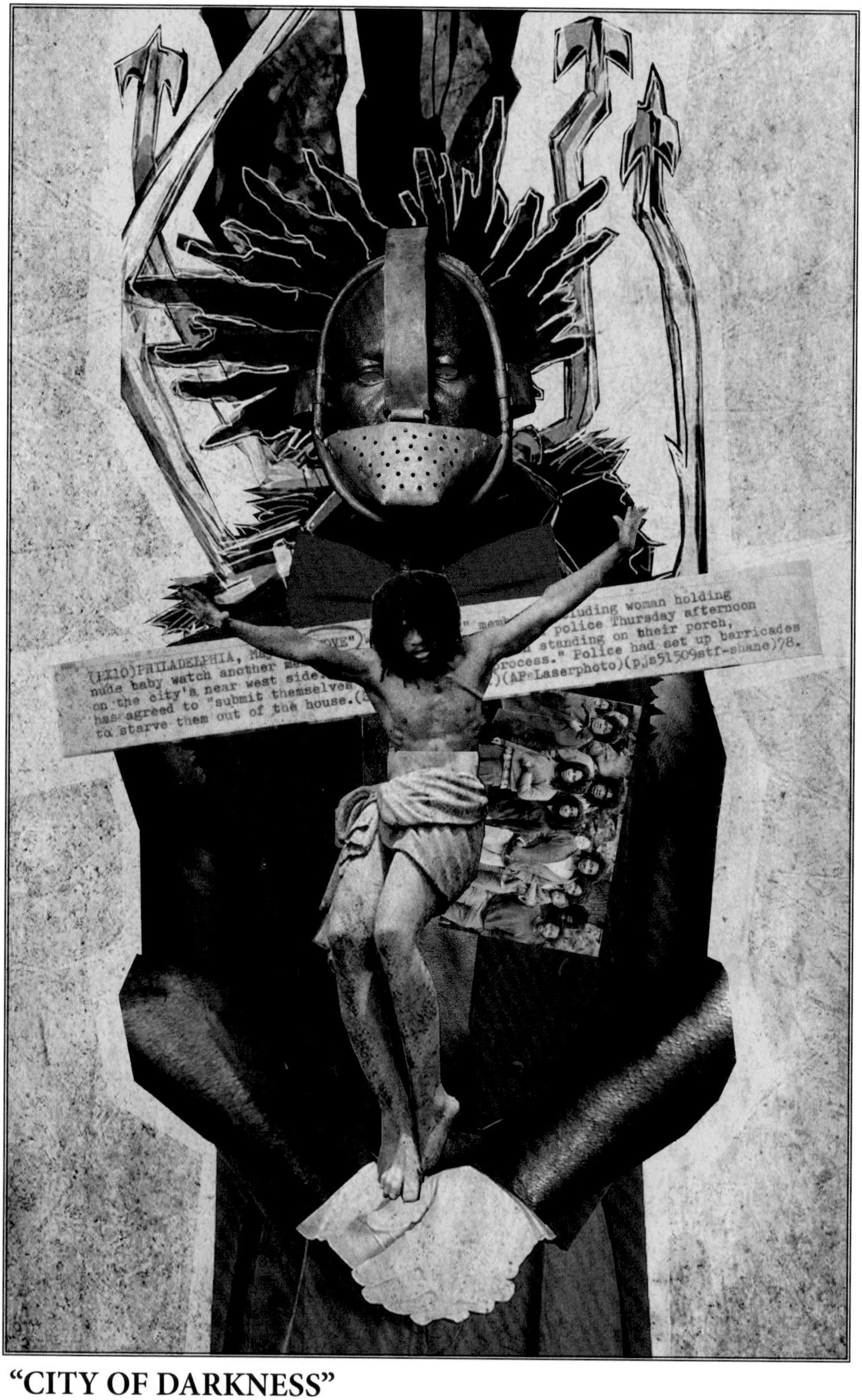
(PX10)PHILADELPHIA, May
nude baby watch another me
on the city's near west side.
has agreed to "submit themselves
to starve them out of the house.(
cluding woman holding
police Thursday afternoon
standing on their porch,
process." Police had set up barricades
)(AP Laserphoto)(pjs51509stf-shane)78.

"CITY OF DARKNESS"

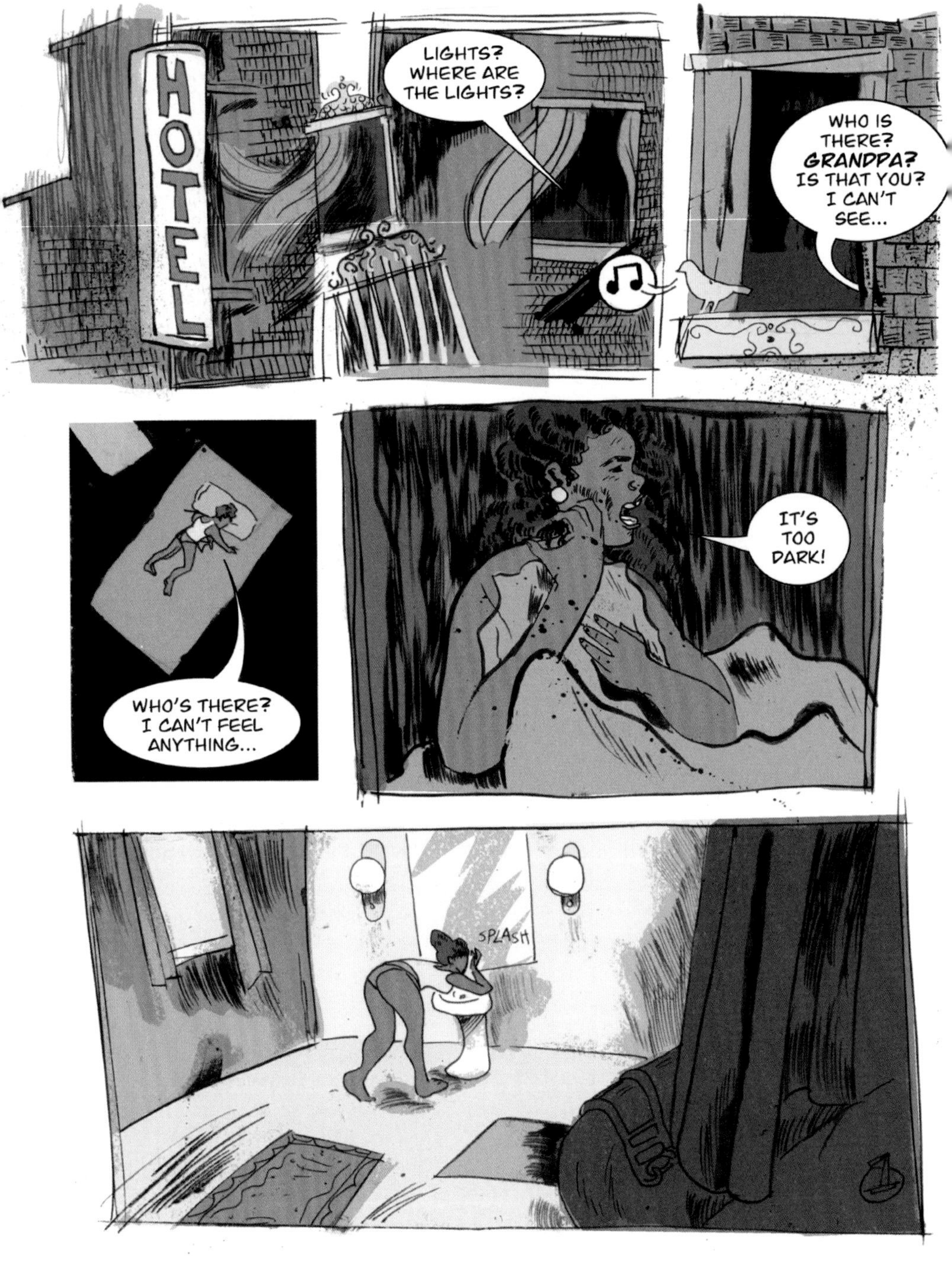
HOTEL
LIGHTS? WHERE ARE THE LIGHTS?
WHO IS THERE? **GRANDPA?** IS THAT YOU? I CAN'T SEE...
WHO'S THERE? I CAN'T FEEL ANYTHING...
IT'S TOO DARK!
SPLASH

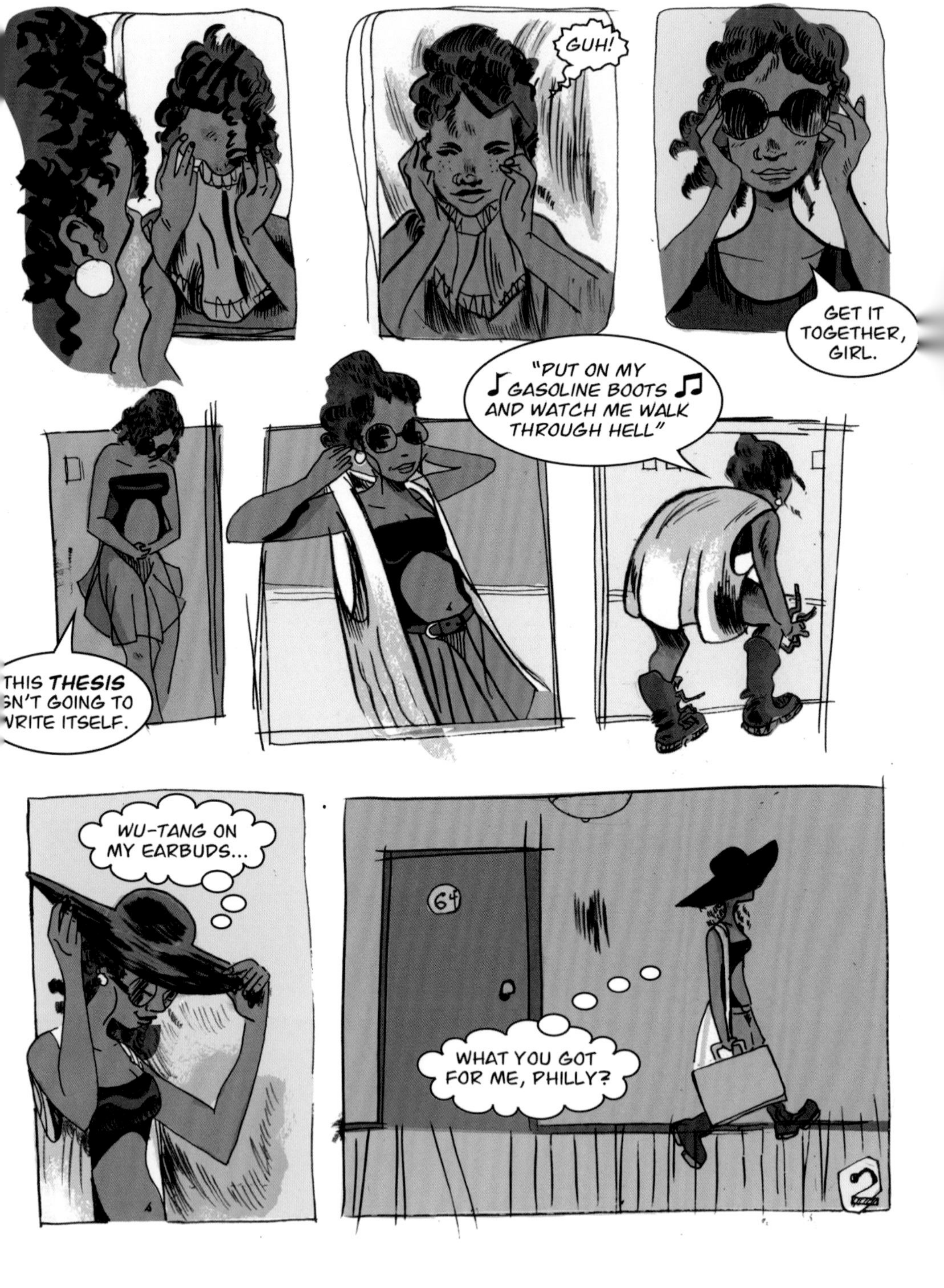
GUH!
GET IT TOGETHER, GIRL.
THIS THESIS
SN'T GOING TO
VRITE ITSELF.
"PUT ON MY GASOLINE BOOTS AND WATCH ME WALK THROUGH HELL"
WU-TANG ON MY EARBUDS...
64
WHAT YOU GOT FOR ME, PHILLY?
2

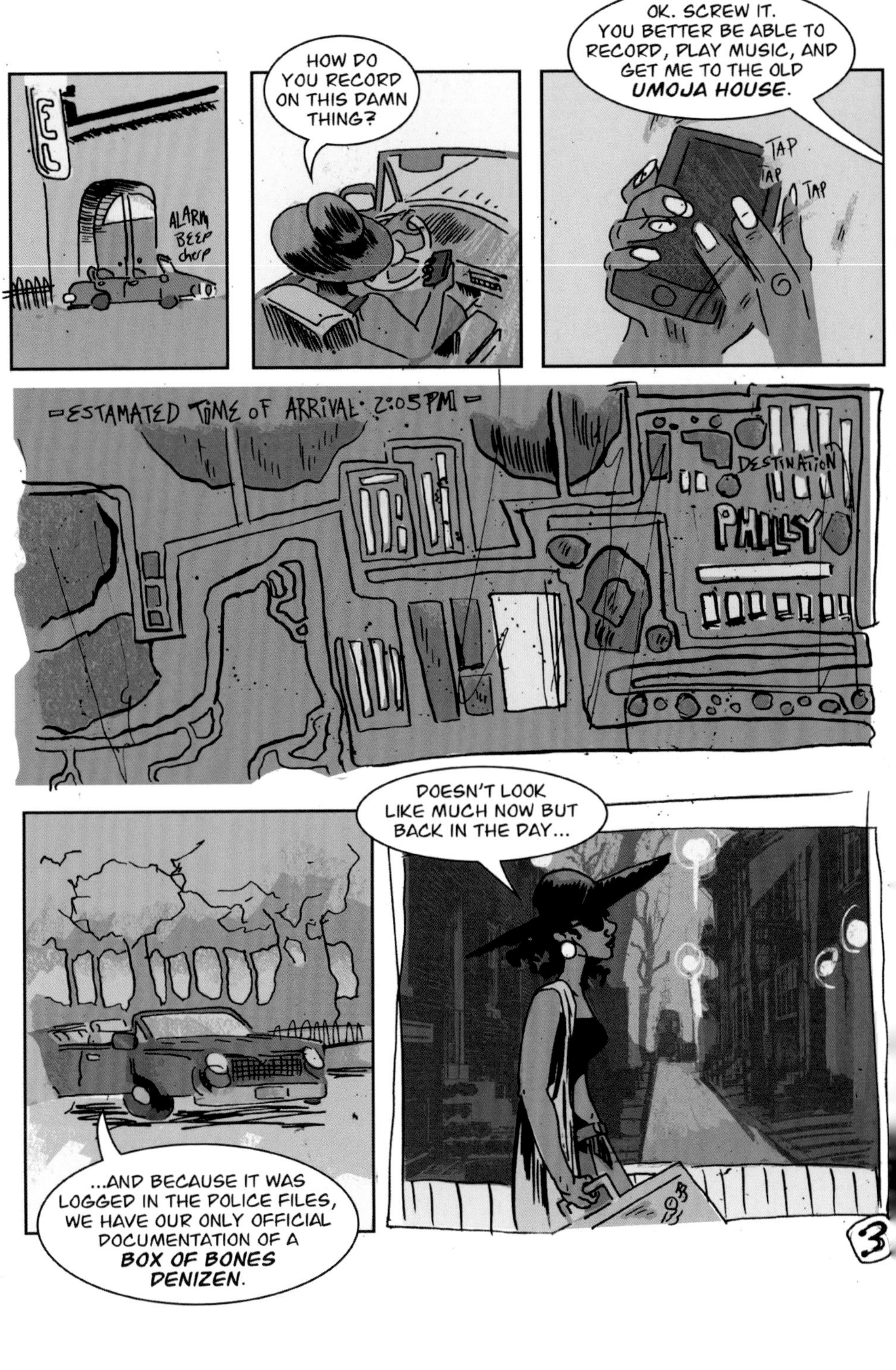
ALARM BEEP chirp
HOW DO YOU RECORD ON THIS DAMN THING?
OK. SCREW IT. YOU BETTER BE ABLE TO RECORD, PLAY MUSIC, AND GET ME TO THE OLD UMOJA HOUSE.
TAP TAP TAP
-ESTAMATED TIME OF ARRIVAL: 2:05PM-
DESTINATION
PHILLY
DOESN'T LOOK LIKE MUCH NOW BUT BACK IN THE DAY...
...AND BECAUSE IT WAS LOGGED IN THE POLICE FILES, WE HAVE OUR ONLY OFFICIAL DOCUMENTATION OF A BOX OF BONES DENIZEN.

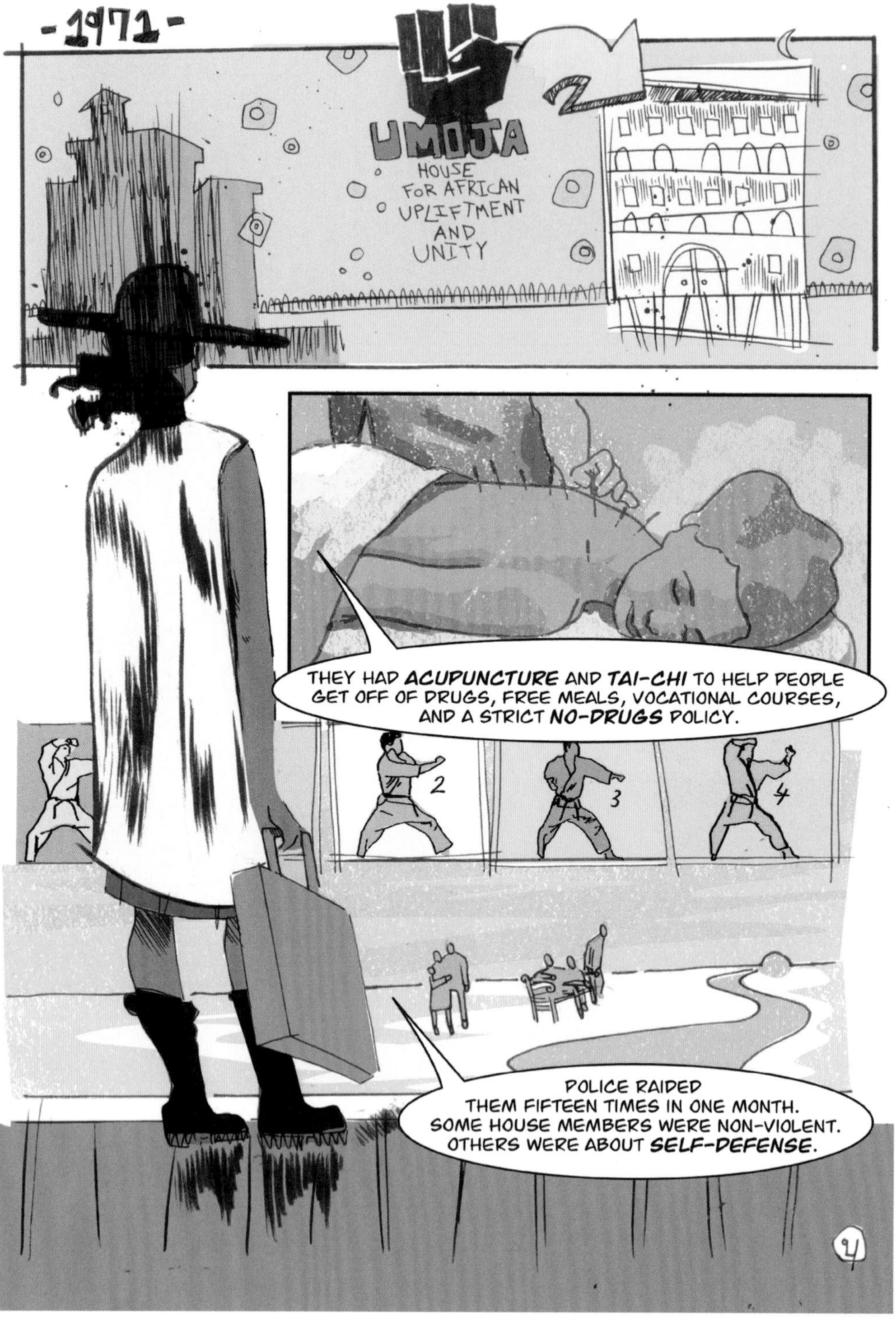
-1971-
UMOJA
HOUSE FOR AFRICAN UPLIFTMENT AND UNITY
THEY HAD ACUPUNCTURE AND TAI-CHI TO HELP PEOPLE GET OFF OF DRUGS, FREE MEALS, VOCATIONAL COURSES, AND A STRICT NO-DRUGS POLICY.
2
3
4
POLICE RAIDED THEM FIFTEEN TIMES IN ONE MONTH. SOME HOUSE MEMBERS WERE NON-VIOLENT. OTHERS WERE ABOUT SELF-DEFENSE.

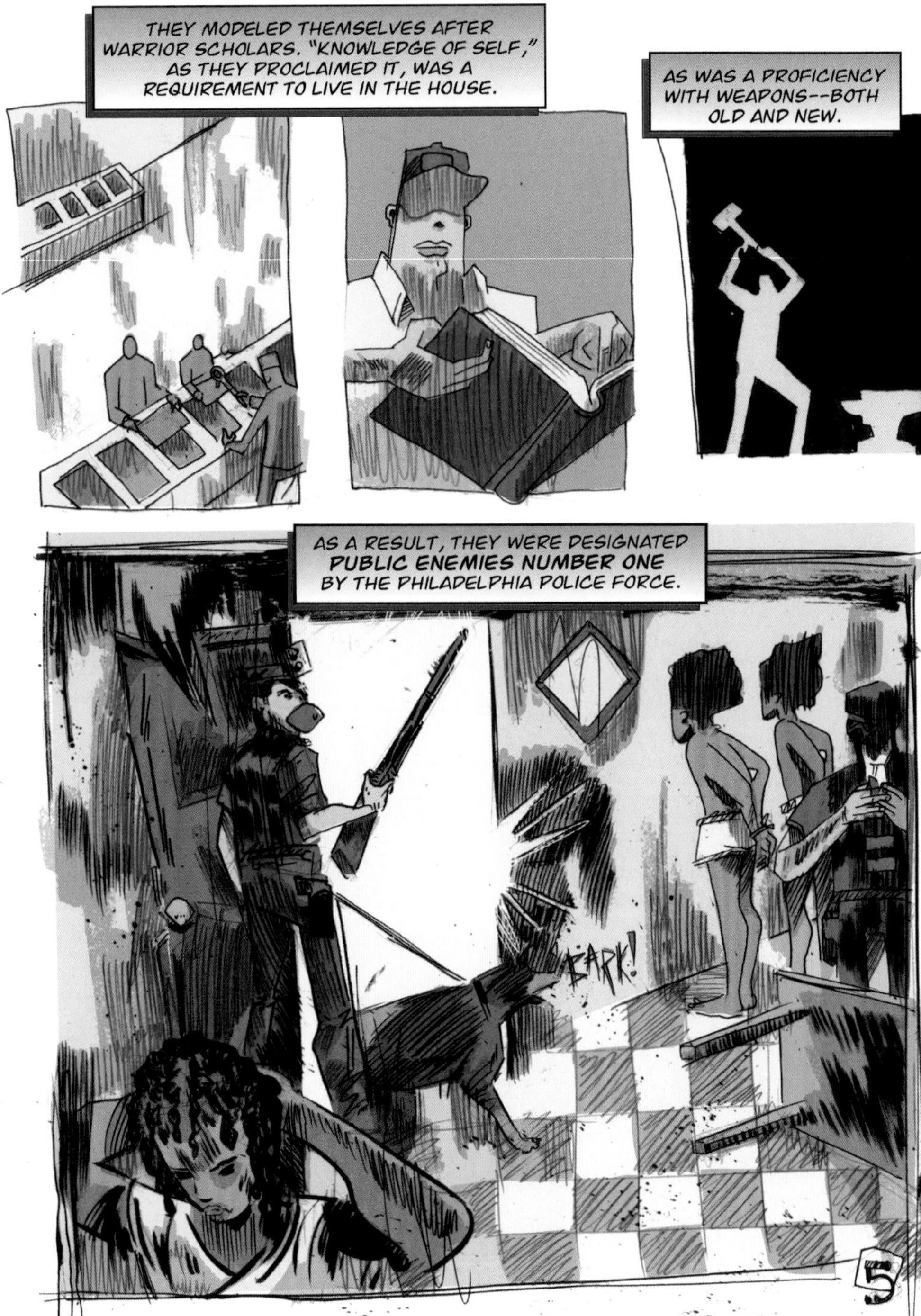
THEY MODELED THEMSELVES AFTER WARRIOR SCHOLARS. "KNOWLEDGE OF SELF," AS THEY PROCLAIMED IT, WAS A REQUIREMENT TO LIVE IN THE HOUSE.
AS WAS A PROFICIENCY WITH WEAPONS--BOTH OLD AND NEW.
AS A RESULT, THEY WERE DESIGNATED **PUBLIC ENEMIES NUMBER ONE** BY THE PHILADELPHIA POLICE FORCE.
BARK!

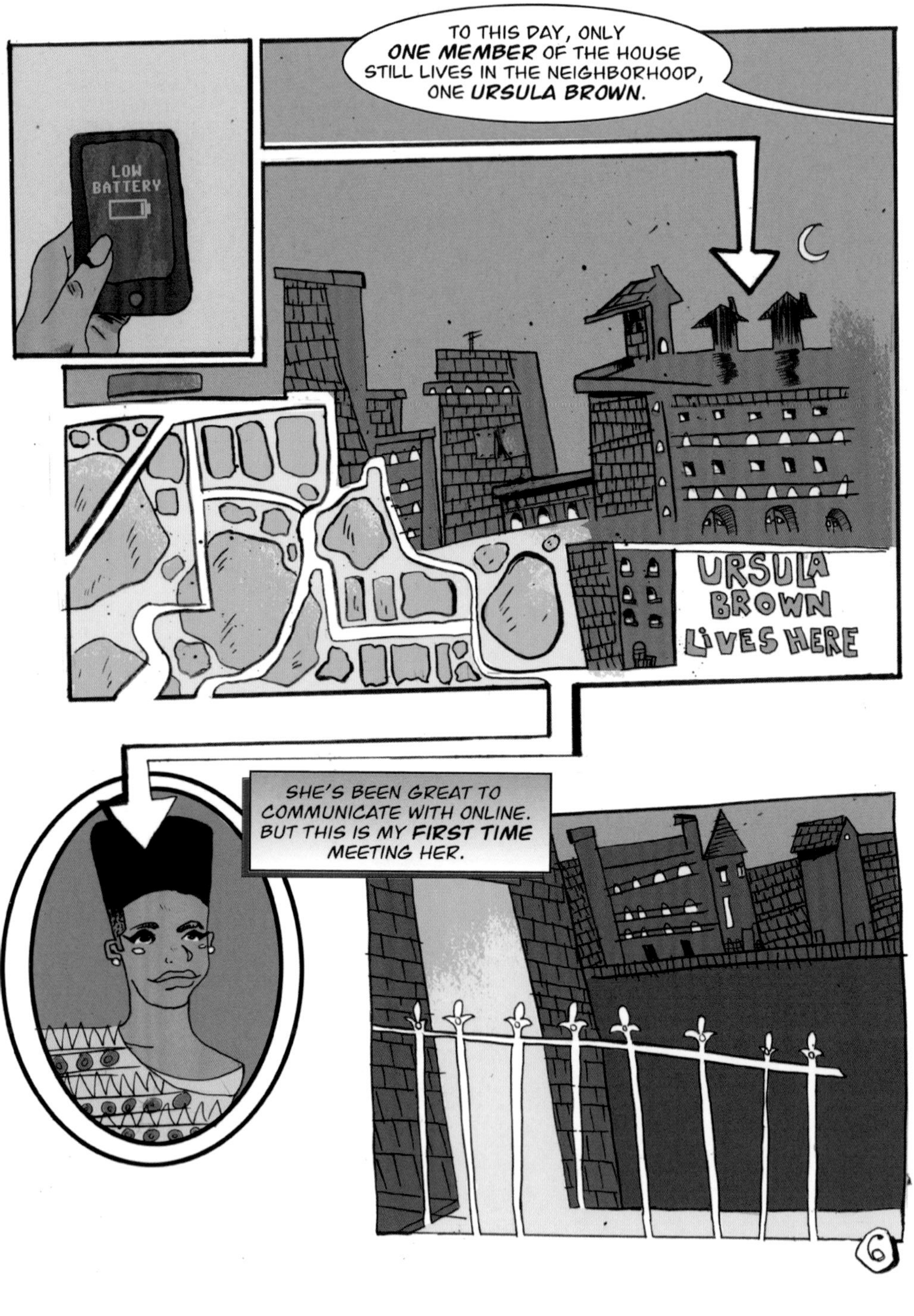
LOW BATTERY
TO THIS DAY, ONLY ONE MEMBER OF THE HOUSE STILL LIVES IN THE NEIGHBORHOOD, ONE URSULA BROWN.
URSULA BROWN LIVES HERE
SHE'S BEEN GREAT TO COMMUNICATE WITH ONLINE. BUT THIS IS MY FIRST TIME MEETING HER.
6

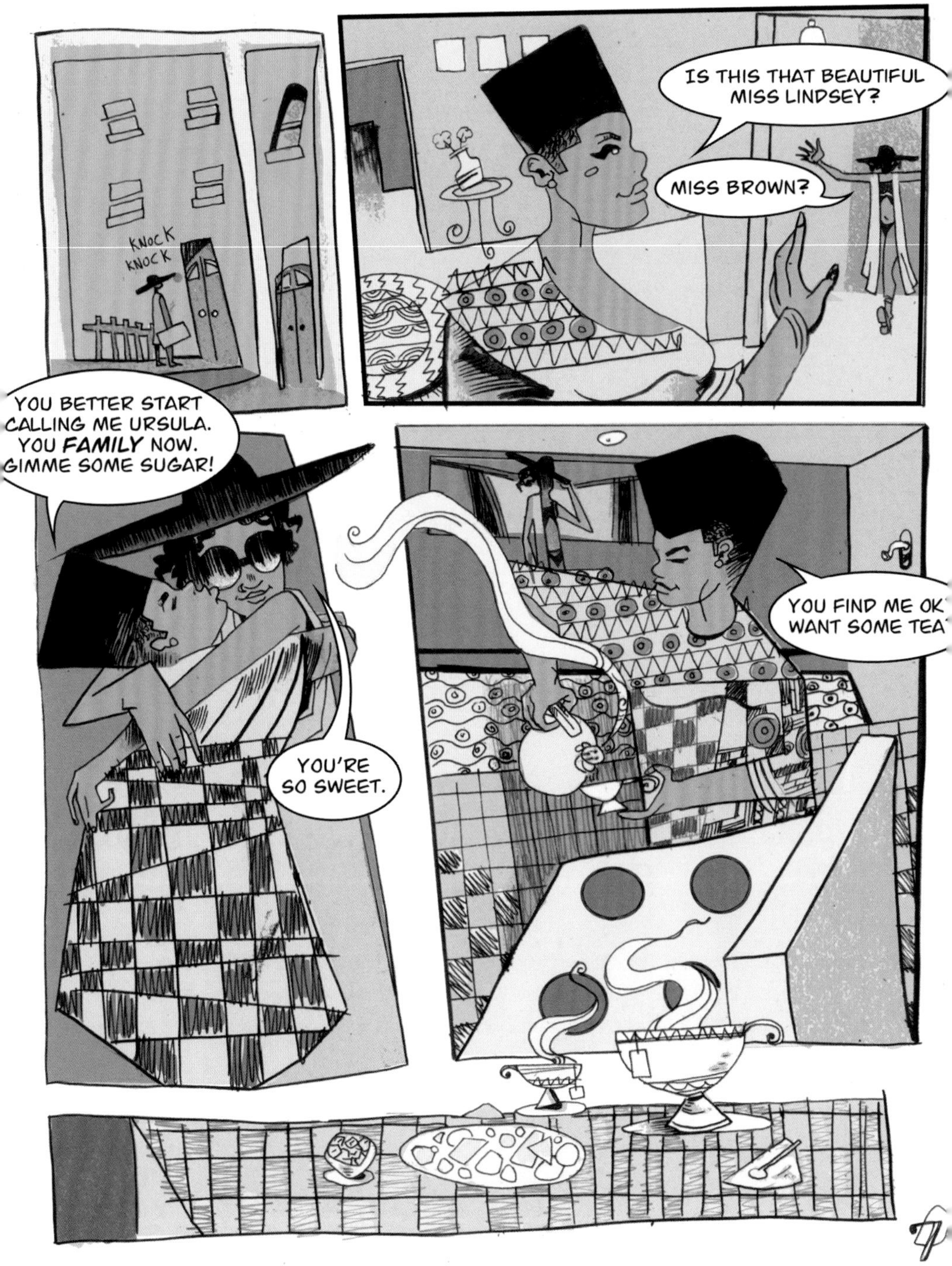
KNOCK KNOCK
IS THIS THAT BEAUTIFUL MISS LINDSEY?
MISS BROWN?
YOU BETTER START CALLING ME URSULA. YOU **FAMILY** NOW. GIMME SOME SUGAR!
YOU'RE SO SWEET.
YOU FIND ME OK
WANT SOME TEA

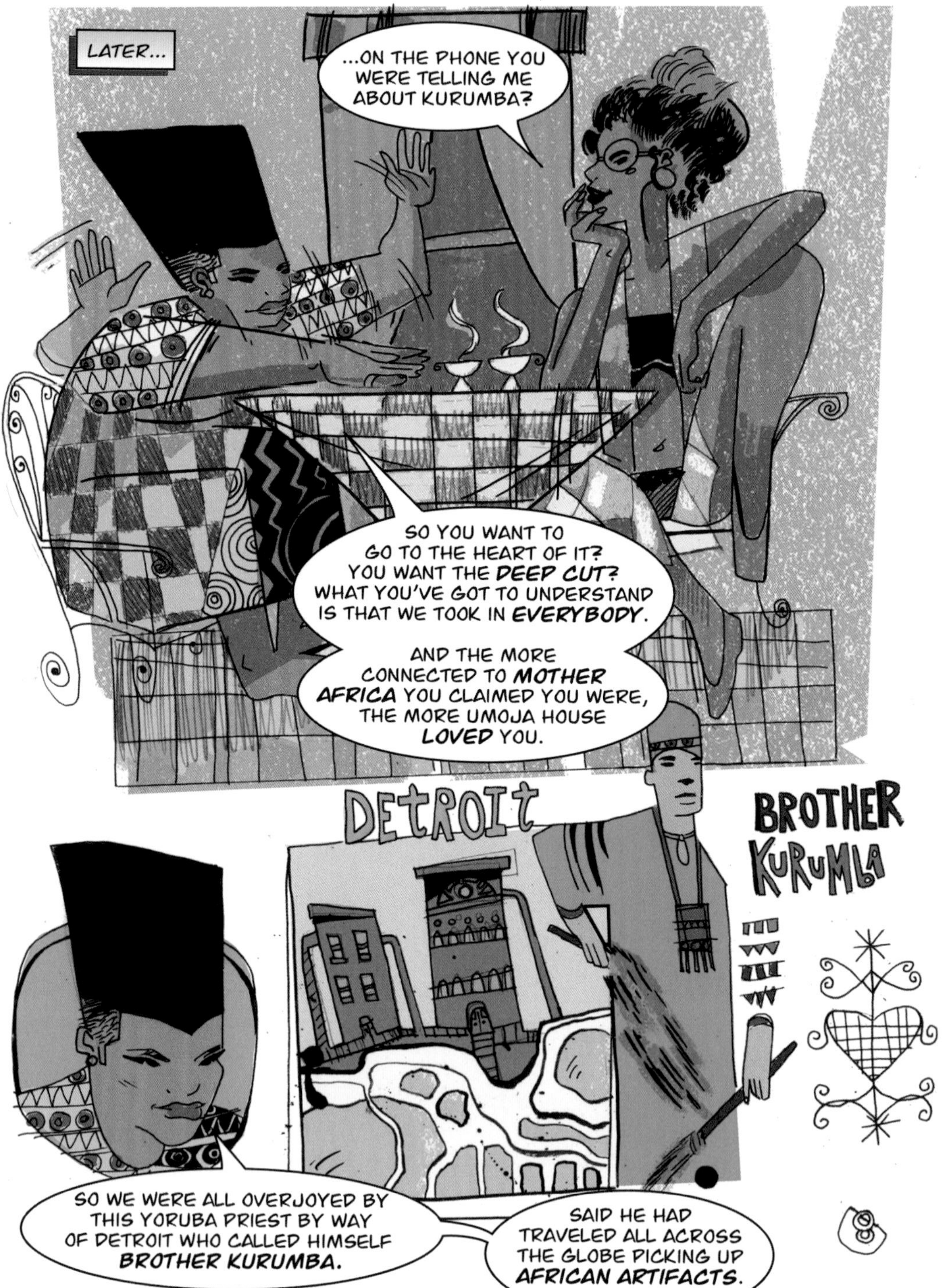
LATER...
...ON THE PHONE YOU WERE TELLING ME ABOUT KURUMBA?
SO YOU WANT TO GO TO THE HEART OF IT? YOU WANT THE DEEP CUT? WHAT YOU'VE GOT TO UNDERSTAND IS THAT WE TOOK IN EVERYBODY.
AND THE MORE CONNECTED TO MOTHER AFRICA YOU CLAIMED YOU WERE, THE MORE UMOJA HOUSE LOVED YOU.
DETROIT
BROTHER KURUMBA
SO WE WERE ALL OVERJOYED BY THIS YORUBA PRIEST BY WAY OF DETROIT WHO CALLED HIMSELF BROTHER KURUMBA.
SAID HE HAD TRAVELED ALL ACROSS THE GLOBE PICKING UP AFRICAN ARTIFACTS.

# AFRICAN ARTIFACTS

HE HAD A **SPEAR** AND **SHIELD** FROM GHANA.

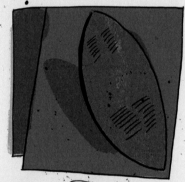

A **WHITE LION'S MANE** FROM KENYA.

HE PLAYED A **TALKING DRUM** HE RECEIVED AS A GIFT FROM AN AFRICAN PRIEST IN THE DOMINICAN REPUBLIC.

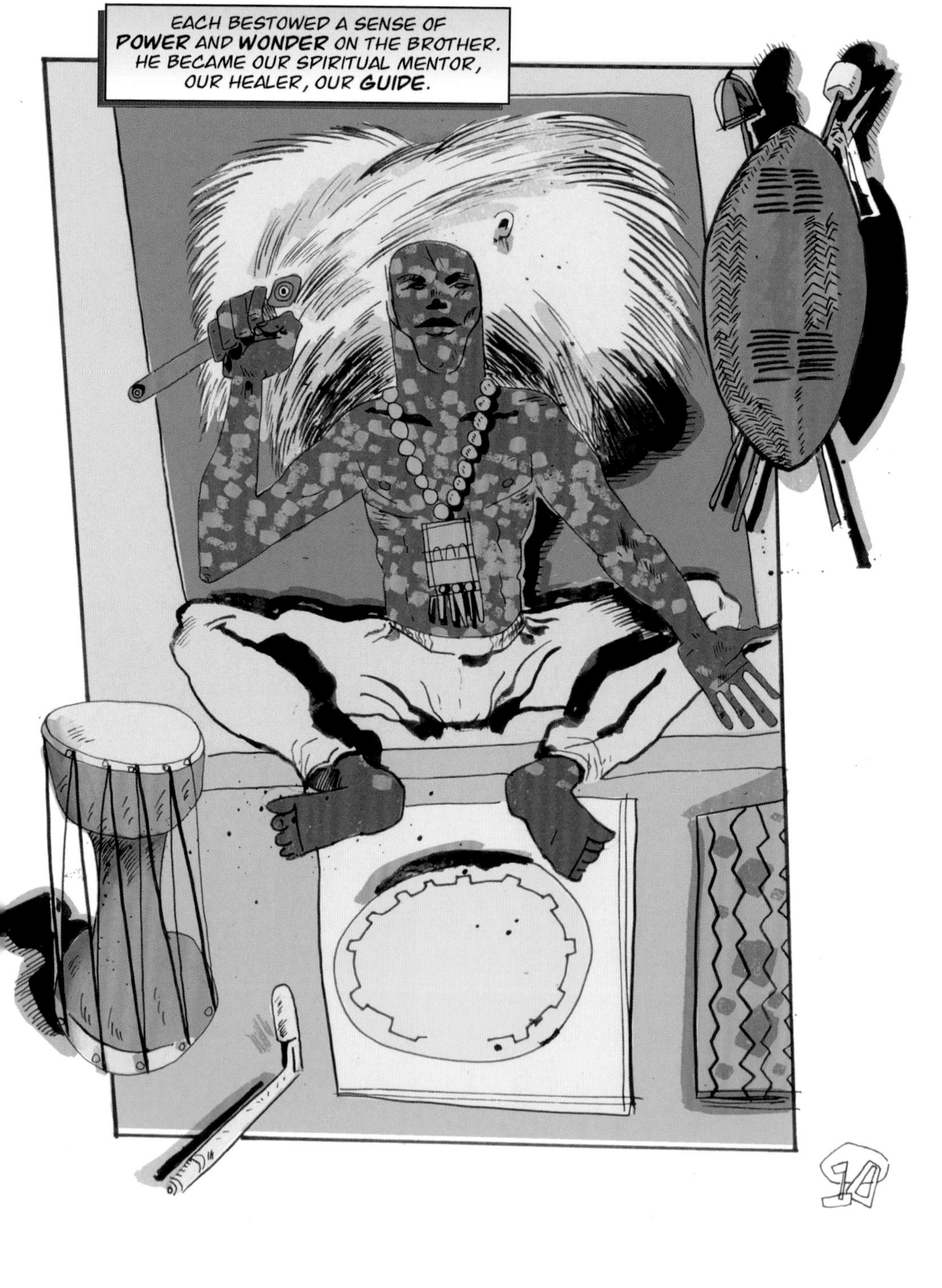
EACH BESTOWED A SENSE OF POWER AND WONDER ON THE BROTHER. HE BECAME OUR SPIRITUAL MENTOR, OUR HEALER, OUR GUIDE.

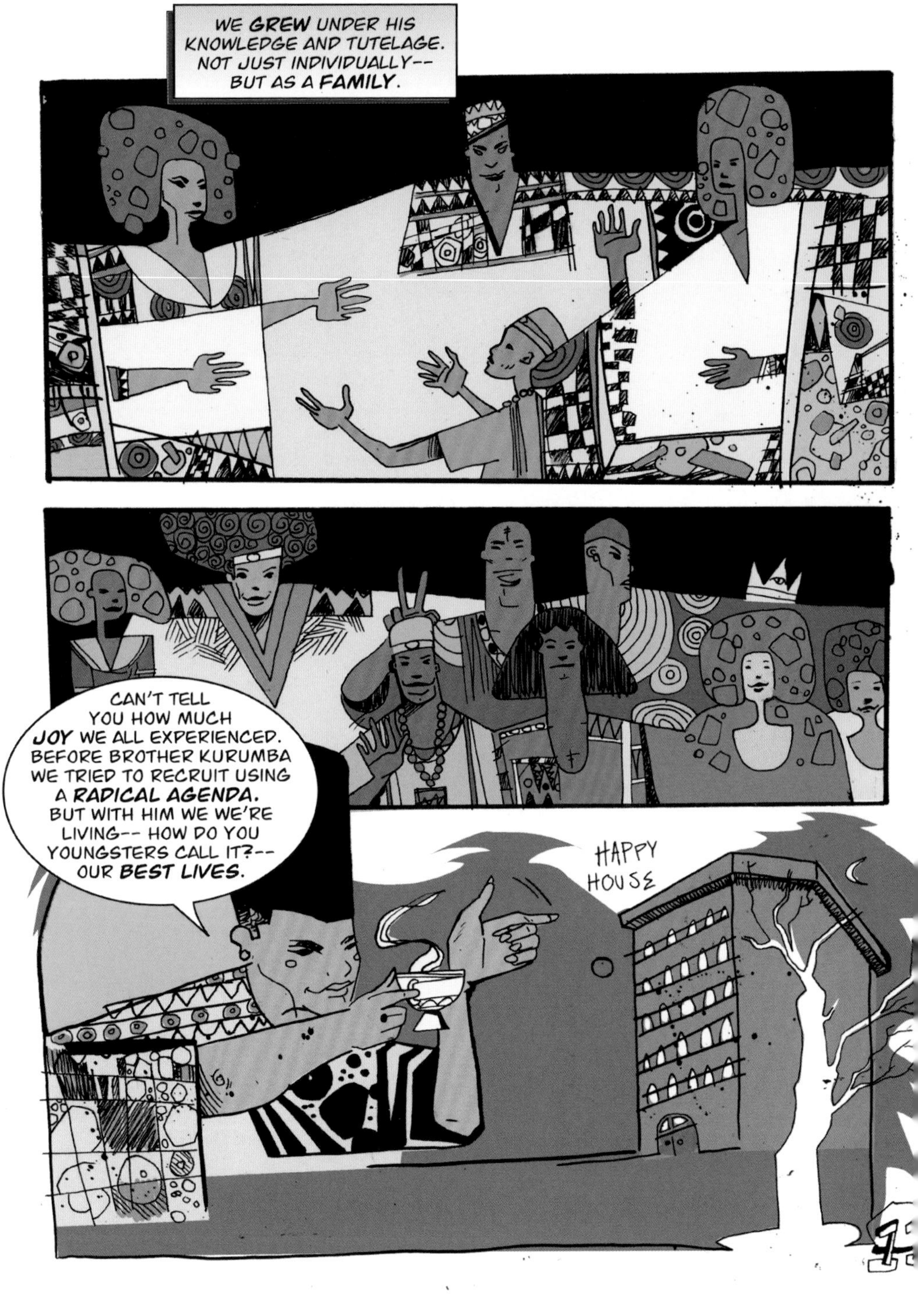
WE GREW UNDER HIS KNOWLEDGE AND TUTELAGE. NOT JUST INDIVIDUALLY-- BUT AS A FAMILY.
CAN'T TELL YOU HOW MUCH JOY WE ALL EXPERIENCED. BEFORE BROTHER KURUMBA WE TRIED TO RECRUIT USING A RADICAL AGENDA. BUT WITH HIM WE WE'RE LIVING-- HOW DO YOU YOUNGSTERS CALL IT?-- OUR BEST LIVES.
HAPPY HOUSE

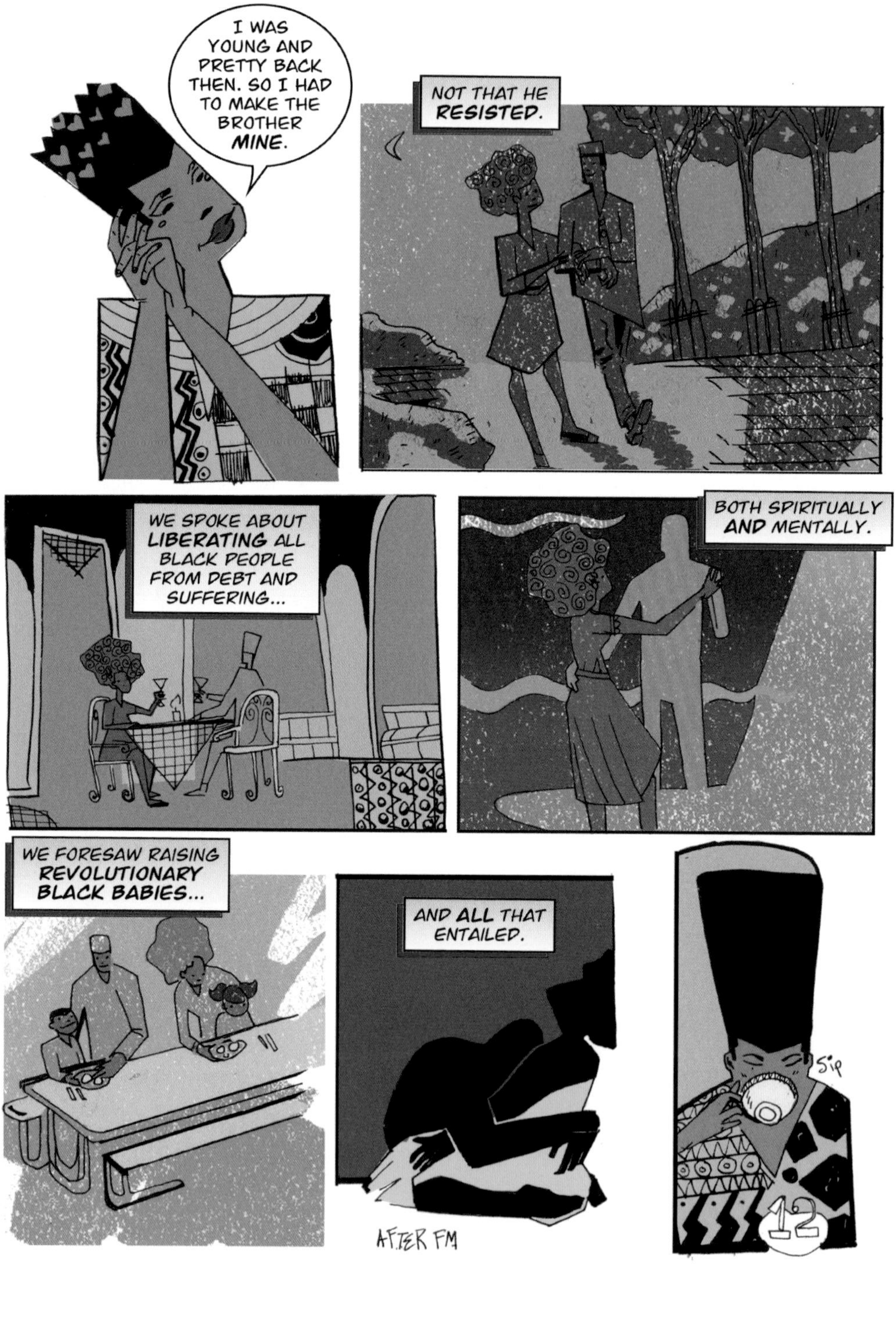
I WAS YOUNG AND PRETTY BACK THEN. SO I HAD TO MAKE THE BROTHER MINE.
NOT THAT HE RESISTED.
WE SPOKE ABOUT LIBERATING ALL BLACK PEOPLE FROM DEBT AND SUFFERING...
BOTH SPIRITUALLY AND MENTALLY.
WE FORESAW RAISING REVOLUTIONARY BLACK BABIES...
AND ALL THAT ENTAILED.
Sip
AFTER FM

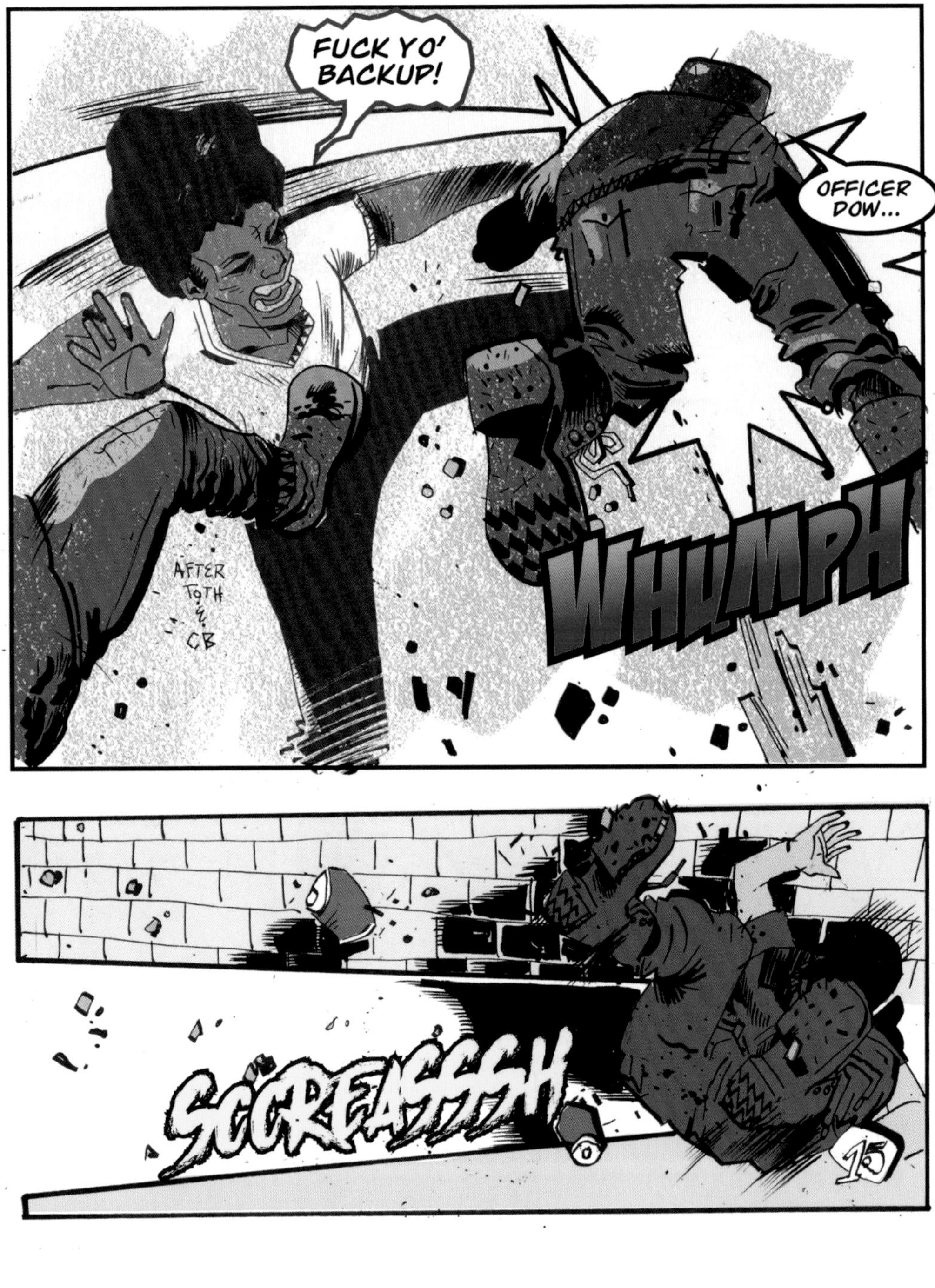
FUCK YO' BACKUP!
OFFICER DOW...
WHUMPH
AFTER TOTH & CB
SCCREASSSH
15

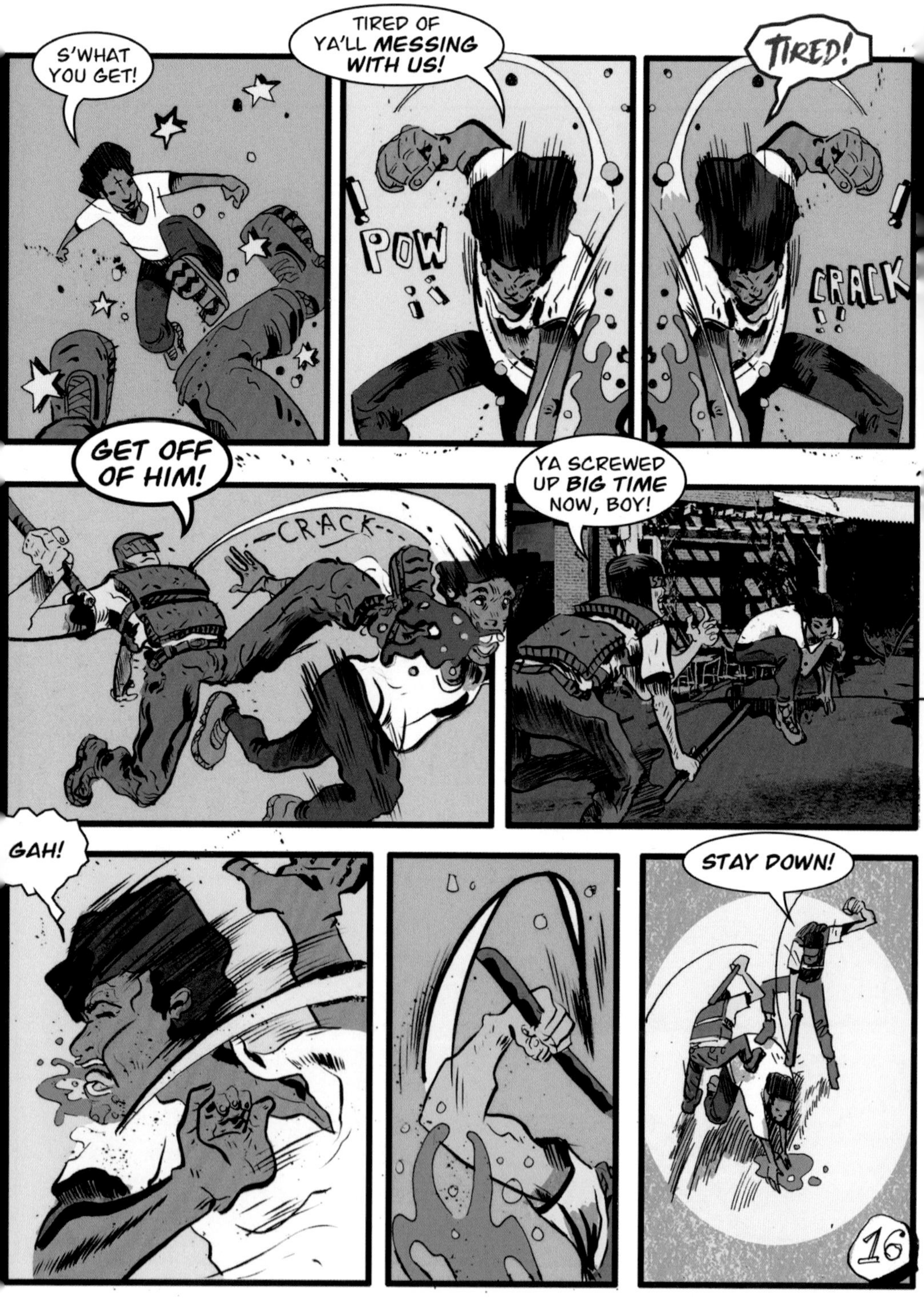
S'WHAT YOU GET!
TIRED OF YA'LL MESSING WITH US!
POW
TIRED!
CRACK
GET OFF OF HIM!
CRACK
YA SCREWED UP BIG TIME NOW, BOY!
GAH!
STAY DOWN!
16

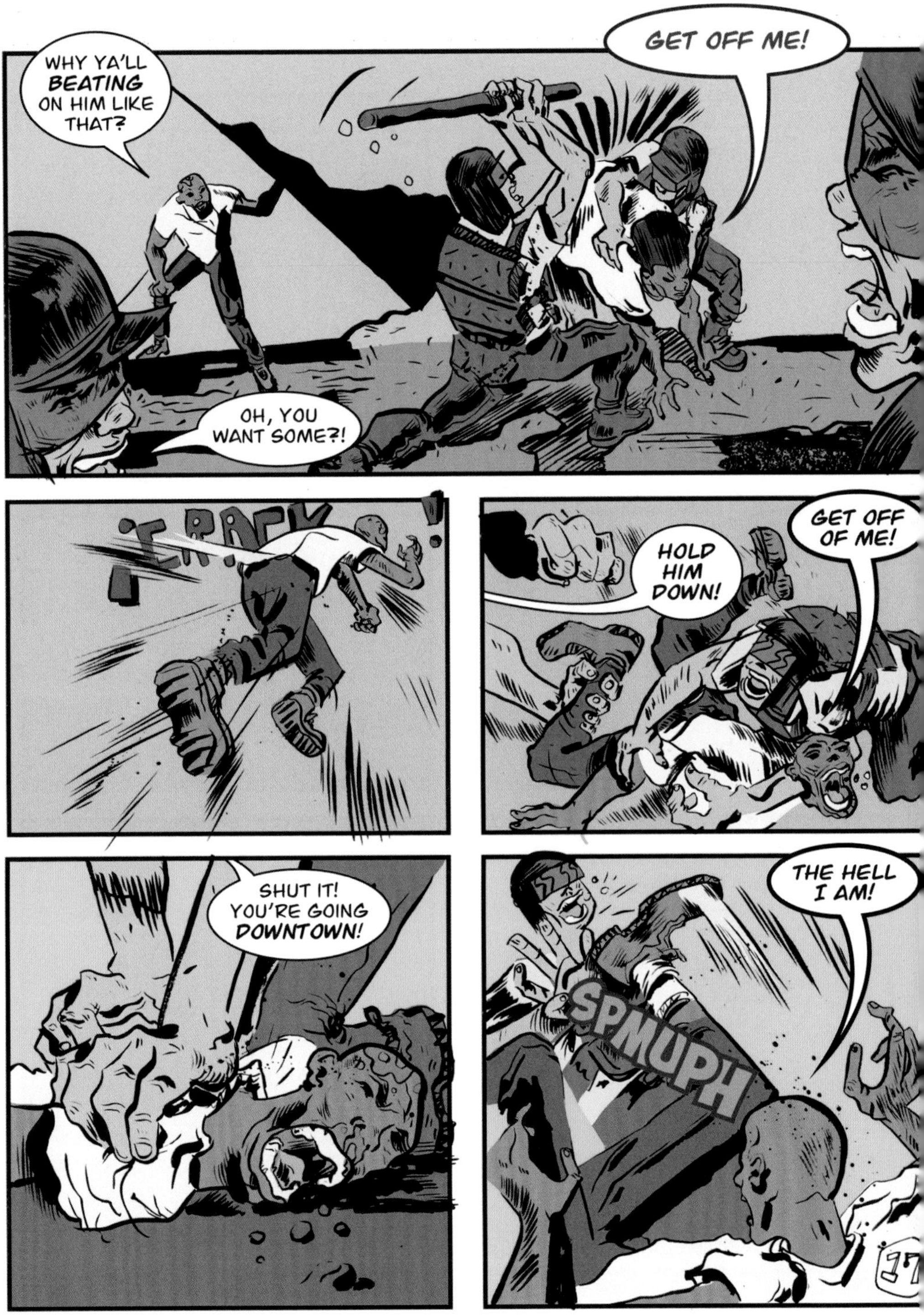
WHY YA'LL **BEATING** ON HIM LIKE THAT?
GET OFF ME!
OH, YOU WANT SOME?!
HOLD HIM DOWN!
GET OFF OF ME!
SHUT IT! YOU'RE GOING **DOWNTOWN**!
SPMUPH
THE HELL I AM!

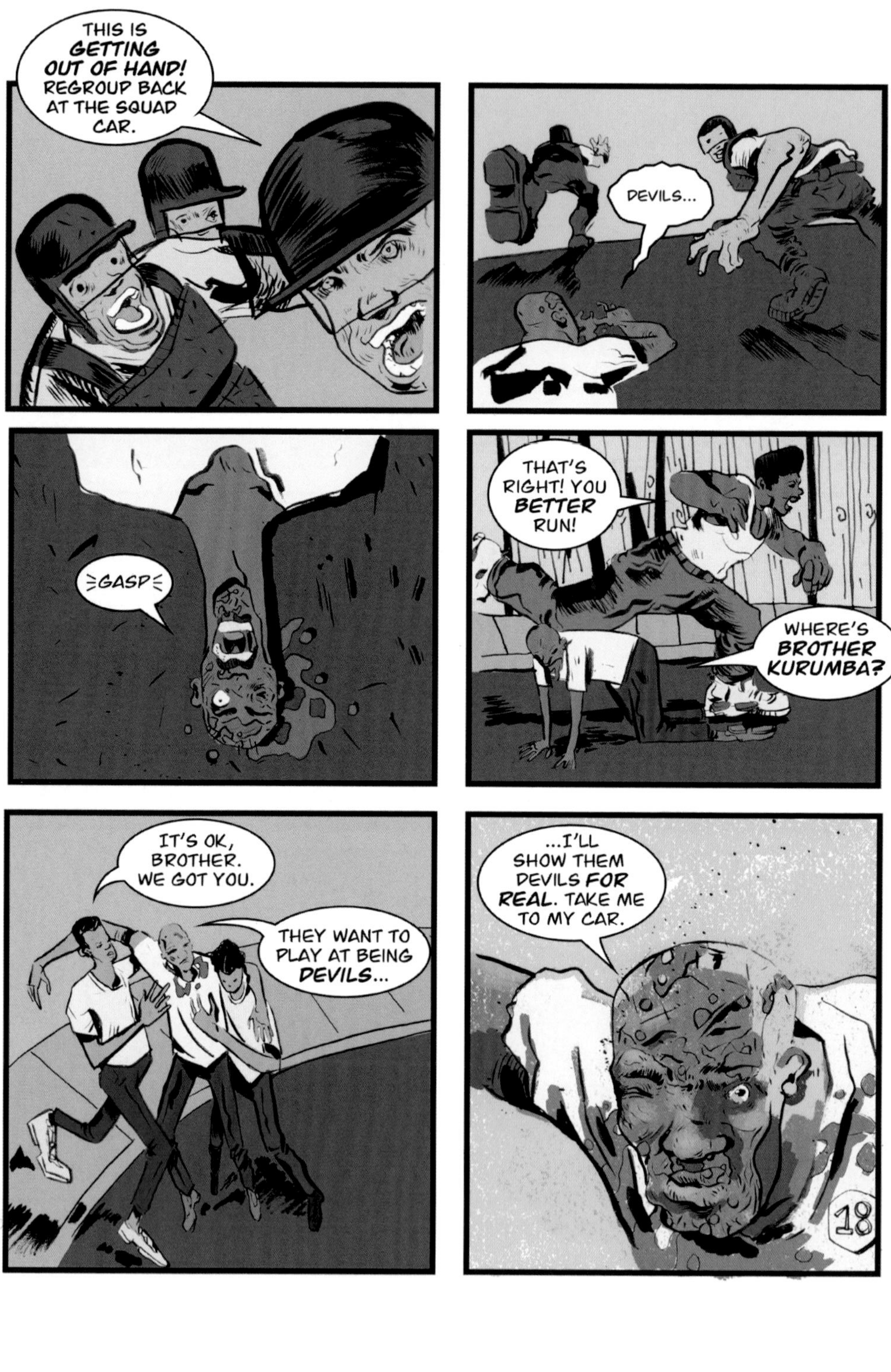
THIS IS **GETTING OUT OF HAND!** REGROUP BACK AT THE SQUAD CAR.
DEVILS...
GASP
THAT'S RIGHT! YOU **BETTER** RUN!
WHERE'S **BROTHER KURUMBA?**
IT'S OK, BROTHER. WE GOT YOU.
THEY WANT TO PLAY AT BEING **DEVILS...**
...I'LL SHOW THEM DEVILS **FOR REAL**. TAKE ME TO MY CAR.
18

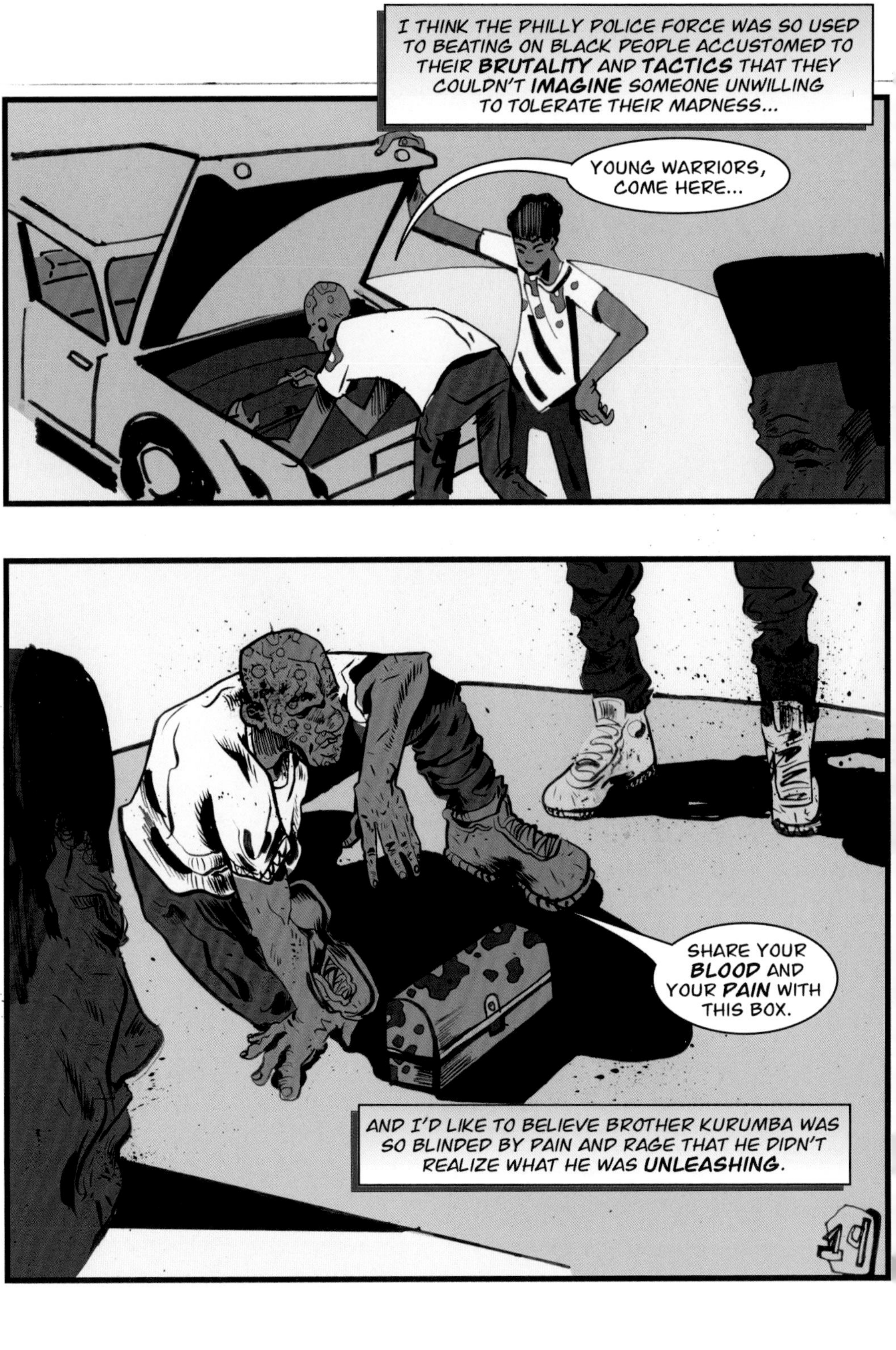
I THINK THE PHILLY POLICE FORCE WAS SO USED TO BEATING ON BLACK PEOPLE ACCUSTOMED TO THEIR BRUTALITY AND TACTICS THAT THEY COULDN'T IMAGINE SOMEONE UNWILLING TO TOLERATE THEIR MADNESS...
YOUNG WARRIORS, COME HERE...
SHARE YOUR BLOOD AND YOUR PAIN WITH THIS BOX.
AND I'D LIKE TO BELIEVE BROTHER KURUMBA WAS SO BLINDED BY PAIN AND RAGE THAT HE DIDN'T REALIZE WHAT HE WAS UNLEASHING.

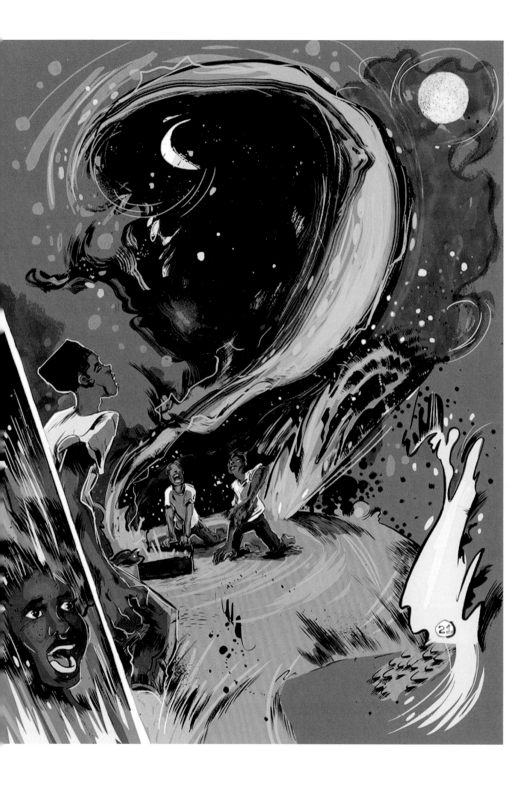

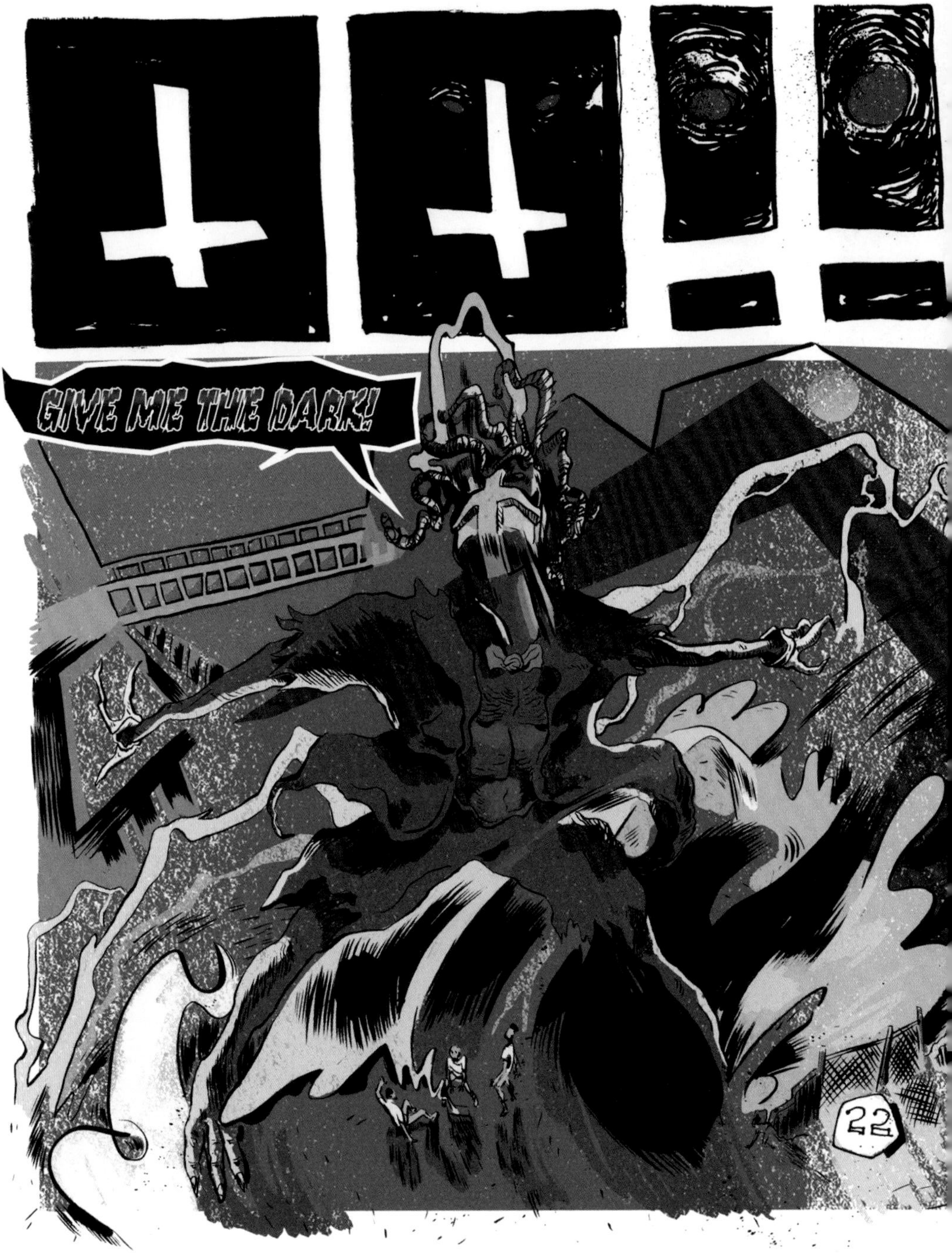
GIVE ME THE DARK!
22

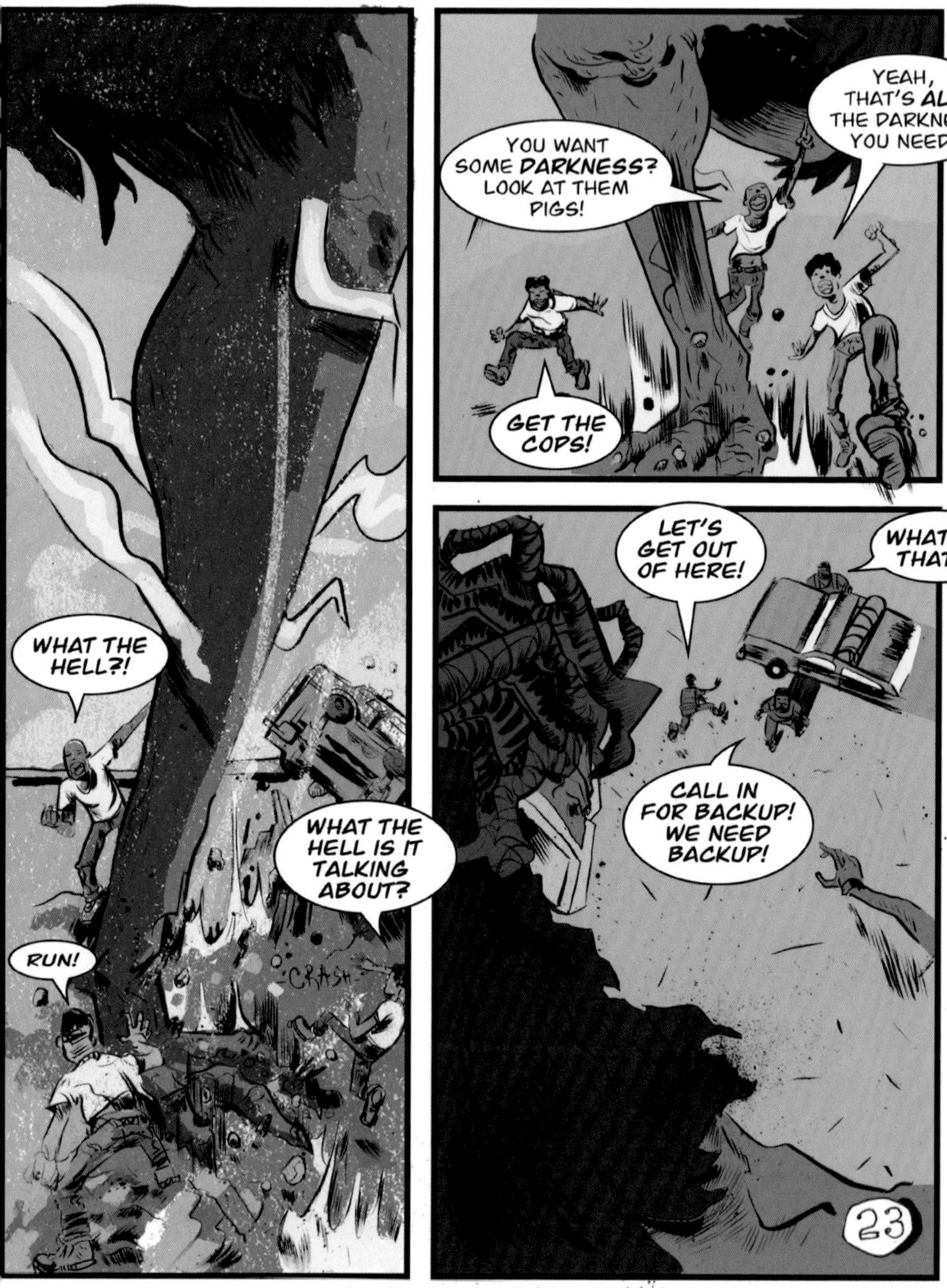
WHAT THE HELL?!
WHAT THE HELL IS IT TALKING ABOUT?
RUN!
CRASH
YOU WANT SOME DARKNESS? LOOK AT THEM PIGS!
YEAH, THAT'S ALL THE DARKNESS YOU NEED!
GET THE COPS!
LET'S GET OUT OF HERE!
WHAT IS THAT?!
CALL IN FOR BACKUP! WE NEED BACKUP!

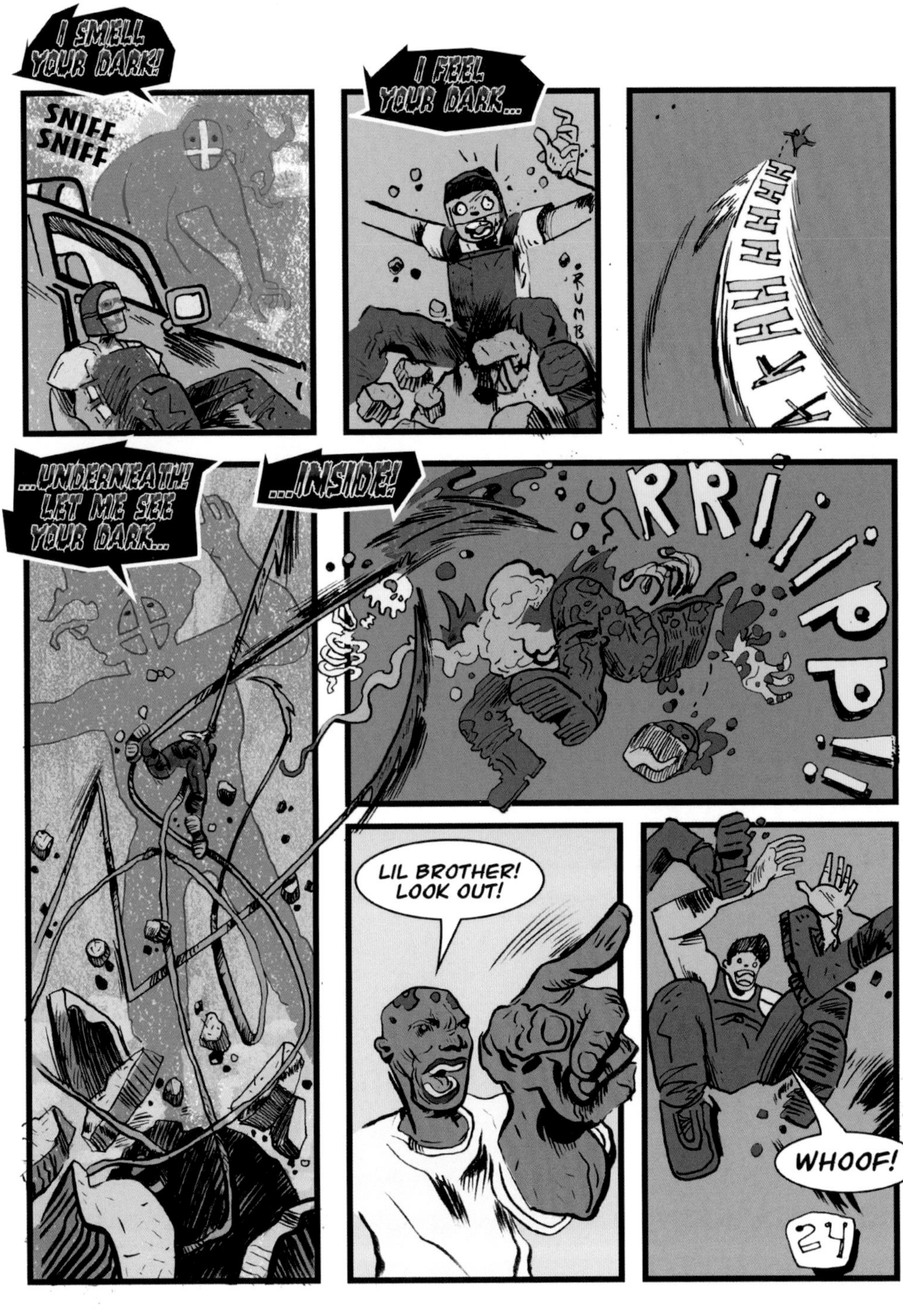
I SMELL YOUR DARK!
SNIFF SNIFF
I FEEL YOUR DARK...
RUMB
AAAHHHHHHHH
...UNDERNEATH! LET ME SEE YOUR DARK...
...INSIDE!
RRIIIPP!
LIL BROTHER! LOOK OUT!
WHOOF!
24

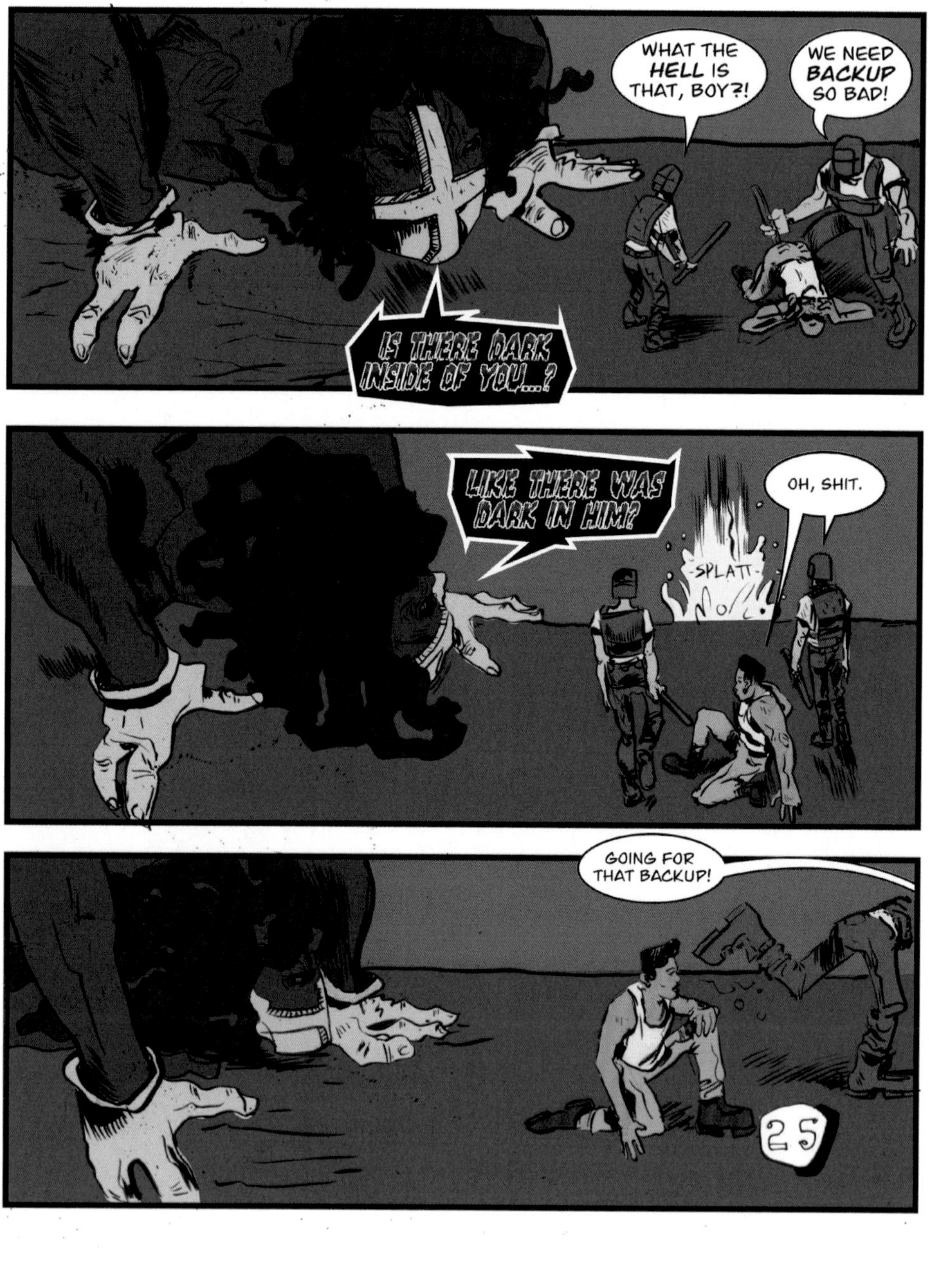
WHAT THE HELL IS THAT, BOY?!
WE NEED BACKUP SO BAD!
IS THERE DARK INSIDE OF YOU...?
LIKE THERE WAS DARK IN HIM?
-SPLATT-
OH, SHIT.
GOING FOR THAT BACKUP!
25

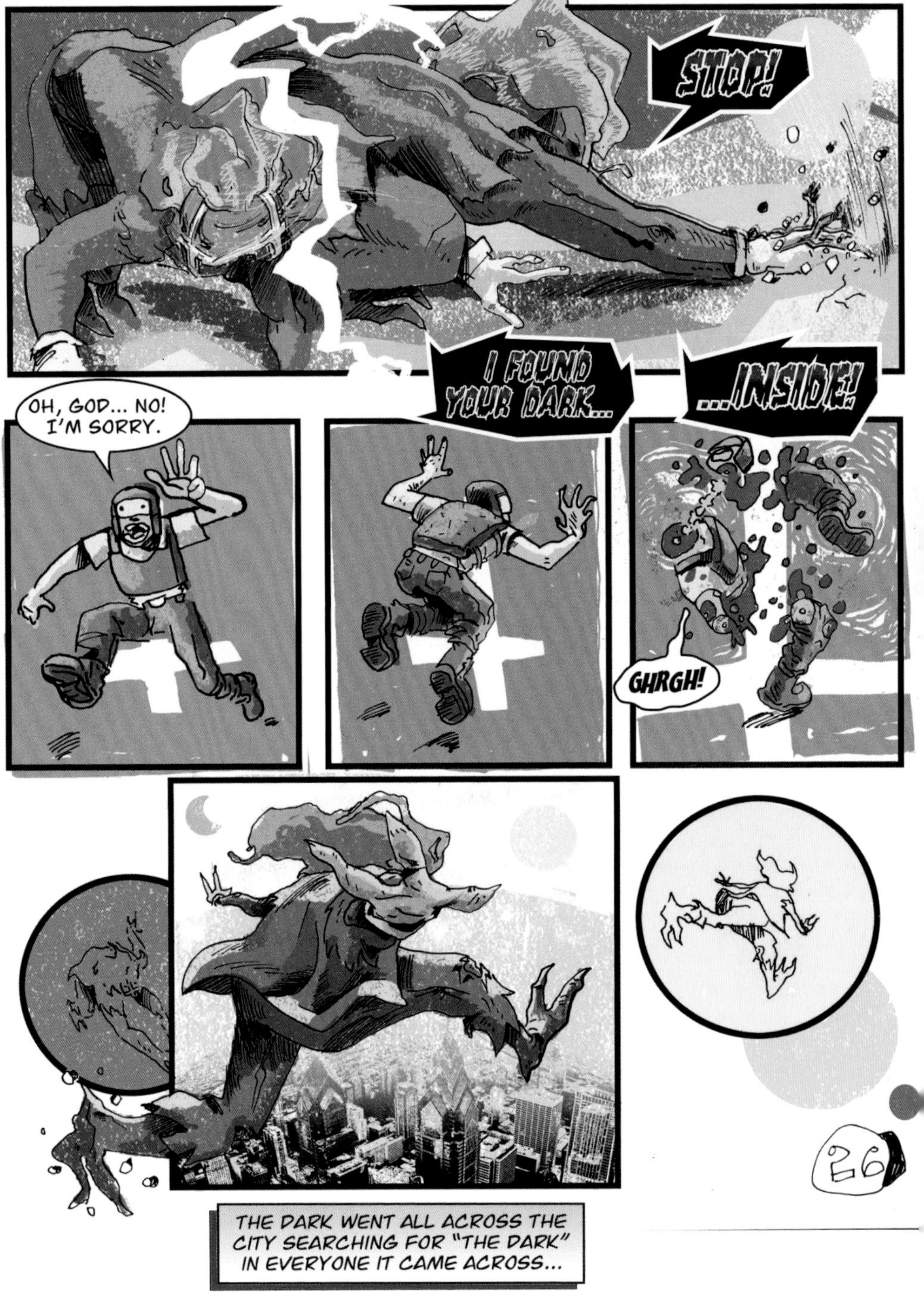
STOP!
I FOUND YOUR DARK...
...INSIDE!
OH, GOD... NO! I'M SORRY.
GHRGH!
THE DARK WENT ALL ACROSS THE CITY SEARCHING FOR "THE DARK" IN EVERYONE IT CAME ACROSS...

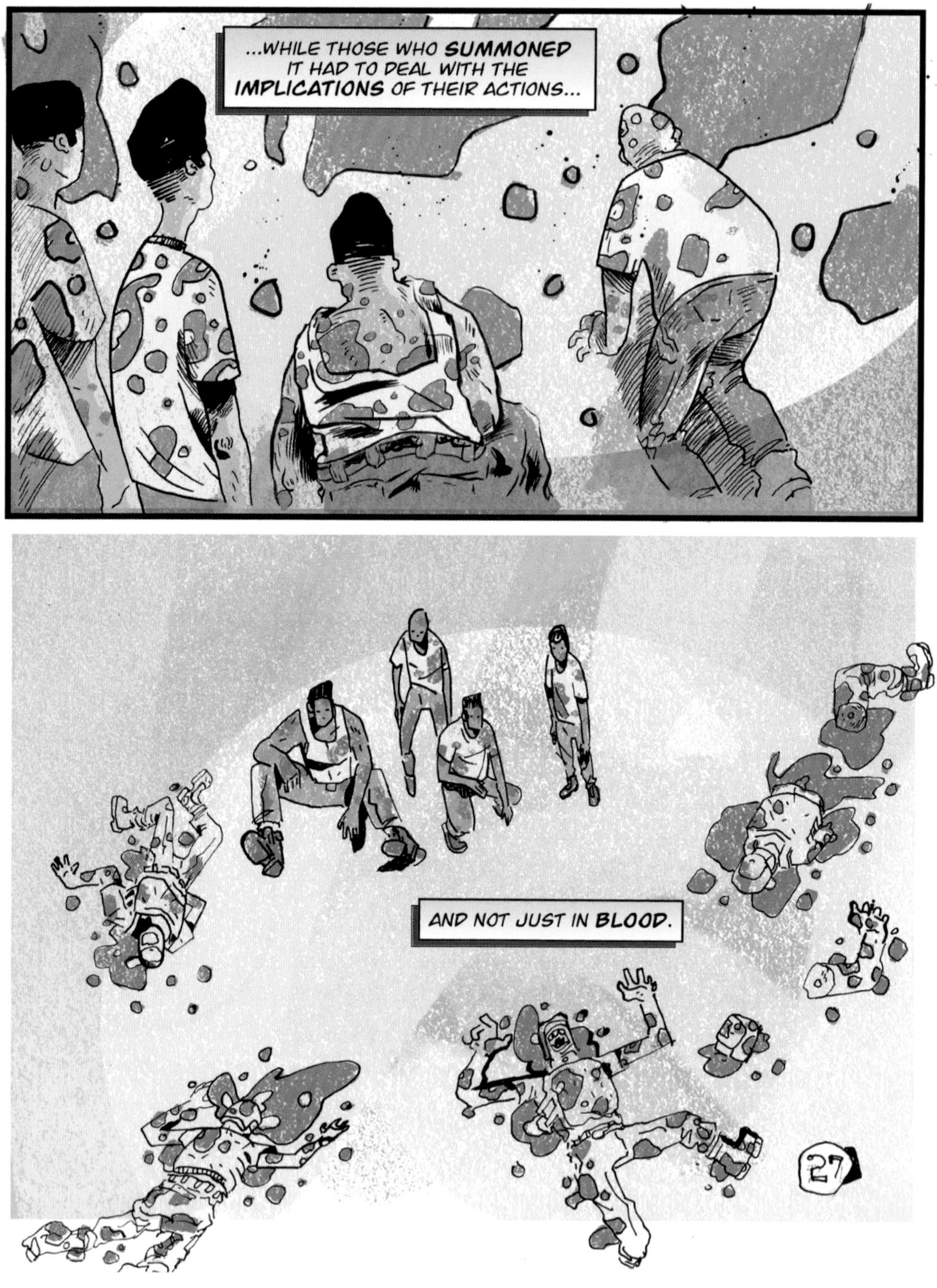
...WHILE THOSE WHO SUMMONED IT HAD TO DEAL WITH THE IMPLICATIONS OF THEIR ACTIONS...
AND NOT JUST IN BLOOD.
27

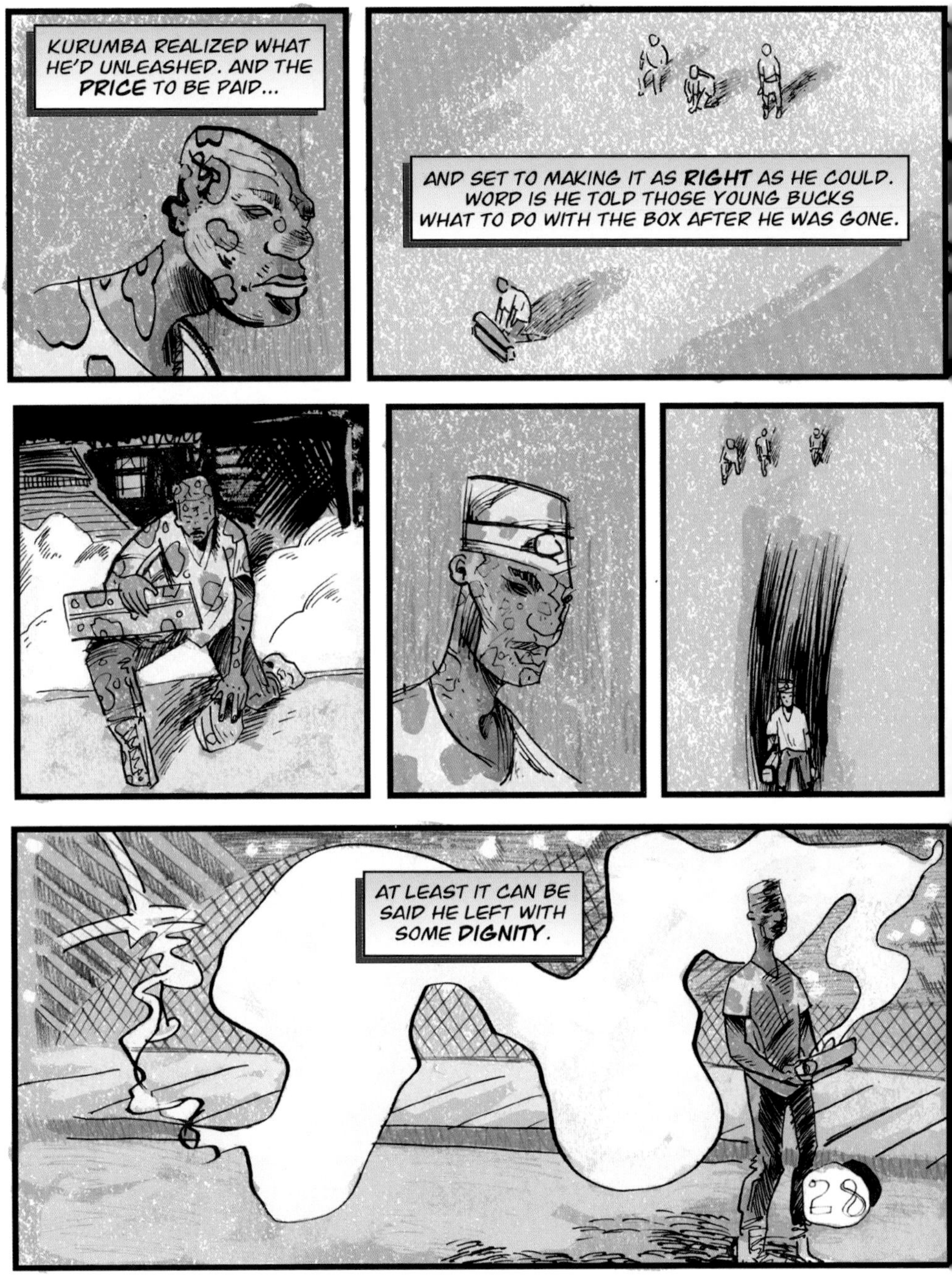
KURUMBA REALIZED WHAT HE'D UNLEASHED. AND THE **PRICE** TO BE PAID...
AND SET TO MAKING IT AS **RIGHT** AS HE COULD. WORD IS HE TOLD THOSE YOUNG BUCKS WHAT TO DO WITH THE BOX AFTER HE WAS GONE.
AT LEAST IT CAN BE SAID HE LEFT WITH SOME **DIGNITY**.
28

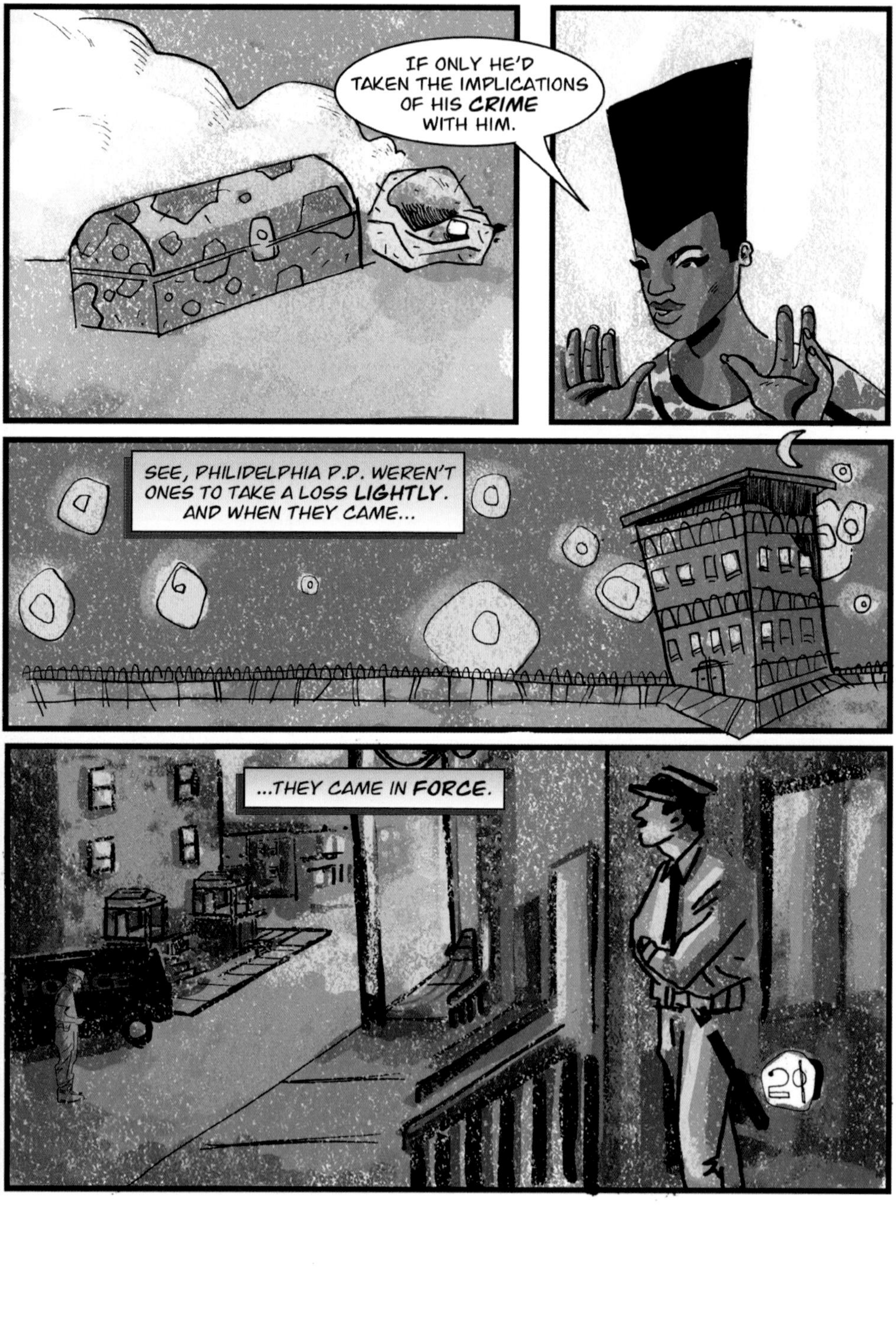
IF ONLY HE'D TAKEN THE IMPLICATIONS OF HIS **CRIME** WITH HIM.
SEE, PHILIDELPHIA P.D. WEREN'T ONES TO TAKE A LOSS **LIGHTLY**. AND WHEN THEY CAME...
...THEY CAME IN **FORCE**.

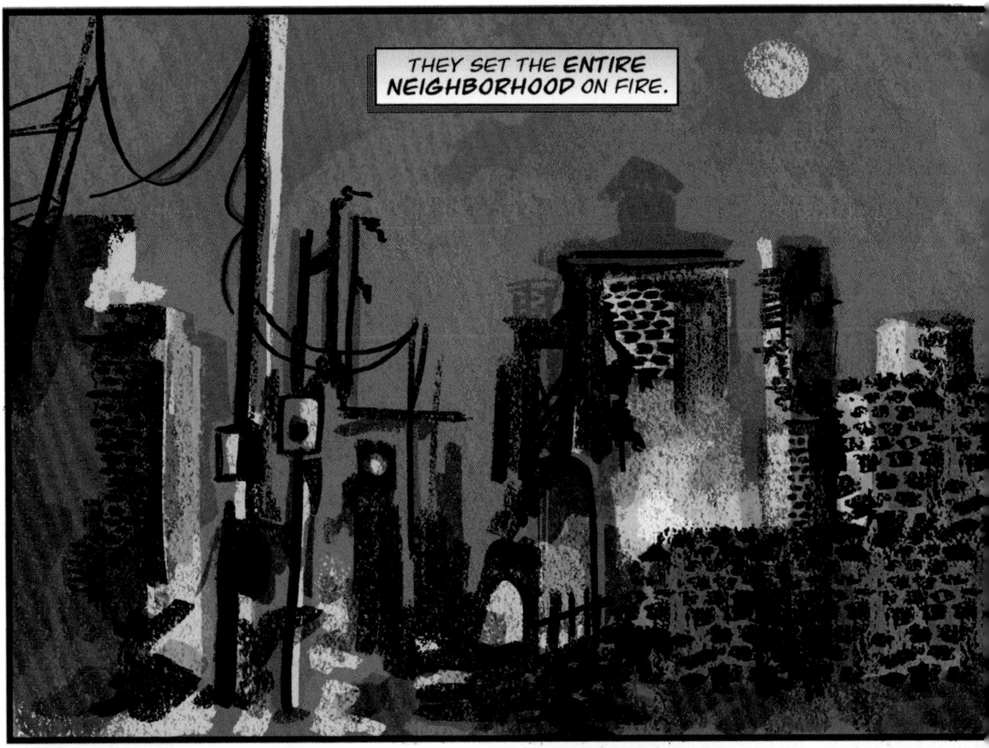
THEY SET THE ENTIRE NEIGHBORHOOD ON FIRE.

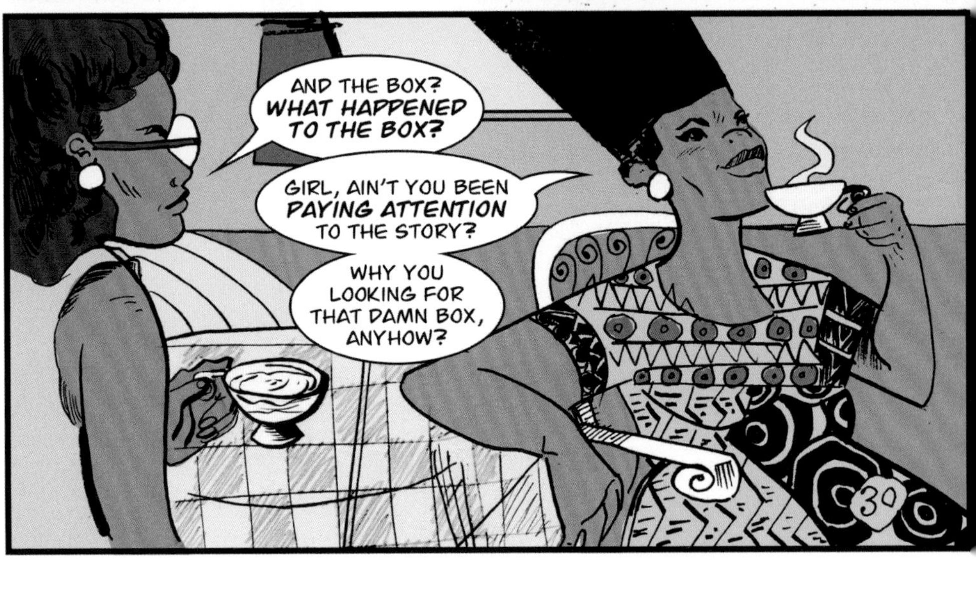
AND THE BOX? WHAT HAPPENED TO THE BOX?
GIRL, AIN'T YOU BEEN PAYING ATTENTION TO THE STORY?
WHY YOU LOOKING FOR THAT DAMN BOX, ANYHOW?

# CHAPTER FOUR

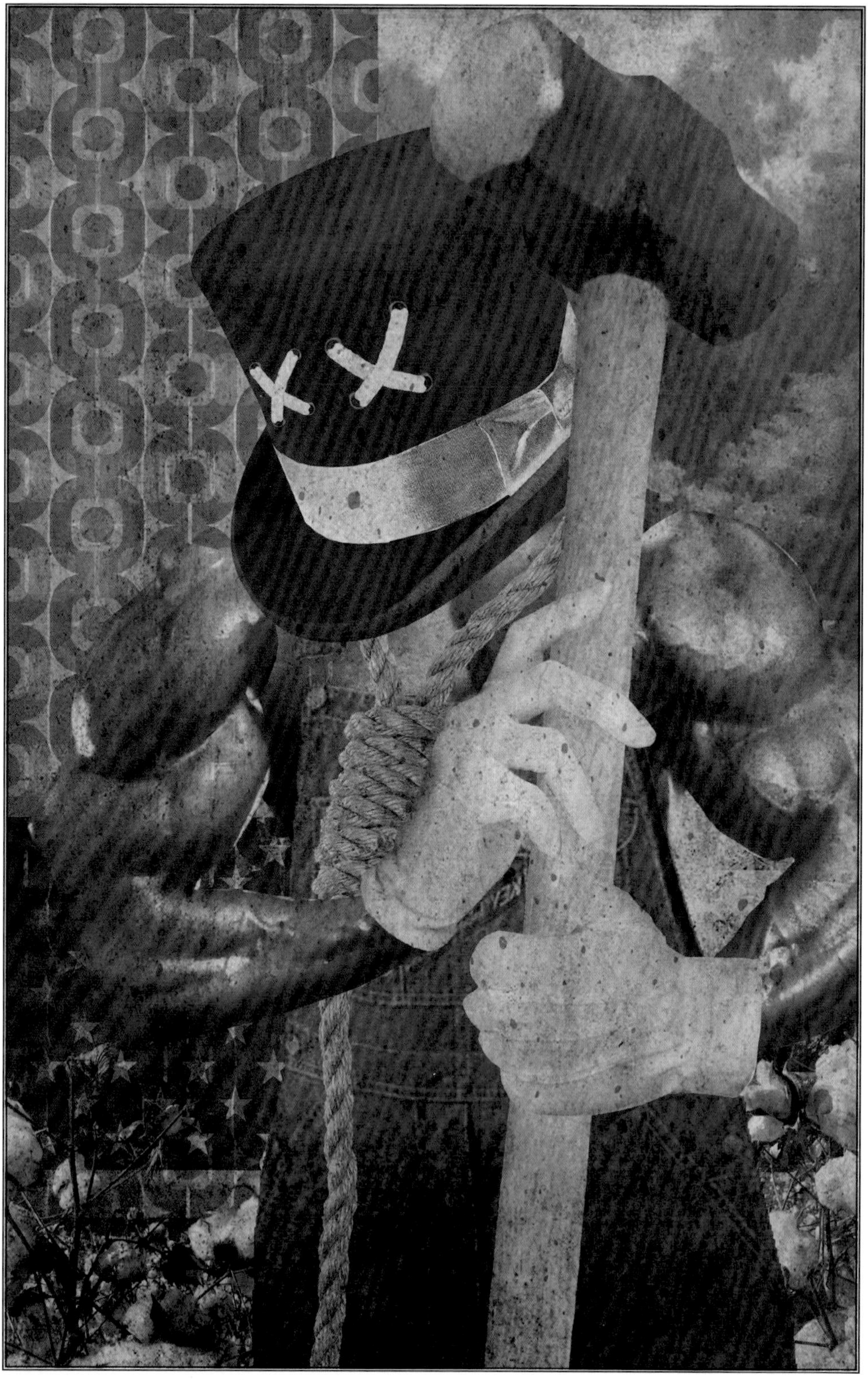

"PLANTATION"

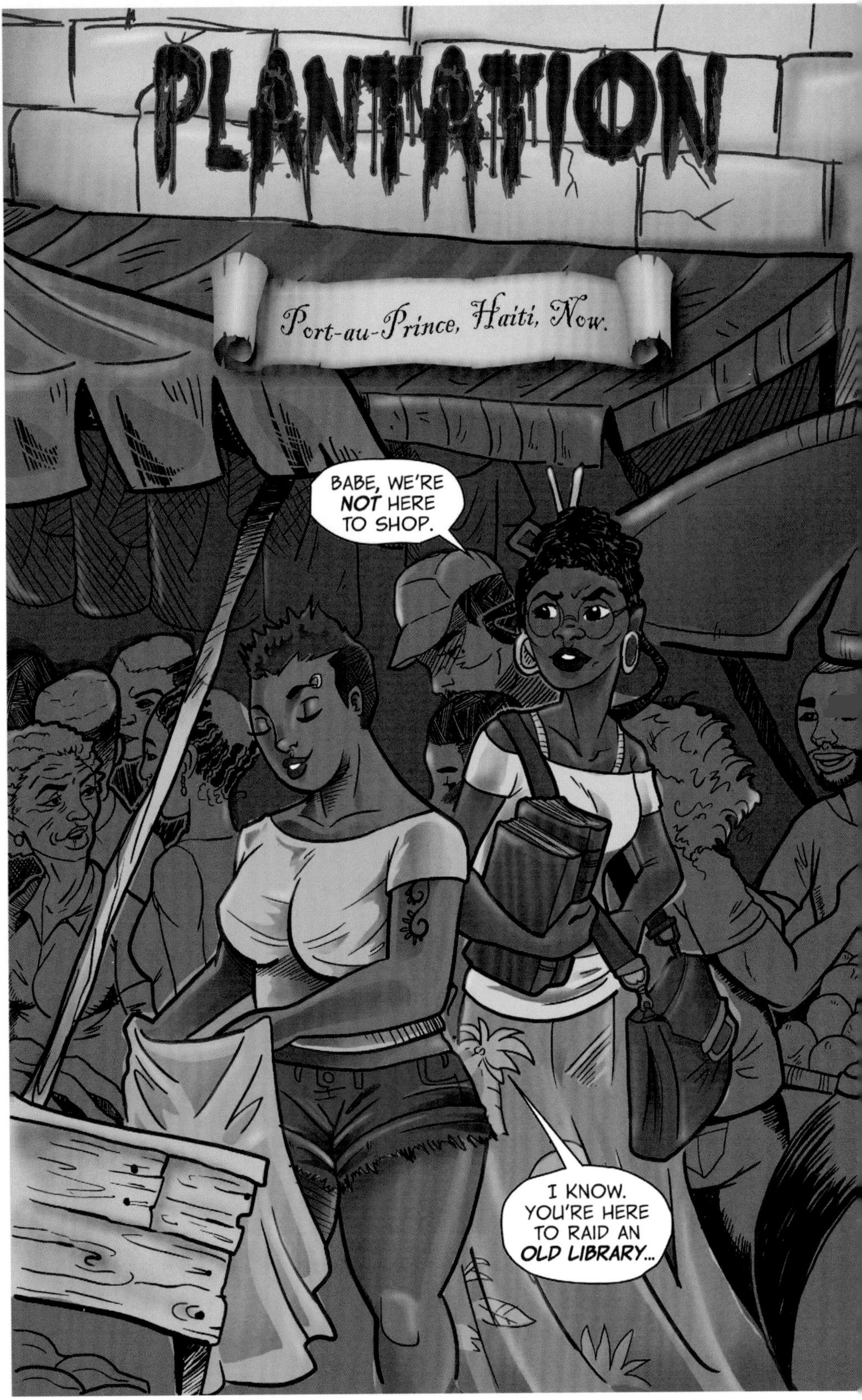
PLANTATION
Port-au-Prince, Haiti, Now.
BABE, WE'RE NOT HERE TO SHOP.
I KNOW. YOU'RE HERE TO RAID AN OLD LIBRARY...

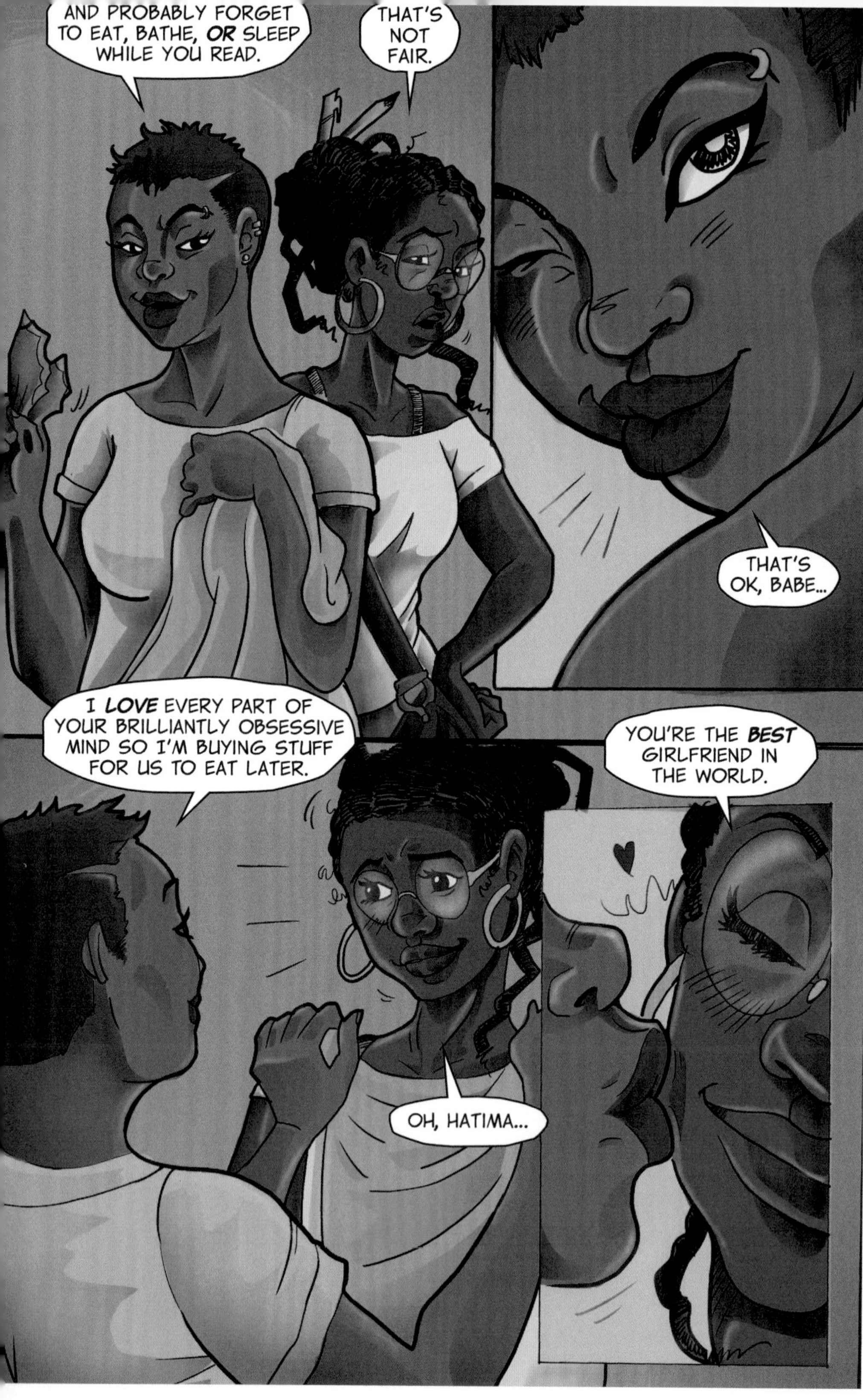
AND PROBABLY FORGET TO EAT, BATHE, OR SLEEP WHILE YOU READ.
THAT'S NOT FAIR.
THAT'S OK, BABE...
I LOVE EVERY PART OF YOUR BRILLIANTLY OBSESSIVE MIND SO I'M BUYING STUFF FOR US TO EAT LATER.
YOU'RE THE BEST GIRLFRIEND IN THE WORLD.
OH, HATIMA...

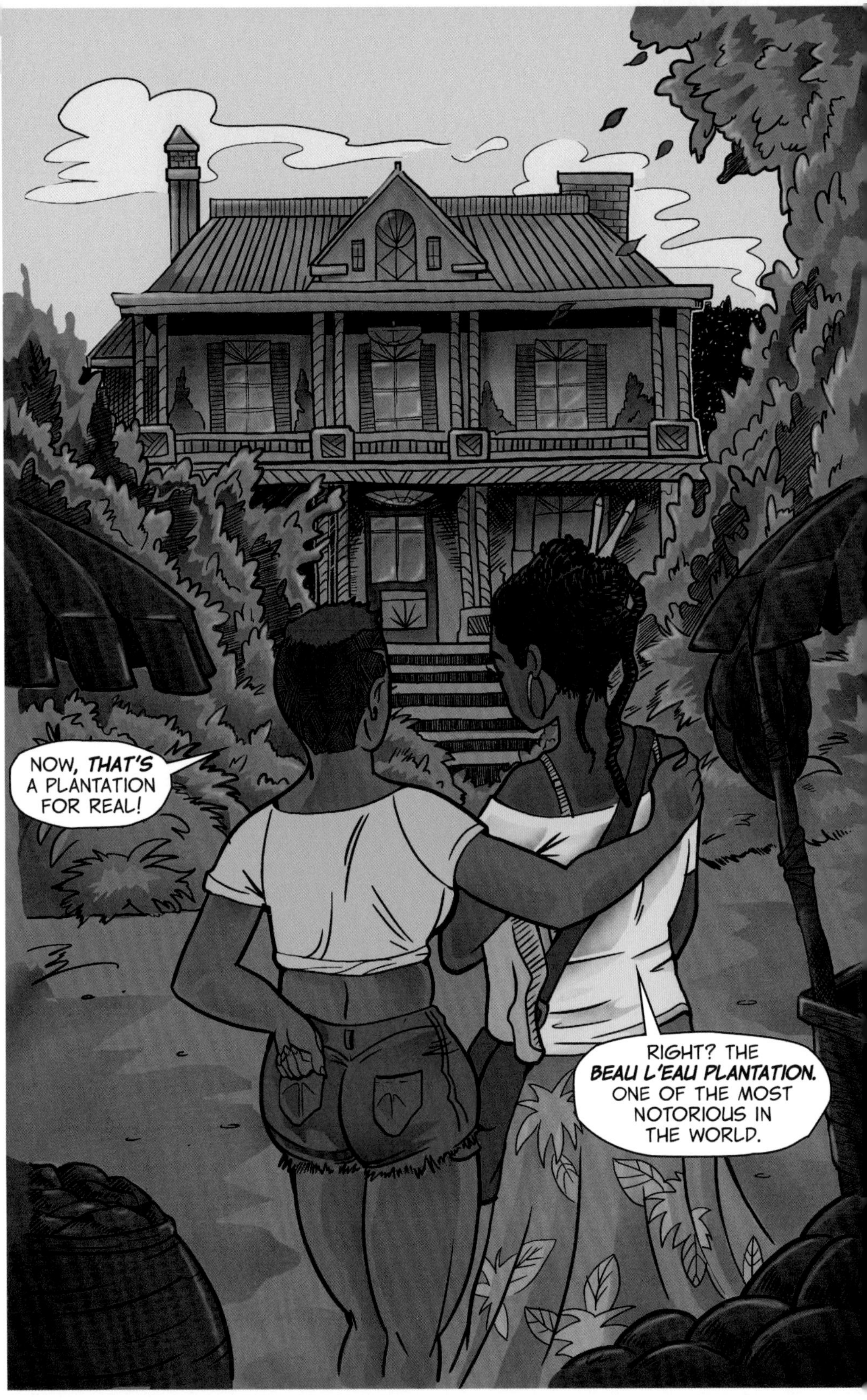
NOW, *THAT'S* A PLANTATION FOR REAL!
RIGHT? THE ***BEAU L'EAU PLANTATION.*** ONE OF THE MOST NOTORIOUS IN THE WORLD.

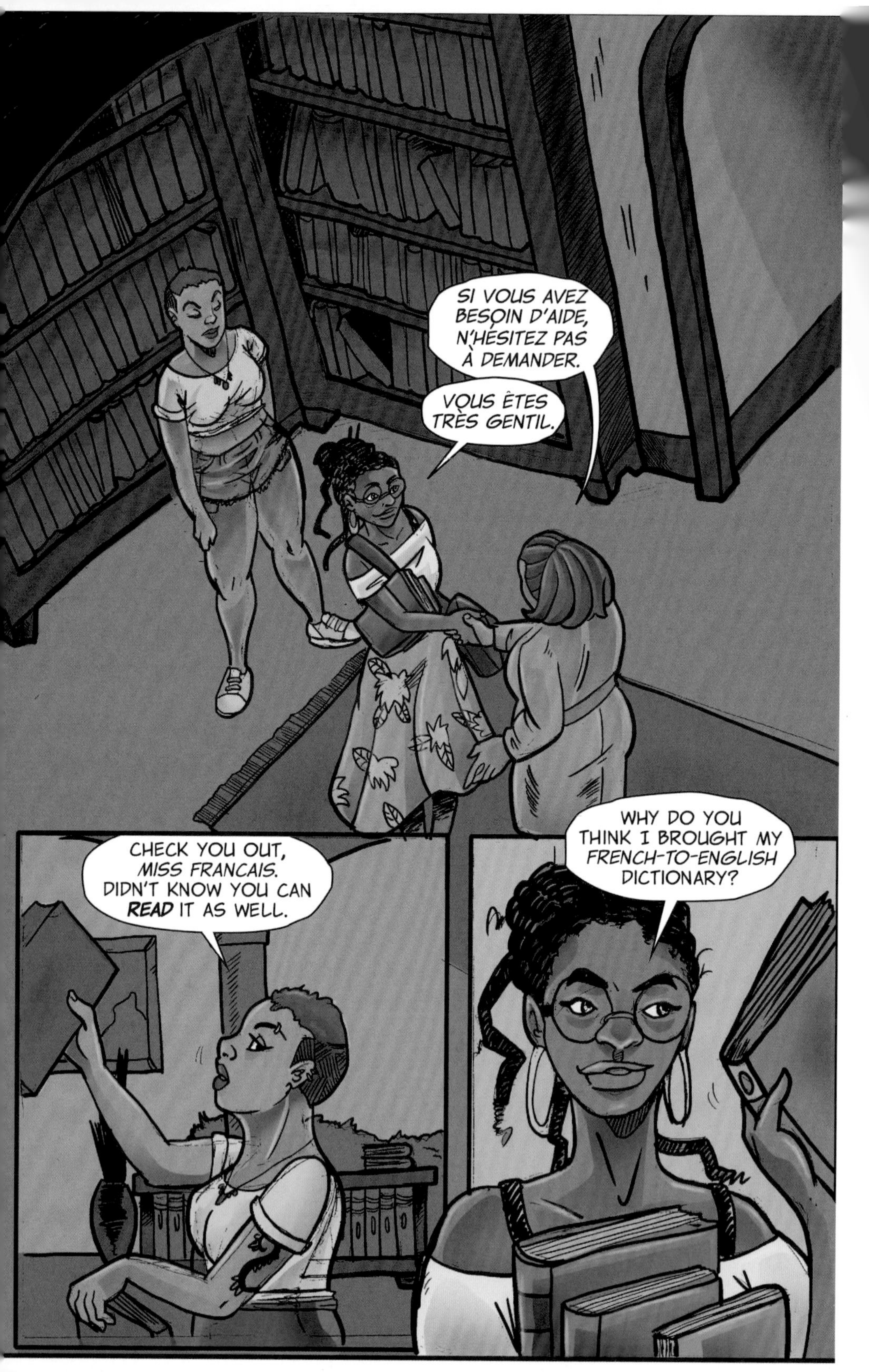
SI VOUS AVEZ BESOIN D'AIDE, N'HÉSITEZ PAS À DEMANDER.
VOUS ÊTES TRÈS GENTIL.
CHECK YOU OUT, *MISS FRANCAIS.* DIDN'T KNOW YOU CAN ***READ*** IT AS WELL.
WHY DO YOU THINK I BROUGHT MY *FRENCH-TO-ENGLISH* DICTIONARY?

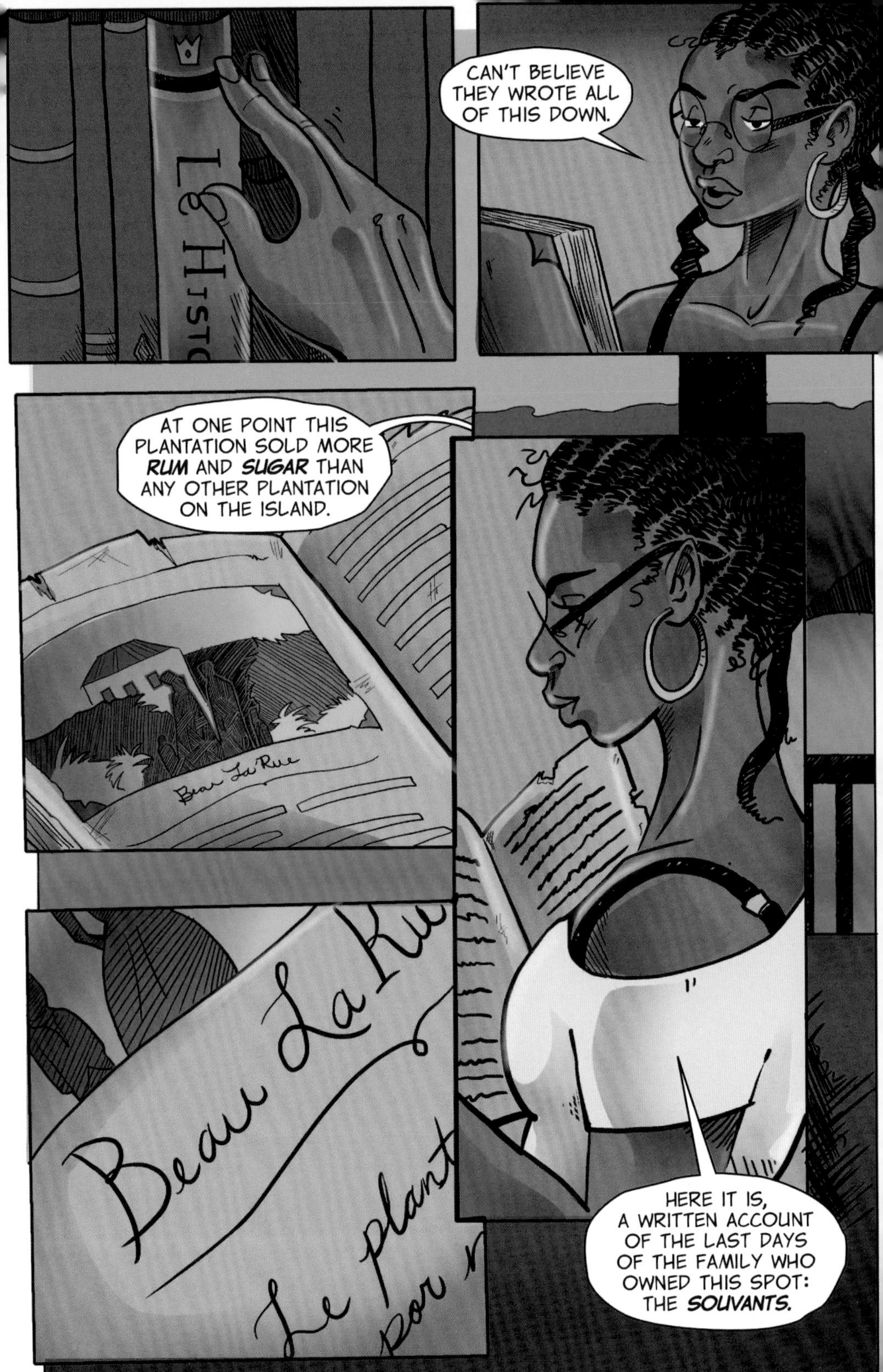
Le Histo
CAN'T BELIEVE THEY WROTE ALL OF THIS DOWN.
AT ONE POINT THIS PLANTATION SOLD MORE **RUM** AND **SUGAR** THAN ANY OTHER PLANTATION ON THE ISLAND.
Beau La Rue
HERE IT IS, A WRITTEN ACCOUNT OF THE LAST DAYS OF THE FAMILY WHO OWNED THIS SPOT: THE **SOUVANTS.**

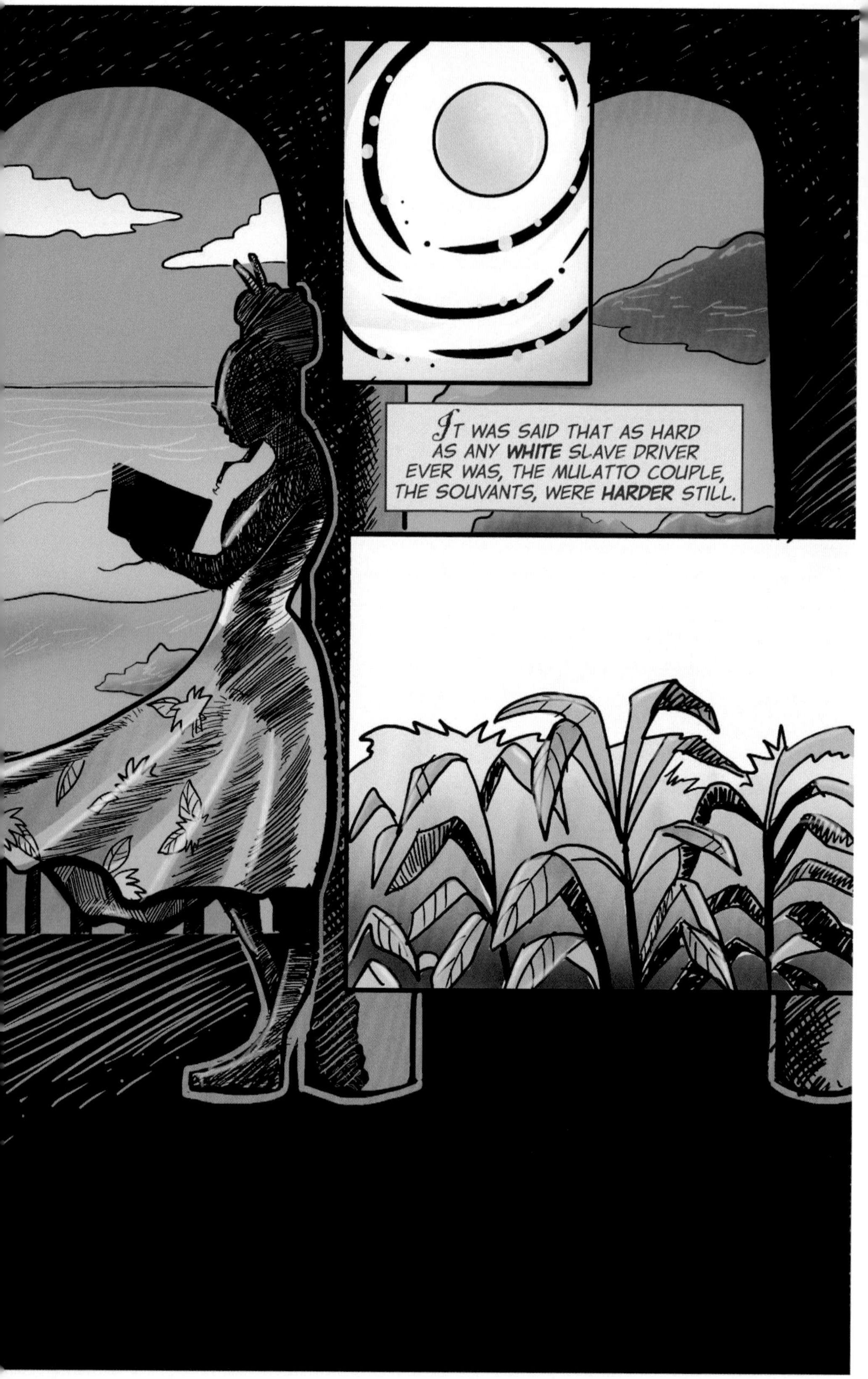
IT WAS SAID THAT AS HARD AS ANY WHITE SLAVE DRIVER EVER WAS, THE MULATTO COUPLE, THE SOUVANTS, WERE HARDER STILL.

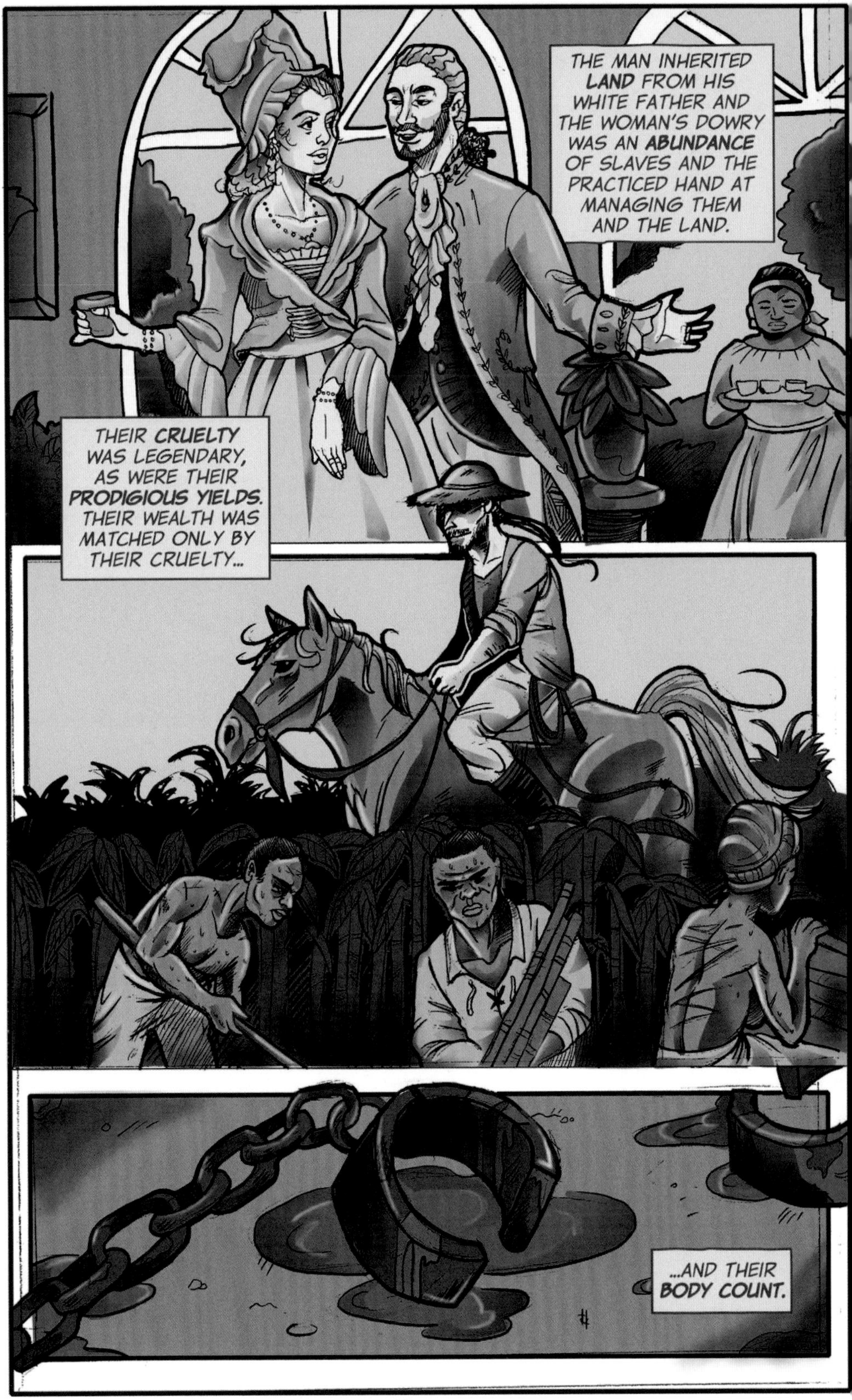
THE MAN INHERITED LAND FROM HIS WHITE FATHER AND THE WOMAN'S DOWRY WAS AN ABUNDANCE OF SLAVES AND THE PRACTICED HAND AT MANAGING THEM AND THE LAND.
THEIR CRUELTY WAS LEGENDARY, AS WERE THEIR PRODIGIOUS YIELDS. THEIR WEALTH WAS MATCHED ONLY BY THEIR CRUELTY...
...AND THEIR BODY COUNT.

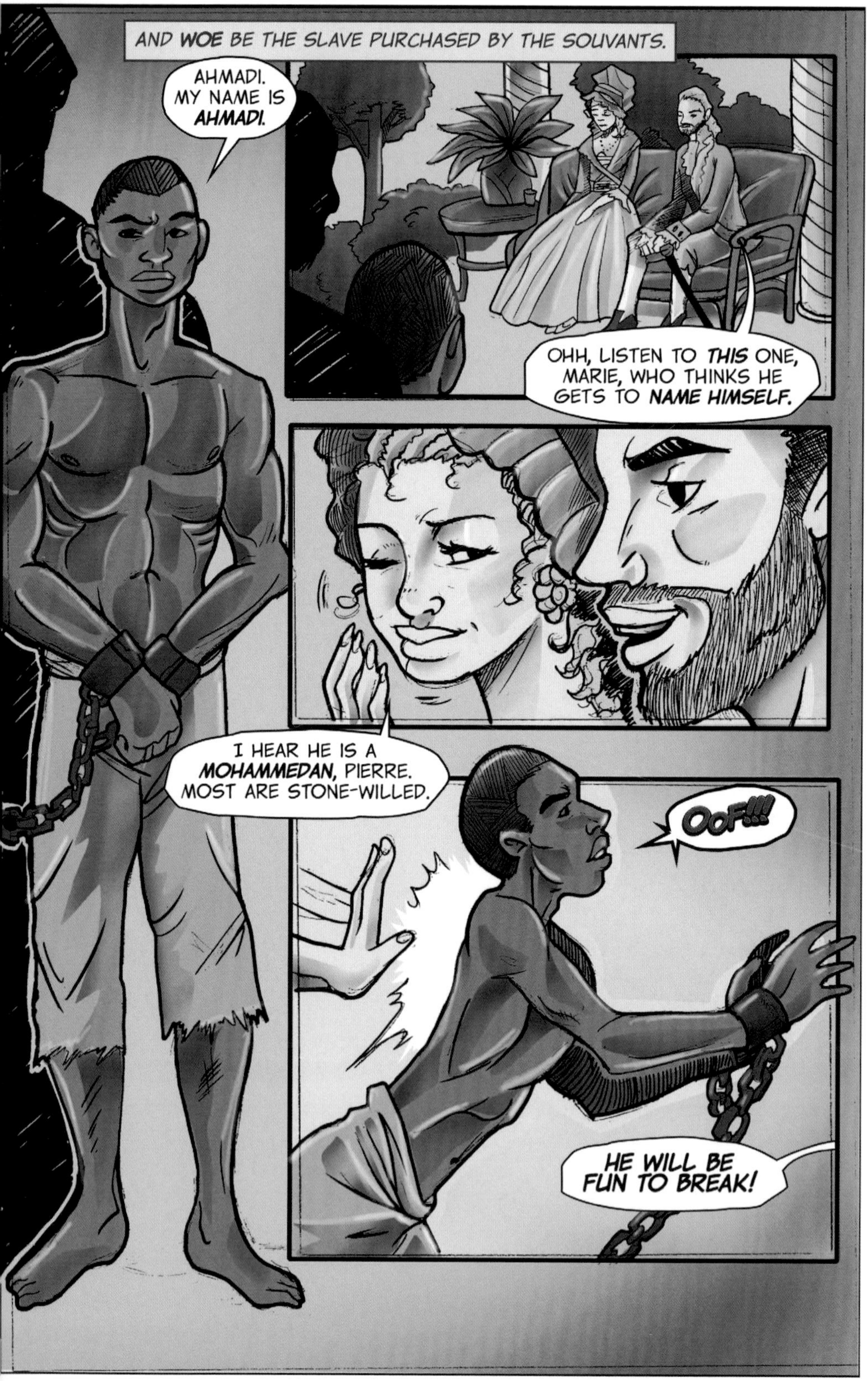
AND WOE BE THE SLAVE PURCHASED BY THE SOUVANTS.
AHMADI. MY NAME IS AHMADI.
OHH, LISTEN TO THIS ONE, MARIE, WHO THINKS HE GETS TO NAME HIMSELF.
I HEAR HE IS A MOHAMMEDAN, PIERRE. MOST ARE STONE-WILLED.
OOF!!!
HE WILL BE FUN TO BREAK!

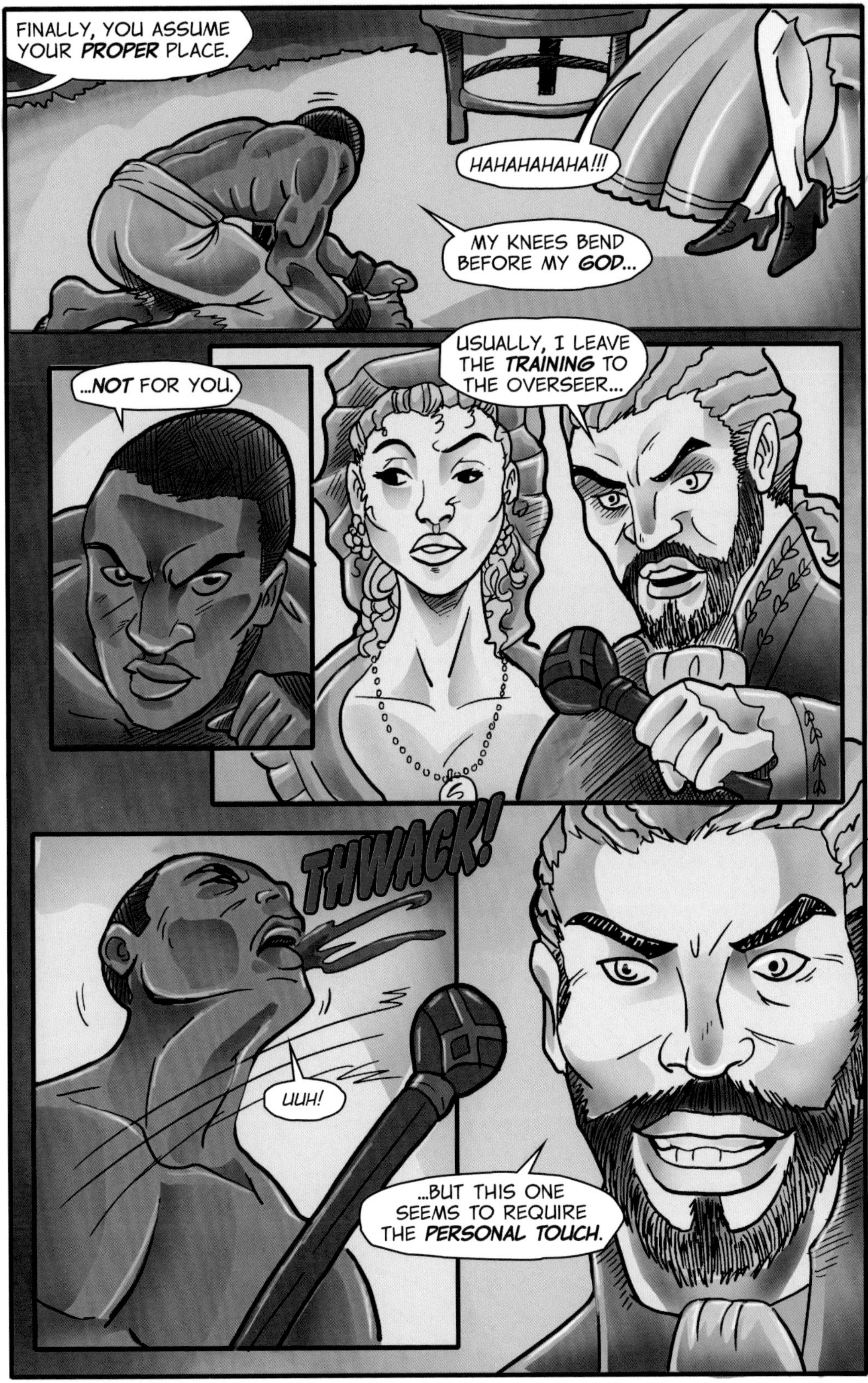
FINALLY, YOU ASSUME YOUR PROPER PLACE.
HAHAHAHAHA!!!
MY KNEES BEND BEFORE MY GOD...
...NOT FOR YOU.
USUALLY, I LEAVE THE TRAINING TO THE OVERSEER...
THWACK!
UUH!
...BUT THIS ONE SEEMS TO REQUIRE THE PERSONAL TOUCH.

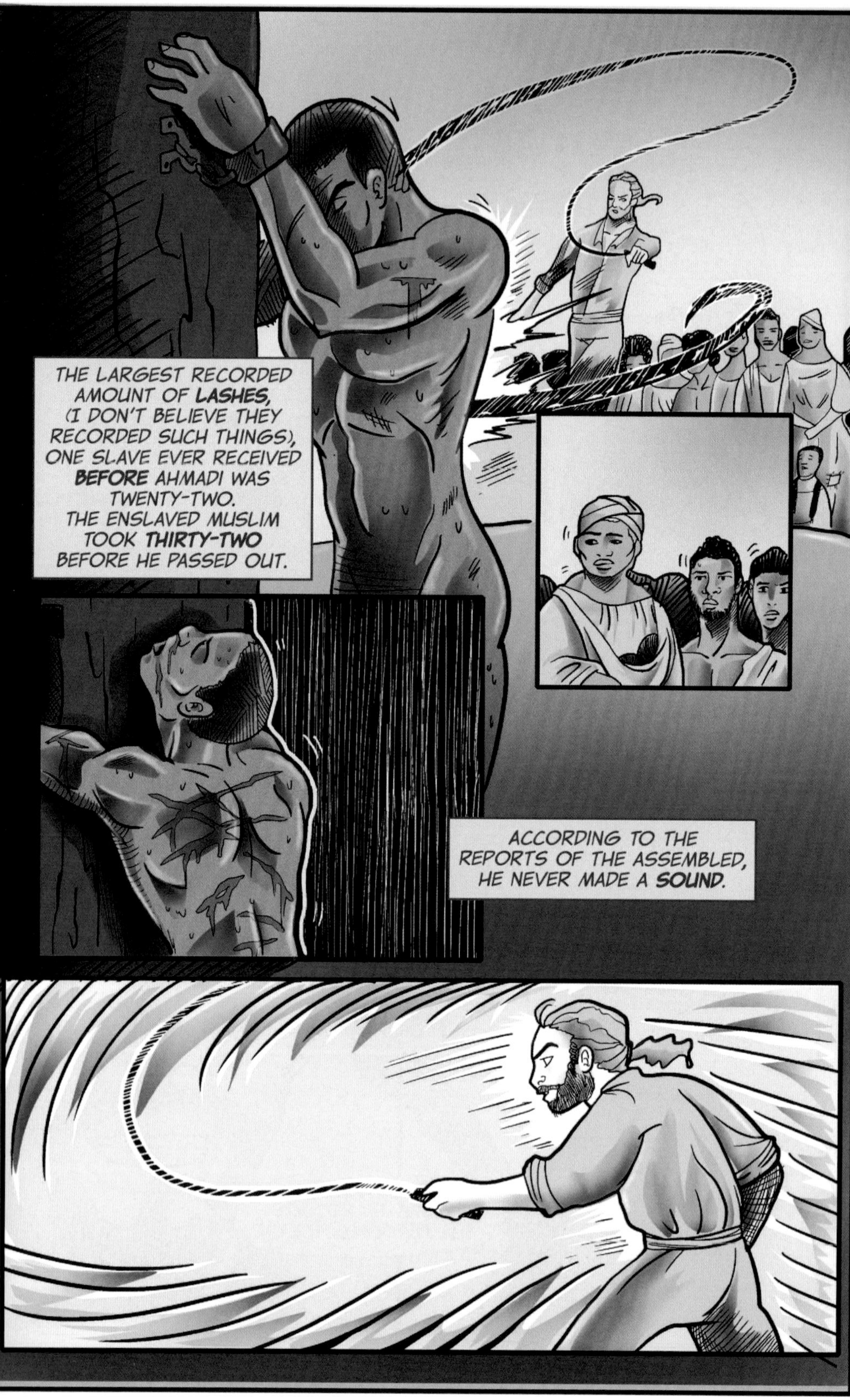
THE LARGEST RECORDED AMOUNT OF LASHES, (I DON'T BELIEVE THEY RECORDED SUCH THINGS), ONE SLAVE EVER RECEIVED BEFORE AHMADI WAS TWENTY-TWO. THE ENSLAVED MUSLIM TOOK THIRTY-TWO BEFORE HE PASSED OUT.
ACCORDING TO THE REPORTS OF THE ASSEMBLED, HE NEVER MADE A SOUND.

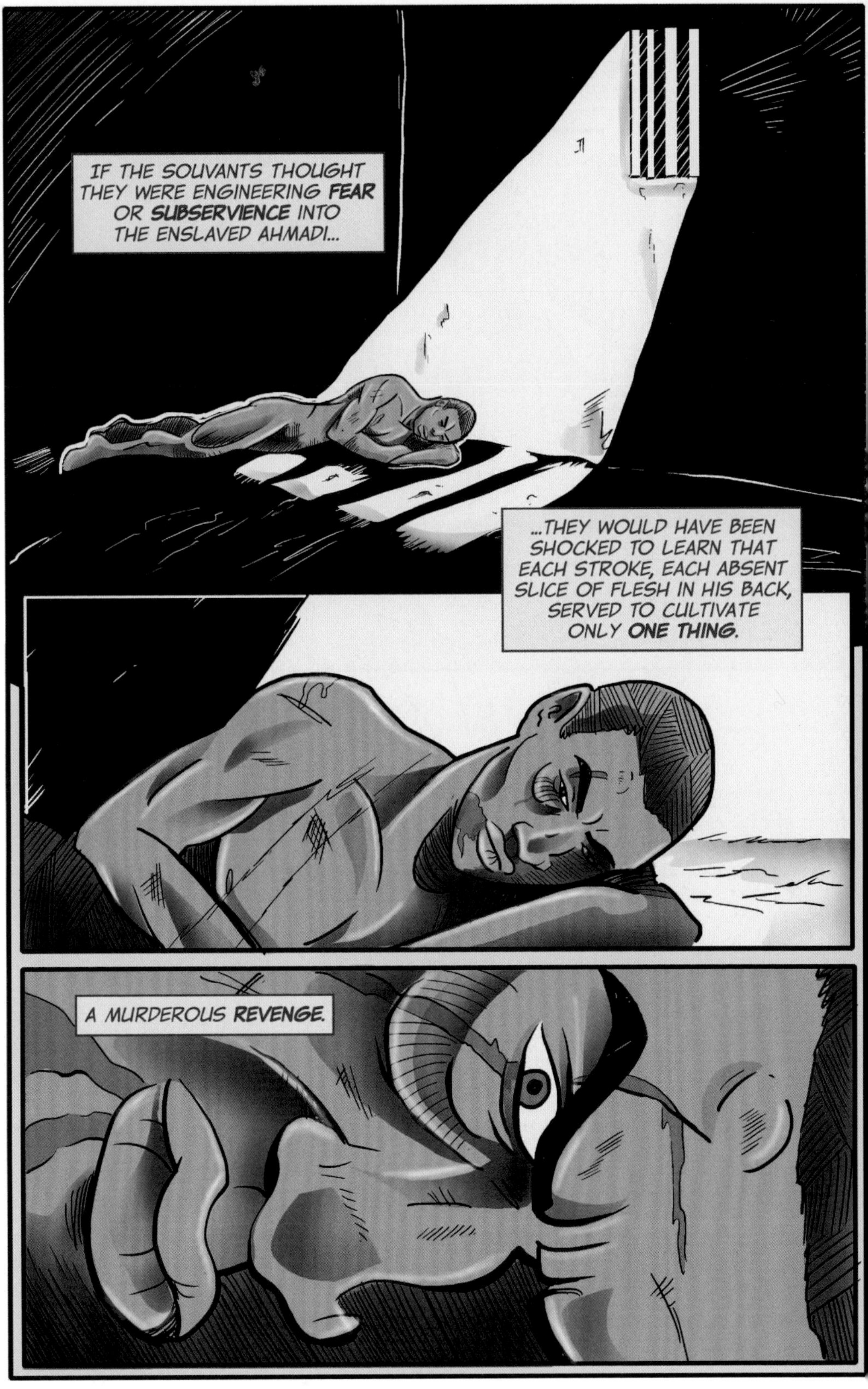
IF THE SOUVANTS THOUGHT THEY WERE ENGINEERING **FEAR** OR **SUBSERVIENCE** INTO THE ENSLAVED AHMADI...
...THEY WOULD HAVE BEEN SHOCKED TO LEARN THAT EACH STROKE, EACH ABSENT SLICE OF FLESH IN HIS BACK, SERVED TO CULTIVATE ONLY **ONE THING**.
A MURDEROUS **REVENGE**.

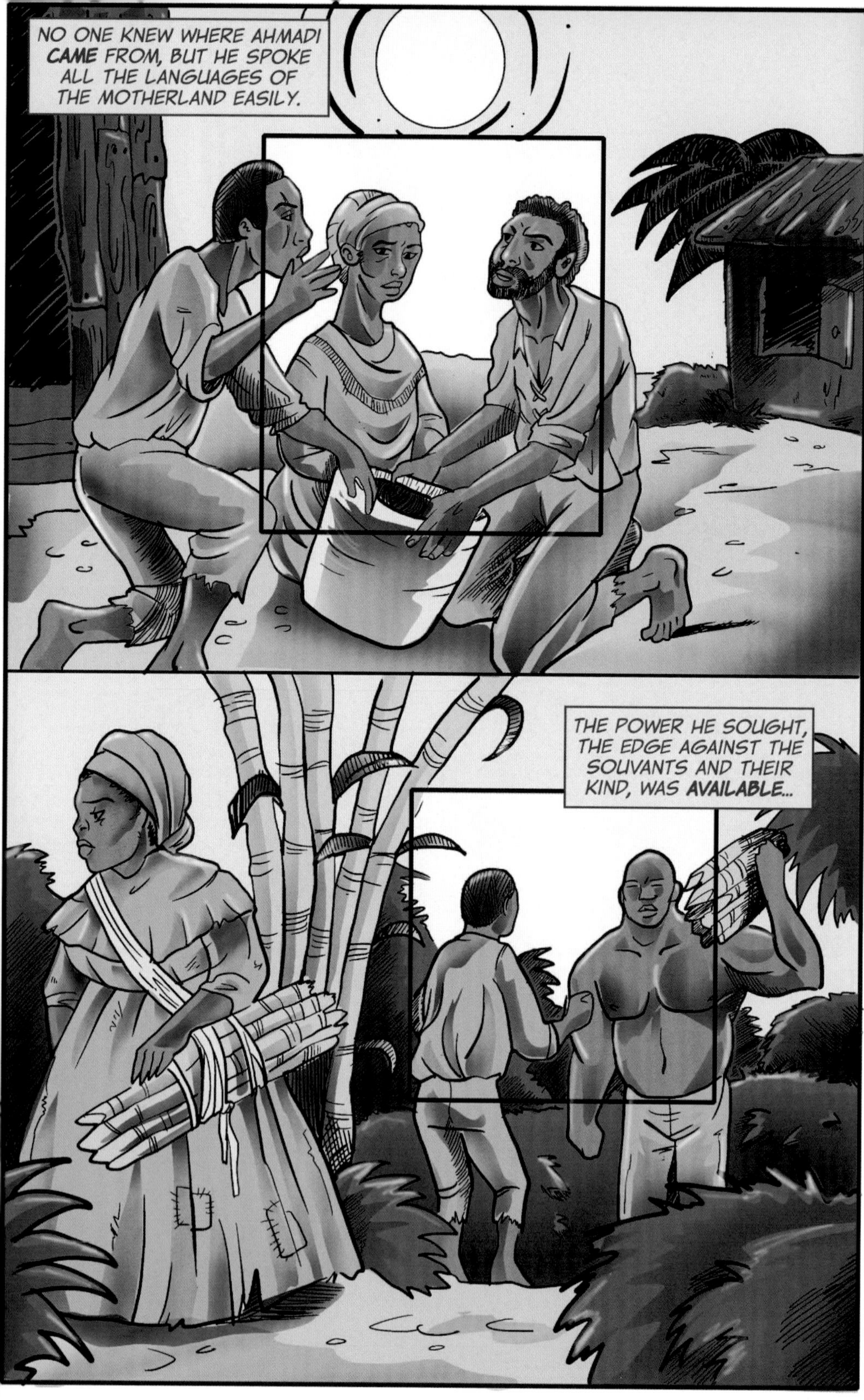
NO ONE KNEW WHERE AHMADI CAME FROM, BUT HE SPOKE ALL THE LANGUAGES OF THE MOTHERLAND EASILY.
THE POWER HE SOUGHT, THE EDGE AGAINST THE SOUVANTS AND THEIR KIND, WAS AVAILABLE...

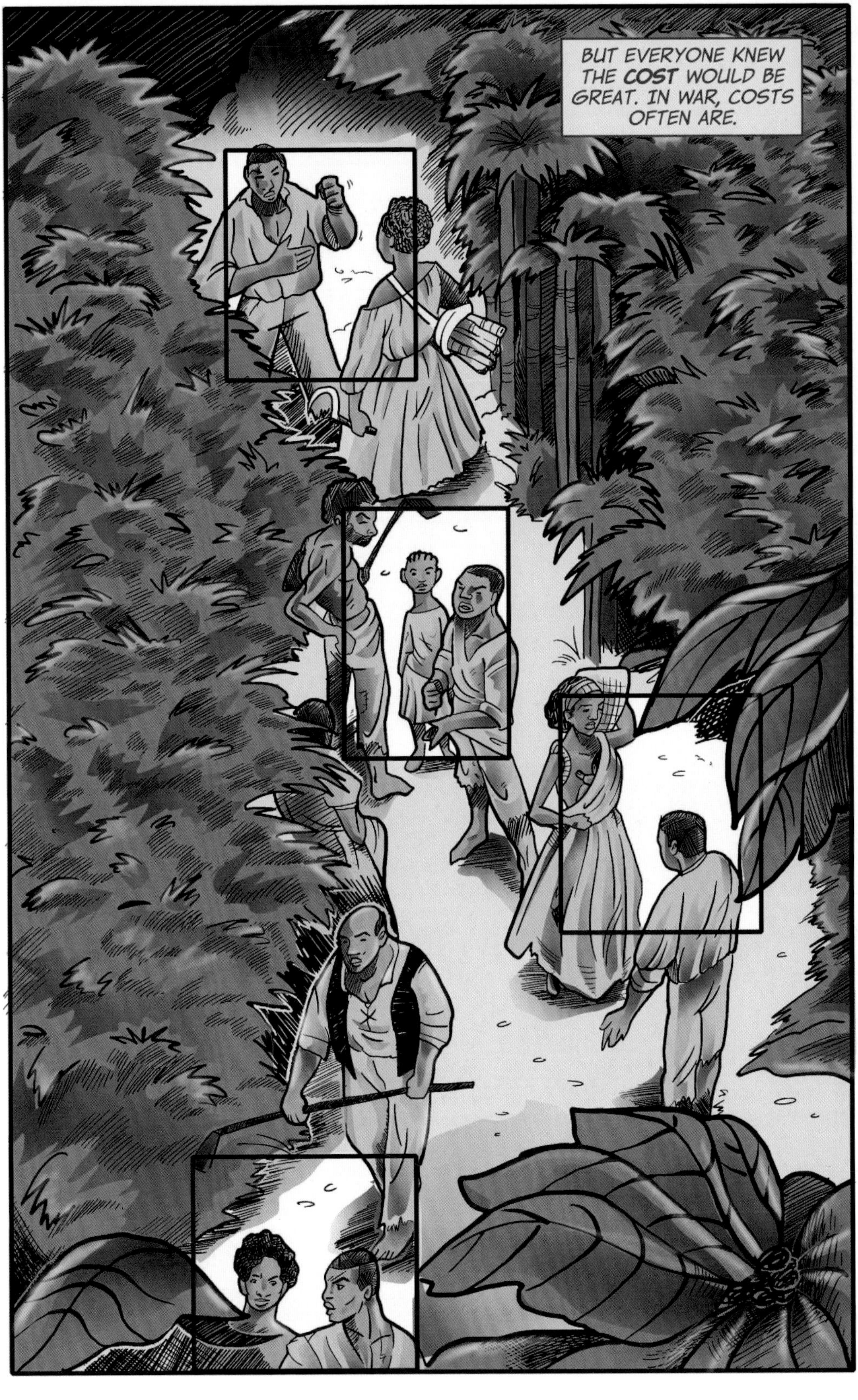
BUT EVERYONE KNEW THE COST WOULD BE GREAT. IN WAR, COSTS OFTEN ARE.

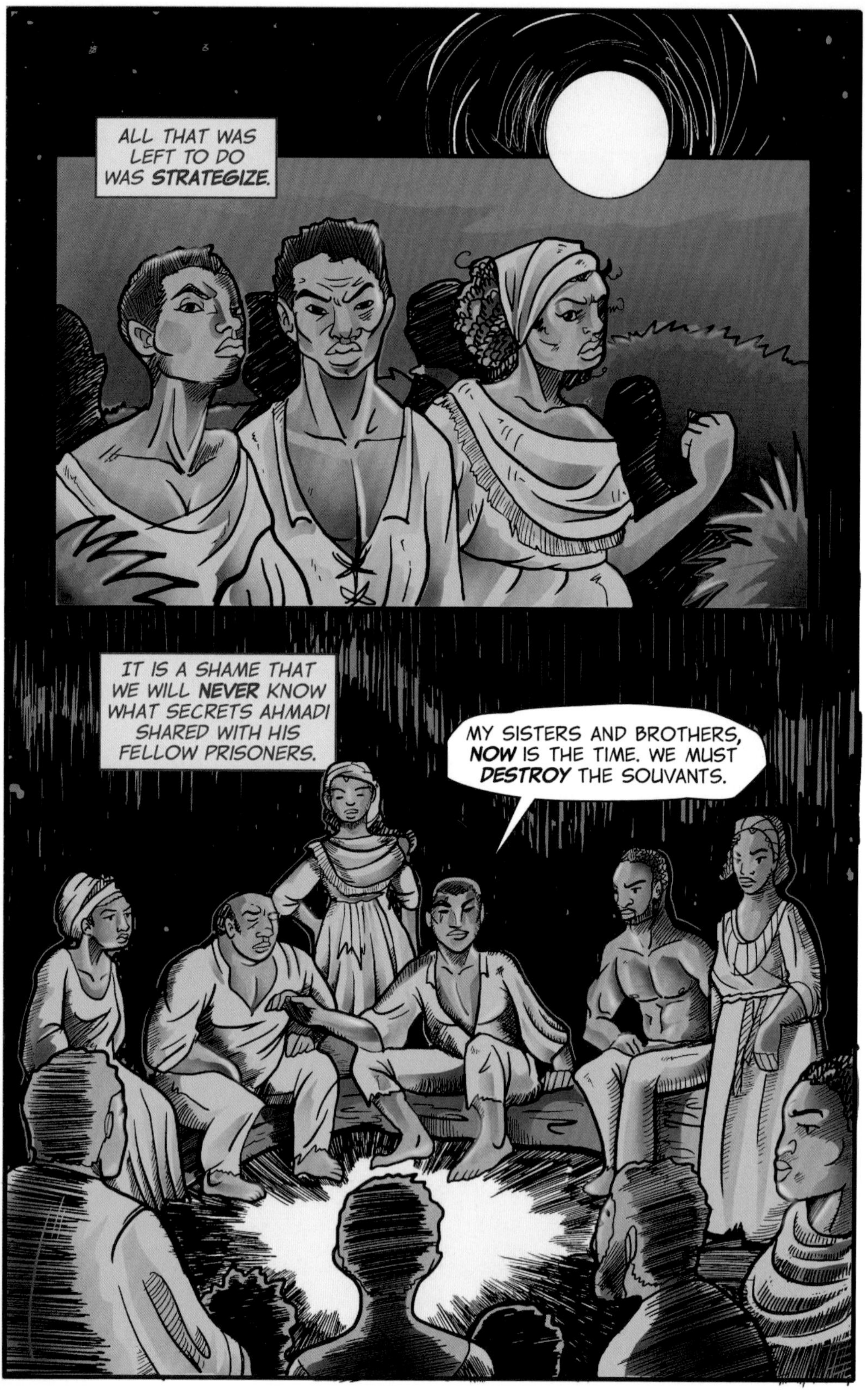
ALL THAT WAS LEFT TO DO WAS **STRATEGIZE**.
IT IS A SHAME THAT WE WILL **NEVER** KNOW WHAT SECRETS AHMADI SHARED WITH HIS FELLOW PRISONERS.
MY SISTERS AND BROTHERS, **NOW** IS THE TIME. WE MUST ***DESTROY*** THE SOUVANTS.

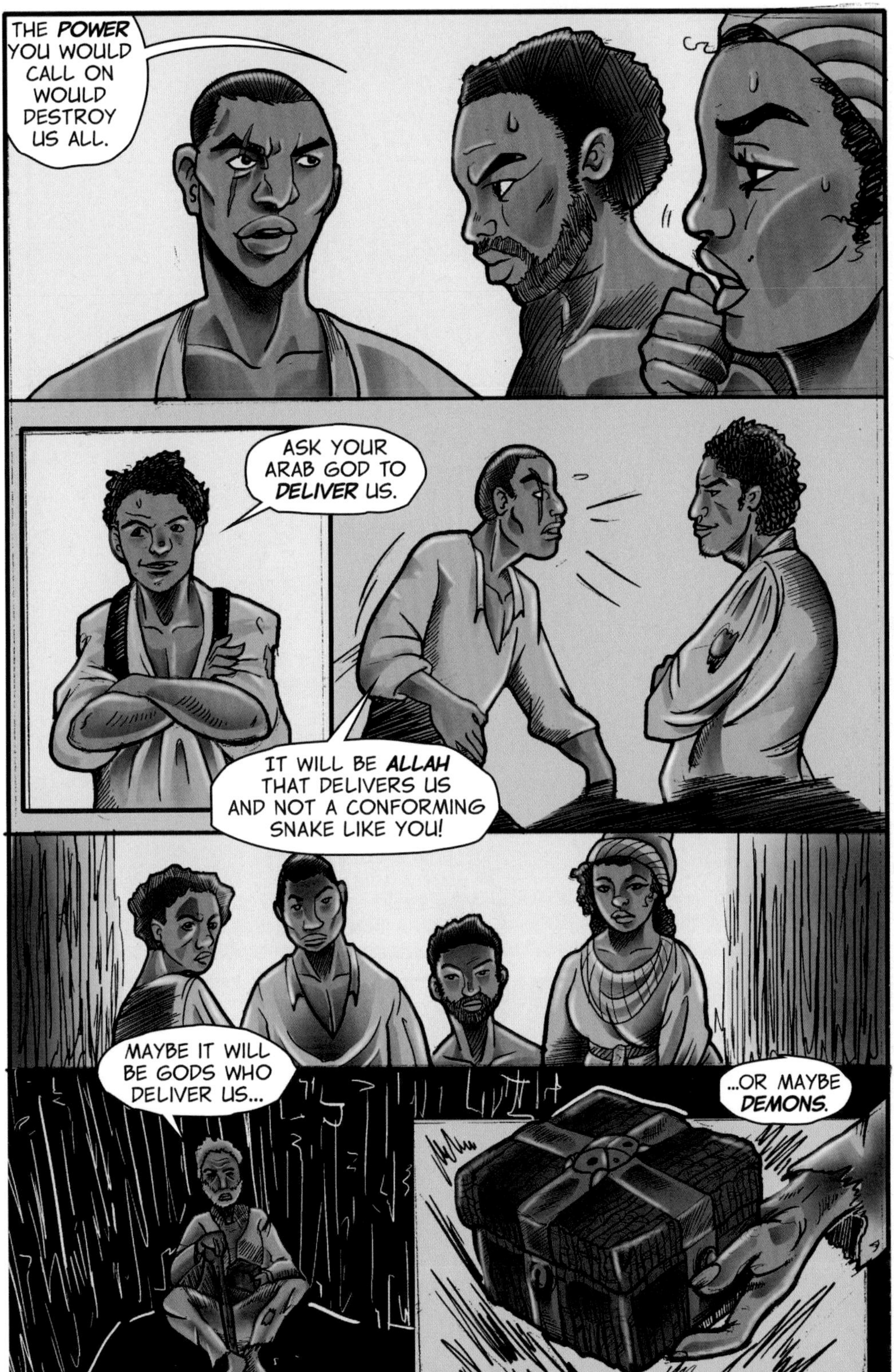
THE POWER YOU WOULD CALL ON WOULD DESTROY US ALL.
ASK YOUR ARAB GOD TO DELIVER US.
IT WILL BE ALLAH THAT DELIVERS US AND NOT A CONFORMING SNAKE LIKE YOU!
MAYBE IT WILL BE GODS WHO DELIVER US...
...OR MAYBE DEMONS.

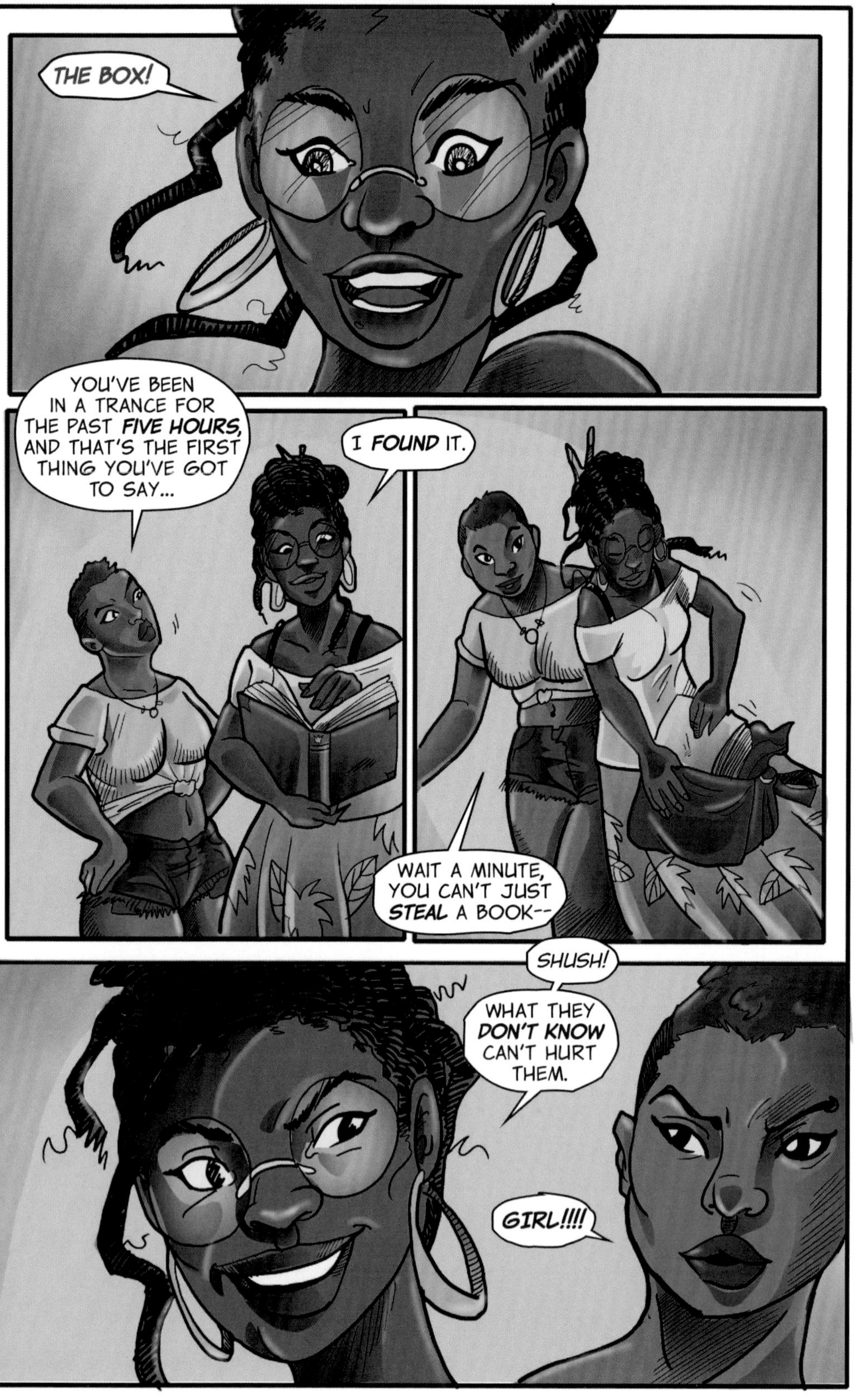
THE BOX!
YOU'VE BEEN IN A TRANCE FOR THE PAST FIVE HOURS, AND THAT'S THE FIRST THING YOU'VE GOT TO SAY...
I FOUND IT.
WAIT A MINUTE, YOU CAN'T JUST STEAL A BOOK--
SHUSH!
WHAT THEY DON'T KNOW CAN'T HURT THEM.
GIRL!!!!

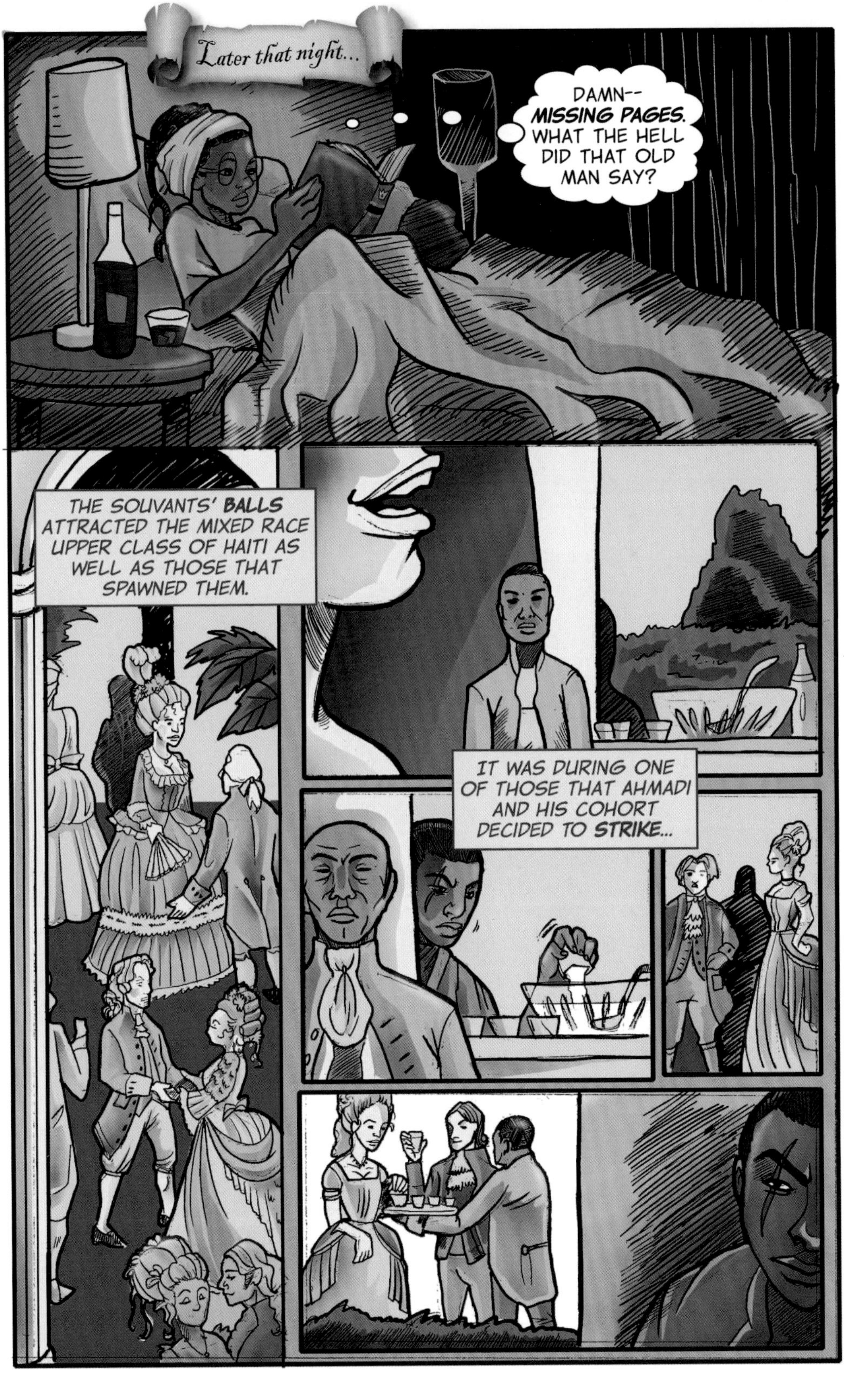
Later that night...
DAMN-- MISSING PAGES. WHAT THE HELL DID THAT OLD MAN SAY?
THE SOUVANTS' BALLS ATTRACTED THE MIXED RACE UPPER CLASS OF HAITI AS WELL AS THOSE THAT SPAWNED THEM.
IT WAS DURING ONE OF THOSE THAT AHMADI AND HIS COHORT DECIDED TO STRIKE...

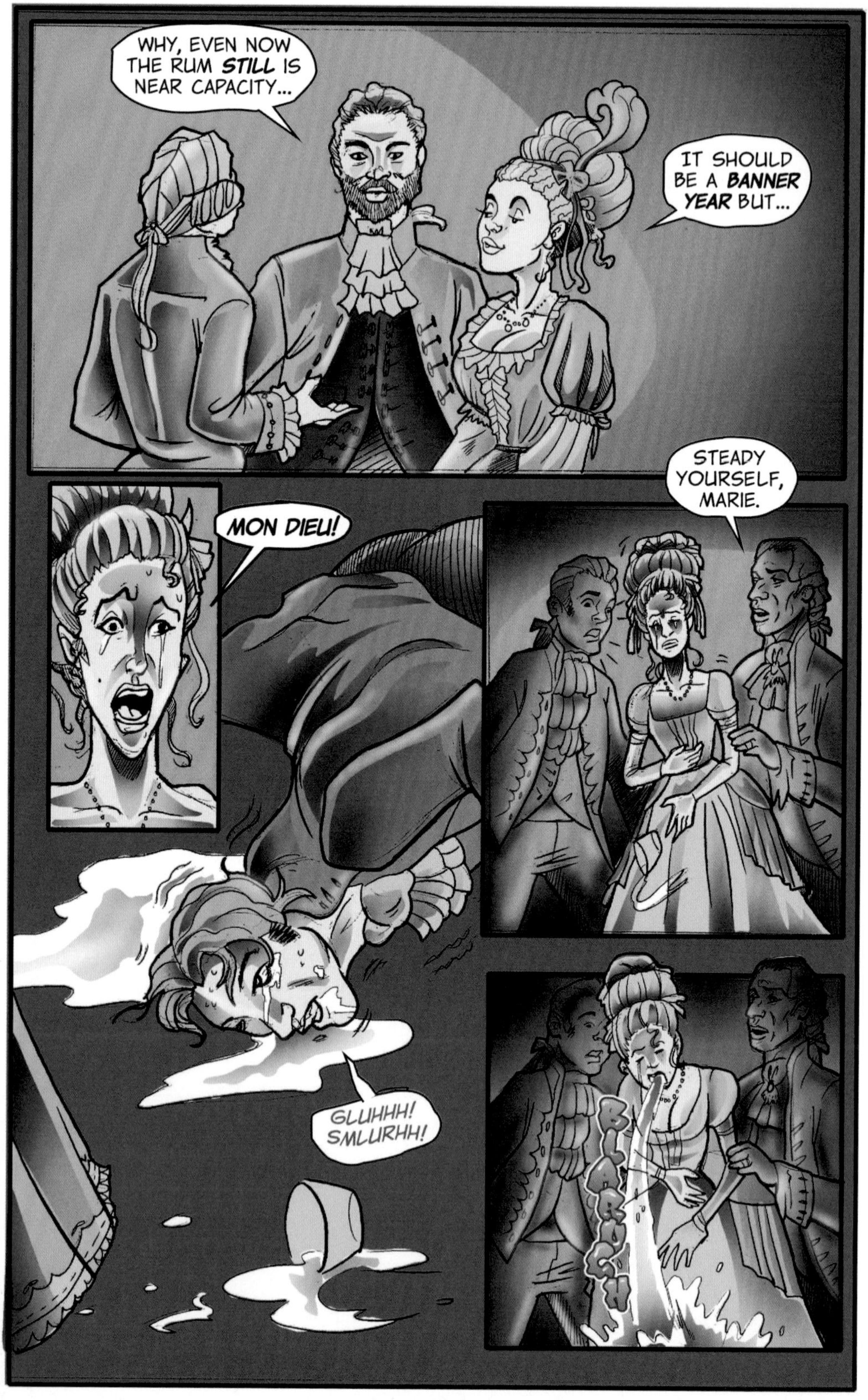
WHY, EVEN NOW THE RUM STILL IS NEAR CAPACITY...
IT SHOULD BE A BANNER YEAR BUT...
MON DIEU!
STEADY YOURSELF, MARIE.
GLUHHH! SMLURHH!

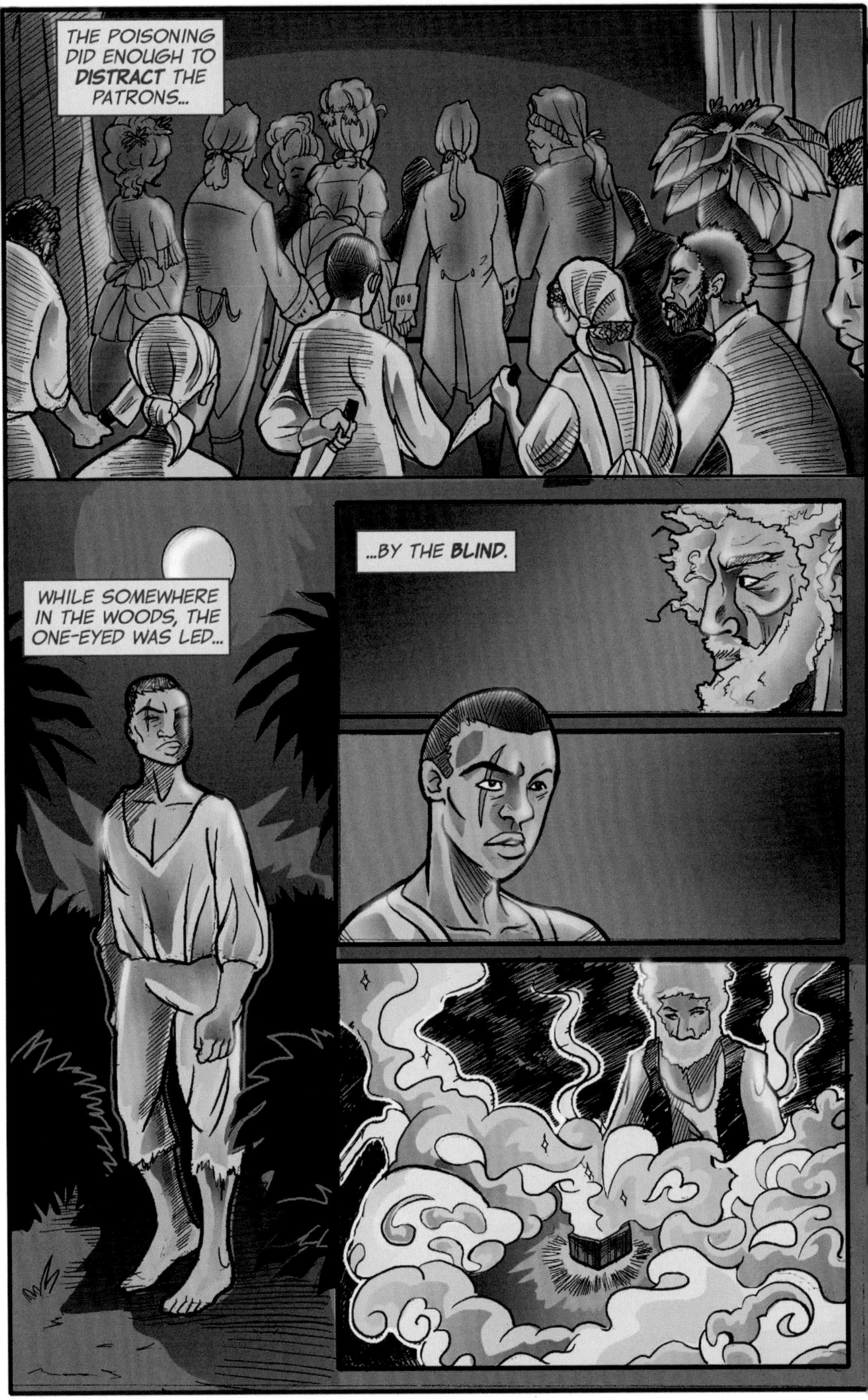
THE POISONING DID ENOUGH TO **DISTRACT** THE PATRONS...
WHILE SOMEWHERE IN THE WOODS, THE ONE-EYED WAS LED...
...BY THE **BLIND**.

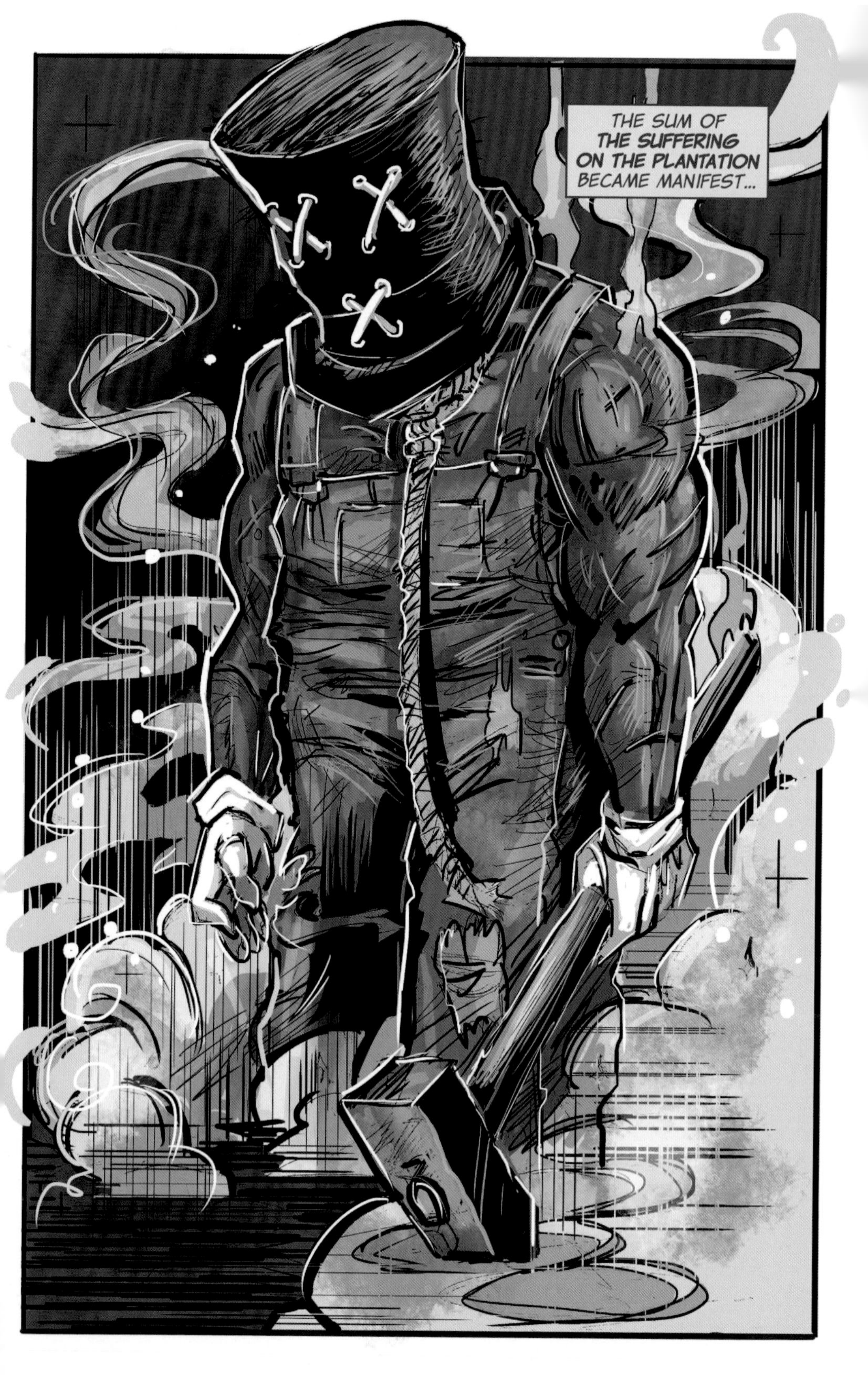
THE SUM OF THE SUFFERING ON THE PLANTATION BECAME MANIFEST...

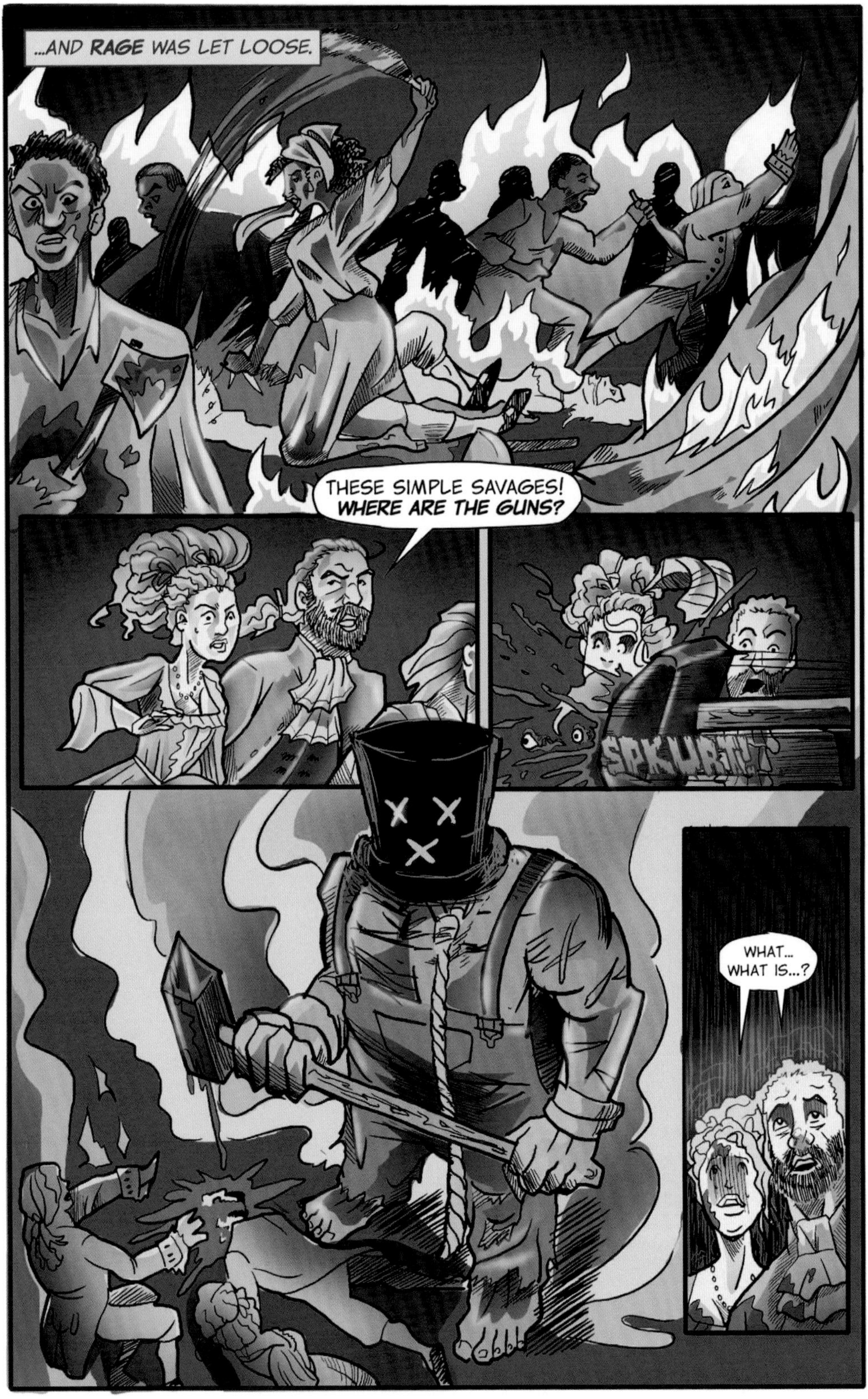
...AND RAGE WAS LET LOOSE.
THESE SIMPLE SAVAGES! WHERE ARE THE GUNS?
SPKURT!
WHAT... WHAT IS...?

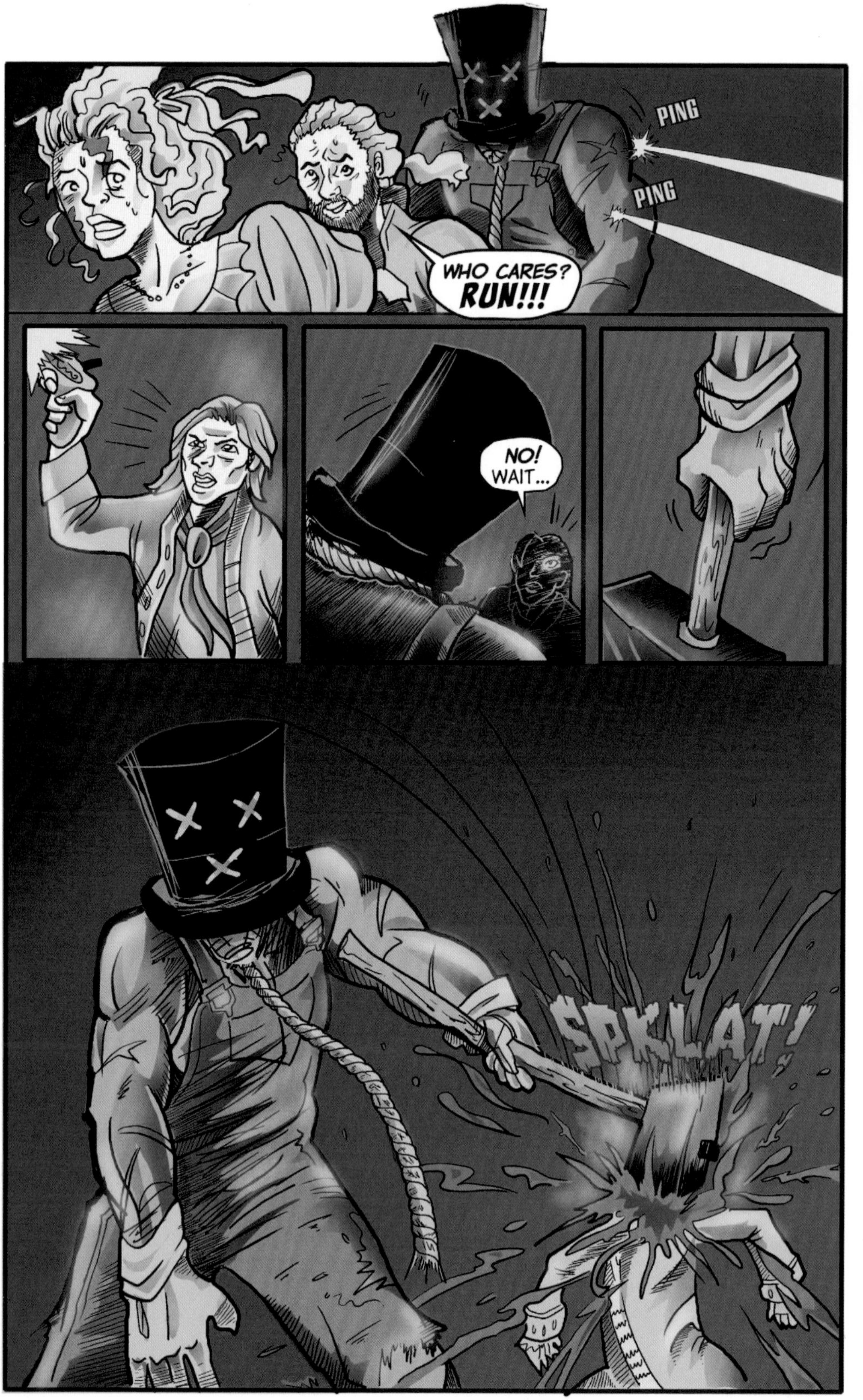
PING
PING
WHO CARES? RUN!!!
NO! WAIT...
SPKLAT!

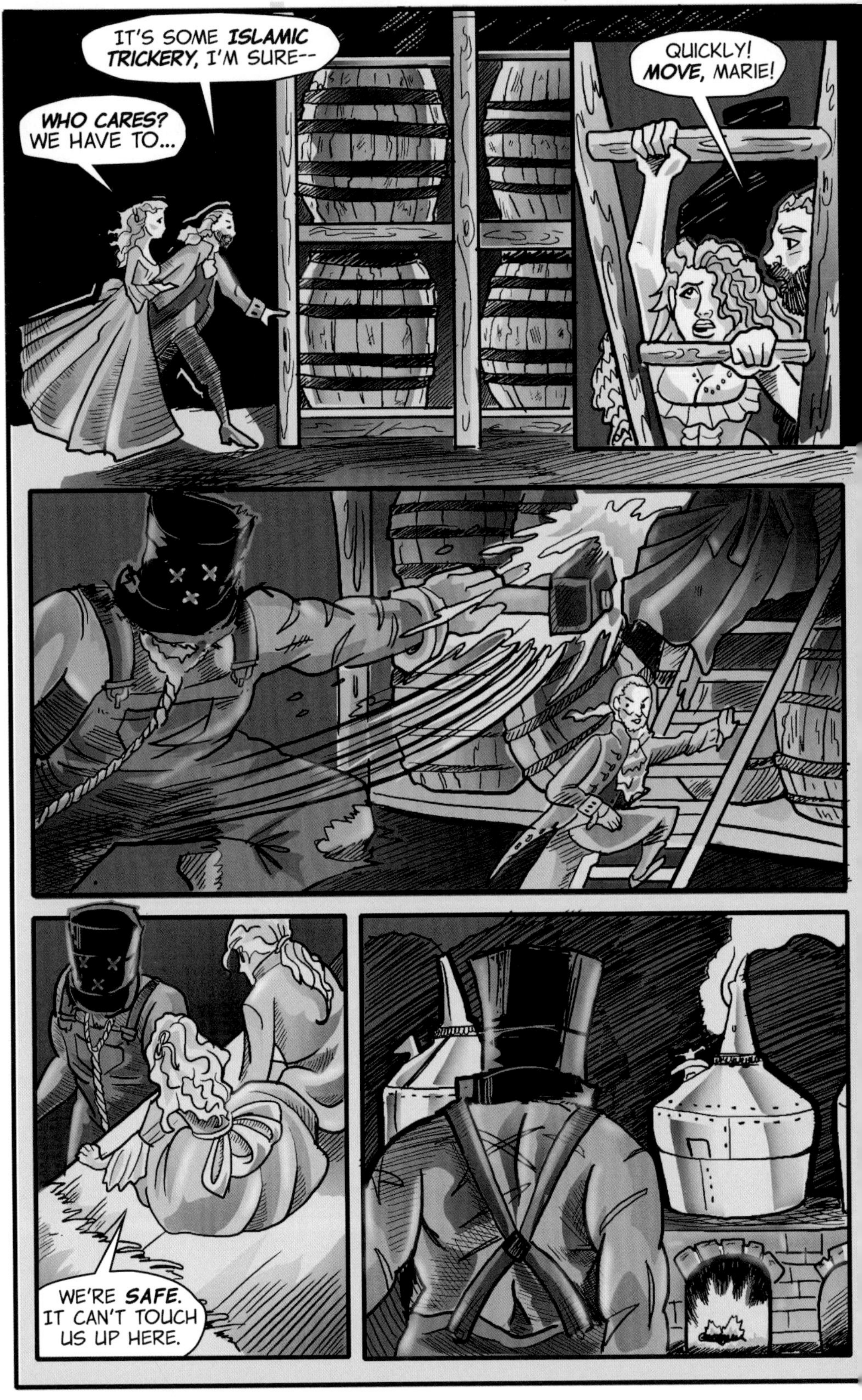
IT'S SOME **ISLAMIC TRICKERY**, I'M SURE--
**WHO CARES?** WE HAVE TO...
QUICKLY! **MOVE,** MARIE!
WE'RE **SAFE**. IT CAN'T TOUCH US UP HERE.

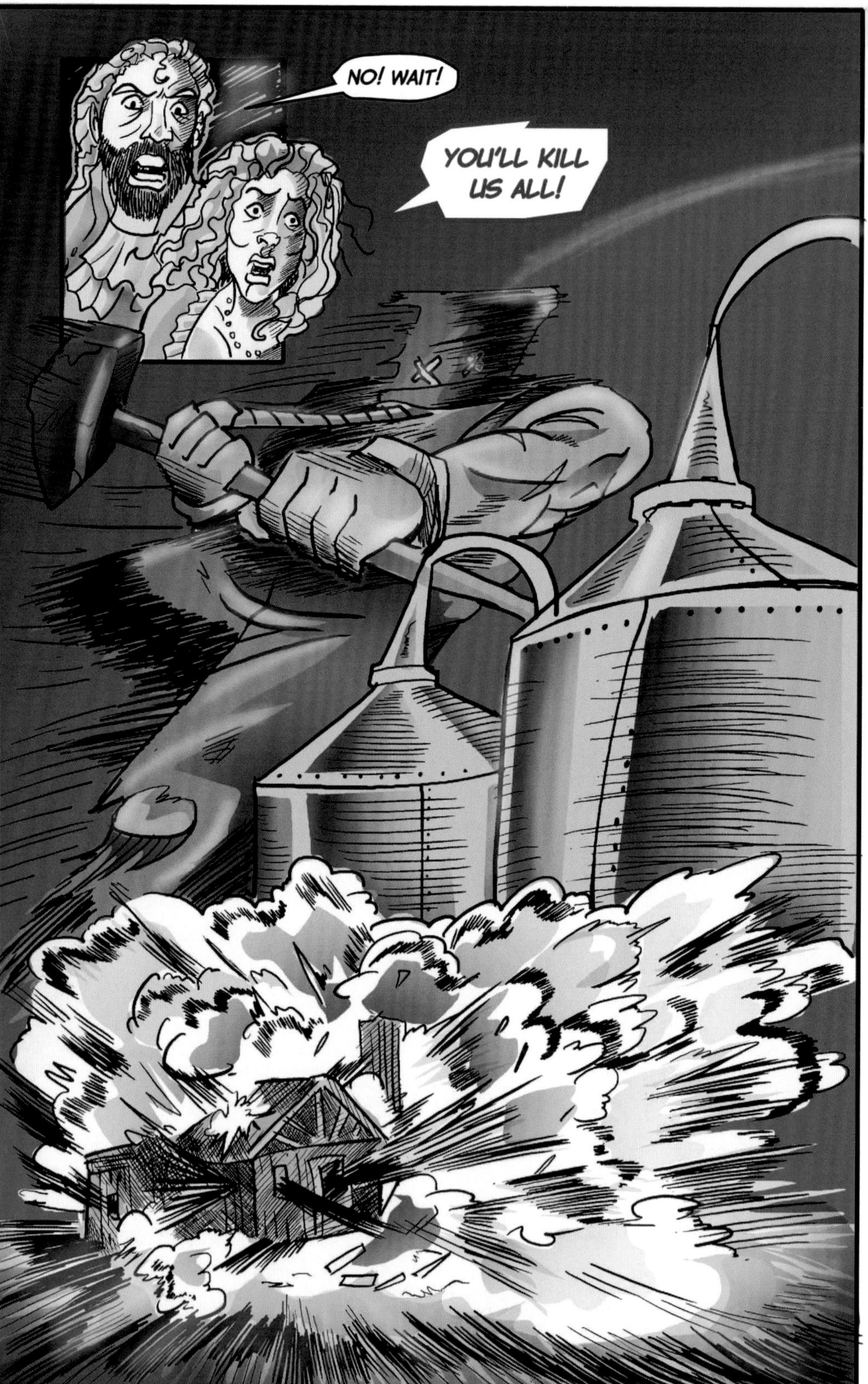
NO! WAIT!
YOU'LL KILL US ALL!

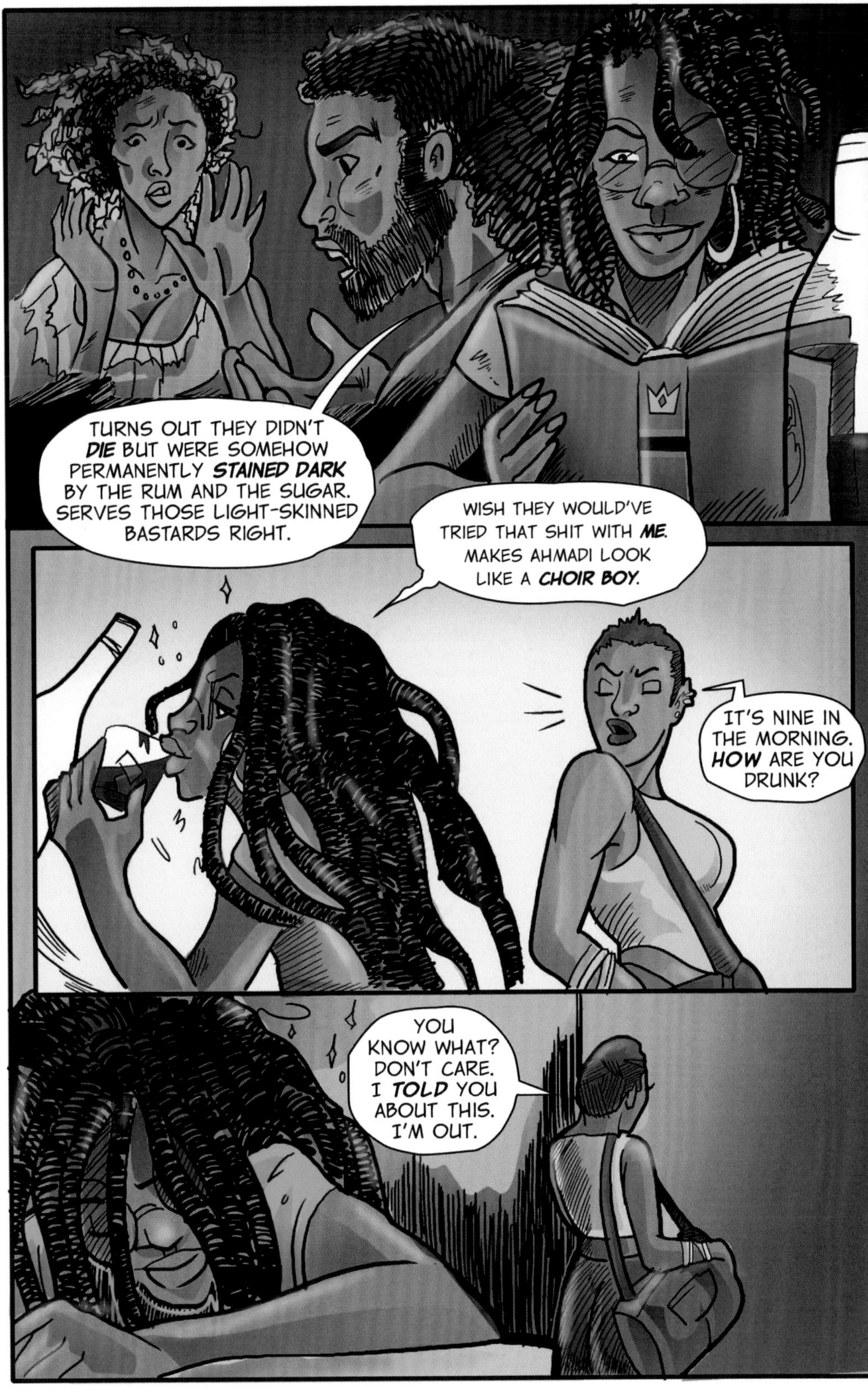
TURNS OUT THEY DIDN'T ***DIE*** BUT WERE SOMEHOW PERMANENTLY ***STAINED DARK*** BY THE RUM AND THE SUGAR. SERVES THOSE LIGHT-SKINNED BASTARDS RIGHT.
WISH THEY WOULD'VE TRIED THAT SHIT WITH ***ME***. MAKES AHMADI LOOK LIKE A ***CHOIR BOY***.
IT'S NINE IN THE MORNING. ***HOW*** ARE YOU DRUNK?
YOU KNOW WHAT? DON'T CARE. I ***TOLD*** YOU ABOUT THIS. I'M OUT.

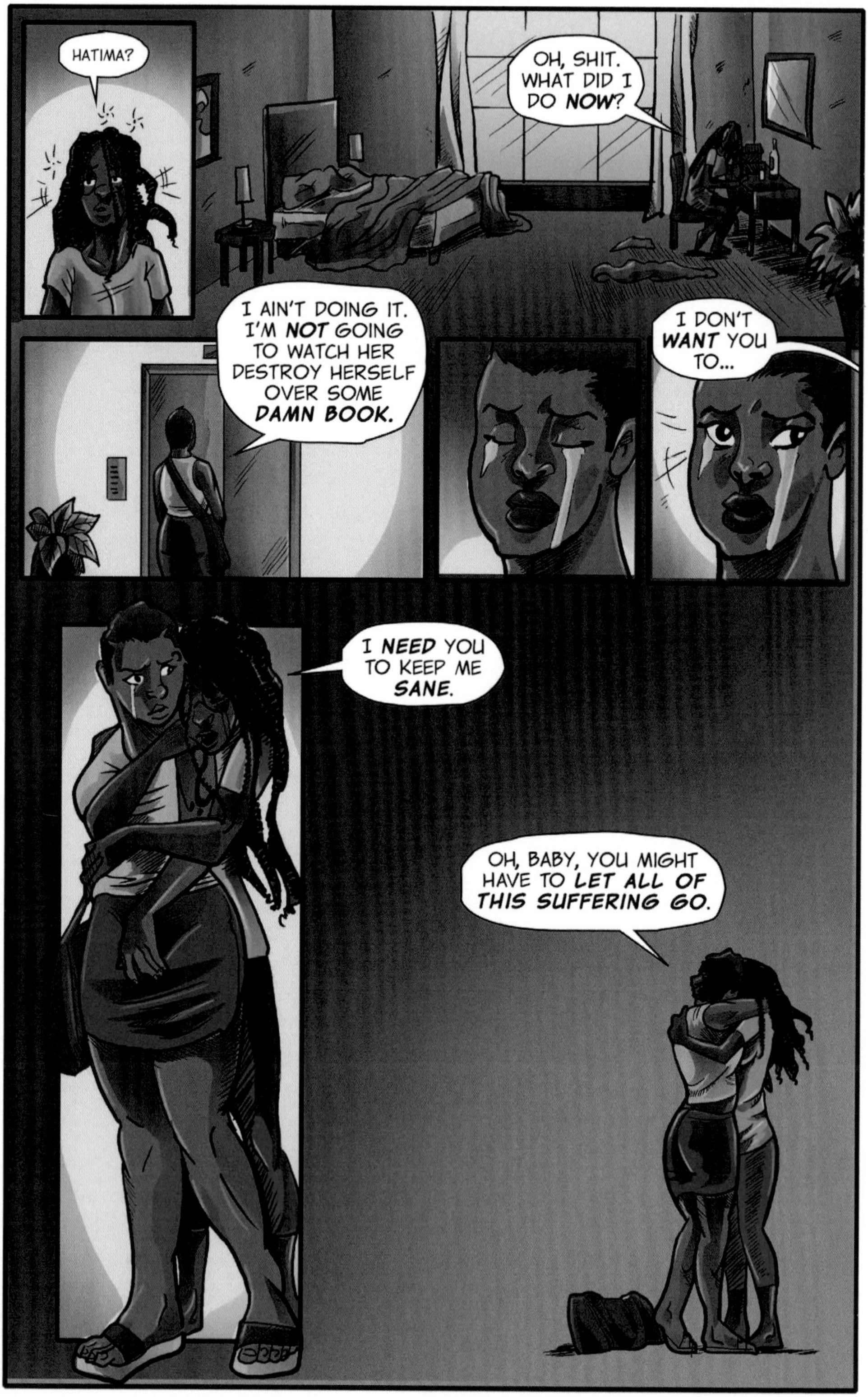
HATIMA?
OH, SHIT. WHAT DID I DO NOW?
I AIN'T DOING IT. I'M NOT GOING TO WATCH HER DESTROY HERSELF OVER SOME DAMN BOOK.
I DON'T WANT YOU TO...
I NEED YOU TO KEEP ME SANE.
OH, BABY, YOU MIGHT HAVE TO LET ALL OF THIS SUFFERING GO.

# CHAPTER FIVE

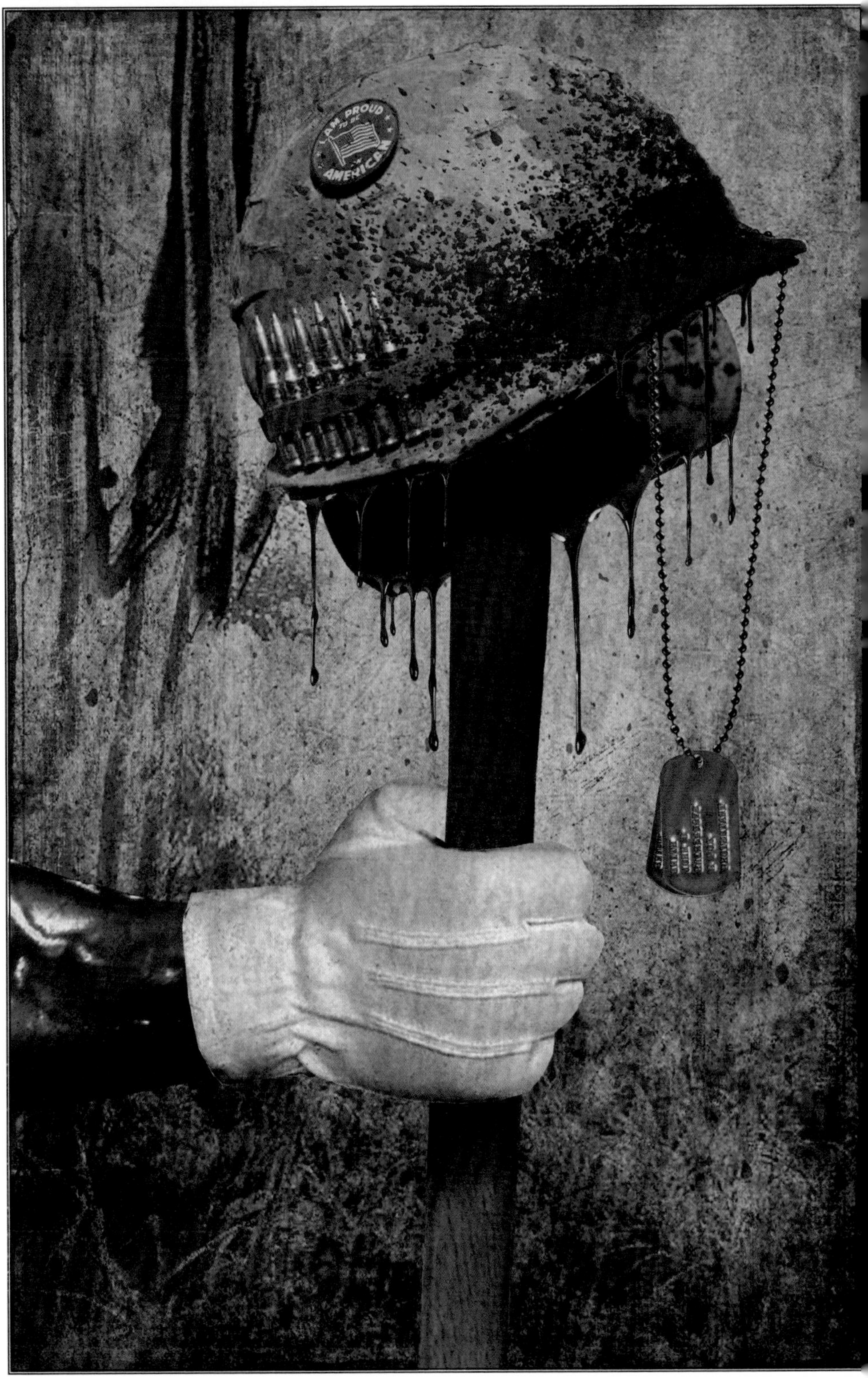

I AM PROUD
TO BE
AMERICAN


# " SUFFERING ON THE HILL"

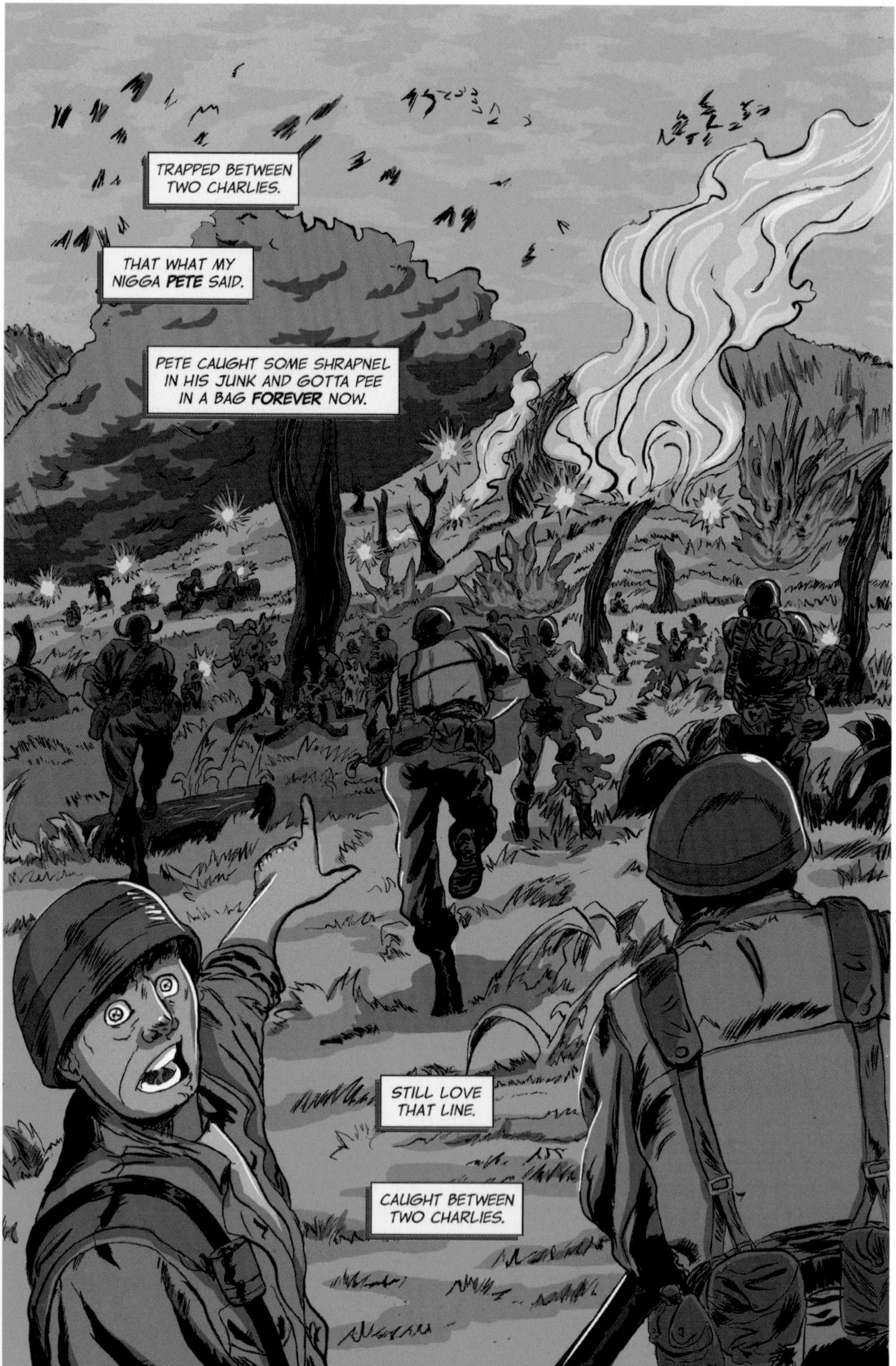
TRAPPED BETWEEN TWO CHARLIES.
THAT WHAT MY NIGGA **PETE** SAID.
PETE CAUGHT SOME SHRAPNEL IN HIS JUNK AND GOTTA PEE IN A BAG **FOREVER** NOW.
STILL LOVE THAT LINE.
CAUGHT BETWEEN TWO CHARLIES.

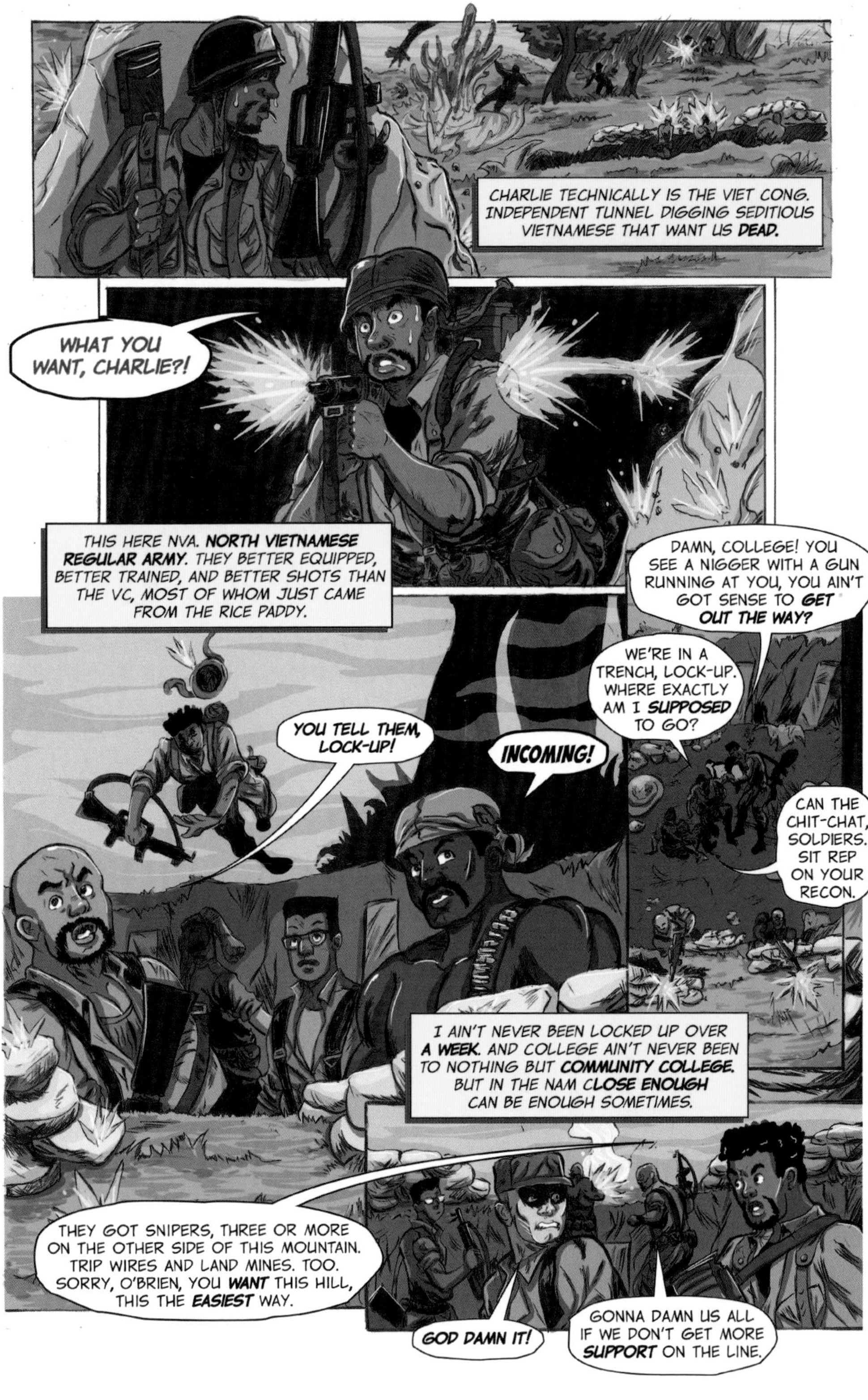
CHARLIE TECHNICALLY IS THE VIET CONG. INDEPENDENT TUNNEL DIGGING SEDITIOUS VIETNAMESE THAT WANT US DEAD.
WHAT YOU WANT, CHARLIE?!
THIS HERE NVA. NORTH VIETNAMESE REGULAR ARMY. THEY BETTER EQUIPPED, BETTER TRAINED, AND BETTER SHOTS THAN THE VC, MOST OF WHOM JUST CAME FROM THE RICE PADDY.
DAMN, COLLEGE! YOU SEE A NIGGER WITH A GUN RUNNING AT YOU, YOU AIN'T GOT SENSE TO GET OUT THE WAY?
WE'RE IN A TRENCH, LOCK-UP. WHERE EXACTLY AM I SUPPOSED TO GO?
YOU TELL THEM, LOCK-UP!
INCOMING!
CAN THE CHIT-CHAT, SOLDIERS. SIT REP ON YOUR RECON.
I AIN'T NEVER BEEN LOCKED UP OVER A WEEK. AND COLLEGE AIN'T NEVER BEEN TO NOTHING BUT COMMUNITY COLLEGE. BUT IN THE NAM CLOSE ENOUGH CAN BE ENOUGH SOMETIMES.
THEY GOT SNIPERS, THREE OR MORE ON THE OTHER SIDE OF THIS MOUNTAIN. TRIP WIRES AND LAND MINES. TOO. SORRY, O'BRIEN, YOU WANT THIS HILL, THIS THE EASIEST WAY.
GOD DAMN IT!
GONNA DAMN US ALL IF WE DON'T GET MORE SUPPORT ON THE LINE.

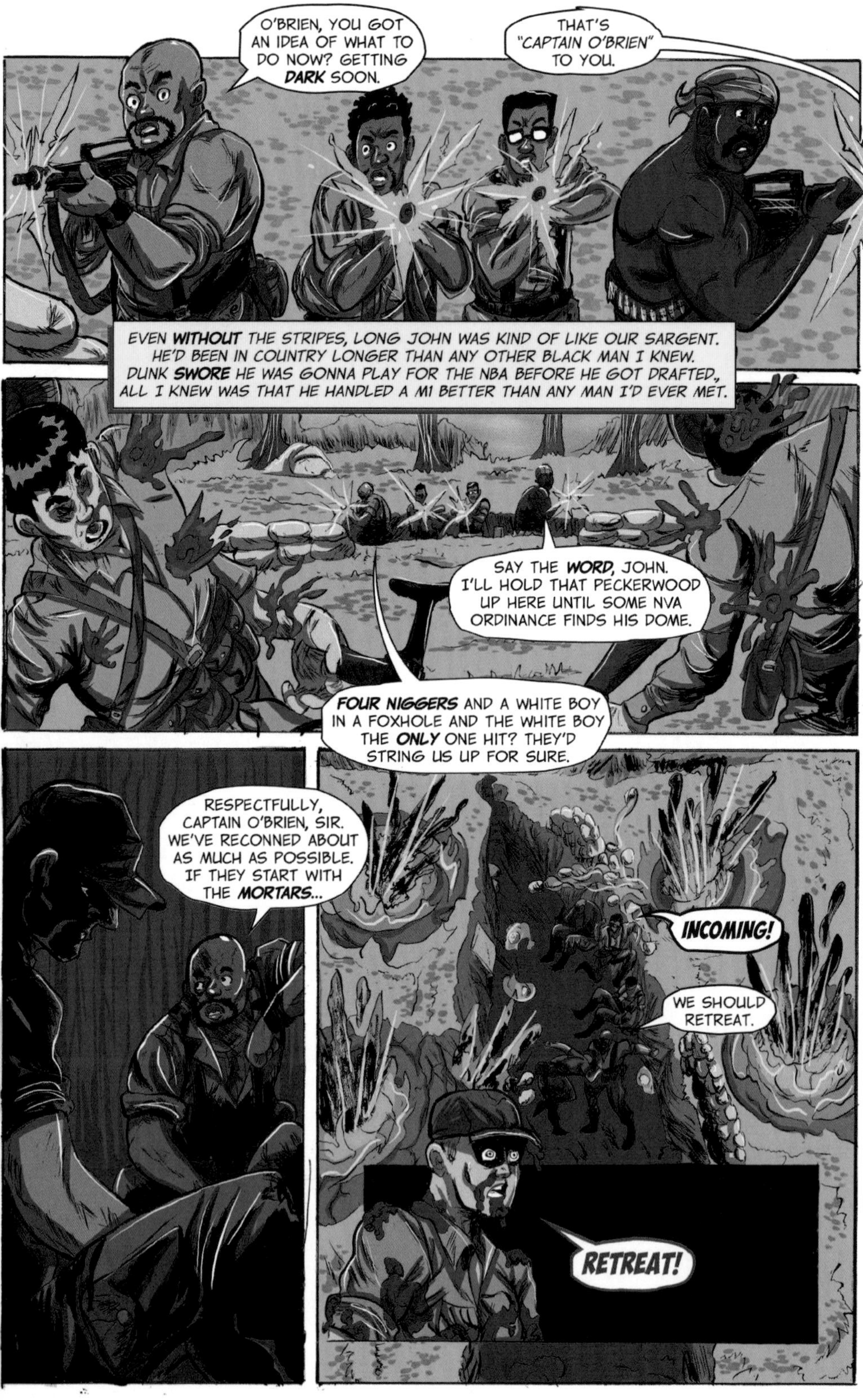
O'BRIEN, YOU GOT AN IDEA OF WHAT TO DO NOW? GETTING **DARK** SOON.
THAT'S "CAPTAIN O'BRIEN" TO YOU.
EVEN **WITHOUT** THE STRIPES, LONG JOHN WAS KIND OF LIKE OUR SARGENT. HE'D BEEN IN COUNTRY LONGER THAN ANY OTHER BLACK MAN I KNEW. DUNK **SWORE** HE WAS GONNA PLAY FOR THE NBA BEFORE HE GOT DRAFTED., ALL I KNEW WAS THAT HE HANDLED A M1 BETTER THAN ANY MAN I'D EVER MET.
SAY THE **WORD,** JOHN. I'LL HOLD THAT PECKERWOOD UP HERE UNTIL SOME NVA ORDINANCE FINDS HIS DOME.
**FOUR NIGGERS** AND A WHITE BOY IN A FOXHOLE AND THE WHITE BOY THE **ONLY** ONE HIT? THEY'D STRING US UP FOR SURE.
RESPECTFULLY, CAPTAIN O'BRIEN, SIR. WE'VE RECONNED ABOUT AS MUCH AS POSSIBLE. IF THEY START WITH THE **MORTARS...**
INCOMING!
WE SHOULD RETREAT.
RETREAT!

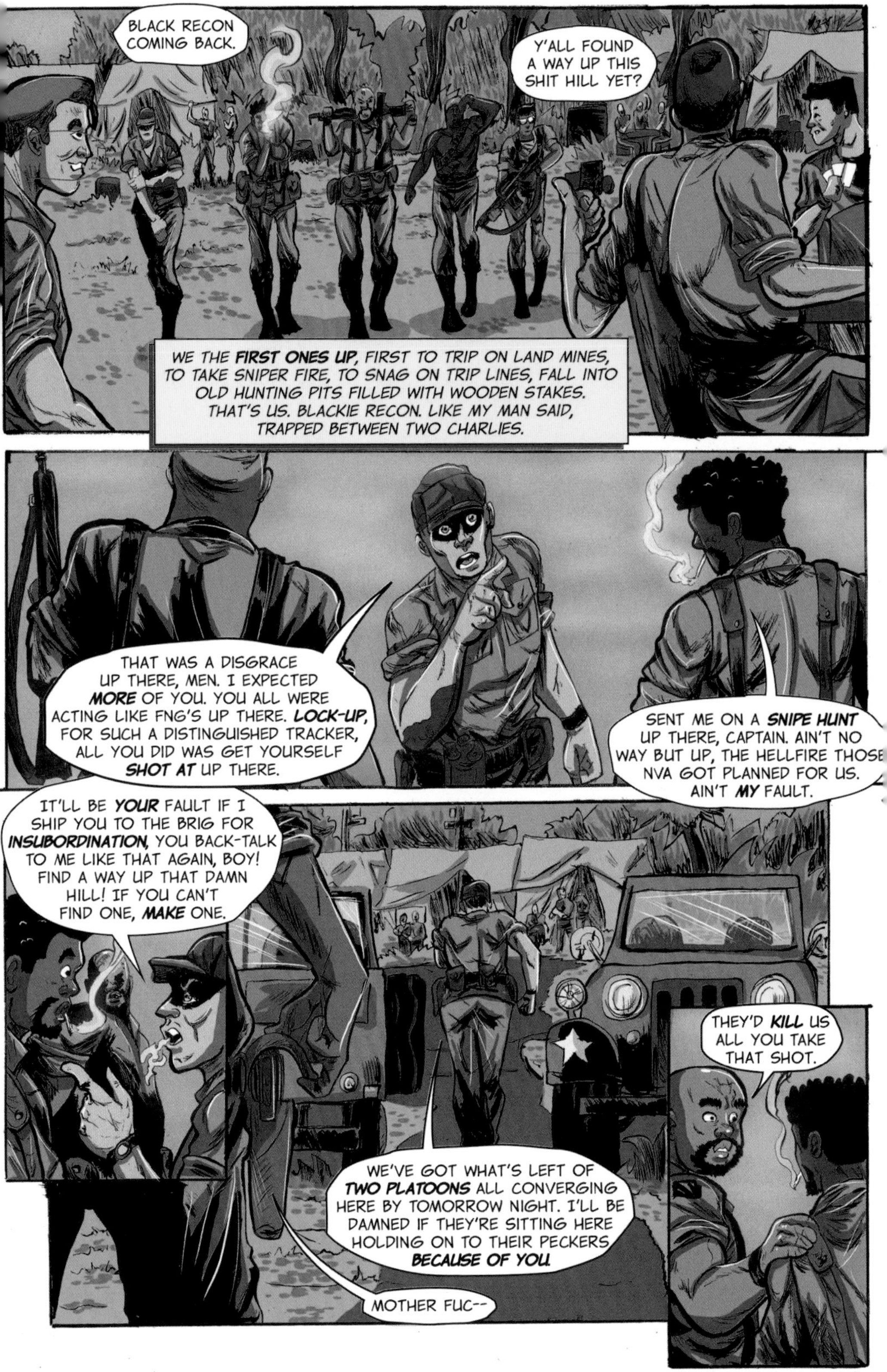
BLACK RECON COMING BACK.
Y'ALL FOUND A WAY UP THIS SHIT HILL YET?
WE THE FIRST ONES UP, FIRST TO TRIP ON LAND MINES, TO TAKE SNIPER FIRE, TO SNAG ON TRIP LINES, FALL INTO OLD HUNTING PITS FILLED WITH WOODEN STAKES. THAT'S US. BLACKIE RECON. LIKE MY MAN SAID, TRAPPED BETWEEN TWO CHARLIES.
THAT WAS A DISGRACE UP THERE, MEN. I EXPECTED MORE OF YOU. YOU ALL WERE ACTING LIKE FNG'S UP THERE. LOCK-UP, FOR SUCH A DISTINGUISHED TRACKER, ALL YOU DID WAS GET YOURSELF SHOT AT UP THERE.
SENT ME ON A SNIPE HUNT UP THERE, CAPTAIN. AIN'T NO WAY BUT UP, THE HELLFIRE THOSE NVA GOT PLANNED FOR US. AIN'T MY FAULT.
IT'LL BE YOUR FAULT IF I SHIP YOU TO THE BRIG FOR INSUBORDINATION, YOU BACK-TALK TO ME LIKE THAT AGAIN, BOY! FIND A WAY UP THAT DAMN HILL! IF YOU CAN'T FIND ONE, MAKE ONE.
WE'VE GOT WHAT'S LEFT OF TWO PLATOONS ALL CONVERGING HERE BY TOMORROW NIGHT. I'LL BE DAMNED IF THEY'RE SITTING HERE HOLDING ON TO THEIR PECKERS BECAUSE OF YOU.
MOTHER FUC--
THEY'D KILL US ALL YOU TAKE THAT SHOT.

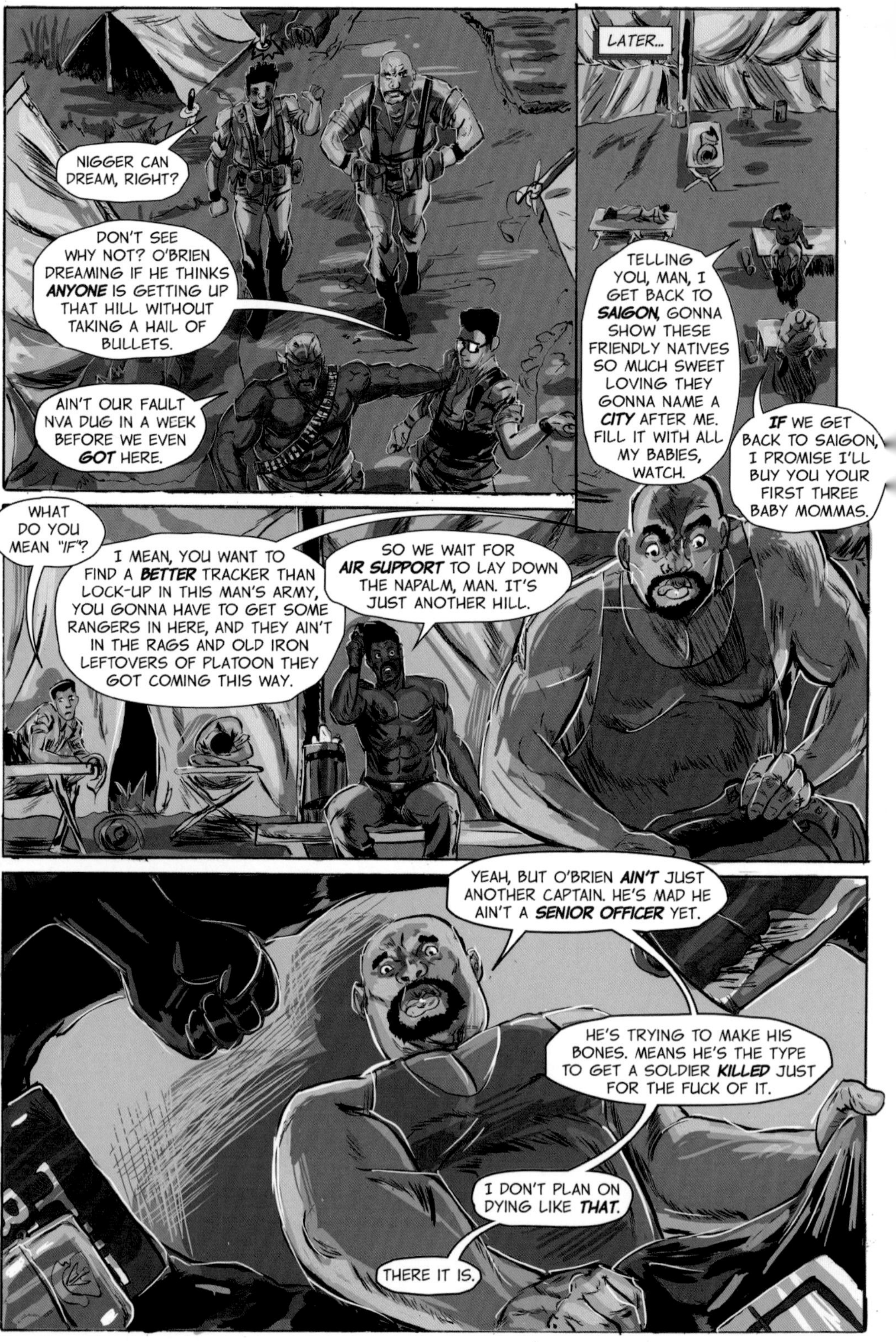
NIGGER CAN DREAM, RIGHT?
DON'T SEE WHY NOT? O'BRIEN DREAMING IF HE THINKS ANYONE IS GETTING UP THAT HILL WITHOUT TAKING A HAIL OF BULLETS.
AIN'T OUR FAULT NVA DUG IN A WEEK BEFORE WE EVEN GOT HERE.
LATER...
TELLING YOU, MAN, I GET BACK TO SAIGON, GONNA SHOW THESE FRIENDLY NATIVES SO MUCH SWEET LOVING THEY GONNA NAME A CITY AFTER ME. FILL IT WITH ALL MY BABIES, WATCH.
IF WE GET BACK TO SAIGON, I PROMISE I'LL BUY YOU YOUR FIRST THREE BABY MOMMAS.
WHAT DO YOU MEAN "IF"?
I MEAN, YOU WANT TO FIND A BETTER TRACKER THAN LOCK-UP IN THIS MAN'S ARMY, YOU GONNA HAVE TO GET SOME RANGERS IN HERE, AND THEY AIN'T IN THE RAGS AND OLD IRON LEFTOVERS OF PLATOON THEY GOT COMING THIS WAY.
SO WE WAIT FOR AIR SUPPORT TO LAY DOWN THE NAPALM, MAN. IT'S JUST ANOTHER HILL.
YEAH, BUT O'BRIEN AIN'T JUST ANOTHER CAPTAIN. HE'S MAD HE AIN'T A SENIOR OFFICER YET.
HE'S TRYING TO MAKE HIS BONES. MEANS HE'S THE TYPE TO GET A SOLDIER KILLED JUST FOR THE FUCK OF IT.
I DON'T PLAN ON DYING LIKE THAT.
THERE IT IS.

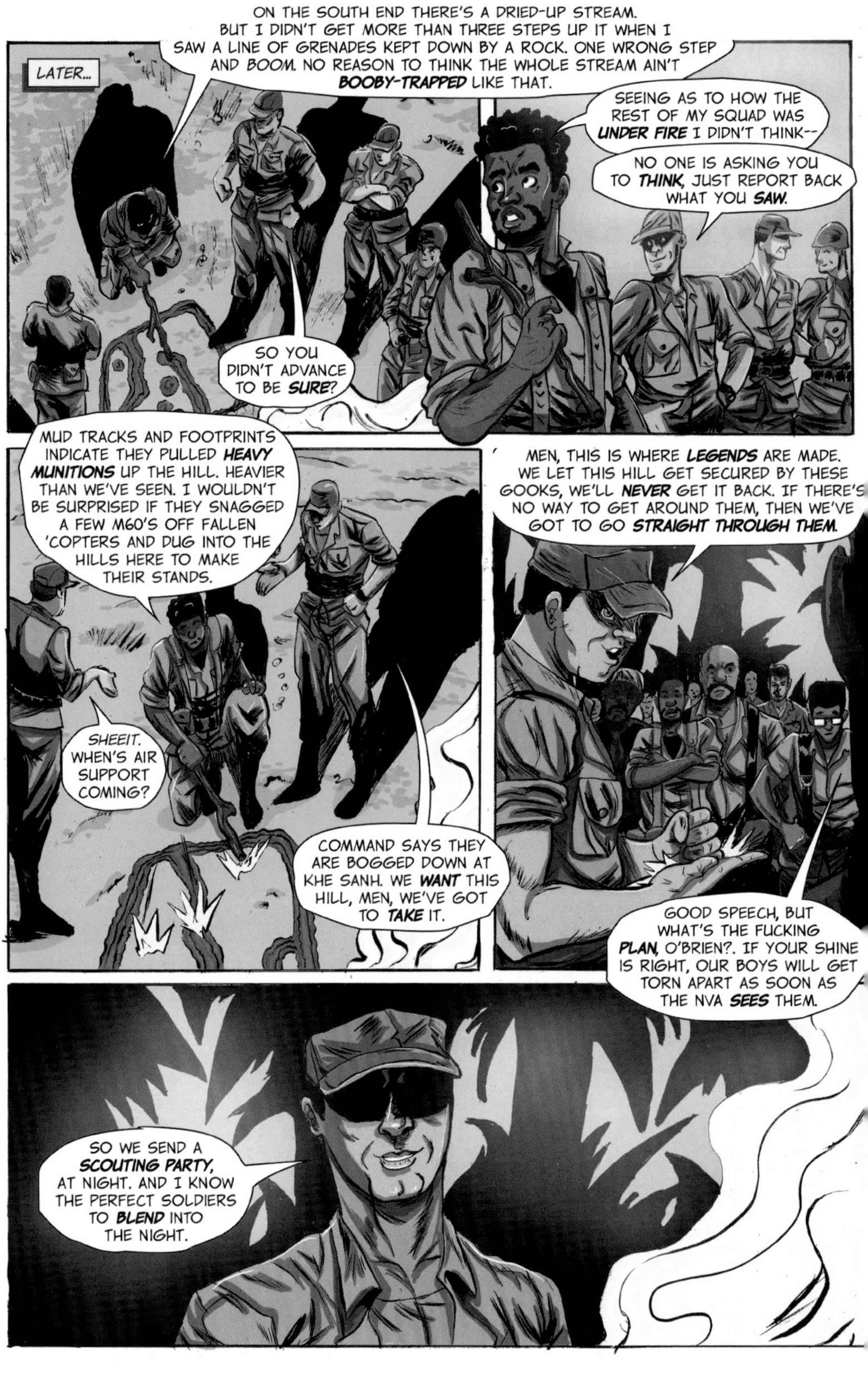

LATER...
ON THE SOUTH END THERE'S A DRIED-UP STREAM. BUT I DIDN'T GET MORE THAN THREE STEPS UP IT WHEN I SAW A LINE OF GRENADES KEPT DOWN BY A ROCK. ONE WRONG STEP AND BOOM. NO REASON TO THINK THE WHOLE STREAM AIN'T BOOBY-TRAPPED LIKE THAT.
SO YOU DIDN'T ADVANCE TO BE SURE?
SEEING AS TO HOW THE REST OF MY SQUAD WAS UNDER FIRE I DIDN'T THINK--
NO ONE IS ASKING YOU TO THINK, JUST REPORT BACK WHAT YOU SAW.
MUD TRACKS AND FOOTPRINTS INDICATE THEY PULLED HEAVY MUNITIONS UP THE HILL. HEAVIER THAN WE'VE SEEN. I WOULDN'T BE SURPRISED IF THEY SNAGGED A FEW M60'S OFF FALLEN 'COPTERS AND DUG INTO THE HILLS HERE TO MAKE THEIR STANDS.
SHEEIT. WHEN'S AIR SUPPORT COMING?
COMMAND SAYS THEY ARE BOGGED DOWN AT KHE SANH. WE WANT THIS HILL, MEN, WE'VE GOT TO TAKE IT.
MEN, THIS IS WHERE LEGENDS ARE MADE. WE LET THIS HILL GET SECURED BY THESE GOOKS, WE'LL NEVER GET IT BACK. IF THERE'S NO WAY TO GET AROUND THEM, THEN WE'VE GOT TO GO STRAIGHT THROUGH THEM.
GOOD SPEECH, BUT WHAT'S THE FUCKING PLAN, O'BRIEN?. IF YOUR SHINE IS RIGHT, OUR BOYS WILL GET TORN APART AS SOON AS THE NVA SEES THEM.
SO WE SEND A SCOUTING PARTY, AT NIGHT. AND I KNOW THE PERFECT SOLDIERS TO BLEND INTO THE NIGHT.

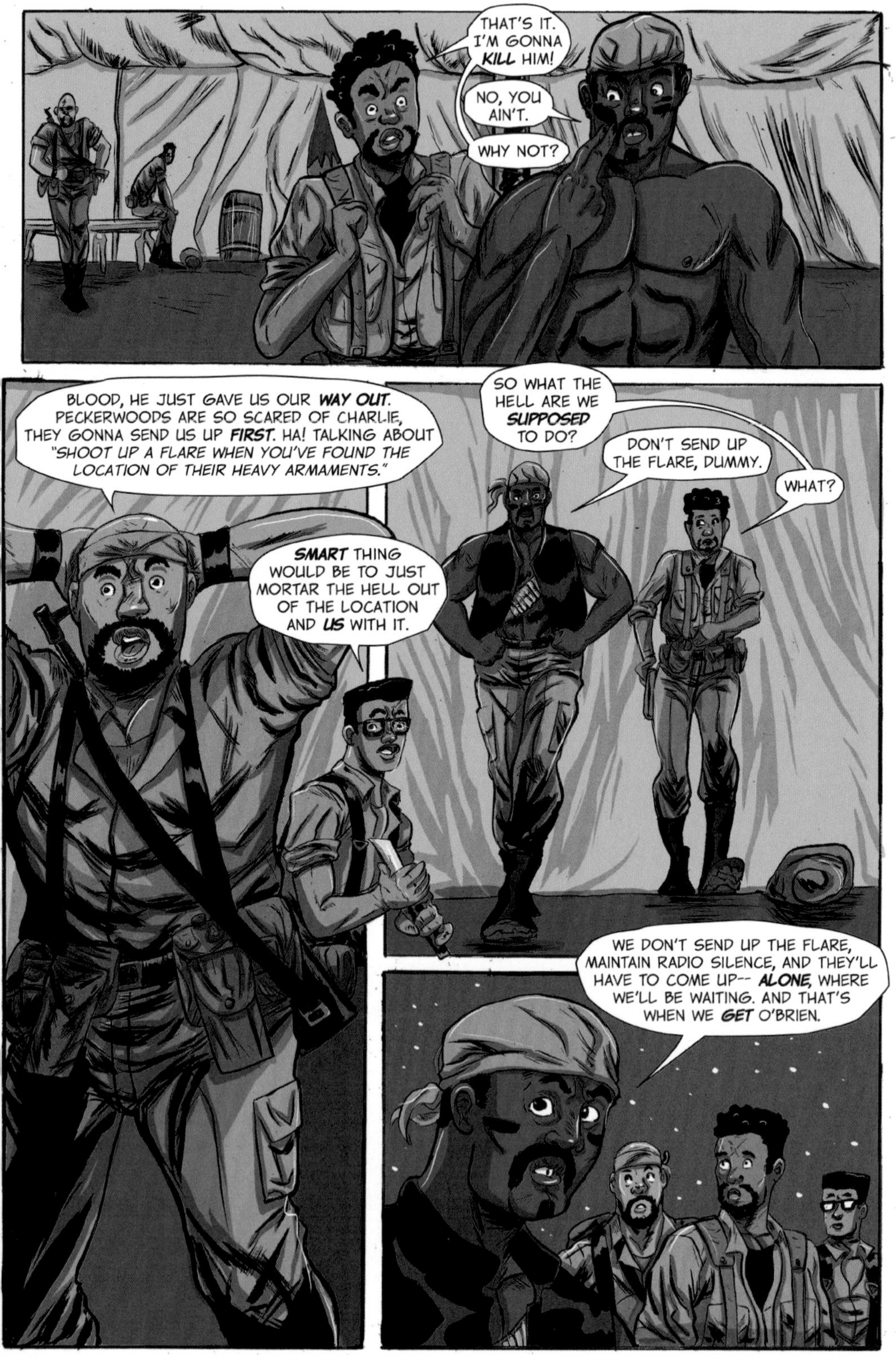
THAT'S IT. I'M GONNA KILL HIM!
NO, YOU AIN'T.
WHY NOT?
BLOOD, HE JUST GAVE US OUR WAY OUT. PECKERWOODS ARE SO SCARED OF CHARLIE, THEY GONNA SEND US UP FIRST. HA! TALKING ABOUT "SHOOT UP A FLARE WHEN YOU'VE FOUND THE LOCATION OF THEIR HEAVY ARMAMENTS."
SMART THING WOULD BE TO JUST MORTAR THE HELL OUT OF THE LOCATION AND US WITH IT.
SO WHAT THE HELL ARE WE SUPPOSED TO DO?
DON'T SEND UP THE FLARE, DUMMY.
WHAT?
WE DON'T SEND UP THE FLARE, MAINTAIN RADIO SILENCE, AND THEY'LL HAVE TO COME UP-- ALONE, WHERE WE'LL BE WAITING. AND THAT'S WHEN WE GET O'BRIEN.

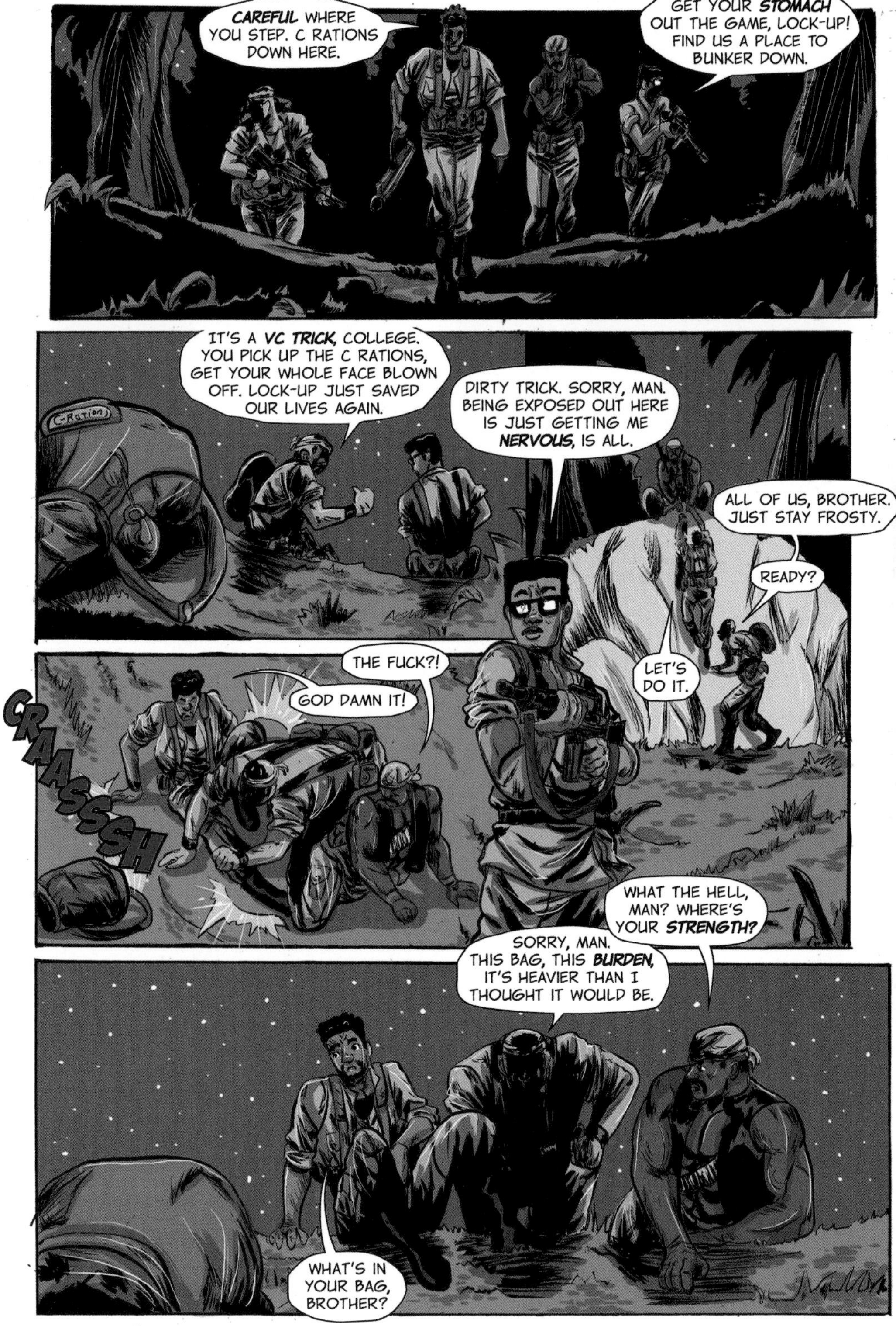
CAREFUL WHERE YOU STEP. C RATIONS DOWN HERE.
GET YOUR STOMACH OUT THE GAME, LOCK-UP! FIND US A PLACE TO BUNKER DOWN.
IT'S A VC TRICK, COLLEGE. YOU PICK UP THE C RATIONS, GET YOUR WHOLE FACE BLOWN OFF. LOCK-UP JUST SAVED OUR LIVES AGAIN.
C-RATION
DIRTY TRICK. SORRY, MAN. BEING EXPOSED OUT HERE IS JUST GETTING ME NERVOUS, IS ALL.
ALL OF US, BROTHER. JUST STAY FROSTY.
READY?
LET'S DO IT.
CRAASSSH
THE FUCK?!
GOD DAMN IT!
WHAT THE HELL, MAN? WHERE'S YOUR STRENGTH?
SORRY, MAN. THIS BAG, THIS BURDEN, IT'S HEAVIER THAN I THOUGHT IT WOULD BE.
WHAT'S IN YOUR BAG, BROTHER?

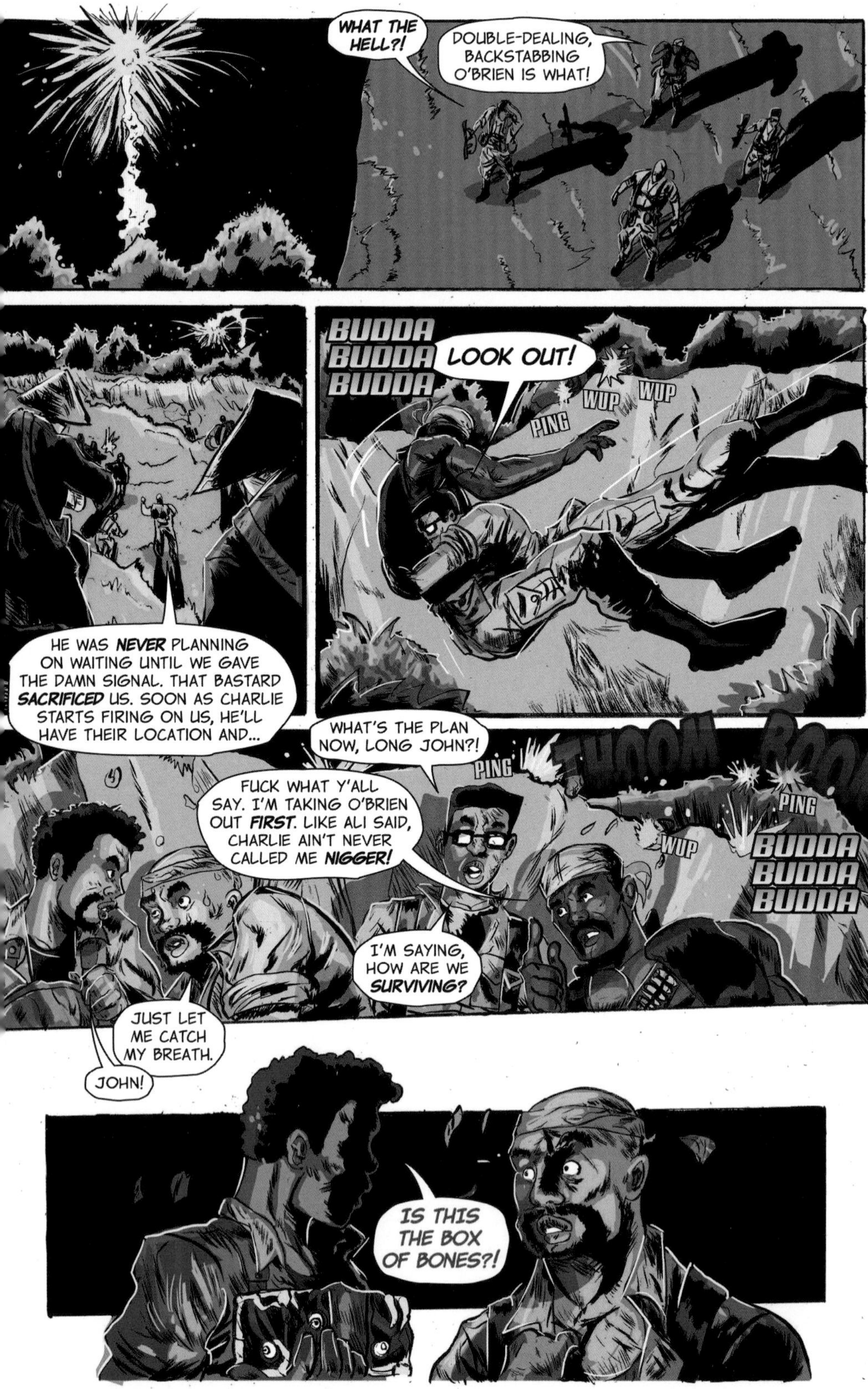
WHAT THE HELL?!
DOUBLE-DEALING, BACKSTABBING O'BRIEN IS WHAT!
HE WAS NEVER PLANNING ON WAITING UNTIL WE GAVE THE DAMN SIGNAL. THAT BASTARD SACRIFICED US. SOON AS CHARLIE STARTS FIRING ON US, HE'LL HAVE THEIR LOCATION AND...
BUDDA BUDDA BUDDA
LOOK OUT!
PING
WUP
WUP
WHAT'S THE PLAN NOW, LONG JOHN?!
PING
THOOM
PING
WUP
BUDDA BUDDA BUDDA
FUCK WHAT Y'ALL SAY. I'M TAKING O'BRIEN OUT FIRST. LIKE ALI SAID, CHARLIE AIN'T NEVER CALLED ME NIGGER!
I'M SAYING, HOW ARE WE SURVIVING?
JUST LET ME CATCH MY BREATH.
JOHN!
IS THIS THE BOX OF BONES?!

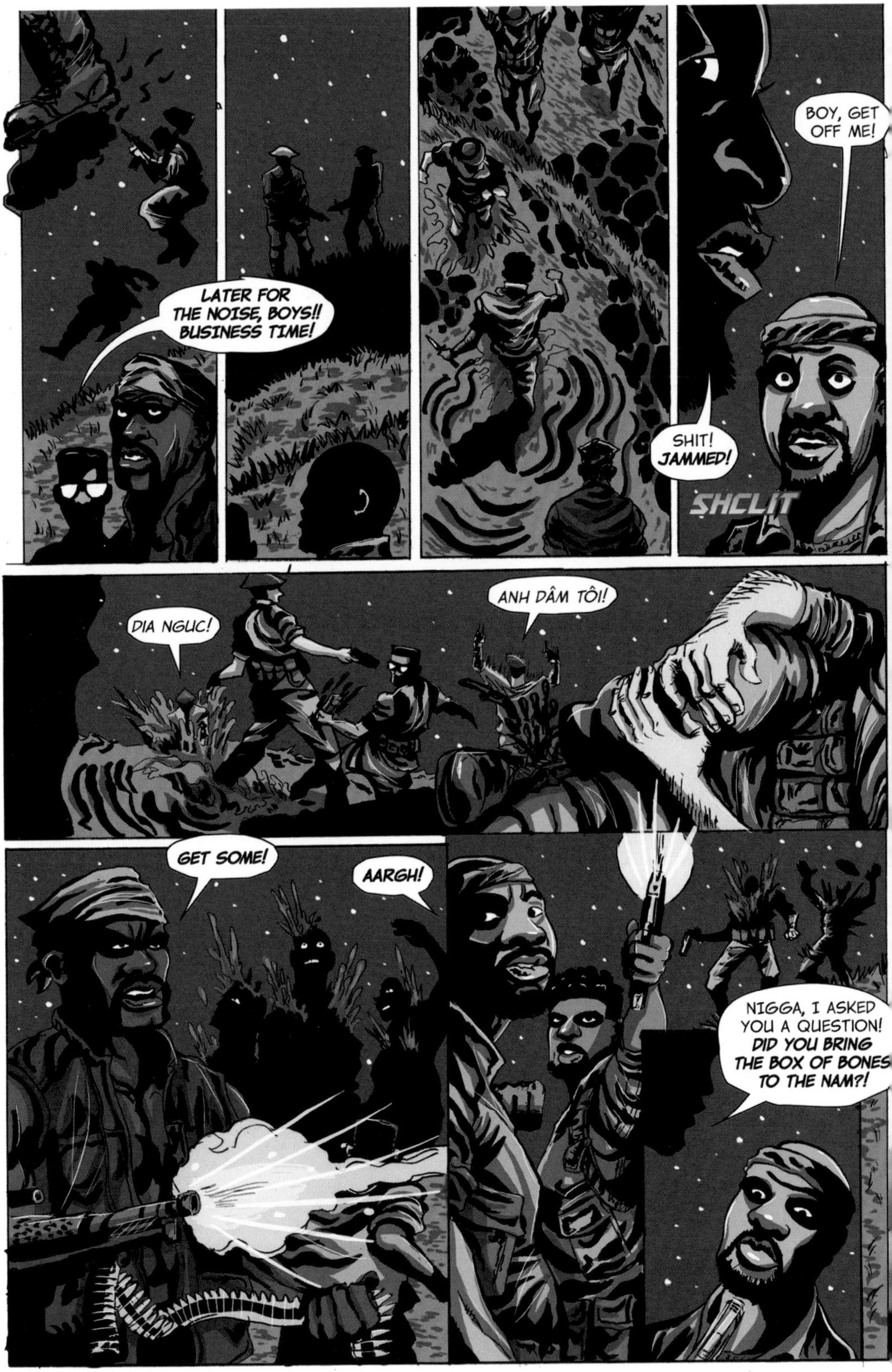
LATER FOR THE NOISE, BOYS!! BUSINESS TIME!
BOY, GET OFF ME!
SHIT! JAMMED!
SHCLIT
DIA NGUC!
ANH DÂM TÔI!
GET SOME!
AARGH!
NIGGA, I ASKED YOU A QUESTION! DID YOU BRING THE BOX OF BONES TO THE NAM?!

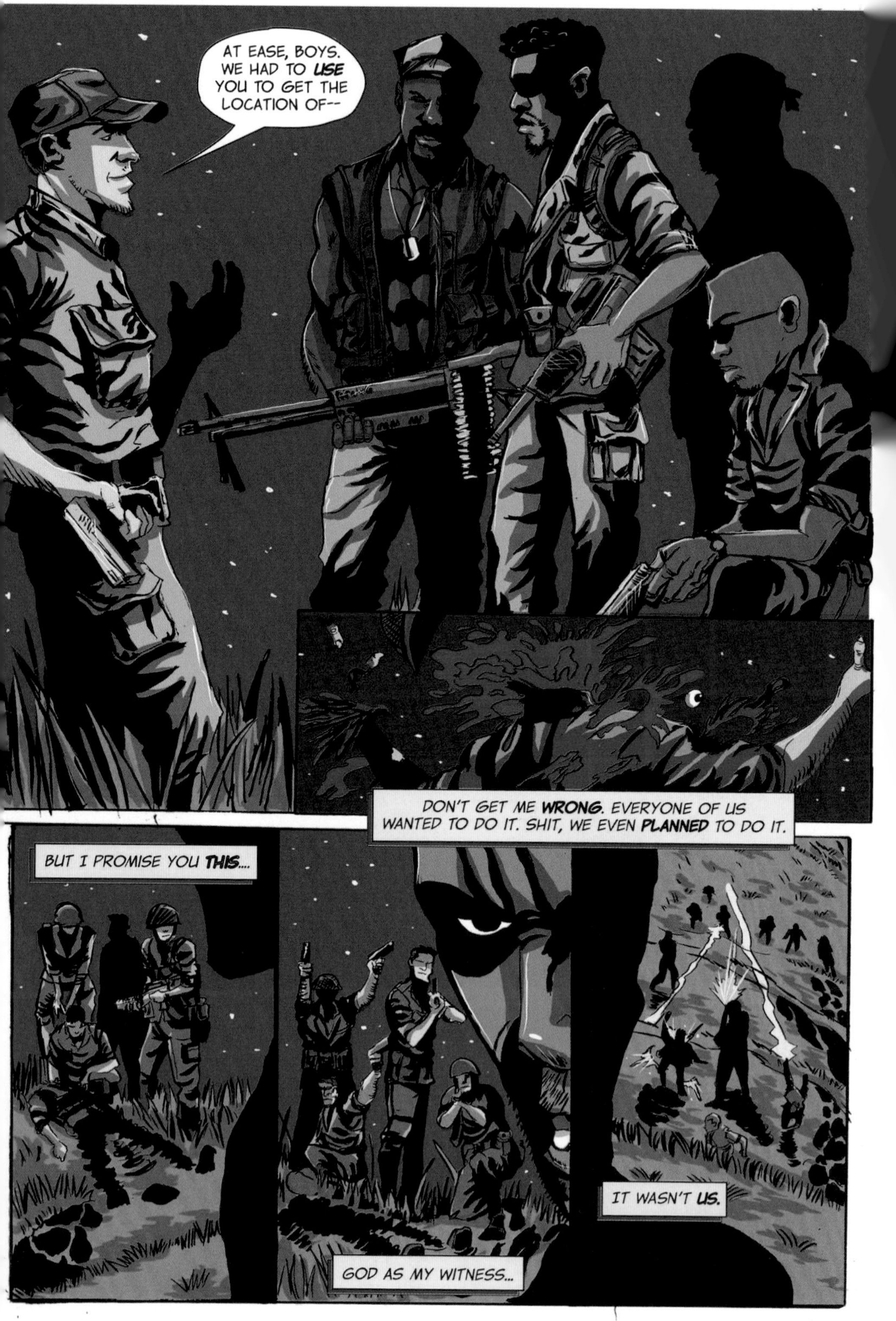
AT EASE, BOYS. WE HAD TO USE YOU TO GET THE LOCATION OF--
DON'T GET ME WRONG. EVERYONE OF US WANTED TO DO IT. SHIT, WE EVEN PLANNED TO DO IT.
BUT I PROMISE YOU THIS...
GOD AS MY WITNESS...
IT WASN'T US.

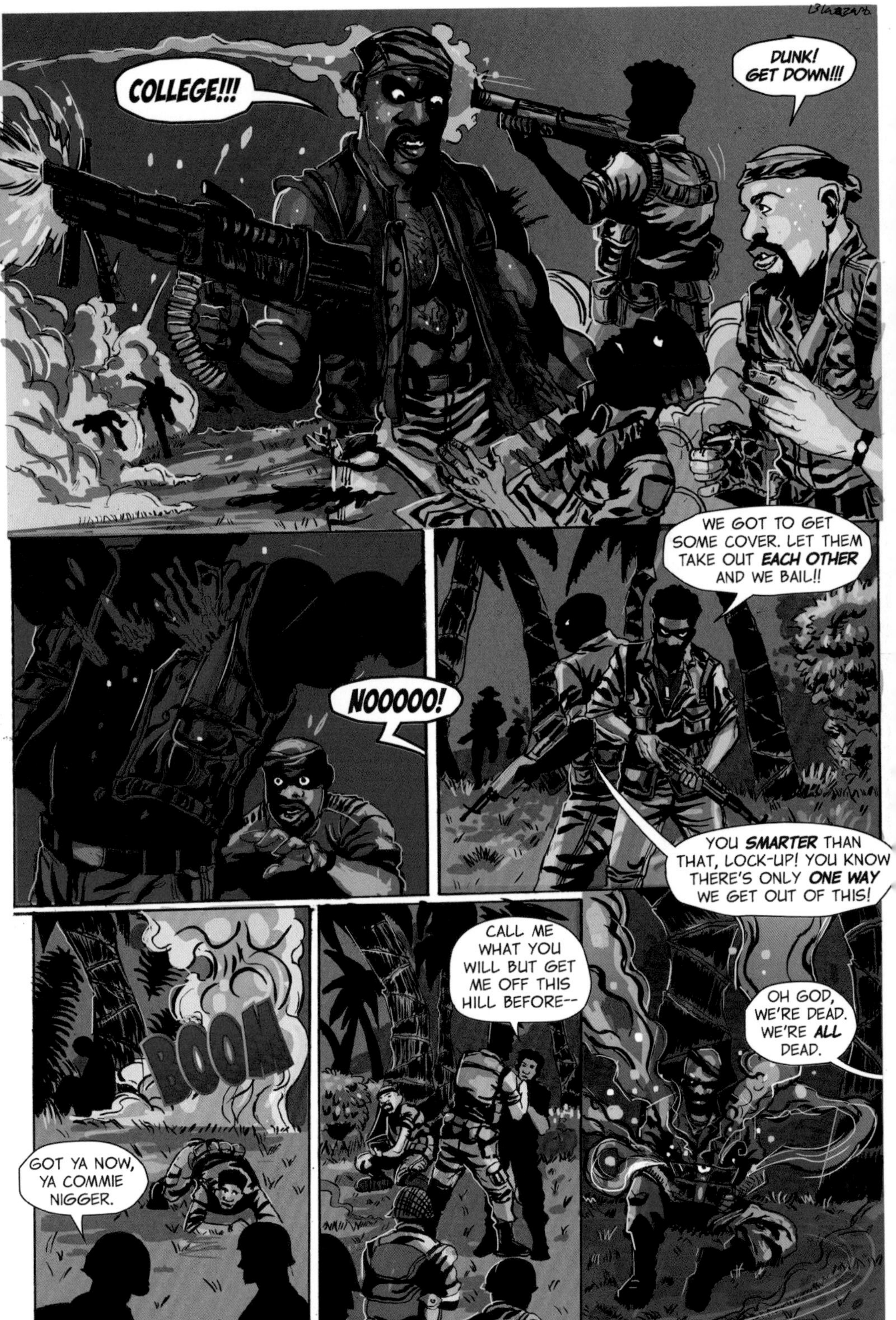
COLLEGE!!!
DUNK! GET DOWN!!!
NOOOOO!
WE GOT TO GET SOME COVER. LET THEM TAKE OUT EACH OTHER AND WE BAIL!!
YOU SMARTER THAN THAT, LOCK-UP! YOU KNOW THERE'S ONLY ONE WAY WE GET OUT OF THIS!
BOOM
GOT YA NOW, YA COMMIE NIGGER.
CALL ME WHAT YOU WILL BUT GET ME OFF THIS HILL BEFORE--
OH GOD, WE'RE DEAD. WE'RE ALL DEAD.

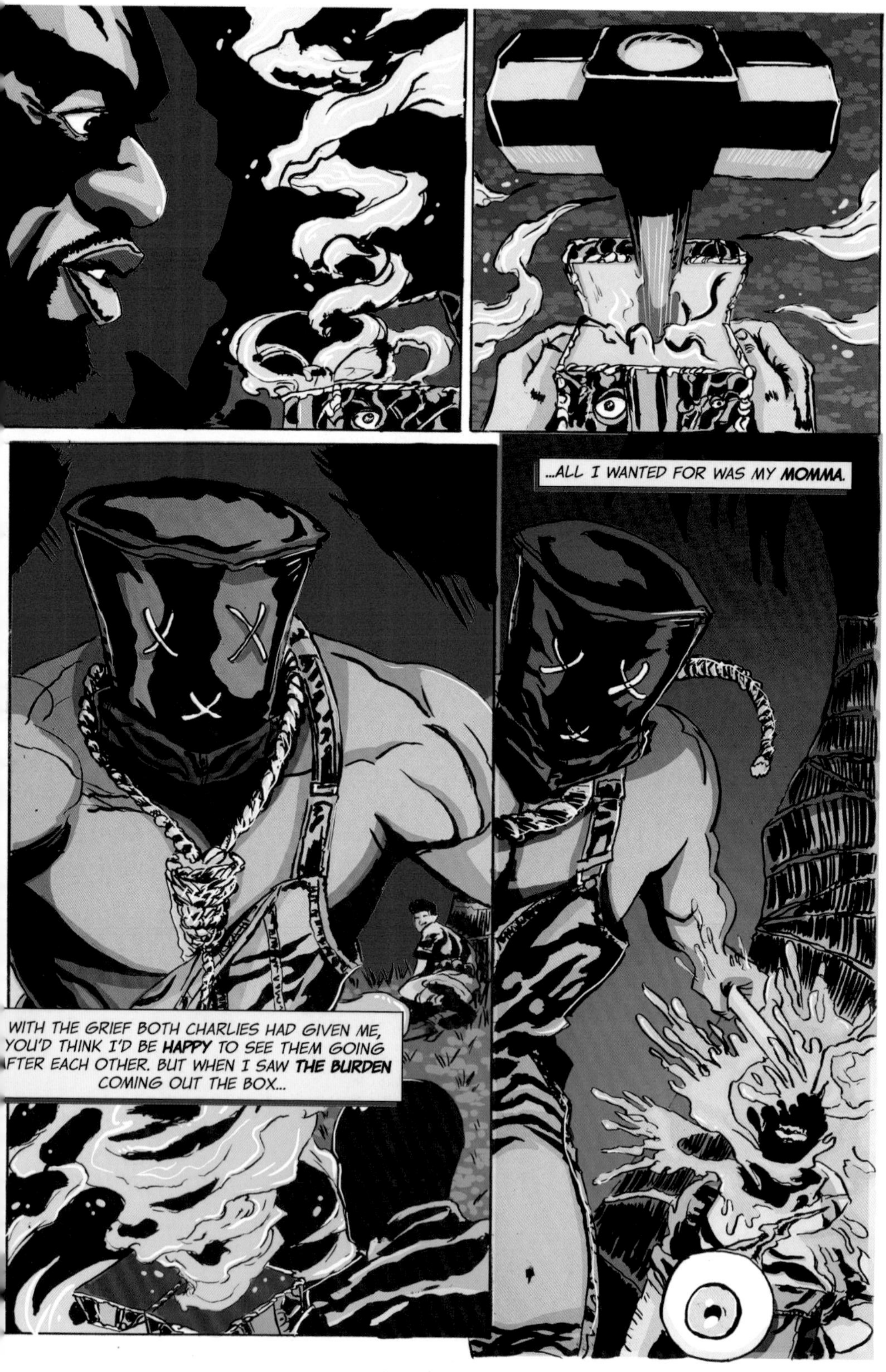
WITH THE GRIEF BOTH CHARLIES HAD GIVEN ME, YOU'D THINK I'D BE HAPPY TO SEE THEM GOING AFTER EACH OTHER. BUT WHEN I SAW THE BURDEN COMING OUT THE BOX...
...ALL I WANTED FOR WAS MY MOMMA.

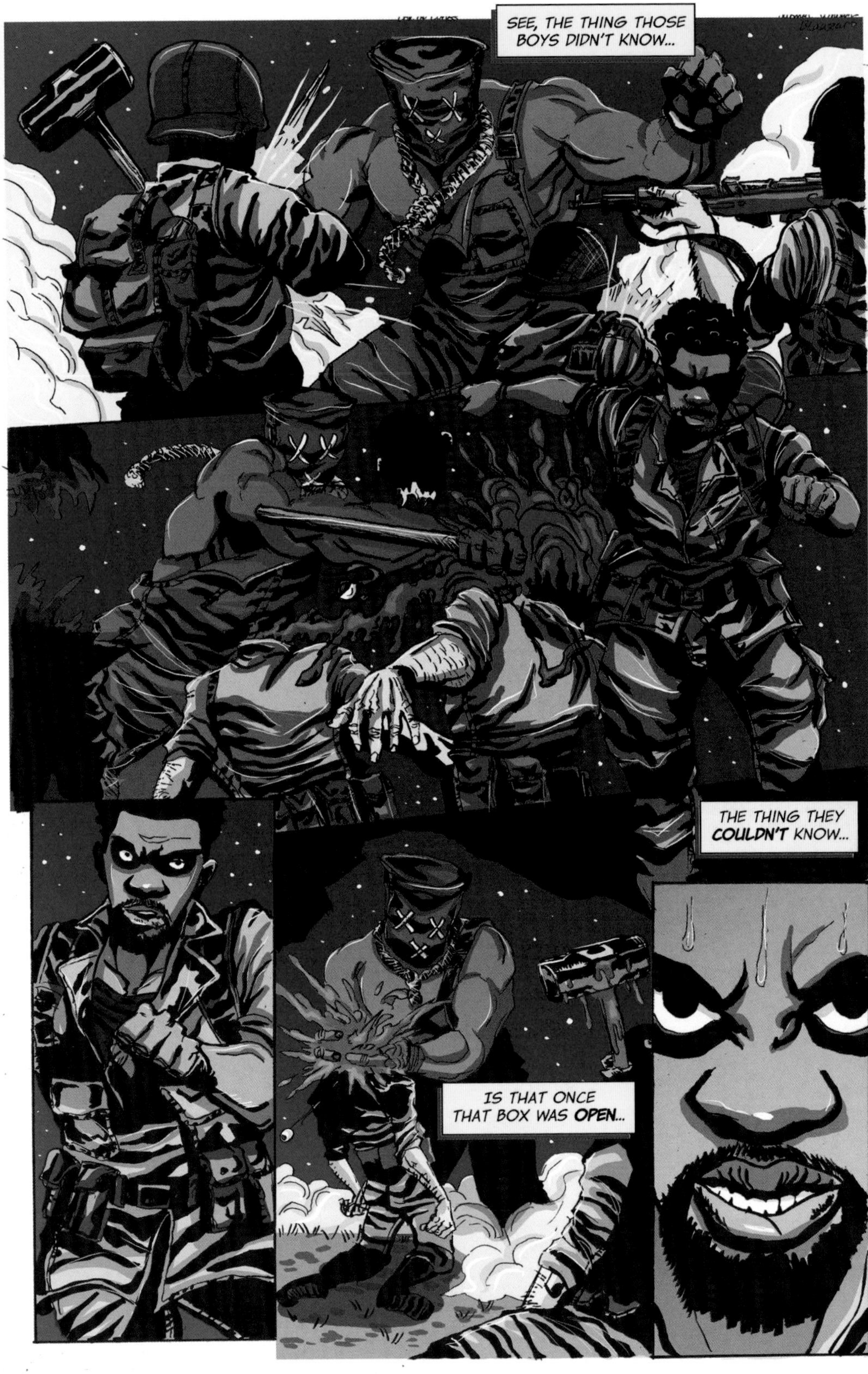
SEE, THE THING THOSE BOYS DIDN'T KNOW...
THE THING THEY **COULDN'T** KNOW...
IS THAT ONCE THAT BOX WAS **OPEN**...

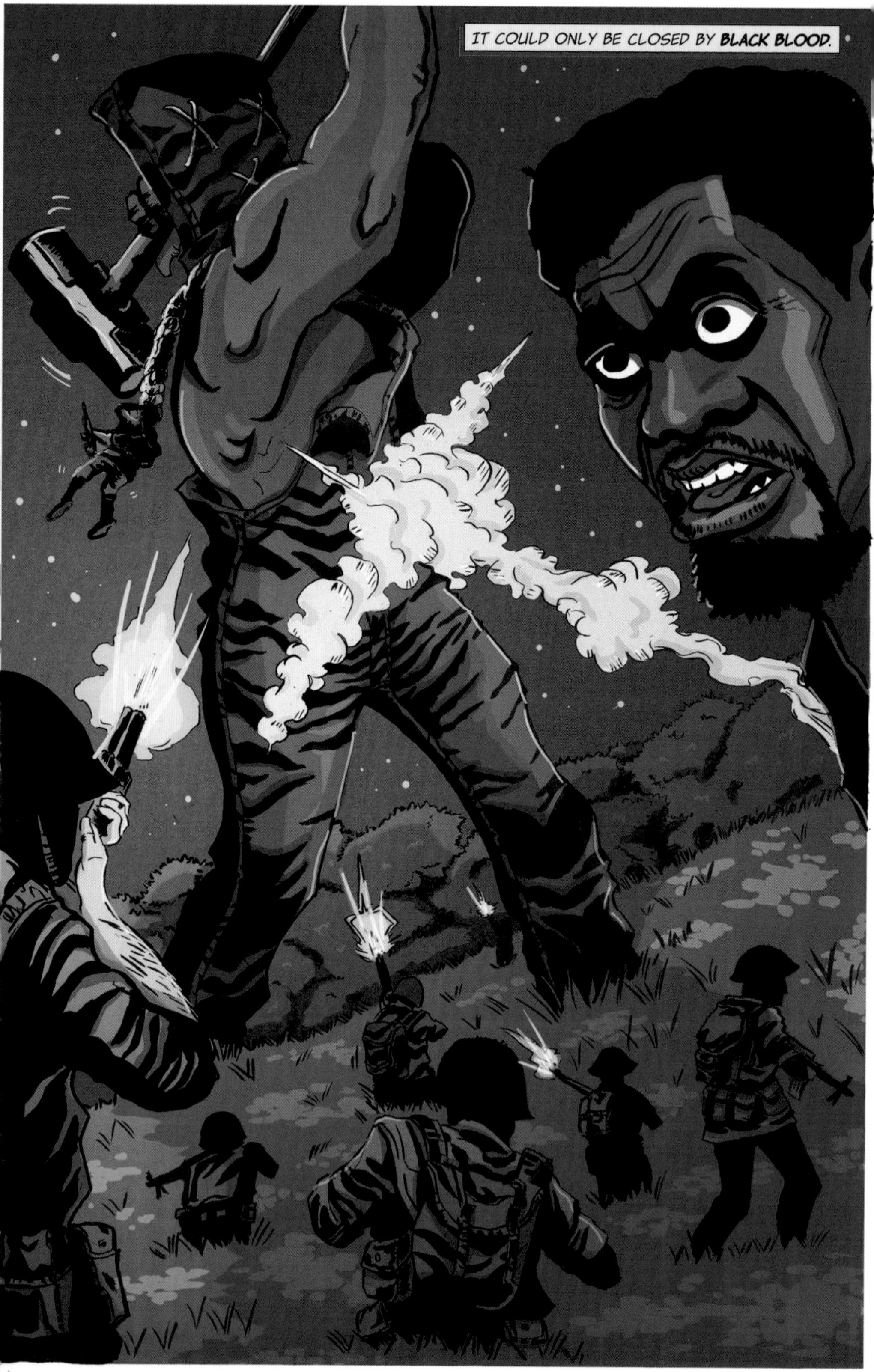
IT COULD ONLY BE CLOSED BY BLACK BLOOD.

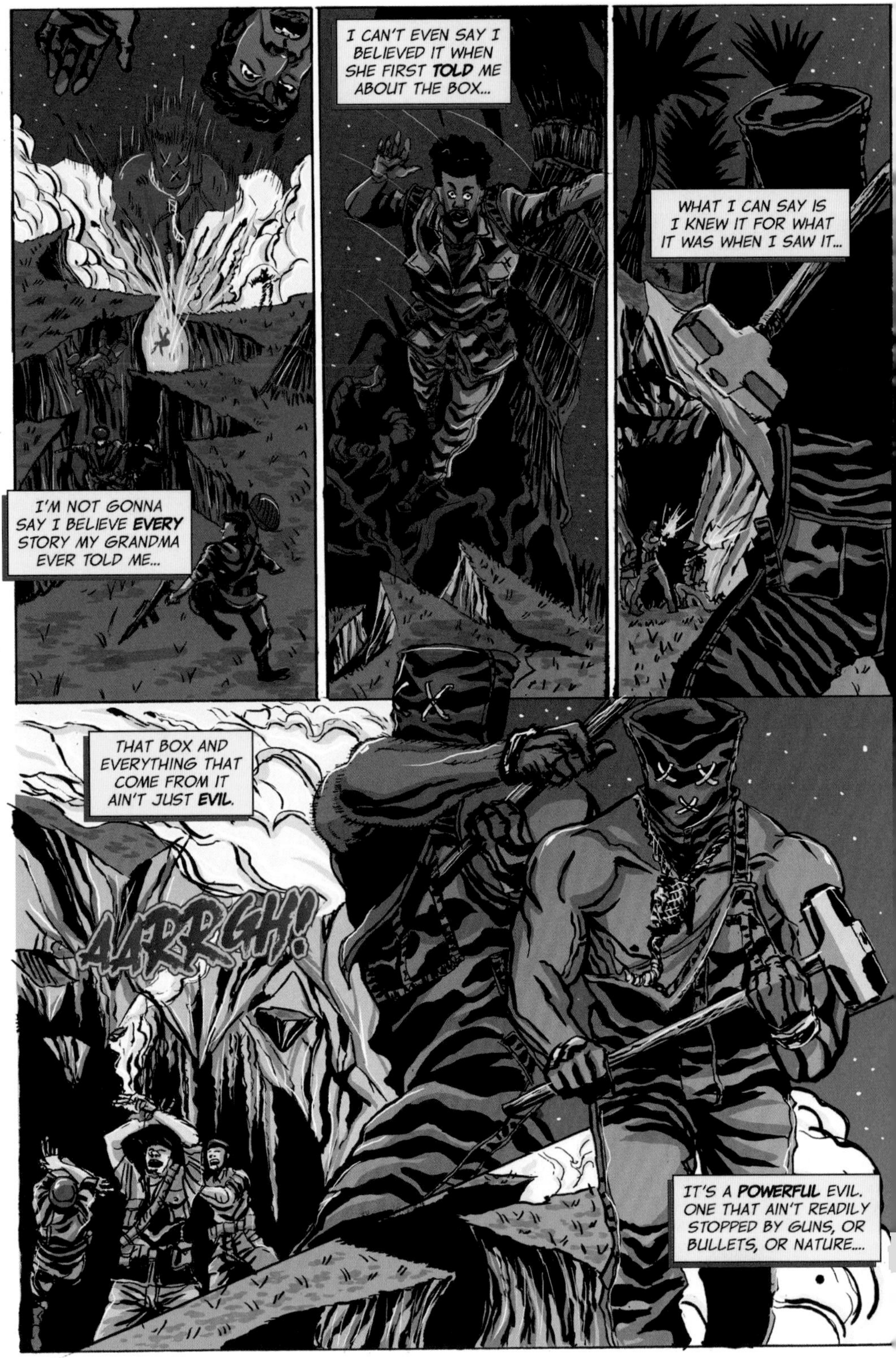
I'M NOT GONNA SAY I BELIEVE EVERY STORY MY GRANDMA EVER TOLD ME...
I CAN'T EVEN SAY I BELIEVED IT WHEN SHE FIRST TOLD ME ABOUT THE BOX...
WHAT I CAN SAY IS I KNEW IT FOR WHAT IT WAS WHEN I SAW IT...
THAT BOX AND EVERYTHING THAT COME FROM IT AIN'T JUST EVIL.
AARRGH!
IT'S A POWERFUL EVIL. ONE THAT AIN'T READILY STOPPED BY GUNS, OR BULLETS, OR NATURE....

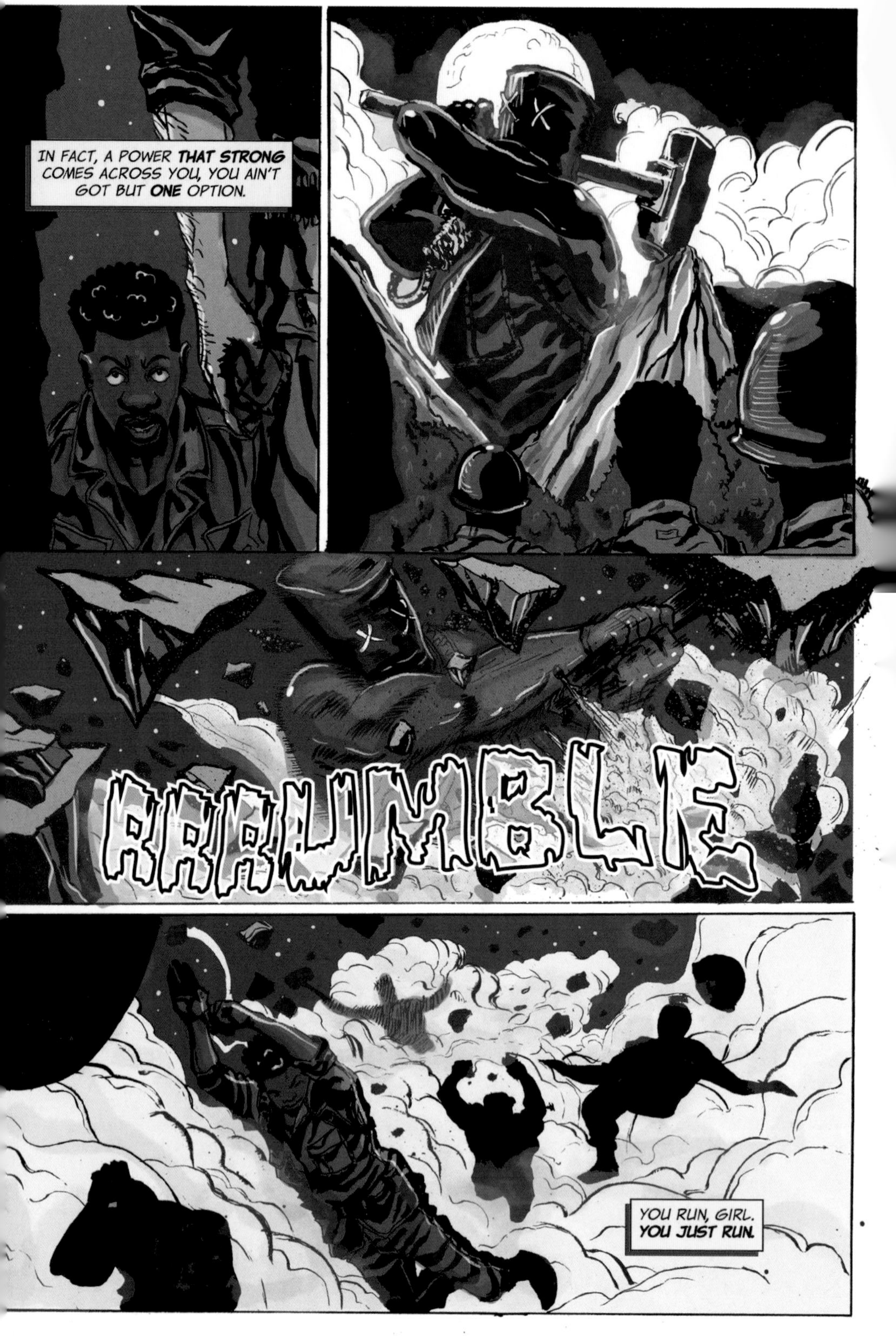
IN FACT, A POWER **THAT STRONG** COMES ACROSS YOU, YOU AIN'T GOT BUT **ONE** OPTION.
RRRUMBLE
YOU RUN, GIRL. **YOU JUST RUN.**

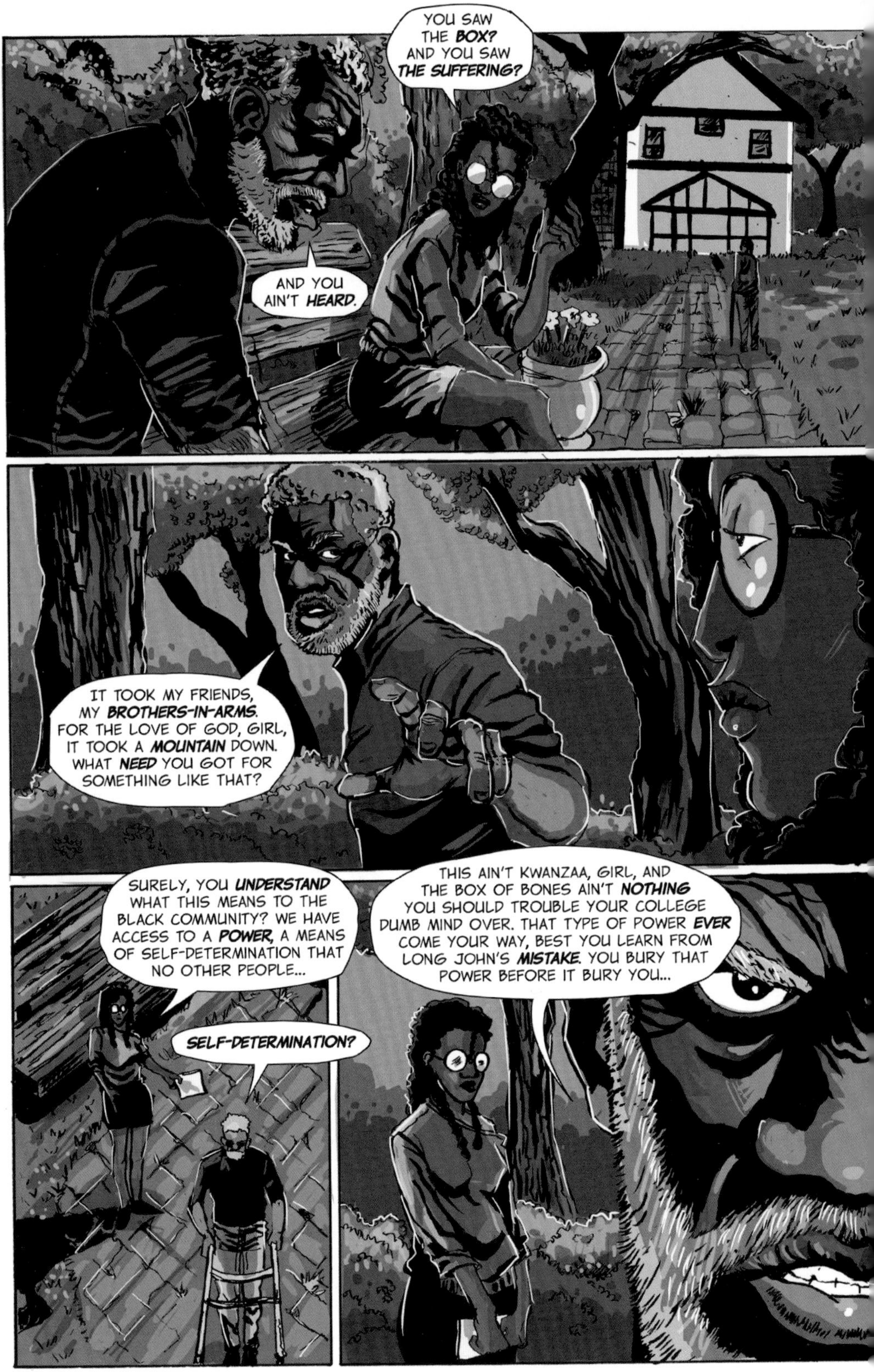
YOU SAW THE **BOX?** AND YOU SAW **THE SUFFERING?**
AND YOU AIN'T **HEARD.**
IT TOOK MY FRIENDS, MY **BROTHERS-IN-ARMS**. FOR THE LOVE OF GOD, GIRL, IT TOOK A **MOUNTAIN** DOWN. WHAT **NEED** YOU GOT FOR SOMETHING LIKE THAT?
SURELY, YOU **UNDERSTAND** WHAT THIS MEANS TO THE BLACK COMMUNITY? WE HAVE ACCESS TO A **POWER,** A MEANS OF SELF-DETERMINATION THAT NO OTHER PEOPLE...
**SELF-DETERMINATION?**
THIS AIN'T KWANZAA, GIRL, AND THE BOX OF BONES AIN'T **NOTHING** YOU SHOULD TROUBLE YOUR COLLEGE DUMB MIND OVER. THAT TYPE OF POWER **EVER** COME YOUR WAY, BEST YOU LEARN FROM LONG JOHN'S **MISTAKE**. YOU BURY THAT POWER BEFORE IT BURY YOU...

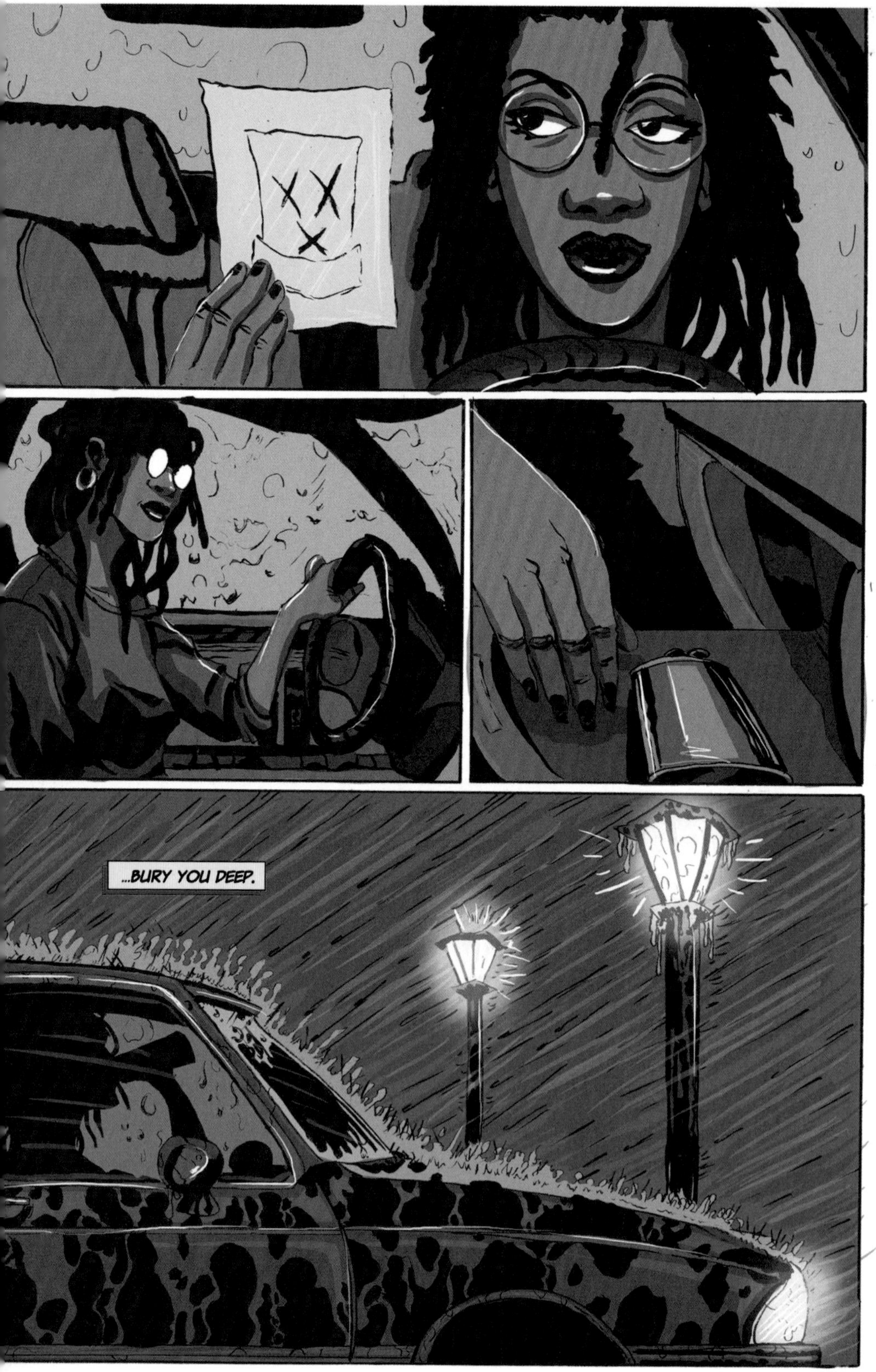
...BURY YOU DEEP.

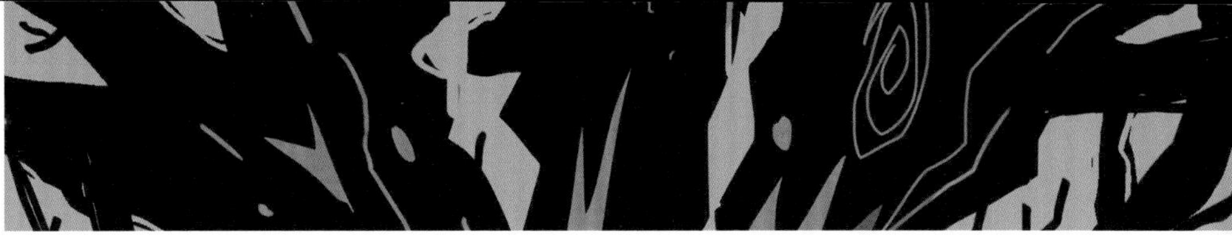

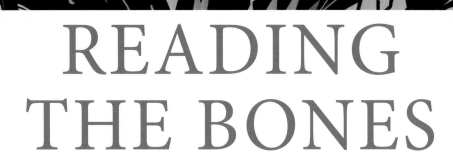

# READING THE BONES

*ESSAYS INSPIRED BY* ***BOX OF BONES***

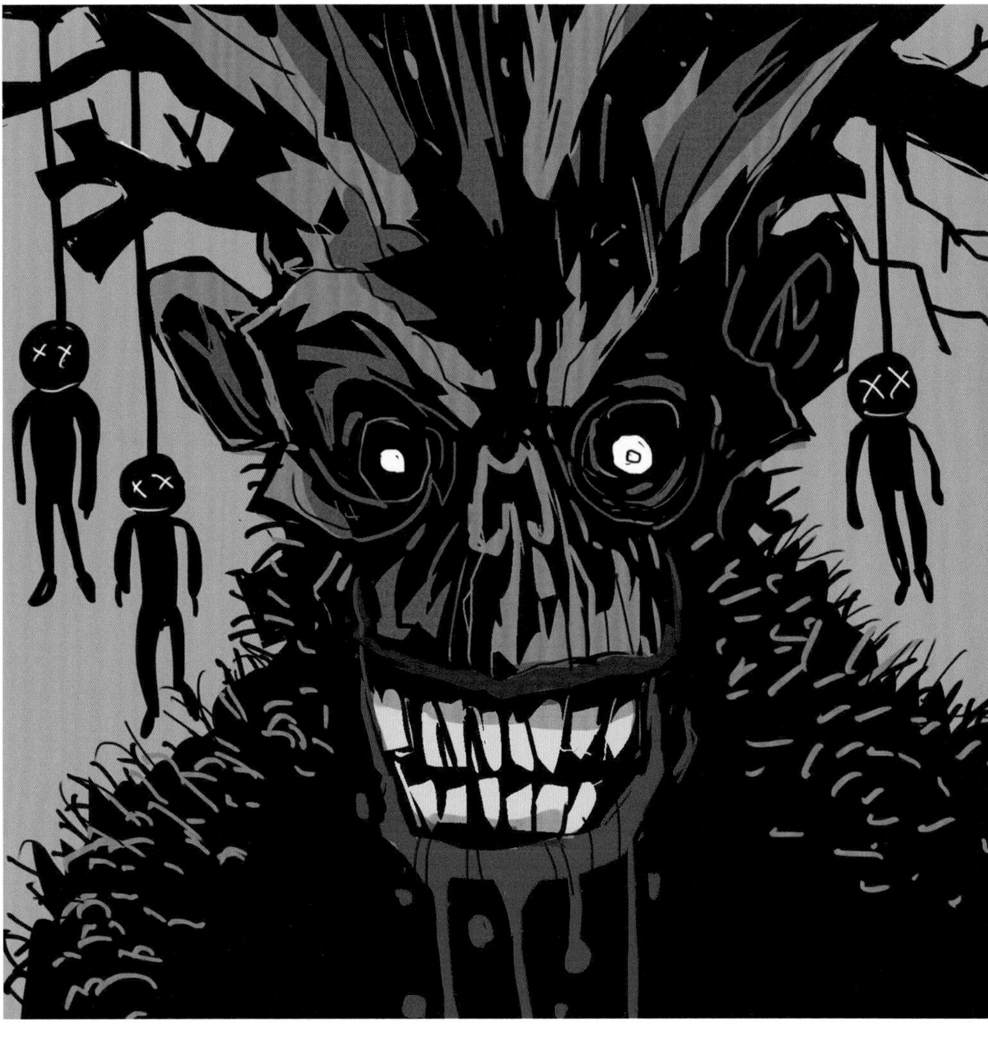

# SOUTHERN HORRORS AND THE BLACK GOTHIC

**Dr. Maisha Wester** is an Associate Professor in American Studies, and African American and African Diaspora Studies at Indiana University. She recently finished a Fulbright felllowship doing research in the UK where she was investigating Black Gothic writing as well as the deployment of Gothic tropes in British discourses on racial and ethnic subjects. Her first book, *African American Gothic: Screams from Shadowed Places* (2012), interrogates Black appropriations, revisions, and critiques of Gothic tropes and discourses. As one reviewer remarks "Nowhere else can readers so clearly grasp in so many examples so well analyzed how African American authors have radically transformed specifically Gothic conventions to make them profoundly symbolic of the horrors and complexities of the black American experience." She is currently completing her second book *Voodoo Queens and Zombie Lords: Haiti in U.S. Horror Cinema* as well as a co-edited collection titled Twenty-First Century Gothic.

American culture is inherently a Gothic culture, haunted by the shadows of an unresolved history that weighs heavily on its populace even as we attempt to repress its disturbing details. The coherence of America's idea of itself as an enlightened and progressive nation embodying the precepts of democracy depends upon repressing conflicting elements of national history—elements that reveal how our very democracy is founded upon the systemic oppression and structural disenfranchisement of minority groups. However, the American mythos is constantly threatened by the eruption of the repressed narratives, buried voices from the past rising to demand recognition of their sacrifice and retribution. Unable to utterly destroy or integrate such troublesome counternarratives into the dominant story, the nation abjects it onto a different space—a location which is not-quite-American. In doing so, the nation can acknowledge and scorn horrific histories of racial violence.

The South proves the location onto which we repeatedly abject histories of racial oppression, specifically between white Americans and African Americans. Deemed both exceptional and abnormal for social, economic, and political reasons, the South is made to embody and speak America's horrific racial past. Consequently, popular discourse creates the American South as a place haunted by the specters of America's racial crimes. Frequently depicted as a ruinous location, the Southern landscape conjures visions of decaying cemeteries ornamented by oaks draped in Spanish moss, dilapidated plantation estates, segregated towns, and desolate rural areas peopled by an impoverished, near skeletal populace. The South, haunted by a terrifying sociopolitical history, is made to function as America's Gothic Other.

Part of the reason for this depiction stems from the ways the South has lagged economically; as the larger nation moved away from agrarianism toward modern factories, the South remained the picture of agricultural society, thus out of keeping with U.S. industrialization and economic progress. A greater rationale for deeming the region "exceptional" is its seeming determination to hold on to its history as a location of political rebellion and difference, even though this history has explicit connections to racial oppression. Southern culture consistently proclaims this difference by championing the Rebel flag, the Rebel yell, and more recently, by commemorating April as Confederate History month in several states.

Notably, the signs of "Rebel history" also prove signs of how the South has placed itself outside the terrain of America's normative image—holding on to the Rebel yell among other historical signifiers means holding on to the defiance of America's idealized self-construction. Most importantly, this "Rebel history" is invariably a history of racial oppression and trauma. Southern gentility and charming culture, which is often the center of "Rebel" nostalgia, was rooted in an economic system dependent upon brutalized slave labor and thrived in a landscape flooded by bloodshed.

For Black writers the South is a gothic location of contradiction—detestable hell and comforting home, unspeakable violence and undeniable beauty, ancestral loss and ancestral origins. Slave narrators were the first to appropriate the Gothic genre to express the grotesque beauty of the South and its complex meanings for Blacks. Henry Bibb, for instance, remarks on how the region's beauty grew out of bloodshed and violence: slaves met with overseers each morning, their pine torches casting a light which looked beautiful from a distance. Jean Toomer's Cane is likewise littered with descriptions of lovely landscapes hiding broken and beaten Black bodies. Its poem "Portrait in Georgia" particularly epitomizes this juxtaposition, personifying the landscape in its description of a beautiful woman while also simultaneously describing the lynching of a Black person. Thus the poem renders the beauty of Southern nature and femininity in explicit connection to Black violation; it acknowledges the way female beauty produces violence against Blacks and, therefore, how such violation is intricately wound up in the landscape's beauty.

Ralph Ellison similarly deploys Gothic tropes throughout Invisible Man, but most explicitly in his depiction of the South. In doing so, he marks the South as a location of contradictions revealing an unresolved racial history that disrupts pretensions of progress. Ellison uses a mock pastoral tone to describe the Black university's grounds, overly emphasizing it as a locale of virginal innocence:

*the buildings were old and covered with vines [...] and wild roses that dazzled the eyes in the summer sun. Honeysuckle and purple wisteria hung heavy from the trees and white magnolias mixed with their scents in the bee-humming air. [....] How the grass turned green in the springtime and how the mocking birds fluttered their tails and sang, how the moon shone down on the buildings, how the bell in the chapel tower rang out the precious short-lived hours; how the girls in bright summer dresses promenaded the grassy lawn. Many times, here at night, I've closed my eyes and walked along the forbidden road that winds [... to] the bridge of rustic logs, made for trysting, but virginal and untested by lovers. (34-35)*

The passage uses overly sublime intonations, consequently turning the pastoral scene into a grotesque spectacle merely through its own inherent excess; its concluding sentence, abbreviated here, is a paragraph long, leaving one literally breathless when attempting to read it aloud. This breathlessness is re-presented in a later paragraph, literally punctuated with gasps: "Oh, long green stretch of campus, Oh, quiet songs at dusk, Oh, moon that kissed the steeple [...], Oh, bugle that called in the morning, Oh, drum that marched us militarily at noon" (36). Beneath such sublime, excessive beauty lies horror. The winding road leads to a ruinous landscape and ruined people: "the cabins surrounded by empty fields beyond red clay roads, and beyond a certain road a river, sluggish and covered with algae more yellow than green in its stagnant stillness; [...] where the disabled veterans visited the whores, hobbling down the tracks on crutches and canes; sometimes pushing the legless, thighless one in a red wheelchair" (35). The description emphasizes the economic and cultural death haunting the region; nothing grows here, and even the unwelcomed algae fails to thrive. Further, the grotesque veterans visiting "sad, sad whores" (35) contrast against the college's untested lovers to foretell the Black students' unfortunate futures.

Black texts are most Gothic in their inability to simply dismiss the South as a location of violence and terror. The South haunts as a crucial part of Black ancestry and culture. Toni Morrison captures this haunting in the recurrent jest about Sweet Home Plantation in Beloved: "it wasn't sweet and it sure wasn't home" (16). Yet as much as Sethe's and Paul D's comment attempts to deny the plantation, Sweet Home was a kind of home, horror-ridden though it was; the slaves formed familial and romantic bonds there, though white masters could rupture these bonds.

Beloved's plantation rewrites the Gothic notion of the haunted house—a home haunted by horrible histories that project themselves into the present moment, resulting in unspeakable violence to and among the family members. Haunted houses embody the Freudian idea of the uncanny as that which is both home(ly) and familiar but also strange and alienating. According to Freud's theory, what's most horrible about the haunted home are not intrusions from without, but the skeletons lurking within and around which the welcoming familial home is built. The Southern region as a whole may be understood as the "haunted house" of the Black Gothic, hiding complex and horrible truths we prefer to forget but also the location that remains "home."

The prefacing pages to Gloria Naylor's Mama Day similarly alludes to and reveals the complexity of the South as uncanny "home." Although the text is a work of magical realism, it too is marked by Gothic turns stemming from the unresolvable history that confronts us in the preface. On the first prefacing page the novel depicts a family tree; the second prefacing page depicts a bill of sale for a slave woman. Juxtaposed as they are, the text suggests that these are two organizing and foundational moments for the novel's story and its characters.

Further, the problem of irreconcilable history haunts throughout the novel in repeated speculations about the events of 1823, particularly the life of an enslaved woman Sapphira and the land that would become a Black town. Characters speculate on whether Sapphira was freed by a master she seduced and poisoned, whether she tricked him into deeding the land to her sons, or whether slave and master were involved in a mutually affectionate relationship. Most importantly, the prefacing pages and speculations about 1823 allude to the ways in which Black experience in the South was complex, consisting of horror, objectification, and violation, but also the location of family and ancestry and where the relationships between masters and slaves may have hidden desires rendered illegible and disruptive to the dominant Black understandings of slavery and the South.

Octavia Butler's *Kindred* further complicates this horror, reproducing the relationship between slave and master as one of unspeakable (sexual) violence while also emphasizing how such violation is necessary to the production of contemporary Blacks. The text's nightmare isn't that the South is a location of such historic horrors but that those horrors too must be understood as constitutive of modern Black existence—Dana has to serve as an accomplice in the sexual exploitation of her Black maternal ancestor if she is to exist in the future.

The lesson of Dana's narrative clarifies another reason the South proves so haunted for Black authors—it's a location that threatens to rupture Black identity and collective memory with repressed and untold narratives surrounding intraracial violence. As much as slave narratives use Gothic tropes to convey the monstrosity of slave masters and the living death of slavery, the narratives are equally haunted by Black betrayal of other Blacks. For example, while authors such as Henry Brown define the rape of Black women as a source of "unspeakable" horror, it's an experience repeatedly spoken throughout the narratives; less detailed are the moments when slave husbands and fathers abandon their families in search of freedom. Understood together, the male narrator's need and willingness to leave his family utterly unprotected in the face of an institution that essentially encourages rape becomes the violence that is actually unspoken/unspeakable. Later writers, such as Tananarive Due, Alice Walker, and Randall Kenan, further explore this haunting legacy of intraracial violence. However, recognizing such aspects of Black experience in the region proves haunting as it disrupts our tidy narratives of identity, trauma, and history.

Overly marked by a horrendous history—in part by its own choice but also because of our collective fictions of it—the South is made to carry the burden of America's racial guilt. The nature of tourism in the South helps, in part, explain why it functions so readily as a Gothic locale for Blacks and dominant America. Notable in the South are its historic plantations whose narratives emphasize the pastoral life of the white masters. Further, many former plantations have been converted into bed and breakfast retreats—providing locations for lovers to marry and begin a bright future. Lurking just beneath this beauty is the horrific violence Blacks suffered in this region for most of their existence in the U.S.—from slavery through Reconstruction to the Jim Crow era and beyond. Thus visitors and newlyweds wander at the regional splendor while treading across blood-soaked ground. The very erasure of their bodies and losses from contemporary narratives provides Black authors with a shudder.

From Forsyth, Georgia, to Kirvin, Texas, the U.S. South is home to horrific (hi) stories of brutal lynching and sexual assault. Yet, as the brutal deaths of Amadou Diallo, Michael Brown, Eric Garner, Philando Castile, and numerous others reveal, demonization of the South as the Gothic location of exceptional racial violence is in part an invention—outbreaks of racialized violence reveal how the American land-scape has historically been and remains baptized in the blood of minorities. The haunting song of Southern violence, "Strange Fruit," was based upon the lynching of two black men in Indiana. Gordon Parks's variation on Grant Woods's American Gothic is located everywhere and no "where"—posing its lonely Black woman in a stark room against the bar-like stripes of the U.S. flag.

When Black writers turn to the Gothic South for their nightmarish visions, they aren't talking about that haunted region alone, thereby perpetuating notions of re-gional exceptionalism that divert attention from the continuing nefarious system of racial oppression throughout the U.S. Rather Black authors' depiction of the Gothic South should be read as a synecdoche for the larger nation; despite their seemingly specific setting, Black authors often affirm Malcolm X's oft-quoted line: anything south of Canada is The South.

**Works Cited**

Ellison, Ralph. *Invisible Man*. New York, NY: Vintage Books, 1952.

Morrison, Toni. *Beloved*. New York, NY: Vintage International Books, 2004.

**Suggestions for Bibliography**

Edwards, Justin. *Gothic Passages: Racial Ambiguity and the American Gothic*. Iowa City, IA: U. of Iowa P., 2003.

Goddu, Teresa A. "The African American Slave Narrative and the Gothic." *A Companion to American Gothic*. Ed. Charles L Crow. Somerset, NJ: John Wiley & Sons, 2013. 71-83
.

Wester, Maisha L. *African American Gothic: Screams from Shadowed Places*. New York, NY: Palgrave, 2012.

# THE WOMAN WITHOUT SKIN

Dr. Susana Morris is an associate professor of Literature, Media, and Communication at the Georgia Institute of Technology. She is co-founder and contributing writer for the popular feminist blog, **The Crunk Feminist Collective**. Her first book, *Close Kin and Distant Relatives: The Paradox of Respectability in Black Women's Literature*, was published from the University of Virginia Press in 2014. Her most recent books are the anthology *The Crunk Feminist Collection*, which was co-edited with Brittney Cooper and Robin Boylorn (The Feminist Press 2017) and *Sycorax's Daughters* (Cedar Grove 2017), a short story collection of horror written by Black women co-edited with Kinitra D. Brooks and Linda Addison. Morris is also series editor, along with Kinitra D. Brooks, of the book series **New Suns: Race, Gender, and Sexuality in the Speculative**, published at The Ohio State University Press. She is currently at work on her latest academic book project, which explores depictions of Black women vampires, Afrofuturism, and feminism.

I learned early on that there was just a thin veil between this world and the next. As a child of the global South growing up in Caribbean-American and African American communities, regular everyday conversation flitted easily between who recently had a baby or who was sleeping with such and such and who was working roots or witchcraft. My child's ears would perk up and strain to hear how to get rid of the evil eye or what to do if some tried to obeah you. My mother thought I was far too inquisitive and always said, "Little pigs have big ears," when she wanted to keep her adult conversations private. I would pretend to be uninterested and walk away, but I still listened, trying to be quiet as I crouched in the hallway, eavesdropping.

Still, I didn't learn everything through eavesdropping. Often my mother told me stories about back home in Jamaica. She told me stories about that old trickster Anancy and how he was always getting in and out of trouble. She told me about duppies and rolling calves and how to be careful at night, especially around graveyards. I learned early on to be scared of the rippling of the veil, as the sound that woke me up in the middle of the night could be my older self rumbling around for some water in the kitchen or it could be a mischievous duppy making noise to lure me away. Mama's stories told me that the veil between this world and the next one was not only thin, it was also translucent. You could see through it and they, the others on the other side of the veil, could see you, too. And so your late loved one might come to you in a dream and tell you which numbers to play or show up at your back doorstep ready to take you away—who was to say how a jumbie might behave. You just had to stay ready. It didn't matter that we were here in a new place. The veil was here, too. The Black people we lived around, whether they were West Indian or transplants from the South, had the same stories. And the same restless dead.

There was one story in particular that has always stayed with me. According to my mother, years ago there once was a rich woman who lived in a big fine house. She had a husband who was a strong, domineering man. He was also very jealous and made her stay at home all day and not even leave the grounds. But at night, when her husband was asleep, she would take off her skin and fly around town. She could float high above the house, the woodland, even the whole countryside. She would fly free all night long. No one could tell her where to go or what to do. But she would have to get back before sunrise, when her husband would wake up or else he might find her skin before she could slip back into it.

This went on for many years. Over time, however, the husband had begun to be suspicious like when he would roll over and did not feel his wife in the bed with him at night. He decided to investigate: he would pretend to be asleep and see what his wife was up to. Night came and, like usual, the woman shrugged out of her skin and stepped in the night, riding the wind currents up and above the clouds. Imagine her husband's surprise when he saw the shriveled husk of his wife's skin and her escaping him for hours every night. Enraged, the man put hot peppers all over her skin and put it back where the woman left it. He laid in wait for her. When she returned from her nightly flight, she slipped back in her skin. She screamed as the hot pepper melted into her body, burning her from the inside out, killing her.

My mother would then say that, "Every shut eye is not sleep," and that the woman's tortured soul still flew out and that, if you weren't careful, she might come visit you in the night. And that would be the end of you. She would frighten you to death and take your soul. Just like she did to her murderous husband one day.

I would have nightmares about the skinless woman floating above my city, my house, hovering above my bed, or I would think I'd seen her crouching down behind a darkened corner. She was still upset about losing her skin, and she wanted to make the rest of us pay, especially naughty little girls who didn't always listen to their mothers. But when I would look back, the woman would be gone.

Later, though, I realized that the story was more than just a folktale or a way to scare me into being obedient. The flying woman was a cautionary tale about control. This woman was moving freely without anyone's permission, and that made her dangerous.

The peppers were also important, especially as I learned how pepper was used in violent ways to control women. Years ago, particularly in rural areas, Caribbean women who were thought to be adulterers, or even just too outspoken or successful, were sometimes publicly assaulted with hot peppers. This socially sanctioned sexual assault was a way of policing a woman's power and pleasure and could prove fatal. It also proved instructive, reminding the other women watching the cost of being a threat to the social order.

But the tale of the woman without skin is instructive in another way. You could view her as doomed, but in another sense she has come into her own power, despite her husband's wish to kill her. Instead, his jealousy and rage made her a monster of his own undoing. Although she is never able to get back to her former life, she becomes even more powerful and more dangerous.

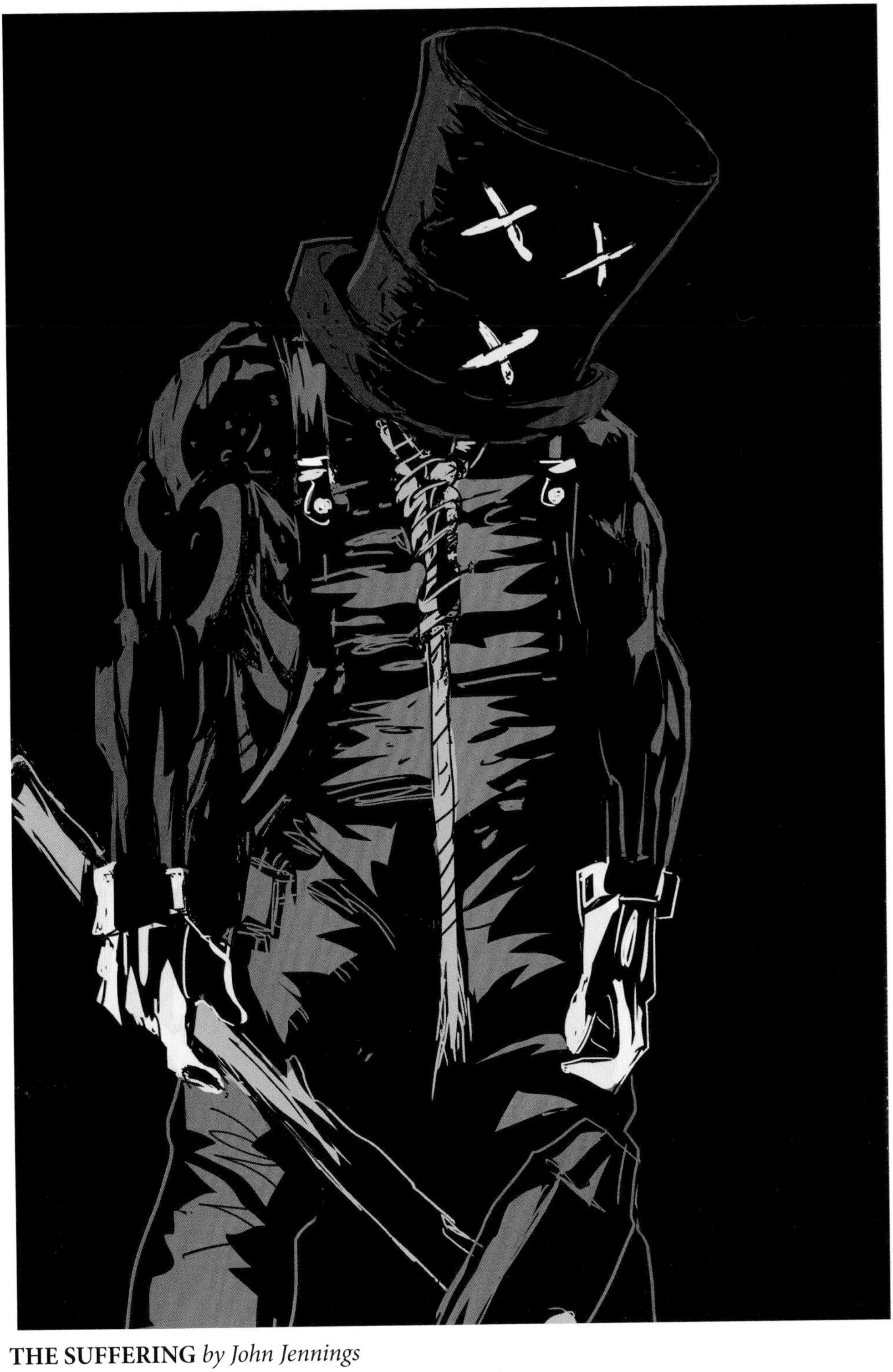

**THE SUFFERING** *by John Jennings*

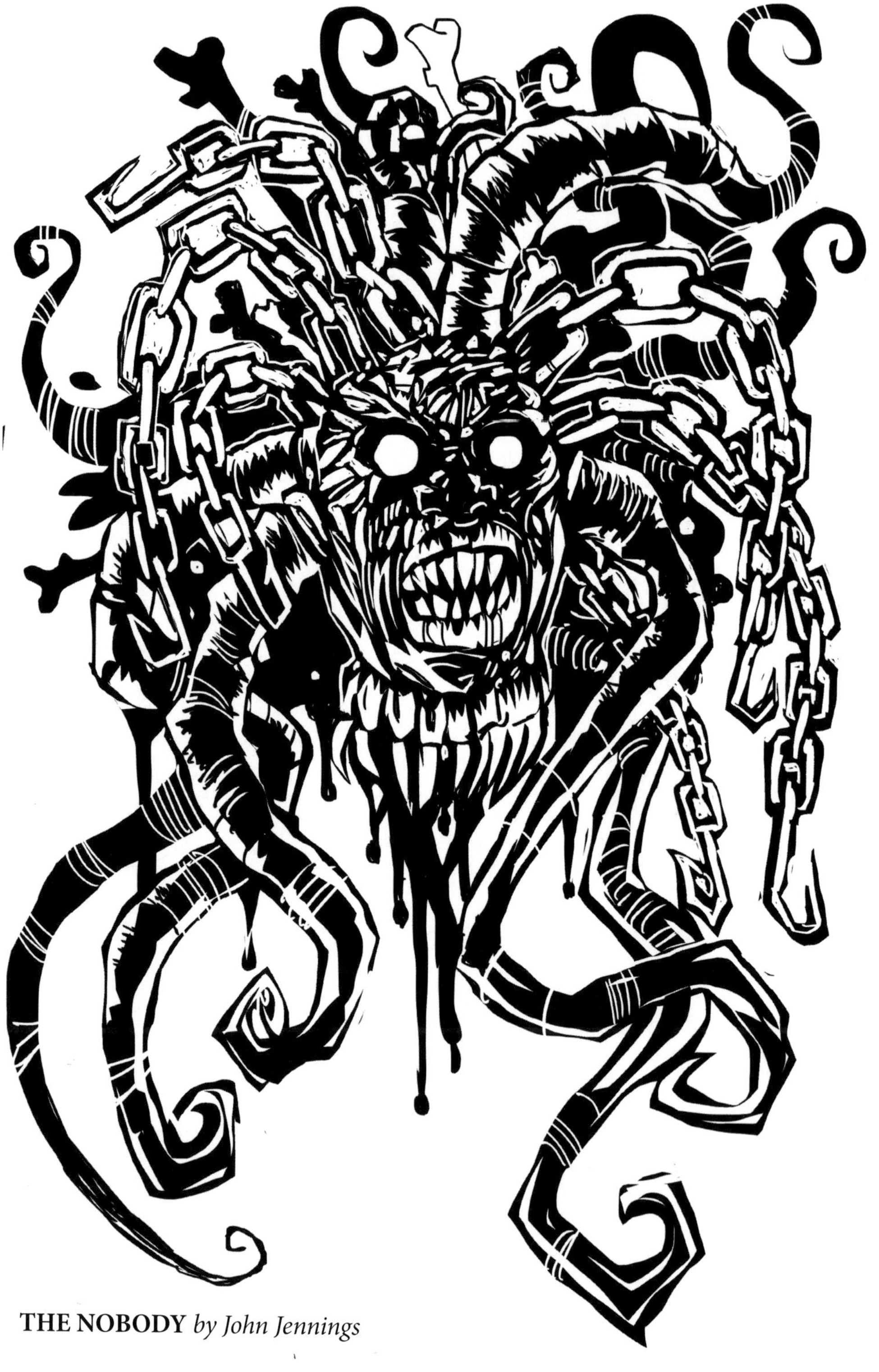

**THE NOBODY** *by John Jennings*

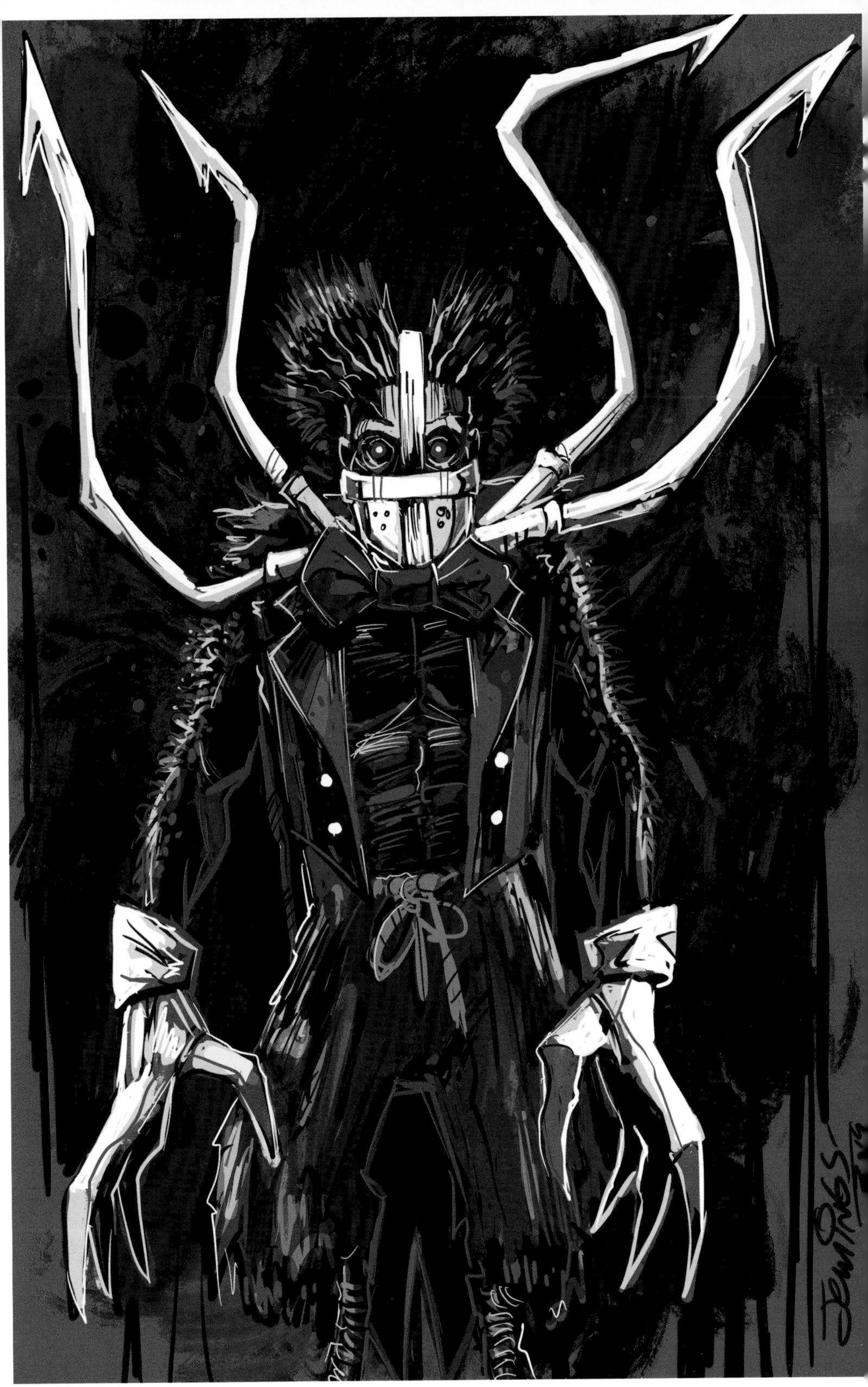

**THE DARK** *by John Jennings*

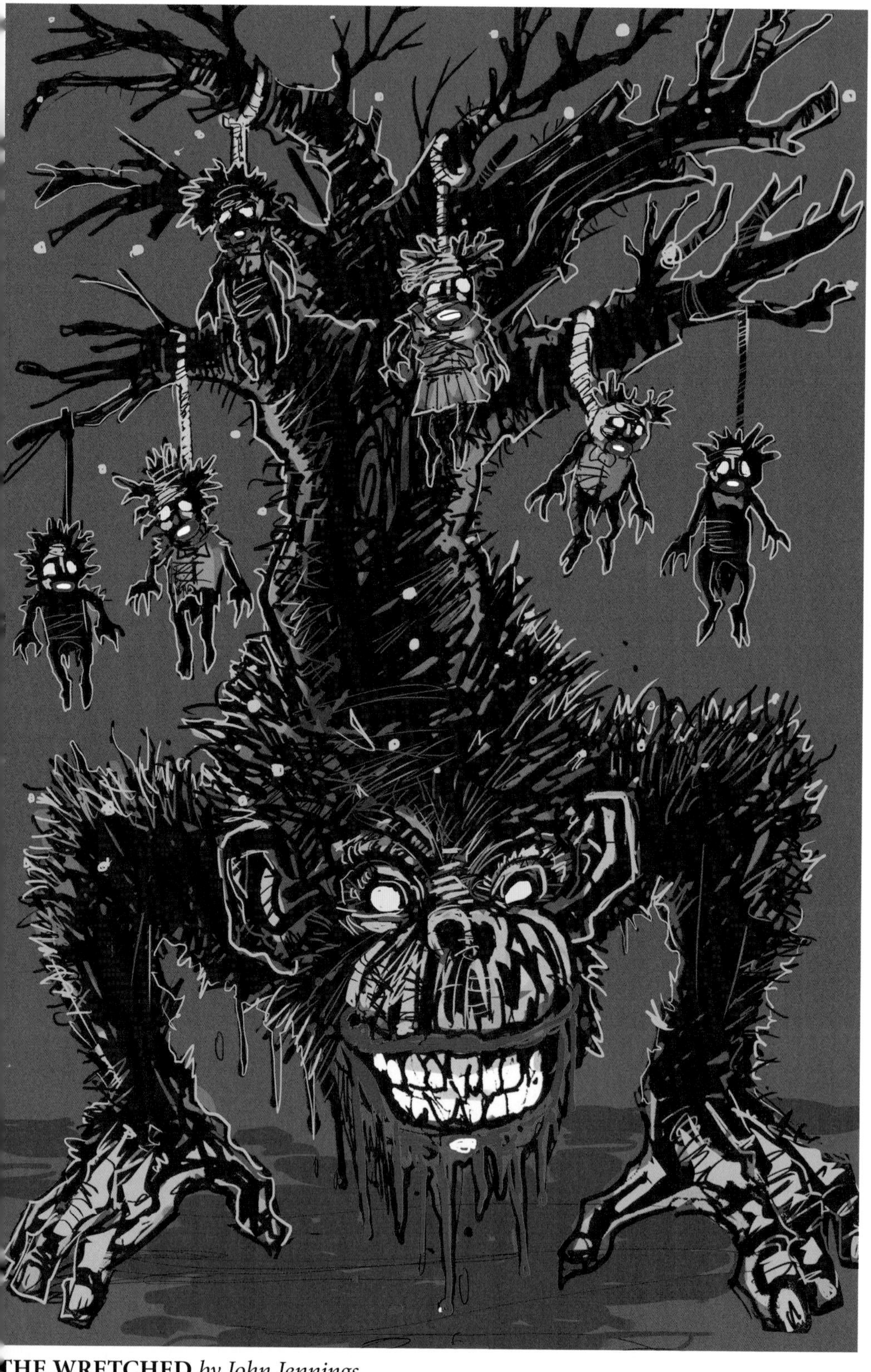

**THE WRETCHED** *by John Jennings*

# ABOUT THE CREATORS

**JOHN JENNINGS** is a Professor of Media and Cultural Studies at the University of California at Riverside. Jennings is co-editor of the Eisner Award-winning collection *The Blacker the Ink: Constructions of the Black Identity in Comics and Sequential Art.* Jennings is also a 2016 Nasir Jones Hip Hop Studies Fellow with the Hutchins Center at Harvard University. Jennings' current projects include the horror anthology *Box of Bones*, the coffee table book *Black Comix Returns* (with Damian Duffy), and the Eisner-winning, Bram Stoker Award-winning, New York Times best-selling graphic novel adaptation of Octavia Butler's classic dark fantasy novel *Kindred*. Duffy and Jennings recently released their graphic novelization of Octavia Bulter's prescient dystopian novel *Parable of the Sower* (Abrams ComicArts). Jennings is also founder and curator of the ABRAMS Megascope line of graphic novels.

**AYIZE JAMA-EVERETT** is an African-American science fiction and speculative fiction writer. He is the author of the trilogy *The Liminal People* (self-published, 2009; Small Beer Press, 2012), *The Liminal War* (Small Beer Press, 2015) and *The Entropy of Bones* (Small Beer Press, 2015). In his review of *The Entropy of Bones*, the writer Charles Yu describes Jama-Everett's work as "resist[ing] easy categorization. [The protagonist's] mixed racial background offers a potentially nuanced look from a perspective that seems underserved." He goes on to say: "If the book veers among different approaches — now a philosophical kung fu master story, now a seduction into a rarefied subculture, now an esoteric universe made from liner notes and the journal entries of a brilliantly imaginative teenager — there's nevertheless a vitality to the voice and a weirdness that, while not always controlled or intentional, is highly appealing for just that reason." Jama-Everett himself sees his writing as a way to heal people who have long been ignored in mainstream popular culture. He asserts: **"There's a big wound in not being seen, in having your reality not being represented in any way."**

Printed in Canada